D1562894

NATION BUILDER

NATION BUILDER

John Quincy Adams

and the Grand Strategy *of the* Republic

CHARLES N. EDEL

Harvard University Press

Cambridge, Massachusetts

London, England

2014

Printed in the United States of America

First printing

*Library of Congress Cataloging-in-Publication Data
is available from the library of Congress.*

ISBN 978-0-674-36808-8

For Kira

and my parents

CONTENTS

Illustrations follow Chapter 3

NATION BUILDER

INTRODUCTION

IN THE SUMMER of 1816, John Quincy Adams rented a country home for his family in the English town of Ealing, located about a two-hour ride from Hyde Park. Removed from the frenzy of official London, surrounded by a garden of laurel trees, and bordered by a fruit orchard, the residence, serendipitously named the Little Boston House, was as comfortable and pleasant a place as he had ever lived.[1] After many years of separation, he had his wife and three sons gathered around him for the most concentrated time they would ever spend together. During the day, they took long walks over the surrounding fields and countryside. With a fire burning to keep them warm at night, they would play cards, perform skits for their own entertainment, and write doggerel to each other.

That summer, much of the Western world felt a similar sense of tranquility. The United States was enjoying a return to normalcy after its recently concluded war with Britain, and James Monroe had been elected president with nearly 70 percent of the popular vote. The election results paved the way for what would be a decade's worth of single-party rule, economic growth, and territorial expansion. Across the Atlantic, Europe had entered its first full year of peace and stability in nearly a quarter-century. Having successfully negotiated an end to the War of 1812 between the British and the Americans, Adams was now serving as U.S. minister to Great Britain in a significantly less antagonistic atmosphere. Reflecting on the changed state of affairs, he wrote, "my special duty at present is to preach peace."[2]

And yet despite recent events and his comfortable surroundings, Adams felt nothing but agitation. Surveying the continental scene, he worried that "all the restored governments of Europe are deeply hostile to us."[3] He observed that some of these governments seemed to believe that the United States was a power whose rise needed to be checked before it could start to challenge the existing Western powers; others that its vast resources and favorable demographics presented a long-term danger to Europe's economic dominance; and still others that the boisterous republic was a growing ideological threat to the monarchies of the Old World. Regardless of the reasons for European hostility, Adams feared that this increasing resentment eventually would produce another violent conflict for his young country.

Holed up in his book-lined study seven miles outside of London, and several thousand miles from Washington, D.C., John Quincy Adams wrapped himself in flannel as he bent over his diary. "The season has been so unusually and constantly cold," he wrote in July 1816, noting that "fires have been kept without intermission in almost every house."[4] Indeed, 1816 would later become known as the year without a summer. Volcanic eruptions the previous year had spread a cloud of dust around the globe, and temperatures had plummeted in the Northern Hemisphere.[5] Even if he did not know the cause, Adams felt the effect, noting that there were frosts in July and August, and newspaper accounts "of snow in harvest, and of ice an inch thick." The "chilling frigidity, of a cold, ungenial, unprolific and churlish summer" had him thinking of the similarities between "New and Old England."[6]

In those cold evenings of England's late summer, Adams's thoughts turned homeward. He worried that an insufficiently powerful federal government would render the country vulnerable to external threats. Additionally, the highly divisive War of 1812 and the New England Federalists' calls for secession at the Hartford Convention had provided ample evidence of the country's centrifugal tendencies. Both of these were troubling in the extreme, but they were not what most concerned Adams. His greatest concern was the habit of so many Americans to automatically, even recklessly, support the policies of the United States. Writing to his father from his study in Ealing, he explained, "I cannot ask of heaven success, even for my country, in a cause where she should be in the wrong." Adams's words were in reply to a popular American toast at that time, "My Country, Right or Wrong!"[7] For, what if the nation pursued a disastrous course, Adams asked. Must the patriot's response always be uncritical support? Adams countered that "my toast would be, may our country always be successful, but whether successful or otherwise, always right. I disclaim as unsound all patriotism incompatible with the principles of eternal justice."[8] Adams believed that while the role of the statesman was to guide America toward power, more important and more challenging was his duty to steer the nation's course toward justice.

Serving as U.S. minister to Great Britain, Adams held the most important American diplomatic posting. However, his tour in

England offered him constant reminders of "how very small a space my person or my station occupy in the notice of these persons and at these places."[9] Whether the smallness he felt was due more to his position, his country's relative insignificance, or the aloofness of the English aristocracy, Adams felt far removed from the councils of his country. Later, Adams would reflect that serving abroad as a diplomat "was merely an incident in the life of a statesmen—a preparation for something else."[10] That was an easy statement to make in retrospect, after he had been appointed secretary of state and was well on his way toward the presidency. But sitting in the quiet of his study and buried in his own thoughts, the path forward was much less clear. He had been posted abroad for more than seven years, and wondered if he had missed the best opportunity of returning home and "presenting myself to the notice of my country." As he acknowledged in letters to his parents, "it was at home alone that I could be in the way of advancement."[11]

Although Adams might have felt that his stay in the English countryside was time in the political wilderness, these solitary months gave him the opportunity to more fully develop his ideas about the direction of America and the necessary strategy required to bring America to a position of preeminence in the world. Adams thought that the young nation offered the world a model of government and society that was new, unique, and special.[12] Yet the republic's key challenge, as he came to understand it, was how to become a great nation without corrupting its core values. Adams struggled with this question his entire life, both on a national and on a personal level. Late in his life, Adams confessed in his diary, "I have not improved the scanty portion of his gifts as I might and ought to have done."[13] And yet Adams's vision of the United States' long-term interests and his strategy for how to counter the various threats arrayed against those interests shaped the official policy of the country and set the nation on a path to continental expansion and hemispheric dominion.

This book explores how Adams conceived of his own and the nation's rise to power, discusses what he did to promote his and the nation's advancement, assesses where he succeeded and where he failed, and examines the contemporary applicability of Adams's thinking. While there have been biographical and policy studies written about Adams, and there have been several books that look at the strategy of the United States in the nineteenth century, this is the first to tie the concept of the grand strategy of the early republic to the life and career of John Quincy Adams.[14]

Using grand strategy as a narrative framework for both John Quincy Adams and the early republic allows for a fully integrated narrative of Adams's life and a comprehensive examination of the evolving strategy that the early United States used to shape its rise to global power. The concept of grand strategy is often invoked but seldom explained in a satisfactory manner. In the broadest sense, grand strategy is a comprehensive and integrated plan of action, based on the calculated relationship of means to large ends.[15] It requires both conceptualizing those large ends and ensuring optimal use of the means available. Its successful practice demands the ability to see the interconnectivity of widely disparate events, to develop the capacity for flexibility and adaptability, and to act when opportunities arise. As a discipline, it originally belonged to the field of military endeavor and political statecraft but has since broadened to encompass a wider range of activity.[16] For a nation, it involves not only defining long-term objectives, but also integrating the military, diplomatic, economic, political, and moral resources of a nation to accomplish its goals.[17] For an individual, it requires the ability both to master discrete subjects and to understand how those separate parts integrate into a larger system.[18] Grand strategy is here understood to operate simultaneously at the personal level (What defines who I am and how I can advance to what I will become?), at the national level (What will it take to secure the country's interests?), and at the moral level (How do I justify all of this to God?).

Adams is an outstanding case study for grand strategy at the personal and national level. His life covers the whole of antebellum America. The eldest son of John and Abigail Adams, John Quincy came of age during the American Revolution. Brought by his father to Europe as his personal secretary, he was exposed to international politics and American policy making from an early age. When he returned to America for college, he was perhaps the most well traveled American at that time. Appointed as the American minister to Holland at the age of twenty-seven, he worked in the foreign service under Presidents Washington, Adams, and Madison in a variety of diplomatic postings in Europe. He then served as secretary of state for eight years under Monroe and is credited with extending American borders to the Pacific. Adams was elected President of the United States for a single term, and then uniquely, after a brief retirement, returned to Washington to serve as an avid antislavery congressman. He remained in that post for the final seventeen years of his life before literally dying on the floor of the House of Representatives. Adams spent time with Benjamin Franklin and Thomas Jefferson as a child, shared the national stage with Andrew Jackson, Henry Clay, and John Calhoun as an adult, and served in the same Congress as a young Abraham Lincoln. Adams's ideas shaped the Monroe Doctrine and influenced both Washington's Farewell Address and Lincoln's Emancipation Proclamation.

Adams's extensive official and unofficial writings reveal that he was nothing if not ponderous.[19] His diary alone, which fills fifty-one manuscript volumes dating between 1779 and 1848, contains nearly seventeen thousand pages. Usually rousing himself from bed between four and five in the morning, Adams sat and recorded his thoughts in his journal. This journal, started at the age of twelve and kept until his death in the House of Representatives in 1848, is a remarkable resource. Nearly every day Adams recorded whom he had met, what they had discussed, and, most importantly, what he had thought. It is an exceptional window into Adams's mind and provides an excellent opportunity to evaluate what he thought he was trying to do.[20]

The availability and the size of this archive make writing about him both straightforward and overwhelming. The challenge to the historian is that Adams's grand strategy for himself and for the country was far from explicit. Even for a figure such as Adams, who wrote about practically everything under the sun, his strategy is something that must be inferred because he never sat down and wrote it out in prose. Yet looking at Adams's remarkable career, his pursuit of America's long-term interests is evident. As a diplomat, Adams worked to insulate America from Europe's quarrels. As secretary of state, he crafted a strategy of continental expansion and hegemony. As president, he attempted to anchor the country's long-term growth in the development of infrastructure, education, and commerce. And finally, as an antislavery congressman, he worked to bring the nation's practices in line with its promise and advocated emancipation from and abolition of slavery. Adams was constantly out in front, and often ahead, of his contemporaries, in conceptualizing and advocating for American interests. While this could simply suggest a man ahead of his time, this book

INTRODUCTION

argues that it was the result of an overarching, prioritized, and sequenced grand strategy.

Looking across his entire career, Adams's grand strategy comes into focus. Adams acted on the conviction that an effective grand strategy required the ability not only to set priorities among competing goals, but also to act on those priorities in the proper sequence. This "you cannot do everything at once" principle dominated his thinking. He possessed a clear sense of the stages of development through which a rising power must proceed and recognized that these stages had to be completed in a certain order. Some things were more important than others—certain events demanded immediate responses, while others could be dealt with later. As secretary of state, Adams reflected on this, writing, "I did not recollect any change of policy; but observed there had been a great change of circumstances."[21]

Adams crafted a grand strategy aimed at reducing security risks to the republic and vindicating republicanism as the form of government best suited to promote human progress and liberty. Each was an end unto itself, but these two great goals supported each other. Without security, the nascent republican principles and institutions would not survive in a world dominated by militarized empires. Without a moral component, America offered the world nothing better than the monarchies of the Old World. Over time, he pursued strategies designed to promote those two ends.

Reducing security threats to the nation required a strategy with three separate, though related, components. To insulate America from Europe's destructive quarrels, Adams advanced a strategy of neutrality. To ensure its lasting peace with foreign powers, he advocated a strategy of enhanced defense capabilities. And to reduce the menace of Europe in North America, he promoted a strategy of continental expansion designed to establish the United States as the predominant power in the Western Hemisphere.

Additionally, Adams believed that while a republic was the form of government most conducive to human flourishing, ensuring such development required a twofold strategy. To further its institutions, he pushed a model of economic growth designed to improve the lives of the nation's citizens. To bolster America's appeal as a political model, it needed to be morally attractive. Adams offered a strategy capable of attacking slavery, and thereby reconciling the contradiction of slavery in a nation based on freedom. Before Adams, political leaders in the United States had a clear enough understanding of goals, but no conception of how to achieve those objectives. Adams was neither the first nor the only national politician to promote strategies for America's rise, but he was the only one who linked, prioritized, and sequenced them into a comprehensive grand strategy that was intended to harness the country's geographic, military, economic, and moral resources. In this, Adams looms large as a nation builder whose particular combination of ideas and policies make him an important bridge between the founding generation of American statesmen and the Civil War-era Lincoln and Seward.

This book traces the grand strategy in the life and career of John Quincy Adams by evaluating five significant phases in his life and showing in each case the relative weight Adams gave to the personal, national, and moral dimensions of grand strategy. These episodes encompass the arc of Adams's career and his unfolding pursuits—keeping Europe at bay; expanding the United States territorially across North America; anchoring the country's long-term development in infrastructure, education, and commerce; attempting to abolish slavery; and finally, evaluating his legacy. Looking at the patterns that emerge over time, many of the seeming inconsistencies in his life and career often reflect the self-conscious sequencing of priorities that successful politicians and strategists instinctively undertake, recognizing that not everything can be accomplished at once.

A common critique of the idea of grand strategy is that a true grand strategy would mean that the whole strategy would have to be developed in advance and executed flawlessly. This, however, is neither realistic nor useful. Arguing that Adams consistently pursued a grand strategy for himself and for the nation does not mean that he had all the issues fully worked out from the start. Nor does it mean that his ideas remained static. Nor does it even mean that he had to be successful (surely he was not in his lifetime) for his strategy to be judged a success. While Adams acted broadly according to his grand strategy, he was also prepared to adjust when necessary. Such tactical flexibility was useful. It also caused him great tension at different points throughout his life and career.

Adams's grand strategy helps explain why America's rise from a confederation of revolutionary colonies to a continental power was not an inevitable result of resources and demographics, but rather the product of a deliberate pursuit. And because grand strategy is assessed not only at the national level, but also at the personal level, it allows for an analysis of what occurred when certain principles, values, and priorities were in conflict. The results, of course, were uneven, as Adams succeeded brilliantly in some areas and failed abjectly in others. But grand strategy is not only about the conception of a vision, but also about its successful execution.

For that reason, a proper assessment of Adams's evolving strategy and a central part of his story mean looking at both consistencies and inconsistencies, and highlighting successes, internal tensions, failures, and unintended consequences. Of these there were many: Adams's personal crises in the 1790s; his turn away from the Federalists in the early 1800s; his privileging of expansion over his antislavery sentiments during the Missouri crisis in the late 1810s; his evolving views on the Monroe Doctrine in the late 1820s; and his partial rejection of continental expansion in the 1830s and 1840s. In these instances, as well as in his pursuit of the presidency and his actions as president, tensions between Adams's competing values and principles, and the personal and national trade-offs required, underscore the problematic nature of both conceptualizing and executing a grand strategy. Additionally, an enhanced discussion of the choices Adams made in several of these instances provides an opportunity to explore alternative paths that Adams and the United States might have taken—and the costs of not doing so.

Tracing the entire arc of Adams's career reveals several dominant tendencies, including the inordinate demands of being an Adams—which meant being both ruthlessly ambitious and selfless in his devotion to the public interest; his use of rhetoric as a means of gaining and exercising power; his belief in progress, but progress of a gradual and not a precipitous nature; his resistance to meddling in the internal affairs of sovereign states; his desire to have the United States replace the European powers in North America; his antipathy toward authoritarian regimes; and his belief that the United States should serve as a positive vision for how a state could improve its citizens' lives.

From the earliest days of American history, Americans have often believed that their own model of democratic capitalism was universally applicable, universally desirable, and more likely to make the world a safer place.[22] Throughout his long career, John

Quincy Adams believed that the United States could serve as a political, economic, and moral model to the rest of the world, but only if it had first developed its own resources effectively. Adams constantly advanced a concept of nation building, but it was one that was firmly concentrated on the domestic front.

At different points in his career, Adams played the role of both the prophet and the politician. His vision of the United States' long-term interests and his strategy for how to counter the various threats arrayed against those interests shaped the official policy of the country. He used political means with varying degrees of success, adapting and learning over time. He understood, and tried to resolve, the balancing act between territorial expansion and individual liberty. In pursuit of his grand strategic vision, Adams laid the groundwork to set the nation on a course to long-term security, stability, and prosperity.

1

THE FIRES OF
HONORABLE AMBITION

The Education of John Quincy Adams

SHORTLY BEFORE BOARDING a ship in May 1785 that would take him back to America for the first time in seven years, John Quincy Adams asked his father "please to present my best respects to Mr. Jefferson . . . and all our friends in Paris. If you see the Marquis, you will inform him, that his Dogs are on board, and shall be well kept, if my attention to them has any effect."[1] While this remark, which concluded a brief letter to his father, John Adams, detailing his seventeen-year-old son's final preparations before setting sail, might have felt casual to the young traveler, it was anything but usual. These were not just any dogs, but seven hounds bred in Normandy by the Marquis de Lafayette and sent as a special gift to George Washington. The younger Adams had already served as his father's personal secretary while he was concluding the final peace treaty that ended the American Revolution, knew Thomas Jefferson intimately, and had spent time living in the same house as Benjamin Franklin. At a young age, John Quincy Adams had already traveled to France, England, Holland, Belgium, Sweden, and Prussia, and at the age of fourteen moved to Russia as a part of a diplomatic mission to the court of Catherine the Great. It is no wonder his father referred to him as the "greatest Traveller of his Age."[2] He knew the most important people in America, possibly had traveled more than any living American, and was well regarded everywhere he went.

Yet, as he set off for his native shores, he felt more trepidation than triumph. "I have been such a wandering being these seven years," he confided in his diary, "that I have never performed any regular course of studies, and am deficient on many subjects."[3] In a sense, Adams was correct. He had received no systematic instruction prior to matriculating at Harvard in 1786. While he did attend schools in Paris, Amsterdam, and Leyden, the rest of his studies had been under the supervision of tutors. His formal education barely exceeded three years. Years later, as a United States senator, Adams acknowledged that his education had been haphazard, lamenting that "though I was always of a studious turn and addicted to books beyond bounds of moderation, yet my acquirements in literature and science have been all superficial, and I never attained a profound knowledge of anything."[4]

This nagging sense of doubt seems to have been an Adams family trait: reflecting on his own education, John Quincy's grandson, the famous historian Henry Adams, wrote that he had a tendency to exaggerate his "weaknesses as he grew older. The habit of doubt" seemed to come to him, as it did to his grandfather, quite naturally.[5] While John Quincy's assessment of himself was characteristically harsh, most of his contemporaries, thoroughly impressed by the young man, disagreed. Just a few months after he had written these nervous lines in his diary, his aunt reported, "I have already discover'd a strength of mind, a memory, a soundness of judgment which I have seldom seen united in one so young. . . . If his applyca-tion is equal to his abilities he cannot fail of makeing a great Man."[6] Spending more time with him only confirmed these views. Young Johnny, she wrote, "is form'd for a Statesman."[7]

But if Adams one day was to become America's greatest secretary of state, he was a long way from there when at the age of nine he wrote his father, "my head is much too fickle, my Thoughts are running after birds eggs play and trifles, till I get vexd with my Self, Mamma has a troublesome task to keep me Steady, and I own I am ashamed of myself."[8] Adams was not born a statesman, but became one. His preparation for leadership required guidance and the pursuit of a position of "painful pre-eminence."[9] His personal development and the values and habits he acquired served as the foundation of his extraordinary record of achievement—and at times failure—as a policy maker. His actions and thought offer clues into the evolution of his theory of America's place, and role, in the world.[10]

Any discussion of John Quincy Adams's education must begin with his parents. John and Abigail Adams instilled in their eldest son the idea that he was destined for great things from an early age. As the two most important influences in his life, they labored to ingrain in him a sense of service to others, a thirst for knowledge, and the drive to excel.[11] Warning his son against complacency, John Adams once admonished young John Quincy that "you come into life with advantages which will disgrace you if your success is me-diocre. And if you do not rise to the head not only of your Pro-fession, but of your Country, it will be owing to your own *Lasiness*,

Slovenliness, and Obstinacy."[12] Abigail was even more blunt. Writing him just after his first Atlantic crossing, she instructed her son to become "an ornament to society, an Honour to your Country, and a Blessing to your parents." She demanded that he strictly adhere to "those religious Sentiments and principals which were early instilled into your mind and remember that you are accountable to your Maker for all your words and actions." In case this was not a serious enough admonition, she concluded, "dear as you are to me, I had much rather you should have found your Grave in the ocean you have crossed, or any untimely death crop you in your Infant years, rather than see you an immoral profligate or a Graceless child."[13]

Evidence of parental pressure on John Quincy is overwhelming and frequently seems excessive. John and Abigail pushed their children to succeed, constantly reminded them of the advantages they had over others, and warned them against complacency. Their ambitions, for themselves and their children, certainly mark them as unique. But in the context of mid- to late eighteenth-century Massachusetts, which retained many of its Puritan folkways, their child rearing loses much, though certainly not all, of its distinctiveness. According to a historian of the period, this was a culture that thought the "first and most urgent purpose of child rearing was . . . the 'breaking of the will.'"[14] In such a culture, personal happiness and individual desires took a subservient role to familial duty and communal obligations.

While their admonitions might seem harsh, this was the Adams creed—through hard work and virtue, excellence, advancement, power, and fame would surely follow.[15] This unwavering drive for excellence and devotion to duty was imprinted on the entire family, but most especially on John Quincy. Already at the age of ten he was parroting the line. "We are Sent into this world for Some end," he informed his younger brother Charles. "It is our duty to discover by Close study what this end is & when we once discover it to pursue it with unconquerable perseverance."[16] It was not much of a mystery what the end was. From his infancy on, his parents repeatedly told him that service to the commonwealth was the first duty of citizenship. And they expected him to become a leader of their new country.

John and Abigail left an extensive written record not only of their own relationship, but also of their hopes, fears, and aspirations for themselves, their children, and their young country— all of which they believed were intimately linked.[17] Not surprisingly, their correspondence is filled with questions of what they should teach their children. The Adamses sought to shape their children, and particularly John Quincy Adams, into statesmen who would play a leading role in the affairs of their new country. This education would be grounded in history, Christian ethics, and civic virtues. In a letter to Robert Livingston, the secretary of foreign affairs under the Articles of Confederation, John Adams described the model statesman. While it was a none-too-subtle hint that he was amply qualified for future diplomatic postings himself, what is more interesting is his description of the proper training for such an individual. The elder Adams thought that a statesman "should have had an education in classical learning, and in the knowledge of general history, ancient and modern, and particularly the history of France, England, Holland, and America. He should be well versed in the principles of ethics, of the law of nature and nations, of legislation and government, of the civil Roman law, of the laws of England and the United States, of the public law of Europe, and in the letters, memoirs, and histories of those great men, who have heretofore shone in the diplomatic order, and conducted the affairs of nations, and the world."[18]

This was exactly the education that John Quincy was pursuing under his parents' tutelage. He learned to speak ancient Greek, Latin, French, Spanish, Dutch, and German. In Greek, he read Homer, Xenophon, Herodotus, Thucydides, and Plutarch; in Latin, Suetonius, Livy, Virgil, Cicero, Tacitus, Juvenal, Horace, and Ovid. He plodded through European history, became versed in the various religions, and devoured political philosophy. He became a daily reader of the Bible and an avid fan of Shakespeare. The great Roman orators taught him wisdom and folly. The story of Abraham and his descendants highlighted "all the vicissitudes to which individuals, families, and nations are liable."[19] But it was the Bard of Avon who surpassed all others as "a teacher of morals." Years later, Adams recalled that his "enthusiastic admiration" of Shakespeare commenced "before the down had darkened my lip." That admiration, "little short of idolatry," stemmed from his belief that the English playwright was "a profound delineator of human nature and a sublime poet."[20] This broad reading was designed to teach him the varieties of human nature, to build his critical thinking capacity, and to teach him to command the English language and bend it to his purposes.

Reading history would stand at the heart of Adams's education. The idea that history should occupy a central position in education was a common one in colonial and revolutionary America. In 1749, Benjamin Franklin wrote that encouraging the study of history was the best way that "the first principles of sound Politicks be fix'd in the Minds of Youth." Thomas Jefferson believed that "history, by apprizing them [students] of the past, will enable them to judge of the future; it will avail them of the experience of other times and other nations; it will qualify them as judges of the actions and designs of men; it will enable them to know ambition under every disguise it may assume; and knowing it, to defeat its views."[21] The founding generation had all read the same Greek, Roman, and British authors and absorbed their lessons. They believed that there were discernible laws of history that, much like the laws of nature, regulated political affairs. They thought that if they read widely and studied deeply, they could understand the patterns of behavior in men, societies, institutions, and governments. Their reverence for history was driven not by romantic nostalgia, but by practical considerations. By comparing historical events and analyzing the results, they believed they could develop a predictive tool for governance.[22]

Among this historically conscious group, John Adams stood out for his views on the value of history as a policy tool. As a youth, he had decided he would form "an exact knowledge of the nature, end, and means of government." He could accomplish this by comparing "the different forms of [government] with each other, and each of them with their effects on public and private happiness."[23] These were the writings of an ambitious young attorney, but this concept stayed consistent throughout his life. His most mature work of political philosophy, the three-volume 1787 *Defence of the Constitutions of Government of the United States of America,* was a historical survey of different types of governments in the ancient and modern world. Adams examined the democratic republics of the Low Countries and Switzerland and compared them to Athens and Thebes. He looked at the aristocratic republics in Zurich and Venice and measured their virtues and vices against Rome's. He analyzed the monarchical republics of England and Poland in light of Homer's monarchies. He considered the political ideas of the ancient Greeks, the Romans, the Enlightenment, and the British Commonwealth men, drawing on authorities from Plato to Tacitus to Machiavelli to Locke and Milton. The point of this broad and often tedious work was to prove Adams's insistence that "all nations from the beginning have been agitated by the same passions." Comprehensively cataloguing those passions illuminated certain principles that were applicable to all men in all places at all times. Adams concluded that "nations move by unalterable rules" and that a close reading of history could reduce governing to a science.[24]

As he developed his thinking on both the science of governing and the central importance of republican ideas, John Adams instructed his son on the importance of reading, above all other historians, Thucydides. "There is no History," Adams wrote, "perhaps, better adapted to this usefull Purpose than that of Thucidides, an Author, of whom I hope you will make yourself perfect Master, in original Language, which is Greek, the most perfect of all human languages. . . . You will find in your Fathers library, the Works of Mr. Hobbes, in which among a great deal of mischievous Philosophy, you will find a learned and exact Translation of Thucidides. . . . You will find it full of Instruction to the Orator, the Statesman, the General, as well as to the Historian and Philosopher."[25]

This is an intriguing letter. Why does Adams say that Hobbes's works contain "a great deal of mischievous Philosophy"? And why is Adams insistent that Thucydides serves a more useful purpose than any other author?

The first answer is fairly obvious. *Leviathan,* which was undoubtedly included in the works of Hobbes, was the standard text on absolute rule and the inviolability, once entered, of the social contract between subject and sovereign, no matter the abuses of the latter. Yet Adams deeply believed in the need to resist tyranny and struggle on behalf of liberty. The second answer rests on Adams's view of Thucydides, suggesting that the ancient Greek historian offered much practical knowledge.

Thucydides intended his work to serve as an aide "to the understanding of the future . . . [and] not as an essay which is to win the applause of the moment, but as a possession for all time."[26] His work was meant to be didactic, not only to his contemporaries but also to future generations of aspiring statesmen and strategists.[27] Thucydides argued that while understanding history meant understanding context, some things, especially human nature, were unchanging. He argued that if a close study of the past was the best method for deducing general truths and discerning recurrent patterns of behavior between men and nations, history would be the best tool for the training of a future statesman. This sounded remarkably like John Adams's own argument for treating the study of history as a science.

Adams found the parallels between the American Revolution and the Peloponnesian War striking enough that he began commenting on this in his letters to his wife. "There is a striking Resemblance, in several Particulars between the Peloponnesian and the American War," Adams wrote. "The real motive to the former was a Jealousy of the growing Power of Athens, by Sea and Land. . . . The genuine Motive to the latter, was a similar Jealousy of the growing Power of America. The true Causes which incite to War, are seldom professed, or Acknowledged."[28] In this comparison, Adams offered his view of what causes conflict in the international system. According to Adams, Thucydides thought that the causes of the

Peloponnesian War were both material—the rise of Athens's navy, commerce, and wealth—and intangible—"fear, honor, and interest."[29] Because "the future Circumstances of your Country, may require other Wars, as well as Councils and Negotiations," John Adams thought Thucydides the best possible instructor in the art of statecraft.[30] Placing the ancient and modern conflicts side by side, Adams showed how without a proper understanding of history, the present would become unintelligible and the future indiscernible. According to this logic, statesmen should use their knowledge of history to order and make sense of the present and as a model for what to do and what to avoid doing in the future. Such thinking would profoundly affect John Quincy, who came to believe that historical knowledge was primarily useful as an aide that furnished "lessons of analogy which have some use for application to every position of affairs among men."[31]

Beyond history, John and Abigail Adams spent a great deal of time thinking about how to instill virtue and a sense of duty in their children. In 1774, writing from Princeton, John reassured Abigail that he had spent much time contemplating this subject. "The Education of our Children is never out of my Mind," he wrote. He instructed his wife to "Train them to Virtue, habituate them to industry, activity, and Spirit. Make them consider every Vice, as shamefull and unmanly: fire them with ambition to be usefull—make them disdain to be destitute of any usefull, or ornamental Knowledge or Accomplishment. Fix their Ambition upon great and solid Objects, and their Contempt upon little, frivolous, and useless ones."[32]

The Adamses stressed the importance of early habits with the hope that certain virtues would embed themselves in John Quincy's character. On child rearing, Abigail would conclude that it was of the utmost importance to instill "the precepts of morality very early into their minds."[33] Her husband shared this sentiment, declaring to John Quincy that "your morals are of more importance, both to yourself and the World than all Languages and all Sciences."[34] The foundation of this ethical education was the Bible, a book John Quincy constantly read and reread. Writing to his own son years later in a series of eleven instructional letters on the Bible's meaning and lessons, he expressed the belief that "when duly read and meditated upon, it is of all the books in the world that which contributes most to make men good, wise and happy."[35] John Quincy later counseled his son that the Bible should be read as history, literature, and a system of morals. He understood it as a practical guide to good conduct, rather than a work founded "upon metaphysical subtleties."[36]

John Quincy wrote that the Bible taught the three cardinal virtues of Christianity: piety, benevolence, and humility. But he cautioned against confusing these attributes with weakness. "Never be tame or abject," he advised his son, adding, "never show yourself yielding or complying to prejudice, wrong-headedness or intractability which would lead you astray from the dictates of your conscience."[37] John Quincy was passing on to his son what he had long ago learned from his parents. It was his own mother who had repeatedly lectured him that "he who will not turn when he is trodden upon is deficient in point of spirit."[38]

It was important to John and Abigail Adams' that their children learned not only the personal morality of Christianity, but also the public virtues of civic duty. While Christianity served as a guide for piety, benevolence, and humility, the Greeks and Romans, or "the heathen philosophers," as John Quincy later called them, taught justice, prudence, and fortitude.[39] John and Abigail insisted that he learn ancient Greek and Latin so that he could absorb the classical authors' views of personal and civic vices and virtues. John Adams declared that "the End of study is to make you a good Man and a useful Citizen."[40] The Adamses saw public and private virtue as mutually reinforcing. Service to the state necessitated high moral purpose; and morality was not private, but public. This sentiment was clearly expressed in a letter John wrote to Abigail after hearing about her mother's death: "Were not her talents, and Virtues too much confined, to private, social and domestic Life[?]. My Opinion of the Duties of Religion and Morality, comprehends a very extensive Connection with society at large, and the great Interest of the public. Does not natural Morality, and much more Christian Benevolence, make it our indispensable Duty to lay ourselves out, to serve our fellow Creatures to the Utmost of our Power, in promoting and supporting those great Political systems, and general Regulations upon which the Happiness of Multitudes depends.... Public Virtues, and political Qualities therefore should be incessantly cherished in our Children."[41]

John Adams wrote from Philadelphia, where he had been away from his family for more than six months, a separation which would only grow longer. While he was understandably anxious about leaving Abigail to run their farm and manage their accounts, he was clearly more concerned about the importance of instilling a devotion to public service in his children, lest they, like Abigail's late mother, end up "too confined." Personal happiness should always be subordinated to the public interest. According to the Adams creed, devotion to the commonwealth was of paramount importance. As John wrote Abigail, if his children did not understand this, if they preferred a life of comfort, ease, and wealth to public endeavor, "they are not my Children, and I care not what becomes of them."[42]

Expressing her agreement, Abigail wrote him that "all domestick pleasures and injoyments are absorbed in the great and important duty you owe your Country 'for our Country is as it were a secondary God, and the First and greatest parent. It is to be preferred to Parents, Wives, Children, Friends and all things the Gods only excepted.'...Thus do I suppress every wish, and silence every Murmer."[43] While certainly exaggerated in sentiment, Abigail's thoughts reinforce the importance the Adamses placed on public duty at the expense of personal pleasure. It is no wonder that John and Abigail's children came to identify love, even familial love, with service to their country. Almost a decade later, John Quincy's older sister came as close as an Adams ever did to analyzing their family's motives, writing to her brother that "the happiness of our family seems ever to have been so interwoven with the Politicks of our Country as to be in a great degree dependent upon them."[44] As if proving the point, before John Quincy took up his first diplomatic posting, his parents advised that he endeavor "to deserve well of your father, but especially of your government."[45]

For John and Abigail, imbuing their children with the idea of duty to country meant instructing them in service to republican principles. John stressed the moral and political obligations that his son had incurred from the sacrifice of others during America's struggle for independence. "I hope that you will remember," he instructed his son, "how many Losses, Dangers, and Inconveniences that have been born by your Parents, and the Inhabitants of Boston in generall for the Sake of preserving Freedom for you, and yours—and I hope you will all follow the virtuous Example if, in any future

Time your Countrys Liberties should be in Danger, and suffer every human Evil, rather than Give them up."[46] To promote these ideals, the Adamses relied upon an extensive and broad-ranging reading of history to instill republican thought.[47]

Chief among these lessons was resistance to political tyranny. The books John Quincy had been reading, in English, Greek, and Latin, were full of such examples. As early as 1774, we hear Abigail telling John that "I have taken very great fondness for reading Rollin's ancient History since you left me. . . . I find great pleasure and entertainment from it, and I have perswaided Johnny to read me a page or two every day, and hope he will find from his desire to oblige me entertain a fondness for it."[48] This is a reference to the popular French historian Charles Rollin, whose *Ancient History* and *Roman History* graced nearly every colonial library—including the one in the Adams household.[49] Rollin's histories urged his readers on with tales of heroic sacrifice and virtuous republicanism, and they were read both as world history and as introductions to the classics.[50] It is not surprising that three years later, in 1777, we still hear of Abigail's admiration for Rollin. "There are two ways says Rolin of acquiring improvement and instruction," Abigail relates to her husband. "First by ones own experience, and secondly by that of other men. It is much more wise and usefull to improve by other mens miscarriages than by our own."[51] Here she comes to the use of Rollin—his history is didactic in nature, offering examples of virtuous and sinful behavior, alternately to emulate and shun. John Quincy often reported on his progress through various works, writing to his father that "I find much entertainment in the perusal of history and I must own I am more Satisfied with myself when I have applied part of my time to Some useful employment than when I have Idled it away about Trifles and play."[52] The ten-year-old John Quincy was already beginning to parrot the family line—industriousness and studiousness—at the expense of pleasure or personal reward.

Reading history and the classical works of literature needed to be supplemented by practical experiences in the years that followed. In late 1777, the Continental Congress, now operating as a sovereign government in wartime, appointed John Adams envoy to Paris. Once there, he would join Benjamin Franklin in securing a Franco-American alliance against the British. Thinking it would be good for their son's education and future prospects, John and Abigail decided that John Quincy should accompany his father. Boarding the continental frigate *Boston* on February 13, 1778, in rough waters, John worried that he had erred in bringing his son on his diplomatic mission to France and exposing him to such dangers. Crossing the Atlantic, the ship encountered particularly violent seas and nearly sank. But, as he proudly reported to his wife, "Mr. Johnnys Behavior gave me a Satisfaction that I cannot express—fully sensible of our Danger, he was constantly endeavouring to bear it with a manly Patience, very attentive to me and his Thoughts constantly running in a serous Strain."[53]

Raising such a young man was their aspiration. In an early letter to Abigail ruminating on how best to educate their children, John Adams wrote that it was their duty to "mould the Minds and Manners of our Children. Let us teach them not only to do virtuously but to excell. To excell they must be taught to be steady, active, and industrious."[54] At times, such advice must have seemed boundless. They told John Quincy what to read, what to value, and what to believe. They counseled him on time management, on not laughing too much, and on the best ice-skating techniques. This last bit of advice was not quite as ridiculous as it might sound. They intended to teach their young son that "every thing in Life should be done with Reflection, and Judgment, even the most insignificant Amusements. They should all be arranged in subordination, to the great Plan of Happiness, and Utility."[55]

Their first son had learned well and conducted himself with a seriousness of purpose. Already, the ten-year-old John Quincy was instructing his younger brothers to put aside their "frivolous amusements" and instead employ their leisure time "gaining a knowledge which will make us useful to our fellow men when we grow up."[56] John Quincy fully had imbibed the Adams creed of industriousness, ambition, high moral purpose, and devotion to country. He also had grasped the value and use of history to the present. And now, he would have a chance to watch diplomacy played out before his eyes. "Poor Johnny is gone you tell me," his old tutor John Thaxter wrote to Abigail Adams shortly after her husband and son had embarked on their journey. But this, he noted, should be celebrated and not mourned. Thaxter concluded, "I think he is now laying the foundation of a great man."[57]

If the initial phase of John Quincy's education consisted of learning his parents' values, the next phase was an education in the affairs of men. This would come cumulatively. As his formal education through books and tutors continued in Europe, he also learned from the practical experience that came from traveling, observing, and mixing with many types of people. When he first arrived in Paris, he lived with his father and Benjamin Franklin. He then studied at Leyden University in the Netherlands, considered the best in Europe at the time. At the age of fourteen, he traveled to Russia as part of a diplomatic mission to Czarina Catherine's court in St. Petersburg. Upon his return to France, his father made him his private secretary while he was concluding the 1783 Treaty of Paris that secured American independence from Great Britain. John Quincy then returned to America to attend Harvard and witnessed the debates surrounding the Constitutional Convention.

Giving John Quincy a practical as well as philosophical education was the motivation for sending him to Europe. The eleven-year-old Adams neither wished to leave his mother's side nor depart his native land. Instead, he had hoped to continue his formal education at Andover Academy. His mother thought otherwise. "In all human probability," she declared, "it will do more for your education to go back to France with your father than to prepare for college at Andover."[58] Compared to European capitals, Boston was a provincial, uncultured backwater. With its theater, arts, and universities, Europe was the intellectual and cultural capital of the Western world. But this was not the primary reason Abigail wanted to send her young son abroad with his father. Dispatched to Europe at the behest of the Continental Congress, John Adams found that his responsibilities included drawing the French into an alliance, persuading the Dutch to finance the American war, and concluding a treaty with Great Britain to end hostilities—in short, ensuring the diplomatic, financial, and political success of the American Revolution. Sending John Quincy along offered a singular opportunity for him to witness history being made. Early in their travels John happily reported to his wife, "my son has accompanied me wherever I have been."[59] For parents hoping to train a future statesman, a traditional education paled in comparison. As John Quincy was learning, future prospects often trumped present concerns, and personal happiness was less important than his adherence to familial duty.

Although these travels necessitated that he forgo formal schooling, his parents made sure that he received as traditional an education as possible. They enrolled him in the best schools they could find, hired tutors, exposed him to the best minds in Europe, and inundated him with reading lists. The authors he read were meant to teach him to communicate his own ideas clearly and forcefully. His father instructed him to read for prose style as much as for content and demanded that he keep a daily journal where he could record the events he saw and advance his "taste, judgment, & knowledge."[60] He used this journal to record his opinions and sharpen his judgments. In addition to providing an excellent documentary record, the diary is a good indicator of his character traits: diligence, keen observation, and capacity for self-reflection and analysis. In the 1783 letter in which John Adams had described his view of an exemplary statesman, he explained that the purpose of a formal and broad education was to train a statesman to think. "A man must have something in his head to say," he wrote, "before he can speak to effect."[61] Abigail demanded of her son, "you must not be a superficial observer, but study Men and Manners that you may be skillful in both. . . . Youth is the proper season for observation and attention."[62]

A significant opportunity for John Quincy arose when Congress dispatched Francis Dana, John Adams's secretary and a significant diplomat and politician in his own right, to St. Petersburg in 1780. Dana's mission was to secure an alliance with Russia. He needed a secretary who could manage his affairs and who spoke French, the language of Catherine's court. The obvious choice was the then fourteen-year-old John Quincy, who was fluent in French and already residing in Europe. And so despite the interruption to his studies and the prolonged separation from his father, his parents enthusiastically volunteered him for this position. John Adams advised his son, "to open your Views and enlarge your Ideas of

Nature, you ought not to neglect any innocent Opportunity."[63] The mission to Russia was exactly the type of opportunity that had motivated the Adamses to send John Quincy to Europe in the first place.

St. Petersburg was challenging for the young John Quincy. It had no schools he could attend, and he was as far away from friends and family as he ever would be. Every day was cold, lonely, and remote. Writing to his mother, he asked her to remember that if his letters were infrequent it was because "I have been all [this] time almost at the world's end . . . in such an *out of the way* place."[64] To his old tutor John Thaxter, John Quincy complained of being homesick and anxious that his time in Russia would adversely affect his education. In his journal he noted the almost complete lack of contemporaries, and that the frigid winter temperatures often prevented him from leaving the house.

Despite these conditions, or perhaps because of them, John Quincy threw himself into his studies. His letters and journal entries show an increasing sophistication and interest in his surroundings. He observed people and places, and honed his writing style. From his readings, he explored various governments' organizing principles. He recorded opinions on European rulers and judged the chances of political stability in different nations. He listed the agricultural and manufactured goods of different regions and pondered the commercial prospects of various nations. He commented on cities' architecture, read deeply in the literature of several countries, and attempted to analyze Europe's varying national characters. John Adams wrote his son, "I am pleased to see . . . your Judgement ripen as you travel," and found himself bursting with paternal pride that John Quincy's letters evidenced "a judgment beyond your age."[65]

John Quincy recorded some acute observations of the Russian state in a letter he wrote to his mother. Though much of the letter was copied from books in his possession, John Quincy added his own analysis. "The government of Russia is entirely despotical," he noted. "The Sovereign is absolute, in all the extent of the word." This arrangement he thought "disadvantageous" to all involved—the sovereign, the nobles, and the people. For the sovereign, it produced an unstable political system that frequently produced revolution. For the nobles, wholly dependent on the whims of an absolute ruler, it meant that at any given moment their estates could be confiscated and they could be exiled to Siberia. Neither prospect was conducive to a stable order or a productive economy. Finally, absolute monarchy was not conducive to the flourishing of the Russian people. "No body," Adams wrote his mother, "will assert that a People can be happy who are subjected to personal Slavery."[66] His mother approved, pleading with her son to let such observations produce "an abhorrence, of Domination and power, the Parent of Slavery."[67]

John Quincy's observations did more than shape his positive views of America's republic in comparison to Europe's monarchies. He began exploring how best to promote America's commercial, political, and diplomatic interests. On his return from St. Petersburg in late 1782, he made inquiries about the prospect for commercial relations among Sweden, Denmark, and the United States. He observed that the Swedes, while concerned about American iron and steel production, were "very well disposed for carrying on" a "considerable commerce" with the United States.[68] Passing through Hamburg, John Quincy took notes on its commercial prospects and judged it likely to "carry on hereafter a great deal of Trade with America."[69] Detailing these ideas in letters to his father,

John Quincy made the benefits of his apprenticeship clear. No longer was he simply listing which authors and what books he was reading; he was beginning to analyze international relations and calculate the advantages America might derive from relations with various countries.

Her son's growing maturity was less apparent to Abigail. An ocean and several thousand miles separated John Quincy from his mother, who remained in Massachusetts supervising their growing farm, managing the family's finances, and raising the other Adams children on her own. As a result, mother-son correspondence was less frequent, less intimate, and less satisfying. This was especially true during John Quincy's residence in Russia, when he virtually ceased writing letters to his mother. When he did write, he noted that it was out of a sense of obligation. Abigail responded with letters full of exhortations to excellence and morality. The impersonal tone of these letters contrasted sharply with the growing warmth and depth of the father-son correspondence. Proximity helps explains the difference, as it had been years since Abigail had last seen her eldest son. Separated from John Quincy and hardly hearing from him, she continued addressing him in the same tone in which she had spoken to him as a young child of eleven. When Abigail finally sailed to Europe in 1784, their relationship warmed, and their subsequent letter exchanges became more frequent and more interesting, even if they still retained a certain reserve and emotional distance absent from the father-son correspondence.

Upon his return from Russia, John Adams began to treat the fifteen-year-old John Quincy as a contemporary, if not quite an equal, for the first time. "He is grown a Man in Understanding as well as Stature," John Adams commented to his wife after John Quincy's return from The Hague. John was undoubtedly pleased to find his son offering "a very intelligent and entertaining Account of his Travels to and from the North."[70] His father took him on as his personal secretary and closest confidant, and on the occasions when he sent John Quincy abroad to deliver papers, he missed his son terribly. "I want you here," John wrote his son during one of John Quincy's trips to London, "as a Secretary, as a Companion and as a Pupill."[71] While John Adams did not think his son's education was yet complete, he recognized that he had entered a new stage of maturity.

John Adams assessed that it was now time for John Quincy's education to move beyond his books and observations into the real world of statesmen. For this, he would need to learn the art of rhetoric. His father had started this process by urging his son to keep a journal, and his mother had demanded that he write her thoughtful letters. They both encouraged him to learn the basics of style, logic, and structure from the classics. But this was just the foundation. To take the next step, he would need to observe public speakers and understand what was worth emulating. When John Quincy was in London, his father encouraged him to attend Parliament, "a great and illustrious School," hoping he would take lessons from the English parliamentarians and apply these later to his own speech.[72]

Considering the number of significant public speeches John Quincy would make later in his career, it is interesting to note which skills he thought necessary and desirable in political speech. After hearing William Pitt and Charles Fox, he compared the two, writing that "Mr. Pitt, is upon the whole the best, and most pleasing speaker of them all. He has much grace, in speaking, and has an admirable choice of words, he speaks very fluently . . . and he was not once embarrassed to express his Ideas. Mr. Fox on the contrary speaks with such an amazing heat and rapidity, that he often gets embarrassed, and stammers sometime before he can express himself; his Ideas are all striking, but they flow upon him, in such numbers, that he cannot express them without difficulty."[73] John Quincy praised Pitt's fluency, diction, and style, and commended him for presenting his ideas directly and without hesitation. While he found fault with Fox for allowing his emotions to affect his clarity, he does admit the powerful mix of his "heat" and ideas, even when they were jumbled. John Quincy closed his account by asserting to his father that these judgments, even if erroneous, were his own. "In this matter," he concluded, he had followed "the Ideas of no one."[74]

John Quincy was developing strong feelings of self-confidence. In Paris, he was in daily contact with most of the diplomatic corps and internalized their habits and protocols. He had studied at the best university in Europe and successfully traveled independently. Assisting his father with diplomatic and financial correspondence, attending the theater and ballet, and observing various court functions, he found he could more than handle himself in conversation with his elders, the most impressive of whom was Thomas Jefferson, who had recently been appointed U.S. minister to France. Jefferson spent much of his time with the Adamses and became a companion, tutor, and mentor to young John Quincy. "Spent the evening with Mr. Jefferson," John recorded in his diary, "who I love to be with, because he is a man of very extensive learning, and pleasing manners."[75] It is interesting to speculate what political principles Jefferson may have passed on to his young pupil.

But the most important reason for his growing sense of well-being was that for the first time in almost five years, John Quincy was once again surrounded by his family and friends. In 1784 his mother and sister had sailed to Europe to rejoin the Adams men. The reunion was a joyful one, with John Quincy (or "Jack," as his mother referred to him) writing his father, "I will not attempt to describe my feelings at meeting two persons so dear to me . . . I will only say I was completely happy."[76] His mother was equally overcome with emotion, and shocked that her little boy had grown into a man whose manners, behavior, and appearance so closely resembled those of his father. And his sister, with just a dash of sisterly sarcasm, informed a cousin that she did "not find him a monster as I expected."[77]

Despite his happy surroundings, John Quincy realized that he could not build a career as an American statesman in Europe. "The desire of returning to America still possesses me," he wrote his cousin in late 1784.[78] But as he readily admitted, his wish to study at Harvard was only one reason for his desired return to his native country. When he wrote that "my country has over me an attractive power which I do not understand," he was certainly cognizant that returning home would be an astute career move as well.

Just as Abigail had sent John Quincy to Europe to witness the diplomatic birth of the American nation on the international stage, she now pushed him to return to America to complete his education and start his political career. While she was loath to part again with her son, with whom she had spent less than three years of the past decade, she knew it would be "much for his advantage" to return to the United States and attend Harvard. Not only would he make up for educational deficiencies, he would also find himself in the company of his peers for the first time in years. And it was in this setting he would need to excel. "America," Abigail noted, was "the theatre for a young fellow who has any ambition to distinguish himself."[79] The high ambitions Abigail held for her son were linked to service to the young republic. She wanted him to return to America to make a proper study of the nation's interests and to start a public career that "will one day call your services, either in the Cabinet or Field."[80]

Talk of John Quincy's future filled many nights at the Adamses' Parisian home. His sister Abigail, known as Nabby, echoed Abigail's point that if John Quincy wanted to spend his life and career in America, "it was time for him to go there." She shared her parents' view that too long an absence from America would be detrimental to John Quincy's development and future prospects. She saw that her brother knew the customs and history of Europe, which would serve him well as a future statesman. But to gain such an understanding in the "ideas of the Country, People, manners, and Customs" of America, he would need to return and build a career and a reputation for himself there.[81]

While John Quincy realized the necessity of the path before him, he was hardly excited by the prospect of returning to America to attend Harvard and study law. How could he be? For the past decade his life had been a whirlwind as he traveled through Europe and met with the most important figures on the world stage. He had enjoyed a certain proximity to power while serving as secretary first to Dana and later to his father. His life had been exceptional. Now as he contemplated what the next decade would hold for him—several years in college "subjected to all the rules which I have so long been freed from," three years plunging "into the dry and tedious study of the Law," and then four more years of drudgery laboring to "bring myself into notice"—the road ahead looked endless. Writing in his journal, John Quincy noted, "it is really a prospect somewhat discouraging for a youth of my ambition."[82]

But he was an Adams, and the family's ambition had been firmly implanted in him by this time.

Alongside his ambitions and studiousness, John Quincy was developing other, less attractive qualities. Upon his return to America, his cousin found him "exceedingly severe upon the Foibles of Mankind."[83] After meeting Ezra Stiles, the president of Yale College, John Quincy commented that Stiles was "an uncommon instance of the deepest learning without a spark of genius."[84] His disdain applied equally to Harvard. Once enrolled there, he reported that his tutors were "ignorant in Greek" and were "far from being possessed of those qualities which I should suppose necessary."[85] His younger brother Tom told John Quincy that he was perhaps becoming a bit too argumentative, as he seemed "to differ most always from everyone else in company."[86] Whether or not he was following too precisely his mother's advice about great men not smiling, John Quincy was growing into a rather critical young man.

It must have come as quite a blow, then, when Harvard rejected his initial application. After interviewing him, Harvard's president decided that the youth was not quite ready for matriculation. His greatest deficiency, which must have been galling for John Adams to learn, was in the classics. So John Quincy retreated to Haverhill, Massachusetts, to be tutored by his uncle, the Reverend John Shaw, and studied at all hours, often reading at his desk for more than ten hours a day. His aunt reported that the midnight hour found him still crouched over his desk, as "his Candle goeth not out by Night."[87] Much to John Quincy's relief, when he returned to Harvard in March and was tested by the president of the college, four tutors, three professors, and the librarian, he passed. In fact, his exceptionally high exam score and his studies abroad qualified him for admission into the junior class.

Equally concerned with earning parental praise and avoiding their opprobrium, John Quincy brought an intensity to his work that would both astound and concern those around him. His family reported that "he is too much *engaged*" with his studies, and worried that the single-mindedness he brought to them "was of no service to his Health whatever it may have been to his mind."[88] Even his mother recognized that her eldest son's commitment to fulfilling parental expectations was starting to make him "too negligent of those attentions which are due to the World, & which tho they may appear little, & trifling, much of our happiness is found by experience to depend on them."[89] While Abigail might have worried that John Quincy's seriousness was endangering his happiness, he thought it a necessary prerequisite to his success.

Throughout his entire life, John Quincy had heard that he was a preternaturally gifted young man who had been blessed with intellect and opportunity. Now at Harvard, for the first time he could measure himself against his contemporaries. In ambition, it would have been hard to find his equal. Quoting Shakespeare's *Henry V,* John Quincy conceded that "if it be a Sin to covet Honour, I am the most offending Soul alive."[90] But when he thought about the skills he needed to fulfill his ambitions, he found himself wanting. This was most conspicuous in the realm of rhetoric. As he knew from his father, effective use of the written word and speech would be his means of ascent. But he knew that even in his small circle of friends, he did not possess "the faculty of convincing persons."[91] So he worked hard at perfecting his public-speaking techniques. His attempts were criticized at first, but he persisted in his efforts until he became recognized as an expert.

The importance John Quincy attributed to speech can best be seen years later, while he was serving as a senator from Massachusetts and returned to Harvard for a term as a professor of rhetoric and oratory. His lectures covered the history of rhetoric, analyzed various speech techniques, and discussed the significance of speech in a republic.[92] These lectures were almost oddly biographical. John Quincy told his students that in Athens and Rome "eloquence was POWER. It was at once the instrument and the spur to ambition. The talent of public speaking was the key to the highest dignities; the passport to the supreme domination of the state."[93] This might very well have described the young John Quincy's hopes for himself. At the very least, it was his advice to ambitious and public-minded young men that skill in public speaking was a critical component of gaining and exercising power.

Throughout these lectures, John Quincy highlighted his desire to combine his personal ambition for fame and success with his desire to serve the nation. Toward the end of his inaugural lecture he asked whether there is "among you a youth, whose bosom burns with the fires of honorable ambition; who aspires to immortalize his name by the extent and importance of his services to his country; whose visions of futurity glow with the hope of presiding in her councils, of directing her affairs, of appearing to future ages on the rolls of fame, as her ornament and pride?"[94] John Quincy knew that twenty years earlier he had been that youth, burning to direct the affairs of his country and write his name into the nation's history.

Toward the end of his collegiate term, it became clear that Adams was focusing as much attention on public affairs and public speaking as he was on his formal studies.[95] He gave speeches on the function of liberal education in a democratic society and the role of civil discord in fomenting change. He wrote about the virtues of republicanism, the dangers of a government without "sufficient energy," and the importance of servicing the national debt.[96]

From his collegiate writings, it appears that John Quincy meant "republican" as a type of government, an ideological disposition opposed to monarchy, and a moral commitment to communal action. Even though these speeches were works in progress, five significant themes emerged that would run throughout his career. The first was a commitment to the progressive improvement of the country's citizens. In one of his early speeches at Harvard, Adams argued that the purpose of education was utilitarian. Its aim should be to turn the individual's attention from considerations of personal happiness to those of patriotism and wisdom. Similarly, he made the argument that governments ought to be judged by the "degree to which they are useful to and improve society."[97] Second, he often discussed the right balance between liberty and equality, arguing that too much equality was not necessarily a good thing. In an address before the Phi Beta Kappa society and with the growing violence of Shays's rebellion very much on his mind, Adams claimed that civil discord, if managed properly and contained within the political system, could be useful and healthy to public discourse. However, using the same reasoning that Edmund Burke would apply to the French Revolution, Adams cautioned that such civil discord could also spread too quickly and lead to the horrors of a civil war. He did not think that Shays's rebellion would prove such an example, but was fairly certain that it would result in the loss of life. This potential for instability led to a third theme that he, like his father, would stress throughout his political career. John Quincy began to develop a firmly held belief that the best antidote to political instability and violence was a strong and energetic central government.

The fourth thread that emerged in Adams's early writing was his wary admiration of the British system of governance. Specifically, Adams noted the strength of its navy, its commercial system, and most especially its finances. In his commencement address, Adams argued that maintenance of public credit by regularly servicing the national debt was "the foundation upon which the fabric of national grandeur has been erected." Looking to historical examples, he posited that when a nation's credit was perceived as trustworthy by other nations, that country would benefit from foreign investment. Great Britain was the prime example of this phenomenon, as her prudent fiscal policy propped up her strategic ambitions. Adams thought that the British example offered an applicable lesson that if a weak new country like America reliably serviced her debts, she could become a strong nation that attracted capital. Characteristically ignoring the dire political consequences of publicly praising Britain, Adams announced that in handling its affairs, Great Britain offered an "imitation for the American state."[98]

Finally, these early writings contain the foundations of Adams's belief that America's republicanism stood in distinct opposition to the monarchies of the Old World. Having been absent so long from his native land, and having received so much of his education in Europe, he feared that his political sentiments would be insufficiently patriotic. "But, I find on the contrary," he informed his mother in a letter written from Harvard, "that I am the best republican here, and with my classmates if I ever have any disputes on the subject, I am always obliged to defend that side of the question."[99] Rather than thinking that some of Europe's institutions should be imported to America, as his classmates argued on occasion, Adams thought the reverse would eventually be true. As long as the young republic kept its finances in good order, "our eagle would soon extend the wings of protection, to the wretched object of tyranny and persecution in every quarter of the globe."[100] Whether this was meant as a call to export America's revolution or just its republican principles of opposition to unjust and tyrannical regimes was left unanswered. However, starting with his ruminations in college, Adams had already begun to develop his belief that America's mission extended far beyond the country's shores.

But these were grandiose thoughts, and John Quincy had far more immediate challenges ahead. He first faced the question of what to do after graduating from Harvard. As ever, his parents were at hand to chart the course forward, and dictated one that looked remarkably similar to his father's. After graduating from Harvard, John Quincy should read law, start his own legal practice, marry, establish a public reputation for integrity, wisdom, and hard work, and gradually involve himself in public affairs. During his son's junior year, John Adams wrote his financial agent, Dr. Cotton Tufts, asking him, "What are we to do then about John? What lawyer shall we desire to take him, in town or country?"[101] They made arrangements for John Quincy to study with Theophilus Parsons, a distinguished Newburyport lawyer.

Studying law was intended to teach John Quincy a trade, but it was also meant to enable his financial independence and further his professional, and ultimately political, prospects. His father wrote him, "you must prepare yourself to get your Bread," and told him not to count on parental support for much longer.[102] Warning him against complacency, and expertly weaving in both praise and guilt, Abigail admonished her son to "spend those hours which others devote to Cards and folly in investigating the Great principals by which nations have risen to Glory and eminence, for your Country will one day call for your services."[103] His father advised him not to be too social, as "it consumes ones time insensibly."[104] And if parental pressure were not enough, John Quincy continued to be assured by others that great things awaited him. Typical of this was the Reverend Jeremy Belknap, who praised John's commencement address by claiming that it was proof that "your country will have a pledge of a succession of abilities in the same Family still to add to her Cause and espouse her interest."[105]

John Quincy worried that he could not possibly fulfill all of these expectations. He found the social life of Newburyport much more interesting than the tedium of legal studies. Even though he often berated himself for doing so, he spent many nights not at his desk, but with friends in the local taverns drinking, playing cards, dancing, and on one occasion serenading young ladies till three or four in the morning.[106] Knowing that it would be a long time before he could achieve financial independence, he despondently wrote his mother, "my anxiety will be very great, untill I shall stand upon my own ground. At my time of life it is a grievous mortification to be dependent for a subsistence even though it be upon a Parent."[107] He summed up his collegiate experience by informing his mother that "it had reduced my opinion of myself and of my future prospects to a nearer level with truth so that making allowances for the general exaggerations of youth I do not overrate myself more than people in general are apt to do."[108] College had been humbling. After his time in Europe in the company of such luminaries as his father, Jefferson, and Franklin, this was perhaps a good thing. But such humbling experiences, coupled with incessant family exhortations to greatness, were leading Adams to develop a fear of failure.

He addressed his fears in a September 1788 speech he delivered as a young alumnus to Harvard's Phi Beta Kappa society. Entitling his talk "Ambition for a Young Man," Adams began his speech by describing the plight of ambitious youth who looked to their futures with a mixture of hope for success and fear that they would not measure up to others' expectations. These youths, and he included himself as one of them, "soar rapidly upon the wings of a flattering imagination and soon lose ourselves bewildered amidst the magnificent objects with which we have adorned the road around us." But once they graduated from college and embarked upon their careers, they realized that "the path of life becomes rugged with thorns: a thousand obstacles apparently stand before us."[109] This was as autobiographical a talk as Adams ever gave. Standing at the cusp of adulthood, feeling familial pressure not only to succeed but also to become painfully preeminent, Adams worried that he would fall short of the glorious future prescribed for him.

It was at about this time that John Quincy fell into the first and deepest depression of his life. He had trouble sleeping, grew exceedingly anxious, and lapsed into a profound melancholy. On his twentieth birthday, he despondently confessed, "I am good for nothing, and cannot even carry myself forward in the world." The road ahead looked long, daunting, and devoid of pleasure. He had three more years of legal studies and then "how many more years, to plod along, mechanically, if I should live; before I shall really get into the world? Grant me patience ye powers! for I sicken, at the very idea."[110] It remains unclear exactly what set off this acute personal crisis. Perhaps it was the relentless pressure of his parents' high hopes. Perhaps it was his continuing dependence on them. Maybe it was exacerbated by an intense sense of loneliness that dogged him. Mostly though, it seems that suspended between the promise of the future and the drudgery of the present, Adams struggled to define his purpose. In his journal, he wrote that "the question, what am I to do in this world recurs to me very frequently and never without causing great anxiety, and a depression of spirits. My prospects appear darker to me every day." Unable to drag his thoughts away from his future, and deeply afraid of failure, he began, at least in private, to repudiate the family creed. He wrote, "I do not wish to look into futurity; and were the leaves of fate to be opened before me, I should shrink from the perusal. Fortune, I do not covet. Honours, I begin to think are not worth seeking."[111]

The more John Quincy thought about his future, the more debilitating his depression became. As he approached a career, independence, and adulthood, he found himself flailing, suddenly unsure of the path ahead. All he could think about was the distance between his present state and his imagined future, and he found his moods swinging wildly between exuberance and despair. "I am sometimes elated with hope," he recorded in his diary, and "sometimes contented with indifference, but often tormented with fears, and depressed by the most discouraging appearances."[112] His younger brother Charles thought that the pressure he placed on himself was causing him to "raise hills in your imagination more difficult to ascend than you will in reality find them," and encouraged him to "persuade yourself to take the world a little more fair and easy."[113] But these words had little effect, as John Quincy became convinced that despite all the advantages he had been given, and his yearning for fame, power, and recognition, he would succumb to his own sadness and make nothing of his life.[114]

Compounding his anxieties and deepening his depression, Adams had fallen desperately in love with Mary Frazier, a young lady in Newburyport. Struck by her charm, beauty, and intelligence, he visited her, wrote poetry to her, and pursued her. Years later when talking with an old friend, Adams stated that his love for Mary "was a consuming flame kindled by her. Love such as I felt for that Lady is a distressing malady; it made me restless, sick, unhappy; indeed, I may say wretched."[115] This was not the first time that Adams found himself ridden with angst and disoriented by the fairer sex. Earlier, when boarding with his aunt and uncle in Haverhill, he had become infatuated with another young lady. That had been a painful experience for the young John Quincy, who had watched his emotions battle his reason, confiding, "I have heretofore more than once, been obliged to exert all my Resolution to keep myself free from a Passion, which I could not indulge."[116] He resolved not to pursue this woman, exhorting himself not to "indulge" in any relationships for many years to come.

As with most critical decisions of his youth, the decision not to pursue these women was imposed on him by his mother. Hearing rumors of his attractions, she wrote multiple letters to John Quincy demanding that he not let his personal longings stymie his professional development. Reluctantly, he broke off the precollegiate relationship in Haverhill. But now, in Newburyport and in love, John Quincy found his angst amplified by his parents'—though it would be more accurate to say mother's—stern and disapproving voice. Abigail reminded her eldest son of the sacrifices that had been made on his behalf and pointed out the dangers of forming too early an attachment. She cautioned her son that the wrong choice of a partner or too early a marriage could derail his ambitions for advancement. Abigail emphasized that familial duty and personal ambition required him to deny following his desires. And in case she had not underlined the point clearly enough, Abigail emphasized John Quincy's continued financial dependence on his parents. This finally had the desired effect, and John Quincy ended the relationship. However, Adams's depression had become so severe that he withdrew from Newburyport and returned home to Braintree in a nearly debilitated state.

When John Quincy fled to Braintree lost in distracting and solitary thought, his father helped him regain his equilibrium by hunting, walking, riding, and reading at his son's side. When John Quincy complained to his father about his prospects, the elder Adams continued to cheer his son, telling him his anxiety was misplaced. "Confidence in your Talents & Fidelity, must arise by degrees from Experience," he wrote his son. John Quincy had excelled in his studies, but now his career progress was necessarily gradual. His father knew of and identified with his son's overwhelming desire to leave a mark on his country. John Adams recalled his own trials as an ambitious young attorney struggling with a sense of "Ennui" and counseled his son to "take large droughts of Patience" while bending to his work.[117] But his father also emphasized that he needed to do something, not merely be somebody. "Your Name can as yet be no more than that of a promising Youth—They will call you after sometime a growing young Man."[118] Gently, John Adams explained to his son that it did not matter what he had accomplished in his studies, what expectations others had for him, or even what ambitions he harbored for himself. What mattered most would be what he did next.

If ambition had been the cause of John Quincy's melancholy, it was also to be his salvation. He moved to Boston, opened a small legal practice with money loaned to him by his parents, and over the next four years devoted himself to working as an attorney and advancing his name in the public realm. Given his lack of resources, this was probably a prudent decision. But it was not a happy one. His aunt wrote him a comforting letter saying how she could shed "tear for tear" over his sacrifices for "Situation & filial Duty."[119] Adams had proved himself more than willing to please his family at the expense of his own personal desires. Stifling his passions, he turned "to the severer toils" of law, country, and duty.[120] To an already serious and aloof young man, emotional distance was an unfortunate personal habit to acquire. While he had been a talkative and charming youth, he seemed to be transforming into a young man of little social skill or grace. As an aspiring politician, this would be a decided handicap. But as a polemicist, Adams would be well served by his aggressive inclinations.

John Quincy Adams was a child of New England. From this culture he inherited certain tendencies, including a focus on education, morality, and industriousness. Tracing such habits back to their East Anglian ancestors, the historian David Hackett Fischer wrote that the Puritan forefathers "tended to be exceptionally literate, highly skilled, and heavily urban in their English origins. They were a people of substance, character, and deep personal piety."[121] They were also an opinionated and argumentative people. "Resistance to something was the law of New England nature," Henry Adams later wrote. According to Henry, this particular New England mind-set saw injustice everywhere and "viewed the world chiefly as a thing to be reformed."[122] This all translated into a feverish work ethic, an obsession with improvement and progress, and an oppositional nature.

Such inclinations were common enough, but the Adamses took these ideas even further. Because of John Adams's prominent position, it meant being "more conspicuous" and being held to a more exacting standard of conduct than "that of a Common Traveller."[123] In a near-ceaseless refrain from the time he departed America with his father at the age of ten, John Quincy's family reminded him of the "peculiar advantages" that he was receiving. They wrote letter after letter warning him that "it is your own fault if you neglect to make a right improvement of the talents that are put into your hands."[124] Even when they were encouraging their son, they reminded him of his responsibility not to squander his talents and waste his advantages. "When you feel disposed to find fault with your stars," his mother reminded him, "bethink yourself how preferable your situation is to that of many others."[125] John Quincy's reply was telling, responding to his mother's advice that "perhaps the idea, that 'to whom much is given, of him, *much shall be required,*' does not at present tend to alleviate the disagreeable sensations, which . . . prevail in my mind."[126] While hearing that he was more fortunate than others was true, it did nothing to lighten his concerns, and to a young man always eager for signs of parental approval, his mother's words of consolation must have seemed like a rebuke.

Although the Adamses' words might have felt severe to John Quincy, they were intended to help prepare him for the extraordinary pressures and demands of high office. "Whenever a great able and Upright Man appears," John Adams wrote his son, "there will be ever a Swarm of little, corrupt, weak or wicked ones, who will find among the People Such Numbers like themselves, as to form a Body capable of obstructing diverting and interrupting him." Referring to William Pitt in this case, the elder Adams was advising his son on how to serve a mercurial public. With such a "publick," the chance to lead was rare, and rarer still was the statesman who could do so "generally by surprize and against their Will."[127] This was the Adamses' model of a statesman: a disinterested public servant imposing order on a confused electorate and guiding the country to progress.

John Adams was an eminently practical politician, as his actions in the international and domestic realms demonstrated. Yet, to his wife and to his son, he also stressed that it was more honorable to be on the unpopular side of an issue. Hearing that John Quincy had staked out a minority position on a series of rather inconsequential public matters, he congratulated his son, writing, "I rejoice that you have taken the Unpopular Side of the Questions." His paternal pride emanated not "because I love Unpopularity or wish you to be unpopular; but because I believe the unpopular Side in these Instances to be right."[128] As John made clear to his son, being an Adams meant acting in a disinterested fashion, favoring proper conduct and long-term results above immediate political advantage. It is going too far to say that John Quincy Adams deliberately courted controversy in his career. Like his father, he was a politician, and many of his actions demonstrated a desire to seek consensus. However, when he did find himself staking out an unpopular position, which happened regularly enough, his father's appeal to independent judgment would serve as solace and help him condone his own actions. But if that was the model, both John and Abigail recognized that the competitive world of democratic politics also demanded talent, skill, and ambition. As John wrote Abigail in one of his more plainspoken letters, their goal must be to teach their children "not only to do virtuously but to excel."[129] As long as these overlapped, there was no problem. But when they conflicted with each other, as was often the case in politics, the Adamses were less clear in their guidance for reconciling these twin, and often opposed, inclinations.

The Adamses understood that they were placing a special burden on their eldest son. He was meant to stand apart, to act virtuously, and to possess and succeed at exceedingly lofty goals. He was meant to succeed in the face of little, corrupt, weak, and wicked men who would try to steer him from that which was necessary to that which would win him the applause of the moment. Accepting the responsibility of being an Adams drove John Quincy toward extraordinary accomplishment, but also left him ridden with intense anxiety throughout his life. Typical of his fears were the words recorded in a diary entry on his fiftieth birthday, where his thoughts ran "to humiliation which spring from the still recurring questions to what purpose have I lived."[130] This was coming from a man who had just been named secretary of state and was well on his way to the presidency.

The cost of carrying such a burden was high. John Quincy described himself as reserved, cold, and aloof.[131] Visiting his deserted childhood home on his return from Europe, he wrote to his mother of the "strangest sensations. . . . Bereft of its former inhabitants, it appeared to me, in a gloomy, unpleasant light." But as she had admonished him to keep his letters free from sentiment, he would try not to dwell on the fact that much of his childhood appeared solitary and lonely.[132] "Separation from all the dearest connections which give a relish to the pleasures of life, and which alleviate its evils, has been almost constantly my fate from my infancy," he observed in a letter to his sister.[133] This was his course, and one that had been imposed on him from his earliest youth. The result, he concluded in the same letter, was an ability "to regulate my expectations and even my wishes." As he would later note, "I am by nature a silent animal, and my mother's constant lesson in childhood, that children in company should be seen and not heard, confirmed me irrevocably in what I now deem a bad habit."[134] Suppressing his emotions might have been a useful, perhaps even necessary, response, but it warped his personality, transforming him from a garrulous and charming youth into an austere and imposing man. His own son later wrote that he thought his father's inner life was impenetrable and noted that it was as if he were "perpetually wearing the Iron mask."[135]

Much of John Quincy's youth had been spent in the company not of his contemporaries, but of older dignitaries and in foreign capitals that often seemed such *"out of the way* place[s]."[136] From a very early age, he felt the extraordinary internal and external pressure of being an Adams. He knew that his actions would be observed and judged not on their own, but as a comment on his family and on his country. By necessity and through parental guidance, dignity, reserve, and moral certitude governed his conduct. He was also his father's son, and from him inherited a short temper, an inclination toward opposition, a tendency to see those who differed from him as enemies, and an overly developed capacity for reflection and depression. But whereas John Adams had his wife, Abigail, as the most constant and supportive of companions, John Quincy had no one with whom to share his hopes, his doubts, and his loneliness.

His parents had drilled into him an almost inexhaustible capacity for work, an intellect that was catholic in scope, and a belief that his own fate was tied to the nation's. He would set up law offices, build a practice, start a family, bring his name into public notice, and begin his climb in the realm of public affairs. But if the general direction was clear, the path before him was less certain. As he had asked in his Phi Beta Kappa address at Harvard, would the soaring heights of ambition blind him to the more pertinent challenges he faced? Would the obstacles in his path undercut his progress? Would he know when a problem could become an opportunity? And when he encountered such opportunities, would he know what to do?

These questions were as applicable to the nation as they were to Adams. The nation might have pretensions of future greatness, but in the early 1790s it was a small, divided, and defenseless republic with immature, if not nonexistent, institutions. To be sure, there were reasons for moderate optimism—a wide ocean separating America from Europe, a rapidly expanding population with a commercial spirit, and a new government designed to safeguard the liberty of its inhabitants. But those were aspirations rather than established facts; believing in a powerful America that set an example with its republican conduct did not make it so. In Adams's formative years and through his writings, he had sketched certain necessities for America's future growth: security, expansion, a progressive spirit of improvement, and a moral impulse. But how these fit together, and in what sequence, remained shrouded in an impenetrable fog. Soon crises in the domestic and international arenas offered Adams the chance to chart his way forward.

2

CLANS AND TRIBES AT
ETERNAL WAR

European Diplomacy and American Politics

In July 1794, on his twenty-seventh birthday, John Quincy Adams was ushered into President George Washington's office and handed a peace pipe. The president was hosting a delegation of Chickasaw Indians, and Adams, as the newly appointed American minister to the Netherlands, was invited to join them in a ceremonial smoke. While John Quincy Adams's first official act as a public official was certainly a heady experience, domestic and foreign circumstances were hardly as peaceful as the ceremony indicated.

Inaugurated as the first president of the newly formed United States in 1789, George Washington was a year into his second term when he met with the younger Adams. The president was already well acquainted with the Adams family, having worked closely with John Adams since the War for Independence some twenty years earlier and currently leading the new nation with Adams sitting as his vice president. Without any good precedents in the preceding two thousand–plus years over how to behave and how to govern in a republic, much of Washington's first term had been consumed with critical, if mundane, procedural tasks such as determining how to receive guests and debating the appropriate titles of address for government officials.[1] From putting together a diverse cabinet of advisers to promoting a federal assumption of the individual states' debts, most of the substance of Washington's first term consisted of conceiving and implementing the appropriate financial and political infrastructure that would allow the nation to be governed. But the birth of political factions and party politics at home, which coincided with and was midwifed by the outbreak of the French Revolution in 1789, and the descent of that revolution into ideological warfare and terror by 1792–1793, challenged Washington's desire for domestic tranquility.

Against such a backdrop, the president faced two challenges to federal authority as his second term began. Protesting settler incursions onto their traditional lands, a group of Indian tribes had banded together into a confederacy to fight for control of the Northwest Territory. After suffering a number of military defeats, Washington had dispatched Revolutionary War hero "Mad" Anthony Wayne to put down the insurrection. At the same time farmers in western Pennsylvania, many of them Revolutionary War veterans, were protesting the imposition of a tax on the whiskey they used as a medium of exchange and had attacked the home of a federal tax collector. Recognizing this Whiskey Rebellion as a challenge to the authority of the federal government, the president ordered a peace commission to negotiate with the farmers while simultaneously raising a militia of thirteen thousand men in the event he needed to use force to put down the rebellion.

Abroad, events looked even more turbulent. With Maximilien de Robespierre's ascension to power, the French Revolution kicked into high gear and plunged France into a reign of terror. The internal violence of France projected itself beyond the nation's borders as French armies marched across the continent. Having declared war on both the British and the Dutch, France took the fight to the high seas. American neutral shipping became a target of both sides. Beyond Europe, American ships increasingly fell prey to pirates from the Barbary States of North Africa. Meanwhile, Britain had yet to evacuate its troops from a series of forts in the Northwest Territory despite its pledge to do so at the 1783 Peace of Paris. With no navy to speak of, and a small and only recently reorganized army, the United States was at the mercy of its opponents.[2]

From the outset, it was impressed on Adams that his job as America's minister to the Netherlands was one of economic statecraft. While in Philadelphia, he met with President Washington, Secretary of State Edmund Randolph, and Secretary of the Treasury Alexander Hamilton. All three delivered the same message—that the interests of the United States depended on its ability to remain solvent. Specifically, he was instructed to obtain a new loan from the Dutch government and to administer loans already in existence. In a letter to the secretary of state, President Washington commented that Adams's "duties at the Hague, will be few, & simple; chiefly of a pecuniary sort."[3] This message was reinforced in Adams's meetings with both the State Department and Treasury. As Adams reported to his father, "The Secretary of State says that the mission is almost exclusively reduced to a pecuniary negotiation."[4]

Both Randolph and Hamilton recommended that John Quincy read through the official record to familiarize himself with the relevant issues and the current state of affairs between America and its Dutch creditors.

Doing so, Adams found himself reading his own father's dispatches from The Hague some twenty years prior, when the elder Adams struggled to secure Dutch backing for the American War for Independence. Stepping into his father's shoes left him feeling amazed and humbled. But as was so often the case, the inevitable comparison to his father had the younger Adams doubting that his own career would add up to much. In several letters to his father, Adams complained that he had given up a successful career as a lawyer to take on an uncertain path that promised little, and at the outset of his appointment, Adams already found himself thinking about how long he ought to pursue a diplomatic career. Humility, anxiety, and the pose of republican disinterestedness prompted him to declare that "it is proper for me to determine how long I shall bear [this position]. And this is a subject of much reflection and much anxiety to my mind." He wrote his father asking for his advice. "I have stopped short in my career," he continued, "forsaken the path which would have led me to independence and security in private life, and stepped into a totally different direction."[5]

Just as he had consoled his son during his low period studying the law several years earlier, the elder Adams now responded to John Quincy's worries with reassurance. He dismissed the concern that this was an unimportant position because it dealt merely with finance. Seeing a diplomatic posting abroad as simply a matter of "pecuniary Negotiation" gave short shrift to his daily work. For, the "Post at the Hague is an important Diplomatick Station, which may afford many opportunities of acquiring political Information and of penetrating the Designs of many Cabinets in Europe." Daily contact with diplomats, politicians, businessmen, and soldiers would give him access to the most current political intelligence on the continent. If he listened carefully and wrote analytically, he would prove an invaluable asset to his country as it evaluated its prospects and considered its policies. This was not simply the vice president's advice to an ambitious, if nervous, young diplomat—it was also paternal advice. John Adams complimented his son on his clear and forceful writing style, encouraged his prospects for speedy promotion within the foreign service, and, thinking of his son's long-term political prospects, advised that he broaden his network to include "able Men in the southern & middle States as well as in the northern ones." Recalling that he himself had once been a young man in a hurry, Adams counseled his son that he was now playing a long game and that perseverance and patience would be his most significant assets.[6]

Heeding his father's counsel, John Quincy Adams quickly became the administration's most important set of eyes and ears in Europe from his listening post at The Hague. Stepping into a Europe in the throes of France's revolution and revolutionary wars, Adams assessed that "the prospects of Europe are thickening, and a deadly gloom hangs over their futurity." This was largely due to what he saw as the inevitable clash between republican and autocratic systems of governance. The appeal of republicanism in Europe was increasing—but so too was monarchical resistance to and suppression of it. At the same time, it remained unclear what types of governments this republican spirit might produce. In an early observation of the European scene, Adams noted that while "the progress of opinions adverse to the system of hereditary privileges is continuously advancing," it was far too early to predict what the alternatives might be, and whether they were more or less harmful to American interests.[7] The continent's darkening future was also exacerbated by the nature of European political geography. The proximity of its warring states meant that any peace achieved through a rough balance of power would likely prove fleeting. This was particularly true when any one state challenged that stability.

Adams's emerging belief in the importance of American geographic, political, economic, and ideological unity came into starker relief when placed against a backdrop of warring European states. He arrived in the Netherlands as the French armies marched into the heart of the country. Meanwhile, a coalition of hostile states formed to fight the French juggernaut. To Adams, this was not a new story, but a classically European one: a divided European continent meant a perpetually hostile collection of states, which in turn led to a dangerous centralization of state power and the creation of standing armies. In the name of security, these autocratic governments and the military forces that served them posed an existential threat to liberty, prosperity, and peace.

For the newly formed United States, nothing could be worse to its republican ideals than division. To Adams, and to many of the founding generation, there was a fear that any disintegration of the fragile Union would compel the various state governments to build up their own militias as they postured for political advantage and territorial aggrandizement. The political division of the North American continent would then make the individually sovereign states susceptible to European interference and perhaps even intervention. Europe's current state of affairs was the dystopian future America's founding statesmen sought to avoid at all costs.

Adams argued that for America to achieve independence, growth, and power, it had to prevent European divisions from taking root in North America. This was a negative policy aim, but one of supreme importance. And if European division was the ultimate threat, dismemberment of the United States was the proximate danger. Unfortunately, America was particularly susceptible to this danger because of its lack of an ability to defend itself. It had already proved averse to taxing itself; it was politically fractious; it had no navy; and, as Adams would later comment, many Americans held the misguided but sincere belief that international politics was based on reason, not power. As Adams would claim, this was not only wrong, but also dangerous, because it allowed many American politicians to cling to the erroneous belief that right made might in international relations.

Witnessing European high politics in the midst of war and societal upheavals gave Adams a more realistic understanding of the dynamics of power. Later, he would write disdainfully of American politicians who "need a tour of travel [abroad] . . . to learn" certain basic truths.[8] He lamented that American politicians, detached from Europe by the seeming security of the Atlantic, made the potentially fatal error of "confounding the principles of internal government with those of external relations. We suppose the principles adopted for the establishment of our civil liberty extend to our political concerns. . . . It is not many years since a member of Congress, and a very good man too, told me that he rejoiced at the French revolution, because it would prove to the world that men were susceptible of being governed by *reason alone*. He has changed his mind, and so have many others, but the change must be more general. There must be force for the government of mankind, and whoever in this world does not choose to fight for his freedom, must turn Quaker or look out for a master."[9]

Disparaging wishful Quaker-like thinking, Adams would develop into a sober analyst of international politics and a forceful advocate for enhanced security. He came to understand that without security, the nascent republican principles and institutions would not survive in a world dominated by militarized empires. Echoing the thoughts of realists throughout the ages, Adams lamented, "in the present condition of the world, and it is much to be doubted whether it will ever be otherwise, that right is not worth a straw which a nation has without force to defend it."[10] Instead, if the country developed its assets unmolested, it would eventually have the power to defend its interests.

Over the course of his diplomatic and early political career, Adams searched for strategies that would allow the young nation time to develop its capabilities. In order to reduce the nation's security risks, Adams advocated the strategies of unity at home and neutrality in foreign affairs. These twin strategies would steer the nation clear of war and dismemberment—events that he knew would be fatal to the young republic and its developing institutions. To Adams, the obvious benefits of a cohesive and unified polity outweighed the negative aspects of a federated union. For even at this stage of his career, Adams was cognizant of the sacrifices to his and the nation's ideals that political union with the southern states would demand. "Much as I must disapprove of the general tenor of southern politics," he explained to his younger brother Charles, "I would rather even yield to their unreasonable pretensions and suffer much for their wrongs, than break the chain that binds us together." Ironic choice of metaphors notwithstanding, it became a central tenet of Adams's political creed that the road to national greatness ran through political union. If united, the country would "proceed with gigantic strides to . . . national greatness; but that if it is once broken, we shall soon divide into a parcel of petty tribes at perpetual war with one another, swayed by rival European powers."[11] The United States would choose either to pursue national greatness through a strong and cohesive union, or it would fall to rivalry, division, and irrelevance. Union would yield decisive political and economic advantage, which would translate into enhanced security, while disunion promised the opposite.[12]

If union formed the domestic side of Adams's policy, its foreign component was independence. To develop its own capacities, the nation would need to steer its own course, independent of foreign pressures. In concrete terms, this meant that the nation would pursue a policy of neutrality abroad. This was easier said than done, as foreign relations in general, and whether or not the nation would support France's revolution in particular, helped spur the growth of political parties in the United States. But Adams believed that neutrality would insulate America from Europe's fratricidal quarrels. This was particularly important for a weak and relatively defenseless country. He also understood that neutrality was neither a natural nor an inevitable state, and could only be accomplished if the country were strong enough not to be forced into taking sides. He maintained that strength would come from commerce, from industry, and from cultivating a sufficiently powerful armed force. Eventually, it would also come from territorial expansion and from having a stronger, more vigorous government.

While Adams eventually came to embody these ideas on the public stage, it was far from a fully articulated strategy when he met with George Washington in the summer of 1794 prior to his posting overseas. Although he had been exposed to diplomacy and high politics abroad as a youth, and had begun to work through some of his ideas about America's place in the world while he was at Harvard, he had not yet developed the various components of the strategy that he thought would best lead the nation to prominence. Before Adams could refine that strategy, he first needed to go overseas to test and revise his ideas, tempering his intellectual beliefs against real experiences in the competitive world of power competition.

Between his entry onto the national scene with a series of influential political essays in the early 1790s and his appointment as secretary of state in 1817, Adams honed a series of strategies that he thought would allow the young nation to grow in strength and insulate itself from Europe's political upheavals. These years were a period of exceptional growth for Adams. He made his first notable public appearance, impressed George Washington, married and built a family, served as a diplomat in the Netherlands and Germany, returned to the United States and was elected to the United States Senate, broke with his party, was appointed American minister to Russia, led the American negotiations with the British to end the War of 1812, and subsequently took up America's most important diplomatic posting abroad in London. Over the course of this quarter century, Adams grew into personal and professional maturity, displaying his growing policy assertiveness, his political independence, and his advocacy on behalf of neutrality abroad, commercial integration into world markets, and enhanced defense capabilities at home.

In the early 1790s, John Quincy Adams charged into the public arena with a series of political essays meant to exonerate his father's politics, which had recently come under attack, and to establish his own name. These essays built on the ideas he first developed at Harvard and laid out much of the political philosophy that would guide his career. The immediate occasion for the first set of these essays was the publication of Thomas Paine's *Rights of Man,* which Paine intended as a refutation of Edmund Burke's *Reflections on the Revolution in France.*[13] Following the outbreak of revolution in France in 1789, Burke had attacked the idea of revolution and swift social change. While he supported social and political progress, he believed it should be accomplished within a society's history and traditions. Burke thought that a revolution aiming to topple not only governments, but also traditions, hierarchy, and long-established institutions would upend social stability. Further, it would bring chaos, violence, and eventually tyranny. Paine saw Burke as a retrograde defender of the status quo and in response published *Rights of Man.* Paine's pamphlet charged that all social institutions that did not benefit the majority of a country's citizens were illegitimate.

As this pamphlet war between Burke and Paine migrated across the Atlantic, it became part of the emerging divide in American politics. In 1790, while serving as vice president, John Adams wrote *Discourses on Davila,* which condemned the French Revolution and called for restraining public passions through a natural aristocracy. In the battle for control of America's foreign and domestic policy, Adams's work was immediately seized upon as antidemocratic. Leading the charge was Secretary of State Thomas Jefferson, who forwarded Paine's pamphlet to a Philadelphia publisher, commenting that he hoped publication would help correct "the political heresies which have sprung up among us."[14] The printer complied with Jefferson's wish and published Paine's work. He also published Jefferson's note and signature as a preface to the American edition. Considering the political mess it landed him in, and the sycophantic apology he subsequently penned to President Washington, it is doubtful that Jefferson wished to be publicly identified with attacking Adams. Regardless of Jefferson's intention, John Adams declined to engage this thinly veiled attack, deeming it beneath the dignity of a sitting vice president and believing that doing so would be injurious to national unity. John Quincy felt no such compunction. Using the pseudonym Publicola, in just over six weeks he dashed off eleven tightly reasoned essays totaling some sixteen thousand words, which were published in Boston's *Columbian Centinel.*

These essays were as much an intellectual response to Thomas Paine as they were a political refutation of Jefferson's attacks. John Quincy argued that it should not be easy to overthrow a government, cautioning that revolutionary France was inherently dangerous. He defended the Anglo-Saxon political system and outlined what he believed were the necessary components of a constitution. Beyond that, the essays accused Jefferson, more than Paine, of illiberal tendencies. Who was the secretary of state, asked Publicola, to say what was true doctrine and what was heresy? John Quincy argued that those claiming to be liberals were in fact less liberal than their opponents, and would willingly suppress dissent if it did not conform to their views.

Amid the sarcasm and animosity, John Quincy's Publicola essays made two main points. He dismissed Paine's assertion that a majority had the right to do whatever it pleased. Adams argued that Paine had confused the rights of the majority with the power of the majority. He warned his countrymen that tyranny of the majority was as detrimental to republican principles as was the arbitrary rule of a king. Additionally, Adams argued that different histories and cultures produced different societal norms. He believed that societies evolved organically and that what was appropriate for one was not necessarily applicable to another. Hence, America's pre-revolutionary belief in equality "was founded upon an equality really existing among them, and not upon the metaphysical speculations of fanciful politicians."[15] This was not the case in Europe, and trying to impose this kind of equality in the face of tradition, history, and culture would privilege abstract philosophy above reality. In one of his more biting lines, Adams charged that "Mr. Paine seems to think it as easy for a nation to change its government, as for a man to change his coat."[16] Just as he did not think Europe's institutions could be imposed on America, Adams also believed that America's political beliefs could not be imposed on other nations.[17] While he believed that it might eventually be possible for European nations to become republics, he argued that it would only be achieved by organic, indigenous movements in support of "the unalienable right of resistance against tyranny."[18]

John Quincy's essays did not make as deep an impression on the public as Paine's pamphlets, but the Publicola essays were forcefully argued and set off a firestorm of letters on both sides of the Atlantic. They were published throughout the United States as well as in Glasgow, Dublin, and London (in the latter erroneously under his father's name). Even though Publicola stated that the vice president had neither written nor corrected any of the essays, the belief in their mistaken provenance held in many quarters. After reading Publicola, Thomas Paine himself confessed, "I had John Adams in my mind when I wrote the pamphlet and it has hit as I expected."[19] Jefferson reported to James Madison that "nobody doubts here who is the author of Publicola, any more than of Davila."[20] But after a close reading Madison disagreed, paying John Quincy a backhanded compliment by remarking that, compared to the elder Adams, Publicola possessed "less of clumsiness & heaviness of style."[21]

Given how much emphasis his family had placed on writing, rhetoric, and oratory, it was not a surprise that John Quincy first made his mark as a writer. These initial essays show him bringing to bear all of his eloquence, logic, and vituperation. If writing was the means, political involvement was the goal. A close friend noted that with these essays Adams had finally "clasped his sickle to reap in the field of politics."[22] Within a matter of months, Adams, writing under an expanding pool of pseudonyms, was among the foremost commentators on the relationship between domestic and foreign policy.

In a series of essays that appeared in the *Columbian Centinel*, Adams focused on the value of neutrality in foreign affairs and defended President Washington's recall of French minister Edmond-Charles Genêt in 1793. Citizen Genêt, assuming that the Franco-American alliance of 1778 still held, had attempted to use the United States as a staging ground for the French conquest of Spanish Florida, Louisiana, and Canada. He had commissioned several privateering ships and recruited a militia to fight against the British. As even Genêt's defenders acknowledged, his actions had endangered America's neutrality in the war between Britain and France. Despite much American enthusiasm for the nascent French Revolution and popular support for Genêt, Washington had issued a proclamation of neutrality between Britain and France. When Genêt persisted in activities that actively undermined the president, Washington demanded the Frenchman's recall.

In response, John Quincy published a series of essays that attempted to turn the tide of popular sentiment against Genêt by rebutting the charges that America was bound to support France.

He further amplified the importance of Washington's calls for neutrality as a strategy to reduce the nation's exposure to foreign influence. In his first essay, he urged Americans to consider that "as the citizens of a nation at a vast distance from the continent of Europe; of a nation whose happiness consists in a real independence, disconnected from all European interests and European politics, it is our duty to remain, the peaceable and silent."[23] He posited that neutrality in European affairs and European lack of interference in American affairs were key to America's independence. Looking back years later, Adams emphasized the supreme importance of this position, writing that "the duty of the United States in this war was *neutrality*—and their rights were those of neutrality. Their unquestionable policy and their vital interest was also neutrality."[24]

Adams believed that neutrality was consistent with America's interests and values. At a pragmatic level, he argued that supporting revolutionary France would be utter folly. He admitted that America had some prior treaty commitments, but did not think that previous treaties obligated the new nation to support all French policies in perpetuity. As Adams read it, there was "no stipulation contained in a treaty [that] can ever oblige one nation to adopt or support the folly of another." He cautioned those who "advise us to engage voluntarily in the war" that doing so would be "to aim a dagger at the heart of the country." Treaties were not suicide pacts. Adams's Publicola essays had argued that the French Revolution was not a harbinger of republican revolution or liberal government. But even for those who disagreed, Adams warned that "we cannot take part with the French Republic without uniting all of Europe against us."[25] He cautioned his opponents not to let their republican enthusiasm cloud their assessment of America's interests.

Adams also believed that American foreign policy could never be devoid of a moral component owing to the nation's founding principles and republican institutions. Even if France's domestic governing principles were now in line with America's, a claim that Adams disputed, he charged that "there would be something singularly absurd and iniquitous to see the United States support the French in a plan of oppressive administration over their colonies, as a reward for rescuing them from the oppression of Great Britain."[26] Despite the change in France's political system, France continued to govern its Caribbean colonies much the way Great Britain had once governed its American colonies. Specifically, Adams was thinking of Saint-Domingue, the most profitable colony of the French Empire. Inspired by the French Revolution's calls for equality, black slaves on the island had attempted to overthrow their colonial masters. France had responded with a show of force, acting in imperial fashion to try to crush the effort. Adams argued that America was not in the business of suppressing republican revolutions or supporting countries that suppressed the revolutions of others. To do so would be "a total subversion of all moral and political consistency" and "a coalition of liberal freedom with despotic tyranny."[27]

In a second set of essays that also appeared in the *Columbian Centinel,* Adams, now writing under the pseudonym Columbus, argued that out of concern for its own independence, the United States must avoid involving itself in European politics and wars. "Of all the dangers which encompass the liberties of a republican State," he wrote, "the intrusion of a foreign influence into the administration of their affairs, is the most alarming, and requires the opposition of the severest caution."[28] Antiquity illustrated the heightened danger disunity posed to both external security and civil liberty, and one of the main lessons that Adams had internalized was that internal division often presaged foreign conquest. Referring to Genêt's actions, Adams asserted that European meddling in the internal affairs of the United States obviously posed a great danger to America's independence. But in an argument that would grow more robust as his diplomatic career advanced, Adams warned that America should also take pains to avoid becoming overly involved in the internal politics or wars of Europe. Doing so would risk bringing America into regional conflicts, which could then justify European intervention in North America. Here, isolation from Europe's corrupt politics took on new importance. Only by fiercely guarding its independence could the young nation hope to steer clear of Europe's meddling influence in its own affairs.

Soon Adams was offered the chance to apply his ideas. Not surprisingly, his forcefully argued articles had been very popular with the Federalists.[29] As his father recalled years later, "Washington was indeed under obligations to him [JQA] for turning the tide of sentiment against Genet."[30] Impressed, the president wanted to find a suitable position for the young Adams. He first thought of appointing him U.S. attorney for the New England region. That idea was scrapped, but four months later Washington appointed the twenty-seven-year-old Adams minister to the Netherlands.

When news of this appointment arrived in Boston, John Quincy seemed shocked. "This intelligence was very unexpected and indeed surprising," he recorded in his diary, claiming that he had never solicited, and never would solicit, any public office. As this was an Adams family principle "which my father has always rigidly observed," he was sure that his father had not asked Washington for a favor. "And yet," he noted, he was "very sensible that neither my years, my experience, my reputation, nor my talents, could

entitle me to an office of so much responsibility." Fearing charges
of nepotism, he claimed that he wished he had been consulted before the appointment had been made, as he wished "it had not been
made at all."[31]

Perhaps he genuinely felt he was not yet ready for such a position. In 1794 the United States had only five missions abroad. Perhaps he still chafed under the pressure of being an Adams, which
meant he had little choice in forging his own path. Just as his
mother had bluntly informed him of his duties during his brief
love affair several years earlier, she now reminded him that he must
not "look Back; or shrink from your duty however arduous or dangerous the task assigned you[.] You will prove yourself the Genuine
Scion of the Stock from whence you spring."[32] But even if he felt
unready, his increasingly public persona had been expressly designed to bring him into public affairs. In addition, he must have
realized that given his time spent living abroad, the diplomatic
training he had received from Dana, Jefferson, and his father, and
his fluency in several European languages, he was more than sufficiently qualified for such a post.

Unsurprisingly, his parents were less shocked, viewing the appointment of their eldest and most accomplished son as a vindication of their efforts. John Quincy noted that "his [father's] satisfaction at the appointment is much greater than mine."[33] His father's
sentiments were shared by his mother, who, hearing of her son's
appointment, wrote Martha Washington, "At a very early period of
Life I devoted him to the publick."[34] Mrs. Washington's generous
reply undoubtedly swelled parental pride. John Quincy's abilities
and his new job, she wrote, afford him "the fairest prospect [of]
rendering eminent services to his country; and of being, in time,
among the fore most in her councils." Concluding her letter, Mar-

tha Washington informed Abigail Adams that these were not her private opinions, but those of her husband, "from whom I have imbibed the idea."[35]

The fruits of the Adamses' labor had been rewarded. For years they had been hoping that "the time will come when this young man will be sought for as a Jewel of great price."[36] John Adams gushed to his son that this appointment was "Proof that Sound Principles in Morals and Government are cherished by the Executive of the United States, and that Study, Science and Literature are recommendations which will not be overlooked."[37] Privately, the elder Adams was barely able to suppress his pride, writing his wife of his "good and worthy son. . . . All my hopes are in him, both for my family and my country."[38]

For his part, John Quincy believed that this assignment was more a fulfillment of his parents' hopes than his own, writing his mother, "I have indeed long known that my father is far more ambitious for my advancement, far more solicitous for the extension of my face, than I ever have been, or ever shall be."[39] But that did not mean he did not welcome the opportunity. While still harboring some concerns about his qualifications for the posting, he recognized that it did provide him a means of financial independence and advancement. With his new salary of $4,500 a year and a gift from his father of 5,000 Dutch guilders, his financial situation seemed set.[40] Shortly after his departure from Boston, Adams happily reported to a friend that he was "once more my own man again."[41]

With his financial future and professional path secure, there was one more area of his life that demanded attention. While Adams had acceded to his mother's demands that he break off his romance with Mary Frazier several years earlier, it was now time to

find a wife. While in London on official business, the young diplomat found himself spending more and more time at Joshua Johnson's home. Johnson was a prominent and politically connected
American expatriate who had served as consul for the U.S. government and worked with several large commercial firms. He also had
seven daughters. John Quincy found himself particularly attracted
to Louisa Catherine, the second eldest. She was intelligent, witty, fluent in French, musically inclined, and full of laughter. Within days,
Adams believed he had finally found the woman he would marry.

This came as a surprise for Louisa. Initially thinking that he was
attracted to her older sister, Louisa noted, "I never observed any
thing in Mr. Adams's conduct towards me that indicated the
smallest preference."[42] From the outset, John Quincy's difficult—he
would probably say independent—nature was apparent. Compli-
menting him on his appearance, Louisa found herself startled to
find that "he immediately took fire," assuring her that "*his* [future]
wife must never take the liberty of interfering in those particulars,
and assumed a tone so high and lofty and made so serious a grievance of the affair, that I felt offended and told him that I resign'd
all pretensions to his hand, and left him as free as air to choose a
Lady who would be more discreet." Adams apologized, and the
couple quickly reconciled, but John Quincy's flash of anger and reproach left its mark. Although captivated by his learning and earnest
solicitousness, impressed with his energy and his ambition, and sharing a love of poetry, music, and literature, Louisa also found herself
intimidated by his aloofness and dejected by his condescension,
"unnecessary harshness and severity of character."[43]

Accustomed to praise, refinement, and luxury, which she attributed to her father's southern roots and commercial success, Louisa
was suddenly introduced to the Puritan ethos, particularly viru-

lent among Adamses, of duty, sacrifice, and improvement. Once engaged, John Quincy refused to set a date for their marriage, informing Louisa that their engagement was "for an indefinite term . . . which might be in one year or in seven." With his diplomatic appointment winding down, he assured her that he had to wait until he was more financially secure and better able to support a family. To Louisa, this seemed the first of many tests to which she was subjected. Mimicking his own parents' commands, John Quincy recommended that Louisa "attend to the improvement of [her] mind, and laid down a course of study." While well intentioned (this was after all how the Adams clan showed affection to each other), John Quincy instead exacerbated Louisa's sense of insecurity, as she constantly "felt my folly and my insignificance" every time she answered his letters. Nevertheless, Louisa bent to her fiancé's requests, hoping that through diligent study she could "lessen the immense distance which existed in point of mind and talents between myself and my future husband."[44]

When Abigail learned of her eldest son's romantic interest, she attempted to intervene, worrying that Louisa was too young, too European, and not experienced enough with the realities and hardships of the world. She wrote her son, concerned that he was falling for a "Syren," and a non-American "half Blood" at that.[45] This letter was too much for John Quincy, and finally drew a rare rebuke from her exasperated son. If he waited for her to approve of his choice, he wryly noted, "I should have been certainly doomed to perpetual celibacy."[46] Realizing that she might have alienated her son, and understanding that at the remove of several thousand miles there was little she could do, Abigail apologetically wrote her son, "I consider her already as my daughter." The two finally wed in London in 1797, after John Quincy had been informed of his appointment, and subsequent raise, as U.S. minister to Prussia.[47] Considering John Quincy's prickly temper and single-minded focus, this was a romance that had its fair share of tempests and storms. But it was also one that would be singularly advantageous to his life and his career. In contrast to his brooding nature and tendency toward solitude, Louisa was effervescent and reveled in company and conversation. In later years, such differences would bring more than one observer to comment that where Louisa was "a very pleasant and agreeable woman," John Quincy "has no talent to entertain a mixed company, either by conversation or manners."[48] Even the elder John Adams confessed that his son's marriage to Louisa was "the most important event" of John Quincy's life.[49]

In the midst of attending to his matrimonial prospects, John Quincy was thrust into the middle of the debate on the future of American security. After a short and relatively uneventful Atlantic crossing, despite the fact that his ship had leaked its way across the ocean, Adams made his way to London. President Washington had requested that Adams detour so that he could deliver a series of confidential dispatches to John Jay and the American minister to London, who were in the midst of negotiating a commercial treaty with Great Britain that was intended to address the unresolved issues from the Peace of Paris of 1783. The treaty terms being proposed in London were less than optimal, and it was clear that if the American delegation signed the treaty it would be deeply divisive in the United States. Delivering the dispatches to America's most senior diplomat, Adams found himself surprised and quite honored to have his counsel solicited. He agreed that the treaty was not ideal, but not wanting to let the perfect be the enemy of the good, or even the acceptable, he believed that while the treaty was both "inadequate" and "far from being satisfactory," it was nevertheless "better than War."[50] In the mid-1790s, the United States was a young and largely ineffectual state, immature in its institutions and weak in power projection capabilities. Avoiding a war with any great power was an imperative. Adams wrote his father that national honor, while bruised, would be maintained. More significantly, so would the country's growth trajectory. Influencing his father's thinking in the years to come, John Quincy concluded that the United States would "suffer infinitely less than it would by the most successful war we could wage.[51]

While the treaty outraged Jefferson's increasingly vociferous supporters, who charged it with being overly favorable to Britain at the expense of France, it did avert war with Britain. As a result, the United States benefited from a marked uptick in trade with London, as domestic exports doubled between 1790 and 1807 and reexports increased from $300,000 to $59,643,558 during the same period, with the overwhelming growth occurring after the Jay Treaty had been ratified.[52] Now on favorable terms with London and therefore free from the menace of the Royal Navy, American trading ships were soon found in Asian, European, South American, and West Indian ports. As an early American politician and economist keenly observed, "A new era was established in our commercial history. . . . In proportion to our population we ranked as the most commercial nation; in point of value, our trade was only second to that of Great Britain."[53]

This was exactly the intent of the Jay Treaty, as its primary supporter, Alexander Hamilton, explained in an essay defending the imperfect treaty as a means to "defer to a state of manhood a struggle to which infancy is ill-adapted. . . . We ought to be wise enough to see that this is not the time for trying our strength."[54] Such sentiments, reminiscent of the thoughts Adams had first laid out in his Marcellus essays several years earlier, gained traction with Adams the longer he served in Europe. For neutrality's value did not reside in its cause, but in its effects. As the Anglo-French conflict drew more of Europe into its vortex, virtually all the belligerents' commercial ships, save those of England, with its dominant navy, were swept from the seas. What was Europe's distress quickly became a neutral America's advantage, exponentially increasing America's carrying trade, creating a vast European market for its shipbuilding and related industries, and growing its domestic economy. Adams thought that Washington's system of neutrality, if it were to remain the country's dominant strategy, would within ten years make "the United States among the most powerful and opulent nations on earth."[55] But this system would be increasingly challenging to maintain as America attempted to navigate between the Scylla and Charybdis of growing British and French rivalry.

Just as John Quincy arrived in Holland, France embarked on a European campaign that would soon topple the governments of the Netherlands, Prussia, Spain, and Austria. Throughout these crises, Adams remained in Holland, acting as Washington's eyes and ears on the continent. He attended diplomatic functions, met with Americans traveling through the area, and sought out the leaders of the business and political communities. And he wrote. As his job was to collect and convey the latest news, he spent much of his day reading and composing dispatches that analyzed the flow of events. This he found a dull grind, carping to his father that he felt foolish receiving a governmental salary for "*penetrating* the contents of a newspaper."[56] His increasingly detailed diary entries and his long letters home undercut Adams's complaints that these were merely regurgitated news stories. His academic training, his facility with multiple foreign languages, and his astute assessments of military and political movements are all conveyed in his voluminous writings. President Washington found his dispatches "very regular and intelligent," while the secretary of state reported that they were "well digested, well arranged and well connected."[57] It was with more than just fatherly pride that Vice President John Adams wrote his son, "I am delighted with your Facts, your Opinions, your Principles, and your Feelings."[58] The elder Adams also ordered his son to "send me good intelligence from all parts of Europe as you have done."[59] John Quincy did, but his detailed letters to the United States contained more than mere assessments of the European political scene—they contained policy recommendations as well.

As an eyewitness to the growing upheavals of Europe, Adams found his desire for American isolation from European entanglements strengthened. In letters to Secretary of State Timothy Pickering and to his father, Adams assessed the changing dynamics of power in revolutionary Europe. He always considered what this meant for the United States. Adams judged that France was fostering hostilities between Great Britain and America "to draw the United States into it, merely to make tools of them, in order to procure advantageous terms for others, who would leave us in the well, after using our weight to get themselves out of it."[60] The politics of Europe at this time were such that shifting balances of power made some nations pawns in the struggle for dominion by others. In a letter to his father, which John Adams duly passed on to President Washington, John Quincy proclaimed that "above all else I wish that we may never have occasion for any political connections in Europe."[61] Moral aversion to these practices only partially explained John Quincy's distaste for European politics; a pragmatic desire to keep such practices from replicating in North America is primarily what informed all his dispatches.

In college, Adams had claimed that spending his youth abroad made him the best republican among his contemporaries because from afar he could see more clearly the virtues of his own country. Now, returning to the continent and witnessing the violent struggle for European mastery, Adams strengthened his antagonism toward monarchy, his perception of the universal antipathy felt toward the United States, and his appreciation for America's exceptionally fortuitous circumstances. When a British diplomat charged that the cacophony of voices in America necessarily weakened its message, Adams argued the reverse—that political opposition strengthened the nation. In comparison to Europe, Adams declared that America's government was more stable because "Every thing comes out. We have no lurking disaffection that works in secret and is not seen."[62] Surveying the European states in a letter to his father, he reported that they had all been deeply undermined by America's republican spirit, which "must eventually lead to the destruction of the relics which yet remain of the feudal aristocracy."[63] The result was a Europe "inimical to the government of the United States, because it furnishes a constant example to those who maintain the superior excellence of a Republican system."[64] Adams believed that such hostility was ideologically based. But it was also due to the historical development of Europe into separate and distinct, though territorially contiguous, states.

The United States had the unique advantage of developing in a sparsely populated and undergoverned land mass, separated by two oceans from the other world powers. Adams believed that this anomaly, if preserved, might allow his country to escape the normal pattern of historical development that had condemned Europe to centuries of warfare. For in their search for security, the reigning powers had by necessity put a premium on security over liberty. The critical difference, as Adams understood, was the lack of a permanent standing army in America. But if the conditions that existed in the Old World recreated themselves in the new, America could not avoid replicating Europe's violent development and illiberal spirit. In a letter to his younger brother shortly before concluding his tour as American minister to Prussia in 1801, Adams explained the conditions under which such a disastrous scenario might play itself out. "The only occasion which can require a great military force," he argued, would be "to withstand external invasion." But fortunately, this was "a danger to which we shall become daily less exposed as our population and strength increase."[65]

But if he held a generally sanguine view on the increasing prospects for the United States, Adams spent just as much time contemplating the disasters that might befall his country if its path began to resemble Europe's. And, unsurprisingly, the main threat to America's growth to power came from the danger of internal division, which in turn would lead to any number of calamities. In that same letter to his brother, he described in detail the threat that disunion posed. Division would expose the nation to increased foreign assault. And the more divided the country became, the greater the number of states that declared their own individual sovereignty, the more attractive a target the North American continent became for foreign powers to divide and conquer. In such a calamitous future, security would derive not from a common policy and joint defense, but rather from the individual states' strengthened militaries. But this too was a problem, as it was likely to heighten fear and competition between the states, likely setting off an arms race. Adams believed that

> each of the separate states will from the moment of disunion become with regard to the others a foreign power. Quarrels, of which the seeds are too thickly sown, will shoot up like weeds in a rank soil between them. Wars will soon ensue. These must end either in the conquest of one party by the other, or in frail, precarious, jealous compromises and momentary truces under the name of peace, leaving on both sides the burden of its army as the only guarantee for its security. Then must the surface of our country be bristled over with double and treble ranges, of rock hewn fortresses for barriers, and our cities turned into goals by a circumference of impenetrable walls. Then will the great problem of our statesmen, too, be what proportion of the people's sweat and blood can be squeezed from them to maintain an army without producing absolute death. I speak in the sincerity and conviction of my soul in declaring that I look upon standing armies, intolerable taxes, forced levies, contributions, conscriptions, and requisitions, as the unavoidable and fatal chain of which disunion is but the first link.[66]

This dark future could only by averted by making sure that America's development stood in stark contrast to Europe's. It was for this reason that Adams considered "the *Union* of our country . . . the sheet anchor of our hopes, and . . . its dissolution . . . the most dreadful of our dangers."[67] But, as he explained to his brother, union was a complex process that involved both domestic political considerations and foreign policy priorities. Chief among those was pursuing a strategy of neutrality in Europe's wars. Neutrality played to American commercial strengths and its geographic isolation.

The value of Adams's reporting and policy recommendations kept him in Europe longer than he had expected. When John Adams captured the presidency, he planned to recall his son, fearing that charges of nepotism would hobble his administration and derail John Quincy's career. But Washington urged otherwise, writing that it was his "decided opinion that Mr. Adams is the most valuable public character we have abroad." This was not intended as a compliment or as flattery, but rather as sound personnel advice. Washington thought that the "country would sustain a loss" if the elder Adams recalled his son owing to an "over delicacy on your part."[68] The incoming president listened to the counsel of the outgoing one and appointed his son minister plenipotentiary to Prussia. After some delays in the confirmation process, Adams was approved by the Senate, and John Quincy and Louisa Catherine headed to Berlin.

From his perch in Berlin, John Quincy observed that neutrality in Europe's wars had other benefits for America. Although worried that perhaps his father would think him too timid, he wrote that neutrality "is in my mind an object of such inestimable value, and involves so deeply the welfare not of the present age only but of all posterity, that I may perhaps be inclined to see through a magnifying medium everything that can have a tendency to defeat it."[69] He assessed that the present state of affairs in Europe was in many ways beneficial to American interests. "The longer the war continues," the young diplomat reported, "the more that interest will increase, from the double cause of their constant weakening and our continually growing strength."[70] Allowing

Britain and France, the anchors of the largely bipolar world of 1796, to continue fighting meant that they would sap each other's strength, allowing America to grow in strength through the power of its neutral commerce. As much as John Quincy, or John Adams for that matter, would have hated to admit it, this was a Hamiltonian strategy.

As early as 1787, in the eleventh *Federalist* essay, future secretary of the treasury Alexander Hamilton discussed the importance of commerce. Rich in its diversity of natural resources and gifted in manufacturing, the United States was increasingly becoming the object of foreign envy. Commerce and a strong navy, Hamilton concluded, were "a resource for influencing the conduct of European nations towards us."[71] Using trade as a foreign policy tool was in many ways a revolutionary thought that reconceptualized and redefined the traditional terms of power relations. Hamilton knew just how radical this vision was, writing, "we may hope, erelong, to become the arbiter of Europe in America, and to be able to incline the balance of European competitors in this part of the world as our interests may dictate." Hamilton first advanced the view that a strategic use of neutrality in commercial affairs would allow America to build its strength and eventually project its power abroad. While John Quincy was no great fan of the man who had slandered his father during the 1800 election, split the Federalists, and effectively handed the election to Jefferson and the Republicans, he did share his belief in the benefits of neutral commerce and Hamilton's view that neutrality in European affairs was key to building America's strength.[72]

In this Adams saw an instrument of statecraft. Advocating on behalf of American commercial interests convinced him that he had been mistaken when he initially disparaged his posting as simply a "pecuniary negotiation."[73] Adams came to see trade as a weapon that could be extended to or withheld from European partners, and one that would make other nations *feel* the necessity of our friendship." Trade, Adams concluded, could promote the country's growth and compel other nations to "observe a more friendly line of conduct."[74]

But if neutrality were advantageous, Adams also recognized that it was not a natural state. Just as Hamilton had proposed that a sufficiently powerful navy would be necessary in an international system dominated by British maritime supremacy, Adams drew the same lesson from the Anglo-French wars. Writing to the secretary of state in June 1796 from the Netherlands, Adams suggested that "as far as the experience of this country can serve as a guide, it does not appear that the proper mode of resistance against the exclusive ambition of British views is by making war without an adequate naval force to meet them upon the sea."[75] If America wanted to maintain its neutral commerce in the seas despite Britain's objections, it would need the means to do so.

This belief became more acute as hostilities with France increased. While Washington's Proclamation of Neutrality of 1793 had officially declared America neutral in the wars between France and Britain, in practice many saw this policy statement as an act favoring London over Paris. When the Jay Treaty became law in 1794 and commercial contact between the United States and Britain increased, France believed that it had gotten the short end of the stick. Furthermore, the United States refused to continue paying its debt to France, arguing that it had owed the money to the French monarchy, not republican France. The result was predictable; French anger turned into conflict, and French ships began preying on American shipping.

The deterioration of Franco-American relations accelerated after John Adams was elected president in 1796. In the midst of a war with England, France responded to warming Anglo-American commercial relations by unilaterally abrogating its 1778 treaty with the United States, seizing American commercial ships trading with the British in the West Indies, and refusing to receive President Adams's envoy. The French navy attacked American trade, preying upon America's undefended commercial fleet and causing insurance rates on international shipping to skyrocket. While President Adams did not desire a war, damaging as it would be to American neutrality, national honor and prosperity demanded that he respond to these sustained attacks. In a speech to both houses of Congress, Adams declared that such attacks "ought to be repelled with a decision which shall convince France and the world that we are not a degraded people, humiliated under a colonial spirit of fear and sense of inferiority."[76] But as he ratcheted up American anger at the French, he simultaneously extended an olive branch, dispatching new envoys to repair Franco-American relations. French officials solicited bribes from American peace commissioners in what became known as the XYZ Affair. As news of this was made public and American outrage grew, President Adams used the crisis to expand the military, asking Congress to underwrite an expansion of the navy and increase the size of the army.

But even as the threat of outright war increased in response to French aggression, the administration, urged on by the counsel of the younger Adams, remained committed to the benefits of neutrality and remained neutral in word if not deed. Ignoring heated calls for a formal declaration of war from his political allies, President Adams waged an undeclared war against the French navy for just over two years. With a series of victories in the Caribbean, the newly commissioned American navy helped force a French reassessment of its policies. John Adams did not press his advantage. More interested in terminating a limited war than in increasing American demands and involvement, President Adams defied his party and sought a diplomatic agreement to end hostilities with the French. Many factors played a role in this momentous policy decision, but John Quincy's on-the-scene assessments of the possibility of a resolution, and the likely favorable implications in Europe and for America, probably played a great role in influencing his father's decision. This decision, however, had disastrous political consequences for the elder Adams, as it outraged pro-war supporters, split the Federalist Party, and cost him reelection in 1800. But it did lead directly to peace as France, now led by a Napoleon Bonaparte who did not wish to fight both the British and the Americans at the same time, agreed to the Treaty of Mortefontaine in 1800. The treaty terminated America's formal alliance with France of 1778 while allowing it to continue trading with and supplying the French as neutrals.

Watching these developments from Prussia, John Quincy Adams thought that France had forced a navy on the United States. This, though, was not an unwelcome development, he concluded, for the American people were loath to tax themselves at a sufficient level to create armed forces sufficient for defense of the nation. But in a competitive and increasingly turbulent world, Adams cheered anything that would incline the United States in a more realistic direction. Writing to a fellow diplomat in the midst of the Quasi War, Adams asserted that America's independence of action came not from its unique form of "representative democracy," but rather from the "real power" of its "armed force."[77] Republican government was the ultimate policy goal of the United States, but its necessary precondition was a strong military establishment.

Equally important to the nation's development, though perhaps a slightly lower priority, was promoting America's commercial prosperity. And it was to this end that Adams attended during his posting to Berlin. Upon their arrival, the Adamses' coach was stopped and the American diplomat was "questioned at the gates by a dapper lieutenant, who did not know, until one of his private soldiers explained to him, who the United States of America were."[78] Despite this initial confusion, Adams's tour was a successful one. In July 1799, he successfully renewed a commercial treaty with Prussia, granting both countries most favored nation status and neutral trading rights in wartime.

This Berlin mission, though, was perhaps most notable for the personal changes in Adams's life—as he became both a father and an author. He and Louisa Catherine took a three-month tour of Silesia during the summer of 1800. The voluminous letters he wrote to his brother Thomas detailing the region's history, geography, economy, and culture were forwarded for publication by Philadelphia's new literary magazine, *Port Folio*.[79] In addition, trying to master the German language, and becoming increasingly enthralled by its complexities, Adams translated Christopher Martin Wieland's epic poem *Oberon* and rendered the Prussian historian and statesman Friedrich von Gentz's comparison of the American and French Revolutions into English.

The trip to Silesia was taken less as a literary excursion than to help Louisa Catherine recover her fragile health. Berlin was hard on her, and she suffered four separate miscarriages in her years there. Finally, after much anxiety for her and her husband, she gave birth to their first child in April 1801. To help Louisa through her labor, the king had the street around the Adamses' home closed to traffic, while the queen inquired daily as to her recovery. Noting "the unusual kindness shewn," Louisa realized that this was more a compliment to her country's rising power, and "not personally to *me*."[80] Her husband also thought the birth of their first son a fitting opportunity to compliment their nation. In honor of his first political benefactor, and ensuring that his son had much to live up to, Adams named the child George Washington Adams.[81] The highlight of his tour, this was also the end of his foreign posting. With John Adams's narrow defeat by Thomas Jefferson in the presidential election of 1800, the elder Adams recalled his son, wanting to spare him the embarrassment of recall under a new administration.

"My mode of life has of course been altogether various," Adams reflected shortly after returning to the United States.[82] Returning to his native shores after an absence of seven years, Adams was amazed by how much had changed—and how much remained the same. When he had departed the country, he was a bachelor living in Boston who had just begun his career as a practicing attorney and had gained some notoriety as a political essayist. As a married man and a father, he returned to Boston, resumed his legal practice, and found himself itching to join the political fray. Hardly had he settled the family in Boston than he felt the "strong temptation and have great provocation to plunge into political controversy."[83] But Adams was well aware of the prospects that awaited him in the political arena. His father had been rejected by the electorate for keeping the country out of war, and it was hard to imagine that another Adams could galvanize the public.

Indeed, Adams recognized that the present state of affairs called for politicians who would serve the parochial interests of party and region. In a poignant letter of consolation addressed to his father after the 1800 election, Adams praised him for acting against the advice of his supporters but in the interests of the country. The elder Adams had kept the country out of a war for which it was ill prepared, had built up the nation's defenses, and had adroitly piloted the country between France and Great Britain, all the while maintaining "the honor of the American name." He pursued a strategy of armed neutrality, thereby allowing the nation the time it needed to grow and develop. While this policy had been purchased at the expense of the presidency, Adams consoled his father that history would vindicate his policy choices. As for his integrity, Adams noted that by his actions, his father had proved beyond doubt that "you were the man not of any party, but of the whole nation."[84] In his read of the election, John Quincy found his father had lived the Adams creed of disinterested statesmanship. This example was the one he would seek to emulate as he entered politics. It was also an example most certain to steer him into controversy.

In April 1802, Adams was elected a Massachusetts state senator. Because he refused to vote the Federalist Party line, antagonized his fellow senators, and generally proved himself a nuisance, his colleagues kicked him upstairs, electing him to one of the two vacant Senate seats in Washington, D.C. Although elected as a Federalist, Adams quickly proved to be his own man, much to the annoyance of the Federalist Party. Arriving in Washington too late to vote on the Louisiana Purchase, Adams nonetheless came out in favor of it. His support for Jefferson's acquisition was in marked opposition to his Federalist colleagues, who viewed the country's extension to the West as a threat to their dominance in politics. In speeches and writings justifying his vote, Adams admitted that his opponents, almost all fellow New Englanders, were correct in their assessments. As the country expanded, the eastern and Atlantic states would, by necessity, lose their "relative situation" of political strength as the "vibration of the centre of power" moved westward. Adams, however, saw nothing other than parochial interests threatened by this natural development. He urged his fellow New Englanders to support the event as "the acquisition of Louisiana adds an immense force" to the nation.[85] While earning the condemnation of many of his natural political allies, this justification of the nation's enlargement as an "extension of national power and security" was an elaboration of his belief that the future of the United States lay in the direction of territorial expansion across the North American continent.[86] Adams reasoned that there was no better way to hold off division and dismemberment of the country than by subsuming the rest of the continent under a republican system of government.

But before the country could expand in the New World, it faced renewed threats from the old. After the briefest of armistices, Napoleonic France and Britain had resumed their great conflict in May 1803. And as this contest evolved into a European-wide battle for supremacy, American commerce and neutrality came under attack from both sides. With military victories proving inconclusive in the larger conflict, London and Paris employed economic warfare to gain an advantage over each other. Britain bankrolled various allies and in 1806 attempted to blockade the French coast. With the defeat of the French navy the year before at Trafalgar, Napoleon understood that he could not challenge British maritime supremacy. Instead, seeking to undermine the source of that power by attacking British commerce, he issued the Berlin Decree in November and instituted the Continental System. This order attempted to strangle Britain by cutting off access to all European ports and imposing an embargo on British trade. Britain further escalated matters by passing its Orders in Council of 1807, which not only attempted to reverse blockade Napoleonic France and its allies but, more significantly for the United States, restricted and attacked neutral trade. While both France and Britain preyed upon American shipping, it was Britain, with its superior navy and its practice of impressing sailors, that was the more formidable threat.

While these events were insulting to national pride and detrimental to American trade, it took an act of armed aggression to push the United States toward war with Britain. In June 1807, the USS *Chesapeake* was attacked by the British warship HMS *Leopard* off Norfolk, Virginia. When the *Chesapeake* surrendered and four crew members were impressed by the British, a political firestorm erupted in the United States. Adams was in the thick of it. While any disruption to shipping was bound to disproportionately impact coastal New England, this was a challenge to the nationally advantageous policy of neutrality. Allowing Britain to dictate the course of American commerce and foreign policy would make the country subservient to the fiats of London or Paris. This, in Adams's view, was akin to surrendering the country's independence. While loath to act counter to his constituents' interests, he felt that he could not ignore such an affront to national pride and such a challenge to national policy.

Britain's aggression, and the Federalist's response, pushed Adams into the decisive political act of his career. As he was later to reflect, "The really important period of my life began with the British attack upon our Chesapeake frigate, in the summer of 1807."[87] When, in the immediate aftermath of the attack, he could not persuade any Federalists to publicly censure the attack, Adams crossed the aisle and joined Republicans in condemning the act. While the

Federalists quickly realized that they had committed a tactical political error, and subsequently also issued a resolution condemning the attack, the damage had been done. Adams would later write that "this was the cause which alienated me from that day and forever from the councils of the federal party."[88] The feeling was mutual, as most Federalists condemned Adams for political apostasy.

Further infuriating his party, when Adams returned to Washington he sided with the Jefferson administration and, searching for measures short of war, helped draft an embargo act against the British. His vote for the embargo was particularly egregious to his party, as it hit the New England shipping industry especially hard. He realized that this vote would anger his party supporters, writing his father, "my views of present policy . . . are so different from those of the federalists that I find myself in constant opposition to them."[89] Understanding that crossing his constituents and Federalist Party elders would most probably cost him his Senate seat, he vowed that "private interest must not be put in opposition to public good."[90] And, in case his message was not clear that the Federalists were acting in opposition to the national interest, Adams caucused with the Republicans in Congress as they voted to choose their next presidential candidate in early 1808.

As expected, his actions antagonized friends and foes. Louisa noted that "Politics were growing very hot and Mr. Adams was very busy and very anxious."[91] A Massachusetts newspaper quipped that he was "one of those amphibious politicians, who lives on both sea and water, and occasionally resorts to each, but who finally settles down into the mud."[92] But the most damning charges came from within his own family. Still smarting from Thomas Jefferson's treatment of her husband almost ten years later, and very much carrying a grudge on his behalf, Abigail could not believe that her son would abandon his father's party for Jefferson's. "I have considered it as inconsistent both with your principles, and your judgment," she wrote, "to have countananced such a meeting by your presence."[93] In response to his mother's charge that he had violated his political principles, he coolly replied, "My sense of duty shall never yield to pleasure of party," and reminded her that it was her values that required him to put duty to the nation ahead of party loyalty or personal feelings.[94] From his father he received nothing but praise. John Adams celebrated that his son had "too honest a heart, too independent a mind, and too brilliant talents, to be sincerely and confidentially trusted by any man who is under the dominion of party maxims or party feelings." No stranger to antagonizing those with "party feelings," the elder Adams praised his son's integrity and thought he had nothing to regret, though warned that he should expect to be turned out of office.[95]

John Quincy was well aware that after voting and caucusing with the Republicans his political prospects were dim. Responding to his father, he candidly assessed his situation and noted that "being now wholly unsupported by any great party the expiration of my present term of service will dismiss me from my public station."[96] Considering what paths might lie open to him now that a public one was seemingly closing, he pondered filling his time with literary pursuits, educating his sons, and practicing law. Such prospects did not upset him. In fact, he seemed to relish the prospect of playing the role of martyr for what he considered "pure, disinterested and patriotic" governing motives.[97] While he had already predicted that the future of the country increasingly lay with advocates of western expansion, it is hard to imagine that Adams's self-described act of political martyrdom was anything other than political suicide in the near term.

Explaining his decision in such a manner allowed Adams to frame his actions as squarely in line with his family's values. Such positions might align themselves with the nation's long-term interests, but they also made his policy choices unpalatable to his nominal supporters. As Louisa noted, "the Whigs began to be jealous of him, and the old Federalists hated him: so that we were fast getting into hot water."[98] If Abigail had scolded her son for deserting the party of his father, surely in quieter moments she must have recalled that the Federalist Party had quite abandoned her husband in the run up to the 1800 presidential election. Not only was John Quincy emulating his father's example of a disinterested statesman putting country ahead of personal gain, but his actions, as he explained them, were in line with the family's belief in staking out unpopular actions in the service of just causes. With such a rebuke, and with John Adams seeing his son as acting in the correct fashion, Abigail came around, writing that she prided herself "more in being the Mother of such a son, than in all the honours and titles which [a] Monarch could bestow."[99]

Parental approval, however, is an insufficient explanation for such a seemingly suicidal political act. Both ambitious and ideological, Adams's politics were enmeshed within his larger goal of ensuring the rise of the young nation and appeasing his conscience as a disinterested and moral statesman. And neither of these goals could be achieved if he condoned divisive regional politics. Asked by a colleague for his true motives in supporting the administration, Adams returned to the logic he had first expounded while serving as a diplomat posted abroad, explaining that he believed internal political divisions in the face of foreign aggression were exposing the nation to extreme danger. "In case of war," domestic political division "must in its nature end—either in a Civil War, or

in a dissolution of the Union, with the Atlantic States in subservi-
ency to Great Britain."[100] Just as he had been critical in the 1790s
of those who desired to steer America toward France, he now attacked those who counseled what he saw as a "stupid servility" to
Britain.[101]

He was critical of the Massachusetts Federalists for thinking of
regional and not national interests. Their opposition to the coming war with Britain meant that "instead of a nation coextensive
with the North American continent," the small-minded actions of
Federalists would produce "an endless multitude of little insignificant clans and tribes at eternal war with one another for a rock, or
a fish pond, the sport and fable of European masters and oppres-
sors."[102] Here, Adams not only depicted the future destiny of the
United States, but also accurately named an internal division
within the United States or an intrusion by Europe onto the North
American continent as the threats to that vision. Regardless of
how such divisions might arise, they would have a balkanizing effect
on America, effectively turning it into another Europe with frequent
wars.

If Adams needed a reminder of what a divided America would
look like, Napoleonic Europe offered an ominous vision. In June of
1808, Adams resigned from his Senate seat in advance of what was
an almost certain electoral defeat or recall. However, largely due
to his support of Jefferson's policies, he was appointed minister to
Czar Alexander's Russia by incoming President James Madison.
Europe was convulsing with Napoleon's advances, and despite the
high cost of maintaining his ministership there, Adams opted to
stay in Russia during these momentous events.[103] Observing the
threat an expansionist France under Napoleon posed to Russia,
Adams could not help but ponder what a united and aggressive

Europe might mean for the United States. Napoleon had already closed all continental ports to American ships, an act that threatened to destroy American commerce. Much as he had done during his first diplomatic posting to The Hague some fifteen years earlier, Adams promoted commercial trade between the nations. And in Alexander's Russia, a state with vast natural resources and a fledgling commercial fleet seeking to steer clear of the worst ravages of Anglo-French antagonism, Adams found a sympathetic ear for the cause of neutral trade, even though Russia, through 1812 at least, was nominally allied with France.[104] Sensing this, Adams managed to convince Czar Alexander to open Russian ports to American goods. This diplomatic coup illuminates the strategic importance Adams attached to ports as hubs of commercial activity.

The diplomatic posting in St. Petersburg also reinforced Adams's belief that although America might be geographically removed from Europe, it was critical for the country to pay close attention to international developments, lest it be caught unaware and unprepared. Adams became convinced of the interconnectedness of the international system and observed that "a man might profess to be perfectly independent, and to set at naught the opinions and wishes of others; but he could not get along without soon finding inconvenience to himself of such a system. And so with nations."[105] Just as his father had once ordered him to inform Washington of political developments in Europe, Adams tried to both formalize and institutionalize foreign policy reporting. One of his first tasks upon assuming the office of secretary of state in 1817 was drafting instructions to the U.S. ministers serving abroad. Writing to the American ministers in Europe, Adams instructed them to observe and document the relations of the countries they served in, to observe the general state of international relations, to communicate with other American ministers, and to stay on good terms with foreign ministers. If it were to preserve its independence, America needed to have the ability to act in its best interests. This could only come through the knowledge that careful observation in foreign capitals could provide.[106]

If the resumption of a continental war reinforced Adams's belief in the supreme importance of American neutrality, the country's inadequate state of defenses forced him to urge restraint in any conflict with Britain. In a letter to his mother, he lamented, "We have not force to defend our rights upon the sea, or exercise our rights upon it at the pleasure of others."[107] But he was just as cautious about an all-out arms buildup, which he thought more likely to endanger the security of the country. Just as he had warned against taking overly aggressive actions against the British following the *Chesapeake* affair in 1807, as the United States did not have the power to back up bellicose rhetoric, he now recommended a slow naval buildup. To do otherwise would be to wave a red flag in London's direction. In response to his father's strenuous calls for a vastly expanded navy, Adams opined that as relations with Britain were currently at a nadir, London could not see a buildup as anything other than a direct challenge. If the nation wanted to expand the size of its navy, which Adams thought necessary for the nation's security, commerce, and prestige, it would have to do so while it was on good terms with Britain "and when we might seem to be building for a contest against her enemies."[108] To do otherwise was to invite challenge from a much stronger military.

But when the United States found itself fighting Britain several months later, Adams became an enthusiastic, if critical, supporter of the war. In many ways this war was a second American war for independence, as the issues contested—territorial boundaries, fishing rights, and Indian relations—were the same as those at issue in the 1783 Peace of Paris. In other ways, though, this conflict was an outgrowth of the continental wars, as British warships stopped, inspected, and seized American merchants and ships that claimed neutral rights in Europe's wars. Unsurprisingly, Adams framed this war not in terms of commercial "freight and tonnage," but of national independence.[109] From Russia, he wrote that the issue at stake in the conflict was the country's "right as an independent nation."[110] While the Americans achieved some degree of success during the war, their military and strategic failures created vivid perceptions of an insufficiently powerful government. This became painfully clear when the British attacked and burned Washington in August 1814.

The events surrounding the surprise attack on the nation's capital could hardly have been more shocking. As a British observer remembered, "the consternation of the inhabitants was complete, and . . . to them this was a night of terror."[111] An inhabitant of Washington recorded that the night was so horrid that "no pen can describe the appalling sound that our ears heard and the sight that our eyes saw."[112] The *Federal Republican* of Georgetown reported that the enemy "entered Washington at his leisure . . . [and] destroyed the capitol, the president's home, and the treasury office . . . [and later] the War-Office." Somberly and angrily, the newspaper concluded that "in the present situation of affairs, when all is confusion and alarm . . . we can scarcely be said to have a government."[113] As the inhabitants of Washington watched the night sky, "brilliantly illuminated by the different conflagrations," their disgust was not confined to the militia, but extended as well to the government that had apparently abandoned them to the British vandals.[114]

Feelings of anger mixed with a profound sense of vulnerability and insecurity after the war's conclusion.[115] Typifying such sentiment was a *National Intelligencer* article that pointed to the charred buildings of the capital as "a beacon to remind us how much may be lost by false security, or by want of union and energy of action."[116] The problem was whether the nation, lulled into complacency over the past thirty years, had lost its sense of security. Beyond that, larger questions loomed of *why* the nation had been so unprepared and *what* it might do to prevent such an attack from recurring.[117]

Adams knew that antipathy toward a powerful government and a strong military ran deep in the early republic.[118] Prior to the outbreak of hostilities, Jeffersonian Republicans, in power since 1800, had drastically cut the defense budget. They reduced the national debt 43 percent by cutting defense, which had accounted for half of the federal budget in 1799. Under Jefferson, the army shrank from 14,000 to 3,287 soldiers, and the navy's budget was reduced by 67 percent.[119] Jeffersonian military strategy, more concerned about the threat to civil liberties that standing armies could pose, called only for a small regular army, a loosely organized militia still officially controlled by the states, and a tiny navy.[120] Jefferson was aware that this could prove disastrous in the face of an invasion, writing Madison in 1809, "I know no government which would be so embarrassing in war as ours."[121] Notwithstanding Jackson's New Orleans victory, the war with Great Britain proved Jefferson correct. If such "national *humiliation*[s]" as the burning of Washington were to be avoided in the future, Adams thought that wartime measures alone would not suffice.[122] As he concluded in a postwar assessment, "the most painful, perhaps the most profitable lesson of the war was the primary duty of the nation to place itself in a state of permanent preparation for self-defence."[123]

Owing to his distinguished diplomatic record, his expertise in European affairs, and some domestic opposition to other Madison nominees, Adams was appointed chairman of the American delegation to Ghent to negotiate an end to hostilities with the British. Successfully concluding a peace treaty on Christmas Eve that helped preserve the status quo of the prewar boundaries, Adams was named minister to Great Britain. This was the most important diplomatic posting abroad because the United States needed to construct a stable peace with England. But as Adams also knew, a lasting peace would only come if America were sufficiently powerful. During the war, Adams had told Secretary of State James Monroe that strength alone was the guarantee of good relations with Europe, warning, "we shall have no valuable friends in Europe until we have proved that we can defend ourselves without them. There will be friends enough, if we can maintain our own cause by our own resources."[124] In the wake of the recent war, these lessons appeared even starker. "The war may also be instructive to ourselves," he wrote, if "it will teach us to cherish the defensive strength of a respectable navy, to preserve in the encouragement of our domestic manufactures; that it will lead us to a more vigorous and independent system of finance."[125] Stationed in London and sensitive to European balance of power issues, Adams assessed that the restoration of a general peace in Europe "may increase the difficulty of preserving ours."[126] But if the United States had learned anything from the War of 1812, it was that "no nation can enjoy freedom and independence without being always prepared to defend them by force of arms."[127] The United States now needed to build and project military power. "The surest pledge that we can have of peace will be to be prepared for war," Adams wrote to his friend William Plumer, then governor of New Hampshire.[128] Future security for America would be found not only in financial, but also in military, strength.

While the need for a more robust system of defense was one lesson of the war, dire threats to the internal cohesion of the Union were even more prominently on display. The conflict was extraordinarily partisan from the start, with 81 percent of congressional Republicans voting for the war, while the Federalists universally opposed it.[129] The war was especially unpopular in the northern coastal states whose economies depended on trade with Britain. In multiple instances, northern governors refused to call up their states' militias to fight in a war they felt antithetical to the nation's, or at least their own, interests. Adams thought that war had revealed many "projects of severing the Union." While resistance was particularly strong in Massachusetts, it was not confined to the Bay State, and in late 1814 disgruntled Federalists met in Hartford to air their grievances with the war and their growing disillusionment with the drift of the federal government. Although the Federalists ultimately discredited themselves by this action, the threat of secession hung over their actions. While the war's somewhat successful termination had undercut these impulses, the extreme danger that northern secessionists posed and the fact that they were "deeply seated in the political system" of the country necessitated that "they will require to be watched, exposed, and inflexibly resisted, probably for many years."[130] But as Adams himself acknowledged, this domestic political challenge was not likely to go away soon. More immediate were the threats emanating from London, Madrid, Paris,

CLANS AND TRIBES AT ETERNAL WAR

and even St. Petersburg. It was to these threats that Adams would turn when he became secretary of state.

On December 24, 1816, John Quincy Adams received a letter informing him that the president intended to make him his secretary of state. In his diary that night, Adams pondered "whether I am fitted to discharge the heavy and laborious duties of the office."[131] Such doubts resurfaced the night before he accepted the position. Understanding the extraordinary responsibility and weight of the office, Adams wrote that "these are hard knots, with which I am to enter upon the discharge of the duties of the Department of State—a trust of weight and magnitude which I cannot contemplate without deep concern."[132]

This was coming from a man who had just been named secretary of state and was well on his way to the presidency. While such anxiety might have been in keeping with his character, it was also unwarranted. Adams brought more experience and knowledge than any of his contemporaries could have. But his professional success continued to come at a high personal cost to himself and to his family. Louisa Catherine later complained of the "Nation whose honor was dearly bought at the expense of all domestic happiness."[133] When President Madison offered him a diplomatic posting in Russia, John Quincy replied that he "could see no significant reason for refusing the nomination."[134] But when he informed his wife that his duty demanded he accept it, and prudence required that they leave their two oldest sons in America, she reacted angrily, questioning the necessity of always subordinating their personal desires to their public ambitions. Even Charles Francis, John Quincy Adams's youngest and most accomplished son, came to regard public life as "a very disagreeable one" that wreaked havoc on a family.[135]

From the outset of their relationship, Louisa had detected a certain perverseness in John Quincy's behavior. More than anyone she had previously encountered, her husband took pride in his ability to deny himself what he most wanted. It was one thing to honor the republican virtues of selflessness and sacrifice, but quite another to purposefully pursue them. Attempting to live up to the image that had been held up to him from birth, denial became a virtue, and indulgence—even of happiness—a vice. During their courtship, John Quincy had displayed manners "so severe, so cold and so peremptory" that they had deeply wounded his wife's pride.[136] Over time, and especially as their bonds deepened, his behavior toward his wife slowly mellowed. But her initial judgments of his extreme irritability, self-righteousness over matters of propriety, and volcanic temper were well founded, and noted by both friends and foes.

"Of all the men whom it was ever my lot to accost and to waste civilities upon," the British minister W. H. Lyttleton reported, Adams "was the most doggedly and systematically repulsive. With a vinegar aspect, cotton in his leathern ears and hatred in his heart, he sat . . . like a bulldog among spaniels."[137] This is too harsh of an assessment, and it came from an adversary. But even friends found him aggressive and argumentative. William Plumer, a political ally from their time in the Senate, found more to admire. Plumer described Adams as "a man of much information, a bookworm, very industrious." Further, he believed Adams "a man of strong passions and of course subject to strong prejudices, but a man of strict undeviating integrity. He is free and independent. On some subjects he appears eccentric."[138] In matters both personal and political, Adams rebelled against anything he thought might infringe on his independence. This inclination often led him to seek out minority positions, and to feel all the more virtuous for doing so. If not happiest, Adams was certainly most comfortable when he stood in opposition to something or someone. Intellectual and industrious, rigid in his beliefs, and with a propensity to see issues and people in stark terms, in many ways Adams was an odd fit for politics.

And yet Adams pursued politics regardless. He was hard working and a vocal defender of the country. If not always popular, he did possess an astute awareness of and ability to articulate the long-term interests of the nation. When he abandoned the Federalists, he did so because he sensed that the future of the country lay with expansionist sentiment and Jeffersonian politics. Although the voters of Massachusetts punished him, he was ultimately rewarded by Presidents Jefferson, Madison, and Monroe. Adams's political pliability should be understood in terms of his long-term personal, political, and national strategy, as both his and the country's future lay in national expansion.

Adams had been abroad for more than eight years and had risen to the top of the diplomatic corps. During those years, he had refined further his initial beliefs on the country's development. First and foremost, Adams believed that neutrality was the surest way to secure independence, which not only required American isolation from European affairs but also demanded European abstention from American expansion. His essays in the *Columbian Centinel,* his letters to his father advocating a middle path between Britain and France, his official dispatches during the Napoleonic wars promoting a nonbelligerent's access to European markets, and his private ruminations in his diary all attest to the centrality of these beliefs. Only by preserving its freedom to act in its own best interests would America, and not Europe, control the country's future. And at the heart of its interests lay the preservation of the republic's security. Witnessing Europe's squabbles over rocks and fishponds, Adams was determined to defend his country's prerogatives, be they fishing rights or evacuation of British frontier garrisons. Additionally, he knew that Europe was unconstrained by internal wars and that the Spanish Empire was collapsing.

Adams's knowledge would affect his agenda. As insecure and vague borders created power vacuums for hostile powers to threaten U.S. territorial and commercial integrity, stabilizing and securing U.S. borders became Adams's top priority. These goals would sometimes require defensive measures to counteract hostile aggressions. At other times, however, they would necessitate expansive actions to project American force into lawless regions beyond U.S. borders. Adams's first year in office as secretary of state found him engaged in both types of actions.

3

IN SEARCH OF MONSTERS TO DESTROY

The Extent and Limits of American Power

EVENTUALLY, THE PIRATES GOT to the secretary of state. Throughout the fall of 1817, President Monroe's cabinet had been equivocating about what action to take against soldiers of fortune who had captured Amelia Island in the Gulf of Mexico and Galveston Island off Spanish Texas. The pirates, claiming they were acting in support of the fledgling republican governments of South America that had recently declared independence from Spain, had occupied the islands and offered to harass Spanish shipping for the United States. But as it soon became clear, the pirates were more interested in acting like pirates than they were in supporting the revolutions against Spain. The results were predictable, as the marauders menaced Spanish and American shipping alike.

This was not a discrete problem, but part of the larger strategic dilemma, as the United States weighed its policy options toward an increasingly weakened Spain. Prior to the cabinet meeting on October 30, 1817, President James Monroe submitted a series of pointed foreign policy questions concerning the relationship between Spain and the South American republics. Monroe wanted to know if he could acknowledge the independence of states still in the midst of rebellion and not recognized by their parent country. He asked the cabinet to assess whether doing so would give Spain cause to declare war on the United States, and if it was in America's interest to recognize Buenos Aires and other parts of South America in the midst of anticolonial rebellions. Most broadly, he wanted to hear their counsel on how the United States should position itself toward a declining but still powerful Spain. And returning to the pirates, he queried them as to whether the United States ought to attack these belligerents, "it being evident that they were . . . already perverted to very mischievous purposes to the U States."[1]

After four and a half hours of listless talk, Secretary of State Adams exploded: "As it appeared to me that all the gentlemen were backward in giving their opinions upon almost every one of them, I finally gave mine explicitly," Adams scribbled in his diary that evening. To Adams, the cabinet was demonstrating few signs of backbone and even fewer of strategy. He urged that the marauding pirates' bases "ought to be broken up immediately." According to Adams, his forceful words settled the matter. He also "explicitly avowed my opinion that it is not now expedient for the President to acknowledge the Government of Buenos Aires."[2] As both President Monroe and the newly installed secretary of state knew, the pirates were part of a much greater problem—how the United States should respond to Spain's crumbling empire. On this, the president deferred a decision.

In 1817, as secretary of state, Adams's job was not to formulate policy, but to execute it. "For myself," he wrote, "I shall enter upon the functions of my office . . . with a suitable impression that my place is subordinate; that my duty will be to support, and not to counteract or oppose, the President's administration."[3] He repeated this line, at least to himself, regularly throughout his tenure as secretary of state. Six years later, in 1823, he reminded himself that "my object was to give all the aid in my power to his [Monroe's] measures, and I wished not one line of my writing to go forth that should not have <u>his</u> hearty approbation."[4]

This did not mean that Adams would play a passive role in the cabinet—far from it, as his reactions on issues ranging from pirates to Andrew Jackson to Spain's crumbling empire demonstrated. In the confidential setting of cabinet meetings, Adams would argue vigorously to influence the president. But in public he would put as little space between himself and the president's policies as possible. Throughout his career, Adams took an unusual, even perverse, pride in demonstrating his own independence—often at the expense of his political career. So why the "subordinate" role? Two reasons suggest themselves. First, as Adams himself indicated, there was little distance between himself and the president on matters of national security. They both believed that it was the destiny and in the interests of the United States to expand. But there was another motivation behind this strategic convergence. As Adams was well aware, from 1800 on, the path to the presidency had run through the Department of State, as the previous three secretaries of state had all become president.[5] As much as Adams affected indifference to this prospect, he was certainly aware of the stakes. And if it was his goal to become president of the United States, Adams's appointment as secretary of state seemed to confirm that he was on the right course.

To be successful, Adams sensed that his own fortunes would rise and fall with those of the Monroe administration. Upon reading the news of his appointment as secretary of state in April 1817, Adams wrote, "these are hard knots, with which I am to enter upon the discharge of the duties of the Department of State—a trust of weight and magnitude which I cannot contemplate without deep concern."[6] If the administration failed, Adams realized that opponents would point to him as the source of that failure. However, if it succeeded, Adams would be able to claim its victories as his own and as proof of his worthiness for the presidency. On his road to the State Department, Adams had a sense of what he was aiming for and what steps needed to be taken to get there, even when he was confused and unsure of the path ahead. The same was true for his tenure as secretary of state as he pursued a policy of continental expansion. And this policy was a product of how the Monroe administration saw American interests in the world, how it understood the threats to those interests, how it formulated its responses in light of those interests and threats, and how it sought to justify those responses.[7]

Before Adams could begin to make policy, he first had to manage the State Department. Quickly, business became overwhelming and threatened to drown the secretary in a sea of paper and visitors. Instead of a getting up to speed on major world events and the functioning of the foreign service bureaucracy, Adams found the urgent getting crowded out by the immediate. Because there was no system to organize and help set priorities, Adams attended to whatever insignificant detail fell across his desk. Reflecting on this three years into his tenure, Adams noted that "one of the greatest inconveniences that I suffer is the necessity of attending to the minutest details, and of superintending with incessant vigilance even the routine of the office."[8] Lacking a system, work was not only inefficient, it was not strategic. It had little ability to tie together disparate events and weave them into a whole greater than its parts.

In an attempt to get up to speed on the major issues, Adams held several debriefing sessions with Richard Rush, the outgoing minister to Great Britain, who had been acting as temporary secretary of state. When not talking to Rush, Adams was settling into a routine that would keep him in office from nine in the morning until three in the afternoon. During this time, he had a steady stream of visitors, including office seekers and members of the foreign diplomatic corps who would drop by, usually unannounced, to chat. In between visits, Adams attempted to read back through the official files. By the end of his first week in office, Adams was complaining, "I find my eyes already so much affected, that before ten I was obliged to desist from writing and retire to repose."[9]

Over the ensuing months, Adams would take on an ever increasing workload. In addition to holding regular hours during the day in his office on Seventeenth and G Streets, the secretary looked over all the dispatches to and from American ministers and consuls and read all of the notes handed to him by the foreign diplomatic corps in Washington. He drafted almost all of the official responses by hand and usually went through several drafts of each of these letters. Additionally, Congress required the secretary of state to oversee the census; collect, print, and distribute all acts of Congress; prepare an index of congressional legislation at the end of each session; oversee the Patent Office; and monitor the laws of the various states. In case this were not enough, Congress had commissioned the State Department to produce a report on the standardization of weights and measures in use in the various states and assess the prospects for imposing a uniform system on the country.[10] As one historian of the State Department noted, by the 1820s, "Congress reconfirmed the practice of assigning to the Department of State all such responsibilities not entrusted to other departments and agencies."[11] State was the federal agency of last resort. Often it was also the agency of first resort. And it was expected to carry out all these tasks with a staff of ten.[12]

Finding that there were not enough hours in the day, Adams attempted to lengthen the day. At the start of Monroe's administration he was waking up between five and six in the morning. Within the year, he was up at five or earlier, and soon, working almost around the clock to produce his massive report on weights and measures, he would spring from bed almost as soon as his head touched the pillow. As Adams himself knew, this had a negative effect on his work: "The greatest difficulty that I find in rising early and at a regular hour is that when I steadily pursue that intention, I awake earlier every morning than the preceding one, til I lose the due and necessary sleep of the night, the consequence of which is a most painful drowsiness the following day."[13] This painful drowsiness led to some awkward moments. One day, Adams and Harvard president Josiah Quincy, a fellow early riser, attended a law lecture. The lecturing judge invited the two to sit at his side on the podium. Almost as soon as they took their seats, the two fell asleep. Noting their snoring, "the Judge pause[d] a moment, and, pointing to the two sleeping gentlemen, said, 'Gentlemen, you see before you

a melancholy example of the evil effects of early rising.' This remark was followed by a shout of laughter, which effectually roused
the sleepers."[14] Lack of sleep and working to exhaustion were con-
stants in Adams's public career, but these next eight years would
push him as far as he could go.

Time spent at home was often just as tiring as time spent in public. Despite being abroad for many years, under Louisa Catherine's
guidance the Adamses quickly moved to the center of Washington's social and political life.[15] It was Louisa's energy and warmth,
not John's cold reserve, that made their home so popular. But this
reserve was not always aloofness. One evening Adams returned
home from the office to find a group of three Osage Indians sitting
in his parlor. With no translator on hand, Big Bear, Big Road, and
Black Spirit greeted the secretary of state silently. They sat staring
at each other until eventually they began pointing at Adamses' fur-
niture in admiration. This was apparently enough for Adams and
his guests to strike up a mutually incomprehensible conversation
that terminated when the Indian chiefs also admired the waist of
Adams's niece.[16] This young niece was one of many residents of the
Adams household, which at various times included sons, nieces,
and nephews. At one point in 1820, John Quincy and Louisa Catherine had as many as ten teenagers living under their roof.

Hoping to control some of the chaos in his life, Adams tried to
regulate his day and his work. Usually rising several hours before
dawn, he would write in his diary about the previous day's events,
read a chapter or two from the Bible, and, weather permitting, engage in his daily exercises. Sometimes he would walk, and occasionally he found the time go riding. But most of the time he continued
his lifelong habit of heading over to the river and taking a plunge.

Wearing a pair of green goggles and nothing else, Adams would swim out as far as a mile into the Potomac's currents before returning to shore. After one swim, Adams climbed out of the water to find a surprised British minister. In the most famous, and probably most apocryphal, story, Adams found an enterprising female reporter demanding an interview in exchange for the return of his clothes. Embarrassing moments notwithstanding, all of these activities, including his daily timed walks to work, suggest a mind that sought to impose order on a frenetic life.[17] Exercise and regularity offered Adams the opportunity to concentrate his energies on the multiple tasks before him. "In the continual bustle and unceasing occupation of my present office, I feel nothing but the want of time." He bemoaned this, but Adams was a manic spirit; the more he had to do, the happier and more productive he was. To Adams, nothing was worse than an idle and useless life. "I shall want *an object of pursuit*," he wrote to himself, and prayed that he would receive the wisdom and grace to find it.[18] Even if he constantly pined after a simpler life, this period was an especially fruitful one, as his objectives were, if not easy to accomplish, at least clear.

Adams's search for order was as much a part of his professional activities as it was of his personal habits. With a frenetic schedule and much of the Department's information hard to find, Adams needed to impose order both on his schedule and, more importantly, on the way the department was run. Record-keeping had been haphazard, the department's finances were in disarray, and diplomatic correspondence was erratic and unorganized. When Adams first sat down at his desk, he found several letters still unanswered from the previous year. Worse, Adams had trouble locating some important files, including a treaty with Sweden that had gone missing. Surveying his desk, his office, and the department,

Adams concluded that "all [was] in disorder and confusion."[19] Adams realized that he could not begin to stay abreast of the news without a system for handling the large amounts of information. He gradually imposed a system that required all correspondence, both domestic and foreign, to be dated, numbered, summarized, and filed. This indexing and filing would allow Adams, and future secretaries, to find the information they needed and, of greater importance, to prioritize their work. Department-wide, he began a bureaucratic reorganization, assigning each of his clerks a specific task. Attempting to reduce inefficiencies, Adams divided up the workload, giving one clerk the task of handling consular correspondence, another departmental finances, another preparing congressional acts for publication, and another copying patents. Additionally, Adams began the practice of sending American diplomats two sets of instructions. The first was general in nature and covered diplomatic procedure and protocols. The second set of instructions was tailored to the mission and contained specific goals, objectives, and policies.

Writing in his diary about the lack of order and procedure he found at State, Adams came near to setting forth his management philosophy. "As in everything else relating to the business of the Department," he scribbled, "I feel incessantly the want of method—systematical arrangement. I am endeavoring to introduce it gradually; but, as it requires long experience of all the business of the office, as the whole and the detail must be known before a good arrangement of distributions can be made," this systematical arrangement proved elusive.[20] But in this, Adams was being too hard on himself. He had arrived in an unordered environment and quickly set in place structures that would systematize the business of diplomacy. The systems Adams created would serve the State

Department into the twentieth century. And, most importantly, Adams had begun to articulate his sense of grand strategy where the particular and the general, the "whole and the detail," operated simultaneously on each other. Charting a course forward would require Adams both to master the discrete issues at hand and to link them to emerging patterns.

In hindsight, the choice of John Quincy Adams as secretary of state seemed to be a natural one, but it had not been a given after Monroe's election to the presidency. Adams, naturally enough, found his selection not only gratifying, but also a seeming confirmation of both his abilities and his rectitude. In reality, the president's motives were as much political as they were driven by respect for Adams's diplomatic skills. To Monroe, an expansive agenda for the country necessitated national unity, and the first place he sought to strike this balance was in his cabinet. This would send a signal that he was in tune with both the aspirations and the grievances of different parts of the country. Writing to Thomas Jefferson in late February 1817, Monroe laid out his reasons for choosing Adams for secretary of state. Noting that many expected him to choose yet another Virginian (which, in this case, would mean either William Crawford or Henry Clay), the president-elect wrote, "I have thought that it would produce a bad effect, to place any one from this quarter of the Union, in the dept. of State, for [sic] from the south or west. You know how much has been said to impress a belief on the country, north & east of this, that the citizens from Virga., holding the presidency, have made appointments to that dept., to secure the succession, from it, to the presidency, of the person who happens to be from that State."[21] Monroe's reasons for this were political—and they were shrewd. Appointing another southerner, particularly one from Virginia, would unify the country against, not for, the administration. "My wish," the president stated, "is to prevent such a combination." Moreover, appointing a New Englander would demonstrate that the Republicans aspired to be a national and not regional party. The solution was obvious: Monroe turned to Adams. "By his age, long experience in foreign affairs, and adoption into the republican party, [he] seems to have superior pretentions to any there."[22]

Jefferson agreed. The Sage of Monticello is said to have remarked, "They were made for each other. Adams has a pointed pen; Monroe has judgment enough for both and firmness to have *his* judgment control."[23] Writing to Andrew Jackson just three days before his inauguration, Monroe repeated his reasoning. "I shall take a person for the Department of State from the eastward; and Mr. Adams' claims, by long service in our diplomatic concerns, appearing to entitle him to preference, supported by his acknowledged abilities and integrity, his nomination will go to the Senate."[24]

Adams, if we are to believe Monroe's reasoning, possessed the best possible qualifications for this high office.[25] He was senior enough in age and experience to command respect. He was the United States' most seasoned diplomat and brought a keener understanding of diplomacy, negotiation, and European affairs than any other candidate. And, significantly, Adams's expansionist views ensured that he passed Monroe's political litmus test. That said, Monroe knew that appointing Adams, a former Federalist, a man from New England, and the son of the man who signed into law the Alien and Sedition Acts, would displease Jeffersonian stalwarts. To offset this, Monroe appointed many southerners to the cabinet: William Crawford of Georgia at Treasury; John C. Calhoun of South Carolina at War; and William Wirt, from Maryland, as attorney general. By nominating Adams for State, Monroe realized that he might be handing off the presidency from Virginia. But "having form'd my opinion on great consideration," he concluded in his letter to Jefferson, "I shall probably adhere to it."[26]

From the outset, Monroe was the decider. Adams, for the most part, accepted this, observing that the president had "a mind sound in its ultimate judgments, and firm in its final conclusions."[27] A contemporary observer formed the same impression: "It is said, his mind is neither rich nor brilliant, but capable of the most laborious analysis, and the most patient research—not hasty in its decisions, and not easily changed when its decisions are formed. Judgment appears to be his prominent intellectual feature."[28] Echoing this statement, the attorney general noted that Monroe had "a mind neither rapid nor rich, and therefore he cannot shine on a subject which is entirely new to him."[29] These divergent views tend to obscure the picture.[30] Monroe was a strong leader who was influenced by his advisers. He was a self-confident man who was not worried about placing strong personalities and bright people around him.[31] He attempted to make executive decisions by the consensus of his cabinet; this is why he submitted questions ahead of cabinet meetings. But while Monroe attempted to reach decisions by consensus, he set the general direction of policy. This seems especially clear in his inaugural address of 1817, drafted and delivered prior to the appointment and confirmation of his cabinet. In this speech Monroe laid out the broad framework of his administration.

With the American economy growing, political divisions healing, and Europe's wars concluded, President James Monroe found himself operating in a very different world than that of his predecessors. For the first time in a generation, a new administration was assuming office without facing the direct threat of hostilities. The *Courier* of New York reported that the foreign policy concerns of past administrations "have all, or nearly all, vanished; the present incumbent *has the world before him,* and is at liberty to exercise all his abilities for the public good."[32] To Monroe, perpetuating this state of relative domestic and international tranquility would best serve American interests. The means to this goal were twofold: delaying hostilities with European powers and expanding across the North American continent.

Monroe's inauguration, held on Tuesday, March 4, 1817, had all the signs of an auspicious day. Elected with nearly 70 percent of the popular vote, Monroe was a steady, if not spectacular, choice. As his Federalist opponent Rufus King noted, Monroe "had the zealous support of nobody, and he was exempt from the hostility of Everybody."[33] Except, that is, from the Speaker of the House, Henry Clay, who was enraged that Monroe had denied him the opportunity—or right, as Clay saw it—of becoming secretary of state.[34] Clay refused the president the use of the Capitol for his speech, so, taking a risk, Monroe decided to deliver his inaugural address outside. This was the first decision of the new administration, and it proved a good one. Even though it was still early March, a spring breeze blew through the capital, and the sun warmed up the thousands of onlookers.[35] The spectacle of seeing the new president sworn in attracted huge "crowds [that] were seen flocking towards the Capital from every direction." And while delivering a speech in the open air to thousands of visitors presented some acoustic challenges, the press reported that "the delivery was so distinct and the silence of the people was so great, that it was perfectly heard [at] a considerable distance."[36]

Unburdened by war and embargo, which had preoccupied his predecessors, Monroe struck an optimistic note. Peace and commerce were paying dividends. The economy was strong: the recently war-drained treasury now had a surplus of nearly $10 million; the nation's credit was fully restored; exports were up nearly 100 percent since the end of the war; and increased revenues meant that the federal debt was nearly retired. But there were dangers to the present state of peace, prosperity, and popular government. Principally these came from abroad. Monroe reminded his countrymen of the perpetual dangers Europe posed to their young country. It would attempt "to overset our Government, to break our Union, and demolish us as a nation." After the Congress of Vienna the threat had diminished, but it had not disappeared. To think that adversaries could be amicable trading partners was naïve at best and dangerous at worst. True, the president told the audience, "our distance from Europe and the just, moderate, and pacific policy of our Government may form some security against these dangers, but they ought to be anticipated and guarded against."[37] Distance was a safeguard but not a fail-safe.

The point of this assessment was neither descriptive nor analytical, but political. As in the debates that followed the War of 1812, when advocates of expanded governmental power linked expansion to national honor, Monroe attempted to cultivate popular opinion for this purpose. "A people who fail to do it can scarcely be said to hold a place among independent nations. National honor is national property of the highest value. The sentiment in the mind of every citizen is national strength. It ought therefore to be cherished."[38] Resumed turbulence in Europe could bring war and disaster. But, just as important, an insufficient focus on the demands of national security at home would invite aggression. As the president explained it, national honor and prosperity demanded a more activist government. From this justification flowed policy recommendations of increased military spending and internal improvements.

The president had noted that oceans did not necessarily provide free security and had urged his countrymen to build up the appropriate military defenses, but he did not link this argument to one of continental expansion. It largely fell to his secretary of state to define how the United States would gain control of North America. To Adams, expansion represented not only security and prosperity, but also destiny. But such a future was threatened by internal divisions within the nation and from European intrusions onto the North American continent. Regardless of how such divisions might develop, they would have a balkanizing effect on America, effectively turning it into another Europe where the stakes were low and the wars frequent. Long years in the courts of Europe convinced Adams that the republic must steer clear of Europe's entangling ambitions and guard its right to shape its future. However, refusing to get involved "over there" was not enough; the United States had to make sure that Europe did not come "over here" and create a balance of power in the New World, exposing it to power politics, war, and corruption.[39]

The first requirement was to postpone another clash with a great power. This was part of the long-standing American strategy of buying time for the republic's territorial expansion. Alexander Hamilton first articulated it in *The Federalist*.[40] The goal of the newly formed United States was "to become the arbiter of Europe in America, and to be able to incline the balance of European competitors in this part of the world as our interests may dictate."[41] The more the United States was able to project its power in the

Western Hemisphere, the less European imperial powers would dictate the limits of America's ambitions. To Adams, the strategy of balancing European powers in North America was less about balancing than it was about replacing them. The best way to preserve America's independence was to reduce the menace of Europe in North America.[42]

During a November 1819 cabinet meeting, Adams came as close as he ever did to laying out a strategy for the preponderance for U.S. power in North America. He discussed European, and particularly British, complaints that the United States was an ambitious and aggrandizing nation. Rather than disavow such sentiments, Adams stated that such British complaints were warranted. Furthermore, the secretary of state argued that if the United States wanted its territorial integrity respected, "the world shall [have] to be familiarized with the idea of considering our proper dominion to be the continent of North America." The strategy involved undermining other European powers' claims to sovereignty there. Much of this would happen naturally; as the United States continued to develop and expand, surrounding territory, nominally under the control of various European governments, would find it increasingly difficult to resist the attraction of a dynamic state. In this view, the United States' attractive power resembled a gravitational force field. As Newton's second law had posited, the more mass an entity possessed, the greater a force it would exert on surrounding objects. The same was true of the United States:

> From the time when we became an independent people it was as
> much a law of nature that this should become our pretension as
> that the Mississippi should flow to the sea. Spain had possessions
> upon our southern border and Great Britain upon our northern

border. [But] it was impossible that centuries should elapse without finding them annexed to the United States; not that any spirit of encroachment or ambition on our part renders it necessary, but because it is a physical, moral, and political absurdity that such fragments of territory, with sovereigns at fifteen hundred miles beyond the sea, worthless and burdensome to their owners, should exist permanently contiguous to a great, powerful, enterprising, and rapidly growing nation.[43]

This was a sanitized version of American territorial expansion. It reformulated Thomas Paine's argument in *Common Sense* that "there is something very absurd, in supposing a continent to be perpetually governed by an island. In no instance hath nature made the satellite larger than its primary planet."[44] But it was also an apt description of how Americans thought of the North American continent. Such a gravitational strategy dictated that the United States expand where it could, bide its time elsewhere, and make sure that its commitments not exceed its capabilities. Adams's first year in office found him engaged in all of these types of actions. Continuing the conciliatory policies he had pursued as minister to Great Britain, he signed a treaty demarcating a northern border that demilitarized the Great Lakes. Simultaneously, he advanced an aggressive policy of expansion against the disputed southwestern border with Spain's North American holdings.

While American prospects certainly looked bright in 1817, domestic and international tensions threatened Adams's plans for continental expansion. Shortly before his departure from England in 1817, an English acquaintance remarked that "America . . . was the only country in the world enjoying happiness and with prospect of greatness. 'Of too much greatness,' said he, 'if you should remain long united; but you will not. You will soon break up into several Governments: So extensive a country cannot long remain under one Government.'"[45] Such expressions were not unique, echoing many conversations Adams had during his service abroad. This was the problem that confronted America's founders when they devised a system of governing a large and diffuse territory. Keeping the country united was the same challenge that Adams and his generation of policy makers would confront. The threat arose from two sources—one internal and one external. It was the president's job to manage the country's fractious politics and divergent sectional interests lest it be torn in different, and ultimately irreconcilable, directions. At the same time, he had to prevent Europe from establishing a further presence in North America.

Arriving in Washington in September 1817 after a brief reunion with his family in Massachusetts, Adams immediately called at the President's House.[46] The president had just returned from a four-month tour of the Northeast that he had used to promote reconciliation between political factions and geographic interests.[47] But Monroe was not planning on staying long in Washington. Due to the strong smell of fresh paint in the newly rebuilt Executive Mansion—in a euphemistic turn of phrase, Adams noted that it appeared "far restored from the effects of the British visit in 1814"—the president was about to leave for his estate in Virginia. But in their brief chat, the president and Adams began discussing the foreign policy challenges confronting them. In Adams's first face-to-face conversation with Monroe in more than eight years, the president entered upon "some general conversation upon the state of the public relations with Great Britain, Spain, and France."[48]

As Adams briefed the president on affairs of Europe, it was clear that the United States faced a number of threats. Until Napoleon's defeat at Waterloo in 1815, Europe had been almost continually at war since the French Revolution had poured across French borders in 1792. In 1814, European diplomats had met in Vienna in an attempt to determine the shape of Europe. Stability, in the minds of its participants, would come through ending, or perhaps even crushing, the republican revolutions that had been sweeping the world.[49] The clearest manifestation of this was the newly formed Holy Alliance, a coalition between Russia, Austria, and Prussia. Ostensibly formed to promote Christian values, in practice it expressed the solidarity of the absolute monarchies against the ideologies that had sprung from the French Revolution.

Of this Adams was clearly aware. "All the restored governments of Europe are deeply hostile to us," he had written his father from London in 1816. "The Royalists everywhere detest and despise us as Republicans." According to Adams, Europe regarded the United States, and not Revolutionary France, as "the primary causes of the propagation of those political principles which still made the throne of every European monarch rock under him as with the throes of an earthquake."[50] Writing to his friend William Plumer from London in early 1817, Adams emphasized the implications of European hostility. "The universal feeling of Europe in witnessing the gigantic growth of our population and power is that we shall, if united, become a very dangerous member of the society of nations. They therefore hope what they confidently expect, that we shall not long remain united."[51]

But the threat from Europe, as Adams understood it, was not merely ideological. Adams realized that while the Europeans might collectively "detest and despise" the Americans, each country's reasons for doing so were different, and in accord with its own particular national interests. In Britain, the cause was America's naval and land successes in the late war. While Adams cautioned the United States to remain as mindful of its own defeats as of its victories, he noted that the effect of the war on Britain had been to unite both liberals and conservatives against the United States. This was particularly important because in the brief period after the Congress of Vienna, Britain had gained "an ascendancy of influence over the whole continent of Europe" which Adams thought England would use "to inspire prejudices and jealousies against us." The French had an interest in seeing the United States at war "because they flatter themselves that [a war] would operate as a diversion in their favor, and perhaps enable them to break the yoke under which they are groaning." With Spain, the main conflict was over territorial disputes that left the two countries "on the verge of war." And for "giving them battle instead of tribute" the Barbary States owed the United States "a heavy grudge." In sum, America had "enemies in almost every part of the world, and few or no friends anywhere."[52] As Adams probably recalled from his study of Thucydides, fear, honor, and interest combined to threaten American security.

This general hostility toward America had diplomatic and military overtones as well. In the same letter that Adams warned of royalist opposition to republican government, he wrote that "the tranquility of Europe is precarious, it is liable to many sudden changes and great convulsions."[53] A further convulsion of Europe would mean disruption of trade, regardless of America's neutrality. But if Europe's tranquility were not superficial there would be even more ominous dangers for the United States. Europe had been at war through almost all of America's history as an independent country, and America benefited from the distractions and shifting power alliances of Europe. But without distraction, Europe could turn its attention and its reach westward. The "British visit in 1814" served as a powerful reminder of the problems that a peaceful, unencumbered, and quite possibly expansionist Europe posed. As Adams seemed to understand, "general tranquility" in Europe heightened the danger to the republic.[54]

In every direction, hostile foreign powers bordered the United States. To the north, the British controlled Canada and, in the wake of the War of 1812, had engaged in a naval buildup on the Great Lakes. Spain's gradual loss of power, both in Europe and in the Western Hemisphere, led to even greater challenges, as Spain held the key to determining the western border of the United States. While America had paid France for the Louisiana territory in 1803, the Spanish had disputed its extent and boundaries ever since. In the Floridas, the Spanish governor could not control his own territory, leaving it open to pirates, runaway slaves, and the increasingly hostile Creek Indians. Even further south, revolutions in Spain's former colonies raised the prospect of Spanish or French intervention. As if this were not challenge enough, Russia was eyeing the Pacific Northwest with increasingly covetous eyes.

Internally, the twin dangers of faction and slavery had the potential to tear the nation apart, though neither was particularly acute in 1817. Of the two, political division was the more immediate. Monroe sought to cleanse a residue of hostile feelings between Republicans and Federalists in the wake of the War of 1812—war had been declared on almost an entirely party-line vote, and the Federalists had openly spoken of secession at the Hartford Convention—by appointing a geographically, if not politically, diverse cabinet. Fear of partisanship was deeply encoded into the political DNA of the country's leadership. The idea that competing political interests could tear the nation apart ran back to Washington's Farewell Address, where he warned of the dangers of political parties. But nowhere was the fear of faction more clearly expressed than in James Madison's Federalist 10. In his famous essay, Madison had argued that republics necessarily give rise to diversity of interests (factions), but an enlarged republic could mitigate the negative effects. It would necessarily produce more checks on majority rule. Interest group would counterbalance interest group and prevent a majority from becoming a monolithic tyranny. This theory seemed to be proving true with the West emerging as a new political bloc, not necessarily bound to either the commerce of the North or the agriculture of the South. But in 1817 President Monroe did not yet realize that western expansion could exacerbate sectional tensions.

The second threat to internal cohesion was slavery—and it was also linked to western expansion. When combined with questions of party politics and slavery, expansion would become the third rail of American politics. When Missouri applied for statehood in 1818, two questions dominated congressional and cabinet debate: Did Congress have the power to regulate slavery in the territories, and, if it did have that power, was it wise to exercise it? Debate showed what a huge chasm of understanding had arisen between northerners and southerners. In the House, Congressman Edward Colston of Virginia accused Congressman Arthur Livermore of New Hampshire, who had described slavery as a "sin" and "the foulest reproach of nations," of "endeavoring to excite a servile war," and declared that he deserved to be hanged.[55] Thomas Cobb of Georgia warned that these debates had "kindled a fire which all the waters of the ocean cannot put out, which seas of blood can only extinguish."[56] And while the public was not as agitated as was

Washington in 1820 over this issue, the political elite tended to agree with Cobb's assessment, if in slightly less graphic language. In an April 21 letter to John Holmes, Thomas Jefferson wrote that the division of the country created by the Missouri Compromise line would eventually lead to the destruction of the Union: "This momentous question, like a fire bell in the night, awakened and filled me with terror. I considered it at once as the knell of the Union. It is hushed indeed for the moment. But this is a reprieve only, not a final sentence."[57]

In addition to the internal threat that slavery posed to the nation, Adams saw the danger of U.S. missionary zeal outstripping American capabilities. This was particularly true in regard to the rebelling Spanish states in South America. Inspired by the American and French Revolutions, Simón Bolívar and others led the Latin American colonies to declare independence from Spain as early as 1810 and asked the United States to recognize their sister republics. For years the United States delayed recognition, not wanting to offend Spain as it negotiated for large tracts of land and navigation rights. But the ideological appeal of supporting a republican revolution was powerful, and most Americans had a natural sympathy for the fledgling republics to their south.

Moreover, in the spring of 1821 fighting broke out between the Greeks and the Ottoman Turks. At first, it appeared that the Turks would crush the uprising, but by the end of the year the Greeks had united, issued a declaration of independence, and established a republican government. Inspired by the democracies of ancient Greece, thrilled by the republican rhetoric of the Greek rebels, and horrified by Turkish atrocities, Americans took the Greek cause to heart. There were pro-Greek rallies in New York and Kentucky as well as editorials from Washington to the Ohio Valley supporting the Greek rebels, and Congress witnessed grandiloquent orations promoting the advance of liberty and calling for aid to and formal recognition of Greece.

Motivated partly by anger at not having been selected as secretary of state, partly by a westerner's understanding of the commercial benefits of a close relationship with South America, partly by a desire to use the issue for his own political aggrandizement, and partly by ideological sympathy, Henry Clay accused the administration of not doing enough to support both Greek and South American revolutionaries. Clay supported a resolution to defray the costs of an American mission to Greece and urged his colleagues to "speak a cheering word to the Greeks" and offer their encouragement "to a nation of oppressed and struggling patriots in arms."[58] Looking south, Clay saw more patriots "fighting for liberty and independence—for precisely what we fought for."[59] Clay's speeches played on Americans' sense of morality and mission as he lectured his fellow congressmen that "we were their great example. Of us they constantly spoke as of brothers, having a similar origin. They adopted our principles, copied our institutions, and, in some instances, employed the very language and sentiments of our revolutionary papers."[60] How, he asked, could Americans possibly "remain passive spectators of the struggle of those people to break the same chains which once bound us?" Clay implied that such a policy was not only "cold, heartless, and indifferent" towards the struggle for liberty, but antithetical to America's history, traditions, and best instincts."[61]

While Clay's ideology was an early form of what became Wilsonianism in the twentieth century, it was also a useful stick with which to beat the administration. As he looked toward the presidential election of 1824, his brief retirement speech in May 1821 reaffirmed and strengthened Clay's position as the leading Monroe administration critic. Speaking at Higbee's Tavern in Lexington, Kentucky, Clay claimed that the public was out in front of an administration that had needlessly and immorally delayed recognition of the South American republics. Going a step further, he charged that the United States should support the independence of Latin America "by all means short of actual war." In conclusion, he suggested that "a sort of counterpoise to the holy alliance should be formed in the two Americas, in favor of national independence and liberty, to operate by the force of example, and moral influence."[62]

This alliance of fledgling republics was meant to combat the pernicious spread of Old World tyranny. As Clay had outlined in May 1820, his American system, "of which we shall be the centre," was meant to serve as "the rallying point of human wisdom against all the despotism of the Old World."[63] Whether this was to be offensive or defensive in nature was left unsaid. While some have argued that Clay's speech was misinterpreted and taken out of context and was, in effect, much more cautious than its critics made it out to be, a divide was emerging over whether, and to what extent, America should oppose tyranny and aggressively promote democracy.

Nowhere was this danger made clearer to Adams than in an article that appeared in the prominent *Edinburgh Review* in May 1820. Surveying the revolutions breaking out all over Europe, the article concluded: "In Germany—in Spain—in France—in Italy, the principles of Reform and Liberty are visibly arraying themselves for a final struggle with the principles of Established abuse,—Legitimacy, or Tyranny. . . . We conceive, that much will depend on the part that is taken by America . . . we now call upon America . . . to unite herself cordially with the liberal and enlightened part of the English nation, at a season when their joint efforts will in all probability be little enough to crown the good cause with success . . . [America's] *influence,* as well as her example, will be wanted in the crisis which seems to be approaching."[64]

To Adams, this was the same as Clay's demands for a hemispheric counterpoise to the Holy Alliance and congressional resolutions supporting Greek independence. He was against both of them. He thought they were seductive and potentially destructive crusades, and he saw them much as he had France's attempts to draw the United States into its revolutionary wars thirty years earlier. Adams saw these revolutions as dangerous distractions for the United States. Intervention would accomplish little, retard the cause of republicanism, and distract the country from its primary goal of continental expansion. Moreover, fearful that U.S. intentions would outstrip its capabilities, Adams thought that projecting U.S. power abroad would weaken its gravitational force on the North American continent.

The threats the Monroe administration faced were of different natures and emanated from different places. An ideological, military, and commercial threat lurked in Europe and Europe's presence in the Western Hemisphere. But an equally troubling danger sprang from within American society. The American impulse to remake the world in its own image carried with it the danger of leading the country into unnecessary and divisive wars. Adams reacted so strongly to the *Edinburgh Review* article precisely because it "inculcates a political doctrine in my estimation of the most pernicious tendency to this country, and the more pernicious, because it flatters our ambition—the doctrine that it is the duty of America to take an *active* part in the future political reformation of Europe."[65] Adams's tenure as secretary of state was remarkably successful in countering European threats. It was less so at persuading the American people to restrain their impulses.

Adams's response to these threats came in three distinct stages. He sought to secure American hegemony in the Western Hemisphere, soothe internal divisions, and restrain American idealism. Of these, the first proved the easiest. Following the gravitational strategy, Adams worked to push Spanish, Russian, and British interests out of, or nearly out of, North America and project American power all the way to the Pacific. Circumstance guided his actions. At the start of Monroe's presidency two geopolitical trends stood out clearly: a growing rapprochement with Great Britain and Spain's diminishing power. While both represented opportunities for America's expansionist agenda, in 1817 neither of these trends were assured. Moreover, while managing Spain's decline in North America presented Washington with the more immediate challenge, Great Britain was the more formidable.

Of this Adams was well aware. He had just returned from two years as American minister to Great Britain. This was the most important diplomatic posting abroad, as no other country had caused the young republic as much trouble. Britain's projection of power meant that America's access to world markets depended on English goodwill. It also meant that when that goodwill was strained, as it had been during the recent war, England could simultaneously restrict U.S. commerce and menace the distant American coasts. Napoleon's defeat at Waterloo and the postwar settlement reached at the Congress of Vienna exacerbated this threat, the Treaty of Ghent notwithstanding, by freeing England from its European constraints.

It is no exaggeration to claim that in the American popular imagination, the threat of Great Britain in the early nineteenth century held a place akin to the menace of the Soviet Union in the twentieth century, even though the United States was not yet a superpower. It was always present, always lurking, and always waiting to take advantage of the republic. When serving as secretary of state, Adams summarized many of his countrymen's feelings toward the British Empire, claiming that "Great Britain, after vilifying us twenty years as a mean, low-minded, peddling nation, having no generous ambitions and no God but gold, had now changed her tone, and was endeavoring to alarm the world at the gigantic grasp of our ambition."[66]

But despite this animosity, Adams realized that the long-term interest of the United States lay in constructing a stable peace with England. As early as 1816 Adams understood this, writing his father from London, "I am deeply convinced that peace is the state best adapted to the interest and the happiness of both nations."[67] The feeling was for the most part mutual. Meeting with Lord Castlereagh, the British foreign minister, in May 1817, shortly after Monroe's inauguration, Adams told him that he "was instructed in the strongest manner to declare the new President, Mr. Monroe's, earnest and anxious desire to cultivate the most friendly and harmonious intercourse with Great Britain." Castlereagh responded that "the same and an equally earnest disposition and desire existed in this country to cultivate and improve the friendly relations with the United States."[68] Such a rapprochement was mutually beneficial. To Britain, it offered an opportunity to extend its growing commercial empire. To the young republic, it provided an opportunity to minimize the chances of war, shore up its territorial boundaries, and integrate its commerce more fully into Britain's global trade system.

After Ghent, and with Monroe's election, decisions in both London and Washington facilitated a gradual rapprochement. The Rush-Bagot Treaty, signed in April 1817 by acting secretary of state Richard Rush and British minister Charles Bagot, authorized the demilitarization of the Great Lakes and Lake Champlain.[69] Of even greater importance was the Commercial Convention of 1818, which gave Americans the right to fish the waters of the North Atlantic, referred American claims of indemnification of seized slaves to arbitration, established the U.S.-Canadian border from the Lake of the Woods to the Rockies along the 49th parallel, and proclaimed that territory west of the Rockies was to be opened for joint settlement and development for the next ten years. The American Senate voted unanimously in favor of its approval, and Castlereagh commented that with the signing of the treaty "two countries ... should [now] strive to make each other rich and happy."[70] Richard Rush, now serving as American minister to London, held an equally sanguine view: with the convention signed and the long unresolved issues of the fisheries and northern boundary lines finally off the table, "the calamity of a war was probably warded off" and "the seed of future disputes was extinguished."[71] While the treaty faced some public criticism, both governments considered it a welcome opportunity to defer, if not abolish, tensions between the countries.

But in other areas the United States would have to give gravity a push. Possession of Astoria, located at the mouth of the Columbia River in the Pacific Northwest, had been disputed with London since before the War of 1812. This was a valuable, if distant, trade post for which both John Jacob Astor's Pacific Fur Trading Company and the Canadian North West Company were vying. At Ghent, the British promised to return the military fort, which they had destroyed during the War of 1812, to American control. But this promise was slow in execution. Interested in working on a business rather than a diplomatic time horizon, Astor spoke to his good friend, President Monroe.[72] The president promptly dispatched the sixteen-gun sloop *Ontario* around Cape Horn to retake Astoria. Newly arrived in Washington, Adams consulted with Treasury Secretary Crawford about "the authority to take territorial possession at the mouth of the Columbia River."[73] The British caught wind of Adams's intentions and fiercely protested. Adams bluntly informed the British minister in Washington, "In my opinion, it would hardly be worth the while of Great Britain to have any differences with the United States on account of the occupation of so remote a territory."[74] Castlereagh's thinking ran along similar lines. Despite the Americans' efforts to take Astoria forcefully, the foreign minister did not deem Astoria worth a fight and sent off a dispatch to the British naval commander in the area "to obviate a very unpleasant collision."[75]

A crisis was averted, and the Americans nailed up a signpost claiming possession of the area for the United States. Both Castlereagh's and Adams's responses were telling. For the British, the potential rewards of America as a trading partner and ally, if an obnoxious one, outweighed such a minor dispute over territory in a remote area, although the long-term implications of allowing American control of the military post in Astoria could hardly have escaped their notice. For America, this action increased its odds of ascendancy in the region and presented an opportunity for Adams, in his blunt manner, to warn the British off further imperial aggrandizement on the North American continent.

In a humorous if tense exchange with the British minister to the United States, Stratford Canning, in 1821, Secretary Adams wondered just how extensive British imperial and territorial claims ran. "You claim India; you claim Africa," Adams began, "you claim —." Interrupting, Canning suggested "perhaps a piece of the moon." Adams did not miss a beat. "No," he replied, "I have not heard that you claim exclusively any part of the moon; but there is not a spot on this habitable globe that I could affirm you do not claim." One can imagine a dour, if somewhat amused, Adams making the point. But behind this playful repartee were serious matters of policy and ideology. Adams and Canning discussed the territorial claims of the British Empire, and Adams wanted the British to know that "there would be neither policy nor profit in caviling with us about territory on this North American continent." In case this was not clear enough, he bluntly stated American desires: "Keep what is yours, but leave the rest of this continent to us."[76] While this was a restatement of his earlier message, it also highlighted Adams' anticolonial beliefs, which increasingly were becoming a prominent part of his foreign policy. In this case, though, American interests and values were the same: keep Great Britain from further encroachments in North America.

But if the United States' gravitational strategy suggested giving a powerful yet increasingly accommodating Great Britain a shove, it necessitated a full-fledged push in dealing with a truculent and weakened Spain. Interestingly enough in light of future events, the first letter Adams read after receiving news of his appointment as secretary of state in April 1817 was a printed copy of Madison's final message to Congress outlining his administration's accomplishments. Following the Peace of Ghent, Madison proclaimed that it was the government's policy "to remain in unity with foreign powers." Due to recent developments with Spain, however, Madison announced that the United States "may make an exception as to that power."[77]

Spain and the United States had differences to settle. Following the American Revolution, Britain ceded control of Florida to Spain in 1781.[78] While Pinckney's Treaty of 1795 gave the United States navigation rights on the Mississippi and demarcated the Spanish-American border, the Louisiana Purchase again opened up territorial disputes as both Spain and the United States contested its boundaries. This dispute was partially, though not amicably, settled in 1810 when Madison sent forces to occupy West Florida, which had revolted against Spanish rule.[79] But there were still claims of indemnities from seized land and questions about where the western boundary lay. These meant that control of U.S.-Spanish frontiers remained unclear. As Adams came to understand, undefined borders meant insecure borders.

Adams understood the implications of Spain's crumbling empire. After writing Monroe that he would accept the office of secretary of state, Adams reflected on Spain's weakness and concluded that it could not "be very formidable while her revenues should continue to fall short, as they now do, of one-quarter of her expenditures."[80] This did not come as a surprise to Adams. Spain's empire had been in decline since the end of the eighteenth century. The destruction of its fleet under French command at the Battle of Trafalgar and Napoleon's invasion of Spain during the Peninsular War effectively disconnected Spain from its ability to communicate with, defend, and ultimately hold onto its empire. Internal disputes between liberal and conservative forces further weakened Madrid's power. This was of particular concern to Spain as its South American colonies erupted in a series of anticolonial wars. All of these factors contributed to a much weakened Spain whose inability to project power had implications for U.S. border security.

Prior to departing for America in 1817, Adams was offered an opportunity to take care of this security concern through acquisition of Florida and a resolution of the larger U.S.-Spanish border issue. Seeking Adams out, Count Fernan Nuñez, Spain's English minister, assured the latter that he "should be 'tres-content' with Don Luis de Onís [Spain's American minister], and that . . . Spain was firmly resolved to settle all affairs amicably with us. There was much nodding of the head, much significance of look, and much show of mysterious meaning in all this, but nothing specific or precise." Adams concluded that "he meant me to understand him as saying . . . that Spain would cede to us the Floridas, although England was taking all possible pains to prevent it." There was, however, a condition: Nuñez let Adams know that the United States "must satisfy Spain about the South American insurgents."[81] The price for Florida that the Spanish demanded was nonrecognition of the revolutionaries.

Lord Castlereagh offered a different solution to the Florida question. The British foreign minister told Adams that he desired to play the role of peacemaker, and offered his country's good graces to mediate between Spain and the United States. As Adams surmised, this offer was hardly altruistic. Castlereagh suggested to Adams that he could acquire the Floridas for the United States if Washington would accept a firm western border of the Mississippi River. Adams saw this for what it was—a plan to limit the growth of the United States. He confided in his diary that this was "exactly what I should have expected from a British mediator.... In all her mediations, or offers of mediation, her justice and policy will be merely to serve herself."[82] Taken together, these two incidents helped Adams frame the issues for dealing with Spain's claims in North America. Spain would be willing to trade away its claim to the Floridas and to deal with the issue of a western border. But it was the express wish of London and other European powers to restrict American expansion. If the United States were to enlarge its territory, it would do so not with the consent of European capitals, but by its own actions.

As Adams began his diplomatic engagement with Onís in Washington, the War Department ordered Andrew Jackson to the Georgia-Florida border to deal with increasingly violent Indian cross-border raids.[83] This was an order the general had long sought, insisting that "the protection of our citizens will require that the Wolf be struck in his den."[84] In order to strike the Seminole marauders, Jackson advocated pursuing them into their Florida sanctuaries. Pinckney's Treaty of 1795 had bound the United States and Spain to securing their shared border by containing and pacifying the Indians residing in their respective territories. However, the borders remained insecure due both to America's relentless drive to acquire more land and to Spain's failure to meet its treaty obligations. Jackson pushed the administration to let him remedy the problem. Jackson wrote to Monroe on January 6, 1818, that his taking of the Spanish forts could "be done without implicating the Government; let it be signified to me through any channel ... that the possession of Florida is desirable to the United States, and in sixty days it will be accomplished." Whether Jackson received the president's approval to take Florida is a matter of unresolved controversy. Jackson argued for years that Monroe sanctioned his actions, whereas Monroe denied it.[85]

What is a matter of historical record is that on December 26, 1817, Calhoun ordered Jackson to assume command of U.S. forces on the Georgia-Florida border. His orders stated that if the Seminoles refused to make amends for their cross-border attacks, "it is the wish of the President that you consider yourself at liberty to march across the Florida line, and to attack them within its limits, should it be found necessary, unless they shelter themselves under a Spanish fort. In the last event, you will immediately notify this department."[86]

The War Department issued Jackson orders that gave him a green light to cross the international border in pursuit of his enemy. What they did not give him was the right to assail Spanish forts, even if they were found to be providing haven to the Seminoles. In such an eventuality, Jackson was to defer to Washington. While there is much controversy about what additional orders may have said or implied, official channels limited the mission to securing borders, not annexing new lands. Pursuing an enemy into foreign territory Washington could justify. Setting off a major international crisis by attacking Spanish garrisons was a decision that would have to reside in the executive's hands.

Jackson, however, had other ideas. Moving into Florida, the general quickly resupplied at the site of the former Negro Fort, which he later renamed Fort Gadsden for his chief engineer.[87] While there the general wrote Calhoun that he had heard of Seminole activity in the St. Marks region. If the Indians took the fort, Jackson announced, "I will possess it, for the benefit of the United Sates, as a necessary position for me to hold, to give peace and security to this frontier, and put a final end to Indian warfare in the South."[88] Echoing his secret communication to Monroe, Jackson saw this as an opportunity to neutralize the Indian threat and seize Spanish land for the United States. Even if Jackson cloaked his actions in the language of security, his private communication made clear that he sought permission to extend the United States' defensive perimeter. On the march to St. Marks, Jackson burned several Indian villages and upon reaching the Spanish fort arranged for its surrender, claiming the Spanish were arming the Seminole tribes. At St. Marks, Jackson's men captured Alexander Arbuthnot, a seventy-year-old Scottish trader who was much in sympathy with the Indians' cause and whom Jackson accused of agitating the Indians into war. A couple of days later, Jackson's pickets captured Robert C. Ambrister, another Englishman, who had recently lost his commission in the Royal Marines.

To Jackson, the presence of British citizens in a Spanish-controlled Indian village signaled Spanish and British complicity in the Seminoles' war against the United States. Or perhaps he was ready to see it as a sign of complicity, reporting to Calhoun that "on the commencement of my operations, I was strongly impressed with the belief that this Indian war had been excited by some unprincipled foreign or private agents."[89] Regardless, he took the presence of belligerents as a sign of Spanish duplicity. Jackson did not make the distinction between "foreign or private agents." He wrote that either overtly or covertly, "the British government is involved in the agency." In order "to "prove an awfull example to the world" that "certain, if slow retribution awaits those uncristian wretches" who menace U.S. citizens, Jackson convened a court-martial that ended with the execution of the two British citizens.[90]

But Jackson was not yet finished with his self-appointed mission of stabilizing, securing, and acquiring the Floridas. The general charged the Spanish governor of Florida, José Masot, with providing haven and arms to the hostile Indians. When Masot denied these charges and threatened to drive Jackson out of Florida, the general decided to take the city and hold it "until Spain has the power or will to maintain her neutrality" in the war between the Americans and their Indian enemies.[91] After a brief firefight, Jackson captured Pensacola and the nearby Fort Barrancas. Masot's surrender, boasted Jackson in a letter to Calhoun, amounted to "a complete cession to the United States of that portion of the Floridas hitherto under the [colonial Spanish] government of José Mazot."[92] Having secured "the peace & security of the frontier, and the future wellfare of our country," the general informed President Monroe of the end of hostilities in the Seminole War.[93] With his mission completed, Jackson headed home to Tennessee in early June.

While Jackson was engendering Indian hatred, British anger, and Spanish cries of injustice, the secretary of state was busy with the Spanish minister in Washington. Echoing what Adams had been told in London the previous spring, Onís informed Adams that the king of Spain had instructed him to conclude negotiations with the United States. Furthermore, the king had informed England that he "had made up his mind to cede the Floridas to us [the United States], and asked the acquiescence of England in the measure, having had previous engagements with England not to cede any territories in America."[94]

But other factors were tied to the Florida issue, especially the independence of South America. In early May 1818, a representative of the new government in Buenos Aires visited Adams and expressed interest in taking possession of Florida as a means of harassing and pressuring the Spanish. The representative went further, explaining that his government would turn Florida over to the United States in exchange for recognition, and asked if the United States would sanction such an act. To Adams, this sounded a lot like the pirates' offer of the previous fall. Adams answered in the negative and reminded his guest that the United States had "expressly provided that no foreign power could be permitted to take possession of that province, or any part of it."[95] Under no conditions, Adams repeated, would the United States "suffer that it should be taken out of their hands by a third party."[96] Conscious of the danger that lay in European meddling, Adams let it be known that the long-term interests of the United States required the absence of all foreign powers in the lands contiguous to its territory.

Adams's belief in America's neutrality in and independence from Europe's affairs continued to shape his, and the administration's, thinking through the spring of 1818. In a May cabinet meeting called to discuss Spain, Florida, South America, and other foreign policy issues, the president raised the question of whether the United States ought to make any moves in concert with the European powers. Adams vigorously argued against such a course of action, pointing out that "it would be a departure from neutrality" and furthermore would leave the United States at England's mercy "to injure us with the other European powers."[97] Reiterating this point in a letter to Albert Gallatin, the U.S. minister to France, Adams emphasized the significance of America's neutrality between Spain and South America because neutrality alone would allow the United States to act independently.[98]

It was in this atmosphere of heightened sensitivity to foreign influence that news of Jackson's campaign in Florida began to trickle into the capital. Newspaper accounts highlighted the savage nature of the Seminole War, reporting that the general had both taken possession of two Spanish forts and executed two British citizens found among the Indians. In early June, Charles Bagot, the British minister to the United States, demanded an explanation of these acts from the secretary of state. Onís lodged a protest with Adams against General Jackson's proceedings in Florida, and the French minister, Hyde de Neuville, discussed the matter "in a very grave tone, shaking his head and saying it was a very disagreeable affair."[99] Onís informed Adams that he had received new instructions from the Spanish government in Madrid, announcing that Spain would halt all boundary negotiations until Jackson was dealt with. If the secretary of state had any doubts over what was at stake, this exchange should have set them aside. Jackson's campaign, already being questioned as unduly harsh and quite possibly unconstitutional, was now threatening U.S. territorial ambitions. His actions seemed to undermine the United States' ability to obtain the Floridas from Madrid and secure its borders.

Making matters worse for the secretary of state, at this critical moment President Monroe left the capital for his farm in Virginia. Adams's thinking on Florida began to take shape now that he was left to deal with the gathering diplomatic storm on his own. In a letter to the U.S. minister to Russia dated June 28, 1818, the secretary of state attempted to explain American involvement in Florida. "The entrance of our troops into East Florida in pursuit of the savages," wrote Adams, will "easily admit justification." Spain was bound "by treaty to restrain the Indians within her territories from all hostilities against the United States, and her notorious failure to fulfill that engagement rendered those measures on our part indispensable for the protection of our own people against the most barbarous and unrelenting enemies."[100] In this early justification, Adams glossed over Jackson's course of action, instead focusing on the immediate cause of America's violation of Spain's sovereignty.

To Adams, long-term interests dictated that the United States achieve independence of action; threats to this independence must be met. Spain had broken its treaty obligations by failing to restrain the Indians in its territory through negligence, impotence, or outright hostility.[101] Regardless of the reason, the result was the same: insecure American borders that exposed Americans to danger. To Adams, Jackson's push into Florida was an offensive measure taken in the service of a defensive policy. If Spain could not control the Indian tribes living within its borders, the United States would. Adams stated this reasoning explicitly in a letter to the president in early July. Discussing his increasingly rancorous exchanges with the British and French ministers, Adams wrote Monroe that it was "my private opinion you would approve General Jackson's proceedings." He was sure of this because the United States "could not suffer our women and children on the frontiers to be butchered by savages, out of complaisance to the jurisdiction with the King of Spain's officers."[102] By failing to meet the terms of its border obligations, and consequently putting American lives at risk, Spain had forfeited its right to inviolable sovereignty.

Another element emerged in Adams's thinking as he defended General Jackson with increasing vigor. From the start, this was not simply a matter of principle. It was also part of the larger issue of securing territorial boundaries. Disavowing Jackson at this moment would forfeit any diplomatic advantage Adams had gained with Spain over where to draw a western boundary.

When President Monroe convened his cabinet on the morning of July 15, 1818, he faced a growing domestic and international crisis.

Beginning in May, increasingly disturbing reports about General Andrew Jackson's conduct in the ongoing Seminole War had filtered into Washington. Newspaper accounts of Jackson's campaign reported that not only had he attacked and burned several Indian villages, but that he had also crossed the international border from Georgia into Spanish Florida, taken possession of two Spanish forts, and after a brisk military trial executed two British citizens. While most Americans supported the acquisition of Florida, seizing it in such a manner raised more problems than it solved: Had the executive exceeded its constitutional bounds by approving a military act without first seeking congressional authorization? Had Andrew Jackson, at once famous and notorious for his tactics, brought the United States to the brink of war with Spain? Had his execution of two British citizens found among the Seminoles provided England with justification for resuming war with the United States?

To Adams, this incident presented an opportunity to extend U.S. borders by pushing the Spanish out of Florida. Others were not thinking in such terms. Talking with the president, Adams found him "so much absorbed in this subject that he relucts at thinking of any other—so that when I am talking to him about the proposed negotiation in England, or even South America, he stops in the midst of the discourse and says something about Jackson and Pensacola."[103] Monroe might have been the decider, but it was Adams who was able to see the interconnectivity of widely disparate events on the domestic and international scenes. From his standpoint, Adams thought the president was focusing too narrowly on the Jackson issue. What Monroe did not understand was that Jackson's aggressions offered an opportunity to secure American borders against foreign threats.

Adams defended his future nemesis, arguing that Jackson had neither exceeded his War Department orders nor acted in an outlandish manner. As he would record in his diary, Adams believed that "there was no real, though an apparent, violation of his instructions; that his proceedings were justified by the necessity of the case, and by misconduct of the Spanish commanding officers in Florida." The rest of the cabinet, and indeed most of the country if the newspaper accounts flooding the capital were to be believed, wanted to distance themselves from Jackson as quickly as they possibly could. Adams, however, argued for Jackson, stating that his maneuvers were justified, necessary, and defensive. Although he did admit that it was a problematic case, Adams disagreed that the administration ought to "disavow what [Jackson] has done."

To counter the belief that Monroe had acted unconstitutionally, Adams argued that congressional war powers were limited to acts of offensive warfare; defensive actions, such as sending Jackson to Georgia and authorizing him to pursue the enemy into Spanish territory, needed no such authorization. The secretary of state held that "there is no doubt that *defensive* acts of hostility may be authorized by the Executive." If the acts were defensive in nature, "all the rest, even to the order for taking the Fort of Barrancas by storm, was incidental, deriving its character from the object, which was not hostility to Spain, but the termination of the Indian war."[104] With this second claim, Adams answered the charge that Jackson had incited a war with Spain, claiming that the United States had acted solely against the Indian aggressors. While such an argument might have been technically true (which in Jackson's case it was not), it clearly ignored the ramifications of Jackson's expedition.

Although Adams's diary and correspondence remain silent on why he thought it necessary to defend Jackson with increasing vigor, it seems clear that the cabinet meetings were becoming preoccupied with debates over political strategy at the expense of diplomatic wisdom and strategic thinking. While political considerations could not have been entirely absent from Adams's mind, they were only one of several competing factors driving the secretary of state's thoughts. If there were political benefits to be gained from defending Jackson, these were benefits of a distinctly secondary nature. For Adams, how to deal with Spain was primarily a strategic decision. It was part of his long-term strategy for securing America's independence and, as such, required a full justification. Adams started by asserting, "My principle is that everything [Jackson] did was *defensive;* that as such it was neither war against Spain nor violation of the Constitution."[105] If one assumed that the general acted in a defensive manner, it then followed that such action was justified by the facts, by international law, and even by the Constitution. Adams would not justify Jackson's campaign in Florida as a land grab. Instead, he defended the campaign with four different arguments. First and foremost, it had neutralized the Indian threat in the American south. Second, it stabilized U.S. borders. Third, it secured the United States against a weakening Spain. Finally, it swiftly and decisively projected American force against Seminole, Spanish, and British threats. Although it clearly contained political benefits, this was a diplomatic, and not primarily political, argument. Defending U.S. interests provided an opportunity to secure them.

Adams added one more argument to these. He reasoned that Jackson took Pensacola only to fulfill his orders, lest the Spanish governor drive him out of Florida. On this there was little doubt, even to himself, that Adams was stretching his justification to, and perhaps beyond, its natural limit. But even "if the question was dubious, it was better to err on the side of vigor than of weakness—on the side of our own officer, who had rendered the most eminent services to the nation, than on the side of our bitterest enemies, and against him."[106] Throughout the cabinet meetings, Adams insisted that the administration strenuously defend acts that, by all accounts, were largely indefensible. Suggestions of politics, race, and imperialism have all been made and, to be sure, all three played some role in Adams's thinking.[107] But there is another answer.

Adams's entire career had focused on defending his country from threats to its independence. Guarding America's neutrality meant warding off Europe's attempts to involve itself in North American affairs. An impotent Spain left Florida "open to the occupancy of every enemy, civilized or savage, of the United Sates." If the power vacuum in Florida invited threats against the United States, then defense of American independence required that the United States fill that vacuum. Adams attempted to convince the cabinet that this was an opportunity to secure American citizens in the face of foreign aggressors, be they Indian, Spanish, or English. If the government censured Jackson, he argued, it would not only face a backlash in popular opinion, but perhaps more ominously, appear weak in the face of Spanish reprobation. This amounted to "weakness, and a confession of weakness."[108] For someone who had spent an entire career guarding against foreign threats and protecting America's interests, this was an unacceptable course. In an insecure and fluid environment, Adams stressed the importance of projecting force.

Frustrated with the pace of Spanish territorial negotiations, and hoping to break the impasse over Jackson, Monroe asked Adams to compose a letter to the Spanish that outlined the whole history of America's Florida involvement and defended its position. Tracing the Seminole War from its origins, it would begin with the British intrusion into Florida under Lieutenant Colonel Edward Nicholls during the War of 1812 and would continue through the trial of Arbuthnot and Ambrister. As such, it was meant to be written "in such a manner as completely to justify the measures of this Government relating to it, and as far as possible the proceedings of General Jackson."[109] Lest any foreign government mistake Washington's political infighting for weakness, Adams wrote that "the President will neither inflict punishment, nor pass a censure upon General Jackson, for that conduct, the motives for which were founded in the purest patriotism." That was a sop to the popularity of the Hero of New Orleans. He continued that Jackson's conduct was vindicated "in every page of the law of nations, as well as in the first law of nature—self-defence."[110]

As for the Spanish officers' claims that they would have restrained the Indians had they but force to do so, Adams replied that "the right of the United States can as little compound with impotence as with perfidy." The result, and here Adams returned to the broader context, was a menace to U.S. security. Spain could either garrison Florida with a sufficient force, which Adams of course knew they could not, or cede it to the United States. Regardless of which course of action Spain elected to pursue, the present situation was unacceptable. Pointing to Spain's weakness, Adams charged that Florida, as it existed prior to Jackson's campaign, was "open to the occupancy of every enemy, civilized or savage, of the United Sates, and serving no other earthly purpose than as a post of annoyance to them."[111] Adams concluded with a reminder that the United States went into Spanish Florida out of neither hostility nor imperial aggrandizement, but because of Spanish negligence.

Spain was not the only, or perhaps even the prime, recipient of this letter. Adams had copies of this dispatch posted to all of the other United States ministers serving in Europe, intending that they make its contents public. But if he wanted America's aggressive stance known throughout the continent, Adams primarily meant this letter to serve as a warning shot in England's direction. By tracing the history of America's involvement in Florida from the outbreak of the War of 1812, Adams lambasted British perfidy in provoking the Indians into acts of aggression. He cited the British occupation of Florida during the war, Lieutenant Colonel Nicholls's construction and fortification of the Negro Fort, and the hero's reception that the prophet Francis, a Red Sticks warrior, had received during a visit to London.

But Adams reserved a special ire for his indictment of Alexander Arbuthnot and Robert Ambrister, the two British citizens convicted and executed under Jackson in Florida. This indictment, which makes up half of the text, accuses the two British citizens of provoking the Indians into war against the United States and providing them with the instruments of war. But Adams did not stop there. After recounting the particular cruelty and gruesome nature of Indian warfare, the secretary's letter thunders that "Great Britain yet engages the alliance and co-operation of savages in war" even though it denies countenancing or authorizing such actions. He continued more emphatically, tying London to the attacks against American men, women, and children. "Yet, so it has happened, that, from the period of our established independence to this day, *all* the Indian wars with which we have been afflicted have been distinctly traceable to the instigation of English traders or agents. Always disavowed, yet always felt; more than once detected, but never before punished."[112]

Adams concluded that the executions of Arbuthnot and Ambrister would serve as powerful warnings to those who would harm Americans. What Monroe had seen as a crisis, Adams took as an opportunity. Support for Jackson's aggressive actions would serve as a deterrent against hostile actions directed at American borders. Perhaps more importantly, Adams let them serve as an implicit reminder that the United States was increasingly the dominant power on mainland North America and could, at will, either restrain or release its expansive forces.

Charging that the British government had just as much blood on its hands as America's Indian enemies, Adams stood up, at least rhetorically, to British intervention in North American affairs. Moreover, by taking such a strong stance, Adams hoped to break through the stalled negotiations with Spain by intimidating Madrid into signing a treaty. President Monroe urged that Adams soften his language, anxious of "giving offence to the British Government, by referring too directly to their policy in relation to our Indian affairs." But to Adams, this "was precisely in the kernel of the vindication of Jackson's execution of Arbuthnot and Ambrister, and if left out would very much weaken the case made."[113] His argument persuaded the president, and Adams's letter had the desired effect. In London, Castlereagh told the American minister that Jackson's executions of Arbuthnot and Ambrister had so excited public opinion that war would have broken out if the Foreign Ministry had but "held up a finger."[114] Intent on pursuing more favorable commercial relations with the United States, and believing that the force of Adams's letter had temporarily derailed those in his own government who would take a more belligerent approach toward the Anglo-American relationship, Castlereagh ordered his minister in Washington to cease and desist from petitioning the American government on London's behalf.[115] As John Adams Smith (the secretary of state's nephew, who was serving in London) wrote, "There has been scarcely a pistol flashed since the great gun from Washington to Madrid."[116]

The "great gun" was felt on the American side of the Atlantic as well. The *National Intelligencer,* Washington's quasi-official newspaper, published Adams's dispatch to George Erving , the American minister to Spain, on December 30, 1819. Its effects were immediate and decisive. Writing to President Monroe from Monticello, Thomas Jefferson claimed that the letter was "among the ablest compositions I have ever seen."[117] And even though Henry Clay continued to hammer the administration from Congress, the House soundly defeated resolutions to condemn Jackson's conduct and to check executive foreign policy, while the Senate did not issue its own report until two days after Adams signed the momentous Transcontinental Treaty.[118]

Adams's aggressive stance in the July cabinet meetings and subsequent diplomatic exchanges helped yield a favorable outcome. Both the Spanish and the British government backed down from their confrontational stance. By February 1819, Onís signed a Transcontinental Treaty with Adams that extended the U.S. border to the Pacific and officially transferred Florida into American hands. The price of this transfer was Texas. Pushing Spain to acknowledge U.S. territorial claims to Oregon and the Pacific Northwest, at the president's urging Adams offered to relinquish American claims on Texas by drawing the western boundary line at the Sabine as opposed to the Rio Grande.[119] The combination of military threat of annexation and territorial concession was enough to push Onís into concluding a territorial treaty.

But even though Onís had agreed to Adams's terms, the Spanish delayed ratification of the treaty. In fact, it would take until October 1820 and a change in government in Madrid for the Spanish to sign the treaty. In the meantime, the issue of slavery's expansion had exploded in America with the Missouri crisis and had changed the terms of the debate. Originally, most Americans had been very well disposed toward the territorial terms of the treaty. But in the aftermath of Missouri, northerners were hesitant about annexing more lands that could become slave states, be they in Florida or Texas, while southerners were upset that all of Texas had not been acquired.

Subsequently, Adams's critics would charge that through some combination of neglect, weakness, or antipathy toward southern interests, he had unnecessarily ceded Texas in his negotiations. Thomas Hart Benton charged that *the Spanish Government had offered us more than we accepted; and that it was our policy, and not hers, which deprived us of Texas . . .*"[120] In the run-up to the 1824 presidential election, Congressman John Floyd of Virginia declared that Adams had swindled the nation out of Spanish territory that could have provided "two [more] Slave-holding states, and secured to the Southern interest four Senators."[121] These charges would resurface during the congressional debates over the possible annexation of Texas in the 1840s. Historians have made much of Adams's private comment to Illinois senator Ninian Edwards that "as an Eastern man, I should be disinclined to have either Texas or Florida without a restriction excluding slavery from them."[122] While this was a private comment, it does seem to offer support for Adams's aversion to slavery. But it is stretching Adams's words to say that this is conclusive proof that he supported giving away Texas because of his personal aversion to slavery. In hindsight, it seems that Spain would have settled for less than it ultimately received. But negotiations involved concessions. His critics, Adams thought, were "excellent negotiators in theory. They were for obtaining all and granting nothing."[123]

Moreover, both Monroe and Adams seemed keenly aware of the dangers Texas, with its large swath of potentially slave-friendly territory, would present to a nation struggling to maintain its regional balance. Adams worried that the country would acquire Texas "sooner than we should want it."[124] When Jefferson wrote to President Monroe expressing concern that the country was unnecessarily excluding Texas from the treaty, the president agreed that "it would be easy . . . to include as much territory on our side as we might desire. No European power could prevent it." But he did not think such a move in the interests of the country. "The difficulty," he informed Jefferson, did not spring from foreign but rather internal concerns "of the most distressing and dangerous tendency." With Missouri having antagonized regional jealousies, he now thought the nation had gained a brief reprieve for "passions to subside."[125] Thanking Jefferson for his advice, the president informed his old mentor that the nation needed, and he would pursue, a reprieve in territorial acquisition in the West and South. Monroe reinforced this point in a letter to Jackson, counseling that "we ought to be content with Florida for the present, and until the public opinion in that [northern] quarter shall be reconciled to any future change."[126] At the very least, it seems clear that both Monroe and Adams had trouble reconciling expansion with slavery and were extremely concerned with disturbing the sectional balance.

Although Adams was focused on extending the country's official borders, he also knew that it was important not to undercut the nation's reach by exacerbating its internal divisions. Because continental expansion was his primary policy objective, he chose to stay publicly silent on slavery during the Missouri Compromise debates. But, as with most issues, this did not mean that he muzzled himself in the relative privacy of the cabinet. Predictably, the cabinet's responses to the Missouri crisis, like those of Congress, followed sectional lines. In one of the longest and most anguished passages in his entire diary, Adams discussed the arguments made in the meeting and his private reflections on the implications of the vote. Of Congress's ability to prohibit the spread of slavery into the territories he was never in doubt. He was equally sure that the fault lay in the Constitution, "which has sanctioned a dishonorable compromise with slavery. There is henceforth no remedy for it but a new organization of the Union." At this point, however, Adams was not willing to call for such a radical step; as he told the other members of the cabinet, "I did not want to make a public display for it where it might excite irritation, but, if called upon officially for it, I should not withhold it."[127] His opinion was that the morality of the Constitution was suspect and its staying power unclear.

Adams wrote that the Constitution sanctioned "a compact laying the foundation of security to the most sacred rights of human nature against the most odious of oppressions." The inability to square the Declaration of Independence's belief in equality with the Constitution's tacit approval of slavery was the compromise, and the contradiction, at the heart of the republic. "The impression produced upon my mind by the progress of this discussion is, that the bargain between freedom and slavery contained in the Constitution of the United States is morally and politically vicious,

[and] inconsistent with the principles upon which alone our Revolution can be justified."[128] Adams's privileging of the Declaration over the Constitution anticipated Lincoln's arguments some forty years later, as did his concern that southerners had perverted the relationship between labor and servitude.[129]

But why did Adams not press his case further? What made him think that perpetuating this hypocrisy was worth it? In his diary he confessed, "I have favored this Missouri compromise, believing it to be all that could be effected under the present Constitution, and from extreme unwillingness to put the Union at hazard." Given the contradictions embedded in the nation's laws, Adams understood that to push for more would be to risk the breakup of the Union. He had spent his entire professional and personal life working to preserve and strengthen it. But for a moment he peered into the abyss. "Perhaps it would have been wiser as well as a bolder course to have persisted in the restriction upon Missouri, till it should have terminated in a convention of the States to revise and amend the Constitution." Adams did not think the country was ready for such a step. But he recognized this as a contradiction and a cause of future friction: "If the Union must be dissolved, slavery is precisely the question upon which it ought to break. For the present, however, this contest is laid asleep."[130]

Here were two competing goods—territorial expansion and slavery's abolition—that seemed incompatible with each other. In the words of the political philosopher Isaiah Berlin, these were incommensurable goals: choosing one meant you had to forsake the other.[131] Adams's diary entries make clear the tension that he felt, as he repeatedly emphasized his belief that after the Missouri Compromise, "the greatest danger of this Union was in the overgrown extent of its territory combining with the slavery question."[132] But it is also clear what he thought was the lesser evil to be suffered, lest the greater one prevail. This was a corrupt bargain the founders had bound the nation to at its birth. Adams was a politician, not a prophet. For the present, the bargain would continue.[133]

But just because Adams was willing to stay within the political system did not mean that he lacked prophetic visions. Later in 1820, he wrote about slavery and the Union in even more graphic terms. "If slavery be the destined sword in the hand of the destroying angel which is to sever the ties of the Union, the same sword will cut in sunder the bonds of slavery itself. A dissolution of the Union for the cause of slavery would be followed by a servile war in the slave-holding States, combined with a war between the two severed portions of the Union. It seems to me that its result must be the extirpation of slavery from this whole continent; and, calamitous and desolating as this course of events in its progress must be, so glorious would be its final issue, that, as God shall judge me, I dare not say that it is not to be desired."[134] But these sentiments were just as private as those he expressed previously. No matter how upset this made him personally, Adams still believed that it was in the interest of the nation to remain silent, temper morality with pragmatism, and defer the question.

But as Adams attempted to expand U.S. borders to the Pacific, he was also trying to constrain America's expansive tendencies. Anxious to slow American involvement in European and South American affairs and hoping to blunt a growing chorus of domestic and international critics advocating a more activist foreign policy, Adams accepted an invitation by a committee of leading Washingtonians to deliver the annual Fourth of July address in 1821. It was by now a well-established tradition to have a public figure read the

Declaration of Independence aloud and perhaps add a couple of thoughts about its meaning.

But just because Adams, a representative of the executive branch, was speaking in Congress did not mean that he was speaking only to Congress. His speech was open to the Washington public, the press, and the diplomatic corps. The speech was *not* official, and Adams was *not* speaking for the administration. He acknowledged as much, writing six days later that "public expression[s] of my opinions, even upon occasions altogether extra official," required a fair measure of prudence.[135] This address required more prudence than normal, as the principles the secretary of state advocated were ahead of those of the administration. Adams intended his speech to address European critics skeptical of republicanism. More important, Adams used this opportunity to address a domestic audience and lay out his strategy of demarcating America's limitations, lest its intentions outstrip its capabilities.[136]

With this speech, Adams hoped to justify a general principle that supported colonial revolutions without committing the United States to foreign wars. Asking why Americans had made reading the Declaration a national pastime, almost a holy rite, Adams affirmed that its message, "the successful resistance of a people against oppression, the downfall of the tyrant and tyranny itself," was America's message. Adams was not simply justifying the American Revolution, but going a step further. He was defending the principle of republican revolution against tyrannical regimes. This was America's mission, and it had universal application. The American Revolution, embodied in the principles of the Declaration, was the first global ideology "destined," according to Adams, "to cover the surface of the globe. It demolished at a stroke the lawfulness of all governments founded upon conquest. It swept away all the rubbish of accumulated centuries of servitude. It announced in practical form to the world the transcendent truth of the unalienable sovereignty of the people."[137]

Differentiating his view from Clay's, and rejecting the idea of a hemispheric, republican counterpoise to the Holy Alliance, Adams argued that the most the United States could or should do was to protect its image as a city upon a hill. Returning to the question of what America had done for the world, Adams affirmed that America had set in motion a powerful movement that would one day overpower all tyrants. The history of American independence was an example, but not a template. "It will be acted o'er, fellow-citizens," Adams declared, "but it can never be repeated. It stands, and must for ever stand, alone, a beacon on the summit of the mountain, to which all the inhabitants of the earth may turn their eyes for a genial and saving light till time shall be lost in eternity. . . . It stands forever, a light of admiration to the rulers of men, a light of salvation and redemption to the oppressed."[138]

If anyone doubted America's or his commitment to republicanism, Adams directly, if ironically, challenged Old World tyrants. In a not too subtle reference to the European situation, Adams charged America "to renew the genuine Holy Alliance of its principles, to recognize them as eternal truths, and to pledge ourselves, and bind to our posterity, to a faithful and undeviating adherence to them." The Holy Alliance was, of course, anything but republican. Adams turned the Alliance's ideas of sovereignty, legitimacy, and stability on their head, arguing that America's example was "the first solemn declaration by a nation of the only *legitimate* foundation of civil government."[139]

In the fight between liberty and oppression, there was no doubt which side America supported. But Adams recognized that there was a choice between competing priorities. America could either continue to strengthen its own republican institutions or rush to the aid of those around the world who claimed to act in solidarity with America's principles. In what would presage the Monroe Doctrine's noninterference principle, he called on the United States to abstain from interventions in other sovereign states, "even when the conflict has been for principles to which she clings, as to the last vital drop that visits the heart." Adams responded to those who would advocate a more activist foreign policy by returning to the opening theme of the speech. He asserted that America "has seen that probably for centuries to come, all the contests of . . . the European world, will be contests of inveterate power, and emerging right."[140] America would be on the side of emerging right, but not necessarily fighting for it.

The reason America could not actively take the side of republicans around the world led to the speech's most famous lines. Adams proclaimed that

> wherever the standard of freedom and Independence, has been or shall be unfurled, there will her heart, her benedictions and her prayers be. But she goes not abroad, in search of monsters to destroy. She is the well-wisher to the freedom and independence of all. She is the champion and vindicator only of her own. She will recommend the general cause by the countenance of her voice, and the benignant sympathy of her example. She well knows that by once enlisting under other banners than her own, were they even the banners of foreign Independence, she would involve herself beyond the power of extrication, in all the wars of interest and intrigue, of individual avarice, envy, and ambition,

which assume the colors and usurp the standard of freedom. The fundamental maxims of her policy would insensibly change from *liberty* to *force*. . . . She might become the dictatress of the world. She would be no longer the ruler of her own spirit.[141]

In conclusion, Adams mused that if the Almighty were to appear on earth, God would say to "each one of us here assembled, our beloved Country, Britannia ruler of the waves, and every individual among the sceptred lords of human kind; his words would be GO THOU, AND DO LIKEWISE."[142]

While the Russian minister in attendance thought that Adams had made "an appeal to the nations of Europe to rise against their Governments," the concluding lines of the speech were hardly as incendiary as they might sound when taken out of context.[143] While his words were certainly an attack on the legitimacy of monarchy and absolutism, which the Russian minister undoubtedly would take exception to, Adams had insisted throughout his long speech that it was through the power of example, not the power of interference, that America's mission would be fulfilled. Stressing the final sentiment of the speech undervalues Adams's repeated qualification that revolution, even republican revolution, was not something that America would materially support. Rather, Adams emphasized that overthrowing the Old World's monarchs was not something with which America should involve itself, especially as it was not likely to occur any time soon. Adams had co-opted Clay's message and interjected it with restraint. Concluding his speech, Adams basked in the glow of a warm reception, observing that "the crowded auditory who heard me was as great and as favorable as I could have desired—the effect of unremitting riveted attention, with more than one occasional burst of applause."[144] One can imagine Adams marching out of Congress triumphant that his message of caution had been heard.

To Adams, America's founding principles were revolutionary. As long as its republican government survived, America would fulfill its destiny of liberating the world by the power of its example. By overcommitting itself to foreign wars, Adams argued that the country would pervert its mission of promoting liberty. How could a country promote political freedom, Adams wondered, if it were doing so through the barrel of a gun? How would the republic continue extending its dominion westward if it were depleting its energy abroad? The country could best continue in its self-appointed mission by restraining itself. Delivering a message of restraint in foreign wars was Adams's motivation for his famous Fourth of July oration.

Yet this is not what contemporaries remembered about the speech. Shortly after the cheering faded, "criticism fastened upon the writer and upon the work."[145] Many were shocked about the vehemence of the attack on Great Britain by a sitting secretary of state. Although the Russian minister, Pierre de Poletica, skipped the address, he got a copy shortly thereafter and wrote to St. Petersburg that "from one end to another, Mr. Adams' speech was a virulent diatribe against England."[146] This reaction also shocked Adams. People were displeased with *the temper towards Great Britain,*" he noted. "It is said that I have stimulated animosities against the British, even while disclaiming vindictive recollections."[147] Although many contemporaries took the speech as British bashing, this is not the message Adams wished for his audience. Of course, reading the Declaration of Independence aloud could be taken as a sign of antagonism toward Britain. But Adams believed that he had clearly stated, both in the speech and afterward, that it was not his intention to raise the temperature of Anglo-American relations.

Realizing that the effect produced was not the same as the one intended, for the next several months Adams spent considerable time writing letters to colleagues, friends, and critics alike attempting to explain what he had *really* meant to say. In a letter to Massachusetts politician Edward Everett in January 1822, Adams reflected that "neither friend nor foe, so far as I have observed, discovered what was really in the address and what I had thought the most noticeable thing in it."[148] According to Adams, these were the principles of anticolonialism and noninterference in the internal affairs of sovereign nations. The first Adams thought was novel. The second was an update and expansion of Washington's Doctrine, as laid out in the first president's Farewell Address. Both served as part of Adams's developing strategy for keeping Europe out of the New World and limiting America's foreign interventions.

Anticolonialism was meant as both a vindication of colonial revolutions and as an ideological challenge to the conservative regimes of the Holy Alliance. This principle, Adams thought, "places on a new and solid ground the *right* of our struggle for independence." Because colonial establishments, by their nature, undermined the ability of a people to govern themselves, Adams was led to the conclusion that colonial establishments "are but mighty engines of *wrong.*"[149] This was a message for the Old World as well as the new, and when asked about his target audience, Adams wrote that "it was spoken not alone to my countrymen. It was meant also for the hearing of other ears and the reading of other eyes, for other regions and other languages." Again refuting the charges that he was simply trying to twist the tail of the British lion, Adams added that this was a message meant not so much for Britain as for "the

Holy allies . . . and their subjects." Expounding on the anticolonial principle in the same letter, Adams anticipated both the "downfall of the British Empire in India" and, closer to home, the challenges that would confront the United States if it were to annex colonial establishments.[150]

But if the principle of anticolonialism was meant as both an affirmation of American values and a challenge to the durability of the Holy Alliance, other parts of Adams's address *were* meant for British ears, or, perhaps more accurately, Scottish ears in Edinburgh. One of the causes that had convinced Adams to deliver this robust speech was reading the *Edinburgh Review* essay that had suggested that the United States should join English and Scottish Whigs in a crusade against the Holy Alliance. Adams rejected the expansive view of American power. Instead, he argued that to take part in a foreign war, even in "wars for freedom," would "change the very foundations of our own government from *liberty* to *power*."[151] As a cautionary tale he pointed to the Jeffersonians of the 1790s who had advocated that the United States fight with and for their sister republic France. This was a policy that, if adopted, would have changed the mission of the United States to exporting, rather than solidifying, revolution. This would have put it on the side of an expansionist, rapacious, and imperial French nation, thrusting America into the center of "all the wars of interest and intrigue, of individual avarice, envy, and ambition, which assume the colors and usurp the standard of freedom." The impulse, well enough intentioned, had disastrous implications, Adams argued, and only a clear-eyed and sober assessment of American interests could mitigate against foreign adventurism.

Where both Henry Clay and the *Edinburgh Review* erred, in Adams's thinking, was in their insistence that American intervention in either South America or Europe would help promote the cause of republicanism. Adams believed intervention would have the opposite effect. Moreover, such intervention was unnecessary in promoting liberty. "The influence of our example has unsettled all the ancient governments of Europe," Adams wrote. "It will overthrow them all without a single exception."[152] Writing to a political ally, Adams affirmed that "the address is . . . a continued tissue of interwoven narrative and argument . . . in answer to the question, what has America done for the benefit of mankind?"[153] Adams's response to this question was that America had set in motion an inevitable revolution to the established order. But when this revolution would come and under what circumstances it would occur were beyond Adams's grasp and beyond America's power to impose. Looking into Europe's future, Adams guessed that these democratic upheavals were "certainly not within half a century."[154] As a result, Adams argued that America should advocate change, but not upheaval. The latter, Adams knew, was every bit as full of peril as it was of promise, and for those reasons he suggested that change should be gradual rather than radical and sudden.

If Adams's speech championed republicanism as a form of government and cautioned against the perils of interfering in other nations' fights, it was somewhat abstract in terms of policy prescription. While the speech might have muted Clay's calls to assist the South American republics "by all means short of actual war," it was not unusual in championing neutrality. From the very onset of republican stirrings to its south, Washington had studiously avoided drawing itself into the vortex of the South American revolutions. But by late 1823 a series of crises involving the Russians, the Ottoman Turks, the Holy Alliance, and Great Britain gave Adams the opportunity to draw disparate, if not competing, policies into a coherent grand strategy of expansion that most famously found expression in the Monroe Doctrine of 1823.

The troubles stemmed from the challenge the republican revolutions in South America posed. As Adams told Clay in a surprisingly frank exchange of views in early 1821, there was no use in prematurely extending recognition, as "the final issue of their present struggle would be their entire independence of Spain."[155] Furthermore, as Adams and Monroe both recognized, moving forward too aggressively with the South Americans could push Spain into Great Britain's arms—which would almost inevitably result in the transfer of Cuba to the British. Monroe's biographer pointed out that "the all-absorbing problem in foreign affairs during his [Monroe's] presidency was Spain's crumbling empire. Most of his major decisions centered on this issue or had to be closely correlated with the questions it raised."[156] The same held true in this case: while the proximate cause of concern was to the south, the real challenge arose from Europe, and not South America.

By 1822 the case for recognizing these countries had begun to outweigh the costs. Recognition would promote American hegemony in the region and undercut Europe's influence. Additionally, Washington sensed new markets for American exports. Already, South America received 13 percent of U.S. exports, and despite the economic downturn of 1819, exports to the region increased from $6.7 million in 1816 to almost $8 million in 1821.[157] And if these indicators and numbers were not sufficient, Adams received reports of Spanish withdrawal from the region. As he wrote to the Spanish minister in April 1822, "the civil war" between Spain and its American colonies "has, in substance, ceased to exist. Treaties equivalent to an acknowledgment of independence have been concluded" between Spain and "the republic of Colombia, with Mexico, and with

Peru; while, in the provinces of La Plata and in Chile, no Spanish force has for several years existed to dispute the independence which the inhabitants of those countries had declared."[158] As Adams noted, facts on the ground had shifted since 1816—in Florida and further south. If previously there had been a diplomatic rationale for withholding recognition, Adams argued that Spain's de facto recognition of its rebellious colonies undercut it. Now, American interests in promoting republicanism, trade, and a sphere of influence encouraged action. In June 1822, responding to the administration's urging, Congress approved the funding for diplomatic posts to five new countries: Argentina, Peru, Chile, Colombia, and Mexico.

But action also involved risks. Writing to Adams in July 1821, President Monroe expressed concern that Washington had "much to apprehend from the hostile feeling of many of the sovereigns of Europe towards us, and that war with them is not an improbable event."[159] Monroe was referring to the sovereigns of the Holy Alliance, who restored the Bourbon monarchy in France in 1814, forcibly suppressed constitutional movements in Naples and Piedmont in 1821, and in early 1823 did the same thing in Spain, intervening in the civil war between liberals and conservatives in order to crush the revolutionaries. Shortly thereafter, ominous rumors began drifting around Europe and across the Atlantic that the conservative alliance would next turn its eyes toward South America.

Whether this was a perceived or a real threat, George Canning, London's new foreign minister, treated it as authentic.[160] Canning had replaced Castlereagh after the latter's suicide in August 1822. Despite vast differences in conduct and character, Canning continued his predecessor's dual policy of Anglo-American rapprochement and increased distance from the continental powers. Partly this was due to commercial considerations as the British rethought their concept of empire. The British Empire that emerged from the American Revolution and the Napoleonic Wars was less reliant on territorial control than it was on trade. With the onset of rebellions in South America, the British were offered an opportunity to extend their commercial presence into an already profitable South America. So, while London could disclaim any interest in aggrandizing its colonial territories, it could hardly stand exclusive control of these markets by the continental powers.

But it was more than just markets that drove Canning. Equally important was the shifting continental balance of power. Hoping to halt European intervention in the Western Hemisphere, Canning simultaneously threatened France and Spain while attempting to entice America into an alliance. In a letter he soon made public, Canning wrote to his minister in Paris at the end of March that "disclaiming in the most solemn manner any intention of appropriating to Himself the smallest portion of the *late* Spanish possessions in America, his Majesty is satisfied that no attempt will be made by France to bring under her dominion any of those possessions, either by conquest, or by cession, from Spain."[161]

It was in this vein that Canning made public his letter of warning to the French, which served the dual purpose of putting the Holy Alliance on notice and warming Anglo-American sentiment. Canning's actions found their desired audience across the Atlantic. Writing from Washington, Stratford Canning, the British minister to the United States and cousin of the foreign minister, reported that "the course which you have taken in the great politics of Europe has had the effect of making the English almost popular in the United States. The improved tone of public feeling is very perceptible, and even Adams has caught something of the soft infection. The communication of your correspondence with France has also had its effect. On the whole, I question whether for a long time there has been so favorable an opportunity—as far as general disposition and good will are concerned—to bring the two Countries nearer together."[162]

England's soft-power pitch had worked. And "the soft infection" that Stratford Canning detected in Adams was accurate. In the midst of a long meeting with the British minister spent discussing maritime and neutral laws, Adams told his visitor that despite differences, Britain and the United States were undergoing a strategic convergence. Adams's analysis bore out exactly what the foreign minister had hoped: "Great Britain," Adams assessed, "had separated herself from the councils and measures of the alliance. She avowed the principles that were emphatically those of this country, and she disapproved the principles of the alliance, which this country abhorred. The coincidence of principle, connected with the great changes in the affairs of the world, passing before us, seemed to me a suitable occasion for the United States and Great Britain to compare their ideas and purposes together, with a view to the accommodation of great interests upon which they had heretofore differed."[163] Whether or not Britain had emphatically embraced the principles of the United States, or more likely had seen its interests grow in detaching itself from the continental powers, Adams was right to sense an increased harmony of interests between London and Washington.

Reports of Adams's "soft infection," combined with his own belief that an Anglo-American alliance would blunt Franco-Spanish designs, led the British foreign minister to dangle his famous offer to Richard Rush in an August meeting. Canning wondered aloud, "What do you think your Government would say to going hand in hand with England in such a policy?"[164] When Canning received no firm answer from Rush, who realized that he could not make such a large decision without consulting Washington, Canning made the point more explicit.[165] "The simple fact of our being known to hold the same sentiment would . . . by its moral effect, put down the intention on the part of France."[166] As Canning described it, the United States could get something for doing almost nothing. "I am persuaded, there has seldom, in the history of the world, occurred an opportunity when so small an effort of two friendly Governments might produce so unequivocal a good and prevent such extensive calamities."[167]

Canning threw out one more reason the United States should act in concert with England. "Had not a new epoch arrived," he asked, "in the relative position of the United States toward Europe, which Europe must acknowledge? Were the great political and commercial interests which hung upon the destinies of the new continent, to be canvassed and adjusted in this hemisphere, without the cooperation or even knowledge of the United States? Were they to be canvassed and adjusted . . . without some proper understanding between the United States and Great Britain, as the two chief commercial and maritime states of both worlds?"[168]

This was a particularly enticing opportunity and challenge. As Canning framed it, the United States was now a great power and deserved to be treated as such by Europe. But with its recently acquired strength, and given its predominant position in the Western Hemisphere, it also had responsibilities. This was the nineteenth-century version of the responsible stakeholder argument: if the United States wanted to be treated as a major power, it had to act the part.[169] It had particular international responsibilities that, according to Canning, happened to overlap with London's interests in this instance. As Adams sensed, though, there were other British interests promoting a joint declaration of noninterference and colonization, such as wanting to constrain America's future hemispheric growth. In the course of this diplomatic minuet those interests were left unstated. Canning framed the question in ideological terms, asking why should the United States, "whose institutions resembled those of Great Britain more than they did those of the other Powers in Europe, and whose policy upon this occasion was closely approximated to hers, hesitate to act with her to promote a common object, approved alike by both, and achieve a common good, estimated alike by both?"[170]

This was a very good question. As these conversations made their way across the Atlantic, President Monroe wanted to accept this proposal. He asked his mentors Thomas Jefferson and James Madison, both lifelong Anglophobes, if the United States should join with Great Britain. They both answered in the affirmative. Jefferson argued that England's proposal was "the most momentous [question] which has ever been offered . . . since that of Independence" and urged the president to consider that as Britain was the "nation which can do us the most harm of any one, or all on earth . . . with her on our side we need not fear the whole world."[171] Madison, back to flights of Jeffersonian idealism, argued that teaming up with London to oppose intervention in the Western Hemisphere was "due to ourselves & to the world."[172] The president himself was inclined to accept Canning's offer, writing that while the issue at hand was important to London, "as to balance of power, commerce &c, is vital to us, as to government."[173] And, not that surprisingly, when Monroe put this question to the cabinet on the afternoon of November 7, 1823, most members, as well as the president, thought this a compelling offer.

Adams alone disagreed, arguing against "going hand in hand" with the British. Why, he asked, would the United States choose to unnecessarily bind itself to Great Britain? "By joining with her," Adams told Monroe, "we give her a substantial and perhaps inconvenient pledge against ourselves, and really obtain nothing in return. Without entering now into the enquiry of the expediency of our annexing Texas or Cuba to our Union, we should at least keep ourselves free to act as emergencies may arise, and not tie ourselves down to any principle which might immediately afterwards be brought to bear against ourselves."[174] As emotionally appealing as accepting such a pledge might seem, Adams urged Monroe to think beyond the immediate crisis. Giving a pledge now could limit the future territorial growth of the United States. Adams wrote in a letter to Richard Rush that "this suggestion is now made with a view to the future."[175] Continuing to think beyond the immediate crisis, Adams suggested ways in which the current situation could be turned into an opportunity.

Regarding European encroachments in the Western Hemisphere, Adams wanted America to announce its future intentions as loudly as possible. The Russians provided such an opportunity. In early November 1823, reports of Russian "exultation at the counter-revolution in Portugal and the impending success of the French army in Spain" landed on the desk of the secretary of state. Baron Tuyll, the Russian minister to Washington, passed a note to Adams that St. Petersburg rejoiced "over the fallen cause of revolution" and maintained "sturdy promises of determination to keep it down."[176] Adams had little doubt that these statements amounted to bluster. They also sounded a lot like 1821, when the Russians had claimed exclusive control of the Pacific coast north of the 51st parallel, only to back down later from these extravagant claims. But the cabinet did not view Baron Tuyll's note with the same historical perspective. Calhoun, in particular, seemed apoplectic. His anxieties mounting, Calhoun claimed that Great Britain could not hold out against the Holy Alliance on its own, and without help from the United States she "would eventually fall into their views, and South America would be subdued. The next step of the allies would then take would be against ourselves—to put down what had been called the first example of successful democratic rebellion."[177]

Adams, however, was much more sanguine and thought that he could make use of the Russians' declaration of their determination to suppress republican regimes to further America's expansionist aims. In cabinet meetings, he argued that the Russian declaration gave the administration an opportunity to answer not just Canning, but all of Europe: "The answer to be given to the Russian communications," he informed the president, "should be used as the means of answering also the proposals of Mr. George Canning."[178] Adams had already told the president that "the answer to be given to Baron Tuyll, the instructions to Mr. Rush relative to the proposals of Mr. Canning, those to Mr. Middleton at St. Petersburg, and those to the Minister who must be sent to France, must all be parts of a combined system of policy and adapted to each other."[179]

Adams began to weave together seemingly disparate policies in order to advance long-term U.S. interests. The United States had to decide how to respond to Canning's offer and what to do about the prospect, even remote, of European intervention in South America. While no response to the Russians was necessary, Adams wanted to issue a clear defense of republican government that spoke beyond this particular moment, built on his previous policies, and laid out a course for the continued growth of American power. It was to be "our manifesto to the world." And while Adams on occasion exaggerated the magnitude of events, he told Monroe, "I considered this as the most important paper that ever went from my hands."[180]

But before Adams could draft this paper, he had an equally important task—restraining what he saw as the president's naïve idealism. Monroe was, for the most part, a pragmatist as president, though he had never completely abandoned his Jeffersonian enthusiasms for republican revolutions. Earlier in his career, Monroe had been both a small and big "R" republican. It was Monroe who had organized Citizen Genêt's tour of the United States in 1793. In 1796, George Washington recalled Monroe from France for becoming too close to the French and their revolution. Throughout his tenure as secretary of state, Monroe had looked for ways to promote South America's revolutions. And as president he was still seeking a way to advance liberty abroad. In June 1823, the president had written to Jefferson of his desire to pursue a more activist foreign policy. "Our relation to it [Europe] is pretty much the same, as it was, in the commencement of the French revolution. Can we, in any form, take a bolder attitude in regard to it, in favor of liberty, than we did? Can we afford greater aid to that cause, by assuming any such attitude, than we now do, by the form of our example?"[181]

By November 1823 Monroe sensed that he had found both the form and the opportunity to strike a bolder attitude on liberty's behalf. Disturbed by the Holy Alliance's moves in Spain, Portugal, and Italy, the president worried about their possible moves in South America. Monroe wanted to use his annual message to Congress to warn that republicanism was under attack around the world, and that America must stand ready to defend its interests and its principles. In an initial draft of his text, the president dressed down

France, declared Greece independent from the Ottoman Turks, and recommended sending an American minister to Athens.[182]

The president's draft of his annual message was too much for Adams. Extremely agitated by what he read, the secretary of state argued that Monroe's support for the Greeks "would be a summons to arms—to arms against all Europe, and for objects of policy exclusively European—Greece and Spain. It would be new, too, in our policy as it would be surprising." History was on Adams's side, as he argued that from Washington's Farewell Address forward, the United States' policy was consciously to abstain from interfering in European politics. The message that the president now proposed "would at once buckle on the harness and throw down the gauntlet. It would have the air of open defiance to all of Europe, and I should not be surprised if the first answer to it from Spain and France, and even Russia, should be to break off their diplomatic intercourse with us."[183] Adams saw it as part of his job to dampen such enthusiasm by asking the president to calculate the reality of the power dynamics—to weigh his hopes against an objective assessment of the situation. Adams concluded by reminding the president that the United States was not ready for a war, that it would be morally and politically advantageous to let trouble originate from Europe, and that Monroe's legacy would inevitably suffer if he were seen as aggressively leading the United States into a war for which the country was not prepared.

The next day in a private conversation with Monroe, Adams urged him "to abstain from everything in his message which the Holy Allies could make a pretext for construing into aggression upon them." His reasons for pressing home the case were as political as they were strategic. Alluding to "considerations of weight which I could not even easily mention at the Cabinet meeting," Adams noted that this was Monroe's last year in office, and reminded the president that anything he started would be "deliver[ed] into the hands of a successor, whoever he might be."[184] While Adams was clearly hoping this would be him, he was politic enough to note that antagonizing the European powers would present challenges to any of Monroe's successors. Monroe promised to consider Adams's requests, and in fact toned down his language. Perhaps this was the instinct of a career diplomat and not a politician, but Adams's reaction was to frame this as a matter that could be settled through diplomatic channels, rather than as a domestic challenge that required broad public support.

Monroe delivered the Annual Message to Congress on December 2, 1823. He publicly declared America's desires to keep the Western Hemisphere as America's exclusive sphere of interest. But it was Adams's response to the Russians that fleshed out what this meant in practice. The paper that Adams drafted was meant to correspond with Monroe's message, and in Adams's own estimation "it was also intended as a firm, spirited, and yet conciliatory answer to all the communications lately received from the Russian Government, and at the same time an unequivocal answer to the proposals made by Canning to Mr. Rush." But it was more than that. Adams wanted this paper to serve as his "exposition of the principles of this Government, and a brief development of its political system as henceforth to be maintained; essentially republican—maintaining its own independence, and respecting that of the others; essentially pacific—studiously avoiding all involvement in the combinations of European politics, cultivating peace and friendship with the most absolute monarchies" but "could not see with indifference any attempt by European powers by forcible interposition either to restore the Spanish dominion on the American Continents or to introduce monarchical principle into these countries, or to transfer any portion . . . to any other European power."[185]

The letter came very close to doing those things. In it, Adams denied that the United States was a revolutionary power and instead aimed to maintain warm relations with monarchies. Since the days of Washington, the United States had stayed neutral in European affairs, and remained neutral during the rebellions in South America until after the facts had been established. All of this was a prelude to the main message of the note: "To the signification of the Emperor's hope and desire that the United States should continue to observe the neutrality which they have proclaimed between Spain and South-America, the answer has been that the neutrality of the United States will be maintained, as long as that of Europe, apart from Spain, shall continue and that they hope that of the Imperial Government of Russia will be continued."[186]

The United States would remain neutral if the Holy Alliance, excepting Spain, respected the sovereign integrity of the Western Hemisphere. The letter did not explicitly state what measures the United States would deem necessary and appropriate if this "neutrality" were violated, but it did make a veiled threat of military opposition to such a move. Adams did all this without Great Britain's concurrence, as this letter was issued independent of London. It then added in some words of praise toward Russia and Alexander, but in case the point had been missed, Adams ended the letter with an explicit red line: "The United States of America, and their Government, could not see with indifference, the forcible interposition of any European power, other than Spain, either to restore the dominion of Spain over her emancipated colonies . . . or to establish Monarchical Governments in those Countries, or to transfer any of the possessions heretofore or yet subject to Spain in the

American Hemisphere, to any other European power."[187] These forceful words echoed the noncolonization language of the Monroe Doctrine, which Adams had suggested in the first place, and were meant to apply equally to North and South, or, as Adams referred to it, "the American" hemisphere.

Adams intended this letter to serve as a statement of American principles and strategy. The United States was a republic and needed to maintain the ability to act as its citizens saw fit. While this did not rule out America's ability to enter into commercial treaties or temporary alliances, the focus was on independence of action. Any measures, no matter how beneficial, that constrained America's actions were suspect. Additionally, as long as America's independence was respected, it would respect that of others. This somewhat ambiguous phrase was Adams's attempt to keep Monroe from promoting Greek independence or from condoning too harshly actions in Spain or France. In a sense this was an echo of his message of July 4, 1821.

But Adams meant this statement to accomplish two additional objectives: to declare the Western Hemisphere as America's exclusive sphere of influence and to make sure that the administration's objectives did not exceed America's abilities. Absolutely opposed to placing the United States at the head of a crusade against tyranny, and resolute that the nation could export its republican principles by example rather than force, Adams worried that the president's overly broad commitments to advancing republicanism would entangle the United States in foreign fights in which it had no business. He was careful to point out that America could work with absolutist states, stating that even though monarchies and republics were founded on different, if not opposite, principles, "we saw no reason why they should not be at peace with each other."[188] As if in affirmation of this belief, Adams copied Tuyll's complimentary remark the next day "that difference of principle did not necessarily involve hostile collision between them."[189]

All of this was in keeping with Adams's approach to working with the world as it was, not as he would like it to be. But then he did something very interesting. Adams, imagining the future of the Western Hemisphere, not only declared the hemisphere off limits to European colonization, but also further declared that U.S. interests meant that it would oppose efforts to create any new monarchies in its sphere of influence. To Adams, Monroe's "summons to arms" indicated a general inclination to roll back authoritarianism wherever it existed. Adams offered a more geographically circumscribed version of the same: the United States would seek to contain the growth of authoritarian regimes *within* the Western Hemisphere. The challenge in the future was what would happen if republican principles were threatened closer to home, or even at home.

The president ended up striking what he considered Adams's more aggressive language, but left its substance. And, just as Adams had done in his letter to the Russians, Monroe's address *broadened* America's commitments by declaring that "it is impossible that the allied powers should extend their political system to any portion of either continent without endangering our peace and happiness."[190] The president's message, and specifically the section on foreign affairs that in later years would be referred to as the Monroe Doctrine, is usually seen as a unilateral pronouncement of American power. What the cabinet meetings and official state correspondence reveal is something quite different. Less a projection of power, under Adams's guidance the Monroe Doctrine was a statement of principles, an expectation of future growth, and perhaps most importantly, a simultaneous limitation of activity abroad and an expansion of interests.

In late 1822, Adams wrote a letter to his wife summing up what he thought were the Monroe administration's primary accomplishments. Not one for humility, Adams insisted that "all that will be worth telling to posterity hitherto has been transacted through the Department of State." This immodest boast had substantial truth to it. He had concluded treaties with Great Britain, Spain, France, and Russia. He had managed relations with the new South American republics. Through his advocacy, the United States had secured its borders in Florida and extended its claims to the Pacific. As he noted, "They are all events affecting not only the present interests, but the future condition of this people," and they had "been first obtained, I might confidentially say by me."[191] Adams was certainly arrogant, but was he correct? If Adams's priority as secretary of state was to project U.S. power in the Western Hemisphere by reducing the menace of Europe in North America, then for the most part he succeeded. His strategy was based on a long-term bet: as the United States grew, the more attractive and powerful it would become. To be sure, this power was not always morally attractive. Adams's unwavering advocacy of Jackson's moves in Florida suggests an overwillingness to employ and condone force to accomplish political objectives. In this instance, Adams argued that it was a useful, if unexpected, diplomatic tool to push the Spanish out of stalled negotiations and advance America's dominion in North America.[192]

Adams laid down principles that he hoped would guide America's expansion over the coming decades. Following a vision first outlined by the Constitution's framers, he worked to establish a preponderance of power on the North American continent. If this were not the case, so the founders had feared, North America would end up looking like the warring states of Europe, which meant no liberty. Following his gravitational strategy, Adams pushed Spanish, Russian, and British interests out of, or nearly out of, North America. The Monroe Doctrine and the accompanying letter to Tuyll serve as explicit statements of this strategy. At the time of its announcement the doctrine was incapable of being enforced by the United States. Its impact, as Adams had anticipated, was not immediate. Adams put the pieces of this geopolitical puzzle together, but left it to his successors to act on his strategy of continental expansion. To enable it, Adams worked to expand America's territorial and commercial interests while limiting its commitments abroad.

But if Adams had preached a gospel of limitations in his Fourth of July address and in his opposition to supporting Greek and South American independence, he failed to think through the implications of his policies. Adams created a grand strategy of continental expansion and hegemony. As early as January 1820, it was clear that he could not square this with his powerful, if silent, antislavery sentiments. In his Fourth of July speech, Adams proclaimed that the central message of the American Revolution was successful resistance to oppression. If this principle did not serve as America's motivating ideology, both at home and abroad, then perhaps republican governments were not worth the bargain the Constitution required. As it became increasingly clear that expansion of federal territory and power meant the growth of the South's political clout, Adams realized that he would need to recalibrate his strategy to account for this shift.

While Adams was adept at understanding America's long-term interests and aggressively advocating on their behalf within the cabinet, he was less good at reading the mood of the public or understanding the nature of American politics. His most public declaration, the Fourth of July address, influenced the administration's decision to delay recognition of the South American republics. But the press and the diplomatic corps heard something different from what Adams intended. And the speech failed in its larger purpose of restraining America's expansive tendencies. Critical of Monroe during the November 1823 cabinet debates, Adams wrote that "the President is often afraid of the skittishness of mere popular prejudices, and I am always disposed to brave them. I have much more confidence in the calm and deliberate judgment of the people than he has."[193]

Adams's confidence sprang from the fact that he did not have to explain difficult choices. His arguments supporting Jackson in Florida glided over the moral ambiguities of the general's actions. On the hard choice between countenancing the continuation of slavery and advancing territorial expansion, Adams chose to remain silent. And during the cabinet debates preceding Monroe's Annual Message of 1823, Adams wanted strong words in *private* diplomatic channels, while it was Monroe who pushed for a broad *public* assertion of American principles. This was not so serious a problem when serving in an advisory capacity to a popular president. But it would become much more problematic when he became president and had to explain difficult choices to a public that did not always privilege calculating reason over political passion. The nature of how he became president further complicated that process.

JOHN QUINCY ADAMS,
President of the United States.

As secretary of state, John Quincy Adams worked to expand the country's borders and establish a preponderance of power on the North American continent. LIBRARY OF CONGRESS.

Abigail and John Adams instilled in their eldest son the idea that he was destined for great things, placing extraordinary pressure on him. NATIONAL PARKS SERVICE, ADAMS NATIONAL HISTORICAL PARK.

The birthplace of John Adams and John Quincy Adams in Braintree, Massachusetts. NATIONAL PARKS SERVICE, ADAMS NATIONAL HISTORICAL PARK.

George Washington appointed Adams American minister to the
Netherlands when he was only twenty-seven years old. His years spent
overseas, the diplomatic training he had received from Thomas Jefferson
and his own father, and his fluency in several European languages quickly
made him the most valuable American diplomat. JONATHAN SINGLETON
COPLEY, *JOHN QUINCY ADAMS*, 1796, OIL ON CANVAS. MUSEUM OF FINE ARTS,
BOSTON, BEQUEST OF CHARLES FRANCIS ADAMS, 17.1077. PHOTOGRAPH © 2014
MUSEUM OF FINE ARTS, BOSTON.

Louisa Catherine Adams, born in London to an English mother and an American father, grew up in France and England. Intelligent, open, and at ease in company, she helped balance her husband's reserve and his tendency toward self-righteousness. As his father remarked, John Quincy's marriage to Louisa was "the most important event" of his son's life. NATIONAL PARKS SERVICE, ADAMS NATIONAL HISTORICAL PARK.

Concluding the
Treaty of Ghent,
which brought an end
to the War of 1812,
John Quincy Adams
shakes hands with his
British counterpart.
Henry Clay, his
future rival and later
ally, is seated in the
rear. SMITHSONIAN
AMERICAN ART
MUSEUM, WASHINGTON,
D.C. / ART RESOURCE,
NEW YORK.

President James Monroe presides over a cabinet meeting discussing the
Monroe Doctrine. Secretary of State Adams holds forth on the left, while
John Calhoun, the secretary of war, sits to the right of the president.
THE GRANGER COLLECTION, NEW YORK.

A FOOT=RACE

A political cartoon depicting the divisive 1824 presidential race. Front-runners John Quincy Adams, Andrew Jackson, and William Crawford stride toward the finish line. Henry Clay, who has dropped from the race, stands watching on the far right. NATIONAL PARKS SERVICE, ADAMS NATIONAL HISTORICAL PARK.

March 1820

A page from John Quincy's Adams meticulously kept diary. He began keeping a diary at the age of twelve and continued to do so until his death in 1848. Eventually, the diary would fill fifty-one manuscript volumes, containing nearly seventeen thousand pages. MASSACHUSETTS HISTORICAL SOCIETY.

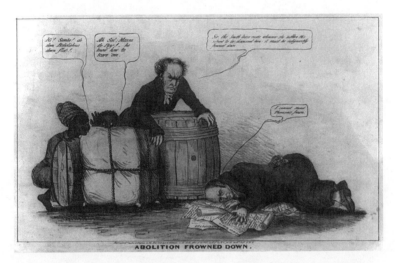

ABOLITION FROWNED DOWN.

Following his presidency, Adams returned to Washington as a congressman increasingly vocal in his opposition of slavery. This satirical representation of the gag rule, which prohibited discussion of slavery in the House
of Representatives, shows Adams lying prostrate before the defenders of
slavery, clutching a series of petitions and a copy of the abolitionist
newspaper the *Emancipator*. LIBRARY OF CONGRESS.

Adams described himself as reserved, cold, and aloof. This 1843 daguerreotype, taken in the midst of his increasingly violent disagreements with proslavery forces, aptly captures his intense nature. This is the earliest surviving photograph of an American president. Albert Sands Southworth and Josiah Johnson Hawes, after Philip Haas, *John Quincy Adams*, ca. 1850, daguerreotype, 12.0 × 9.0 cm. GIFT OF I. B. PHELPS STOKES, EDWARD S. HAWES, ALICE MARY HAWES, AND MARION AUGUSTA HAWES, 1937 (37.14.34). THE METROPOLITAN MUSEUM OF ART, NEW YORK. IMAGE COPYRIGHT © THE METROPOLITAN MUSEUM OF ART. IMAGE SOURCE: ART RESOURCE, NEW YORK.

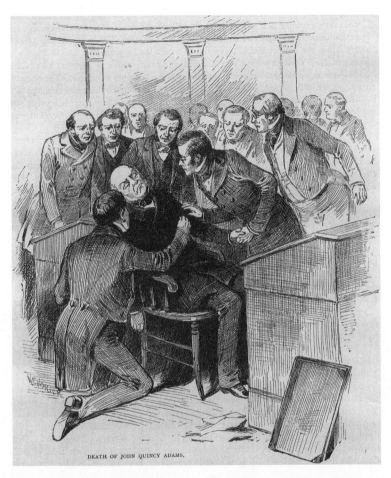

DEATH OF JOHN QUINCY ADAMS.

In February 1848, Adams died in the House of Representatives, having suffered a massive cerebral hemorrhage on the floor of Congress. Downplaying his divisiveness, his colleagues recounted his long, varied, and distinguished career, and mourned his passing as a national loss. CULVER PICTURES / THE ART ARCHIVE AT ART RESOURCE, NEW YORK.

4

THE SPIRIT OF IMPROVEMENT
Economic and Moral Development

TRYING TO POSITION himself as Monroe's natural successor, John Quincy Adams hosted a ball in January 1824 to honor the tenth anniversary of Andrew Jackson's victory over the British at New Orleans. Looking back at Washington life some fifty years later, commentators noted that it was "one of the most brilliant affairs ever given," while another asserted that it was "the great social event not only of that season," but of all seasons since.[1] There was dancing on the first floor, supper on the third, and decorations of tissue paper and evergreen wreaths everywhere the eye could see. Louisa Catherine had hired a Baltimore artist to chalk a victory motif of eagles, flowers, flags, and military emblems, all of which wound around the words "welcome to the Hero of New Orleans."[2] A poem in that day's Washington *Republican* concluded, "Belles and matrons, maids and madams, All are gone to Mrs. Adams'."[3] It certainly seemed that way to those in attendance, who reported that the house was "crowded to suffocation almost."[4] Another noted that "in fact, every body who was any body was there—nearly a thousand persons in all, it is said."[5] The diplomatic corps were all present; all of Congress was invited; and, most interestingly, the various presidential candidates were all gathered under the same roof.[6] At the outset of this election year, no one wanted to miss the first big social and political event.

But even in his own home, Adams played second fiddle to Jackson. When the general's carriage pulled up in front of the Adams house on F Street, Mrs. Adams was there to meet the guest of honor. As she escorted Jackson through the house, all the guests jostled to get close to the nation's first military hero since George Washington. Louisa later noted in her diary that Jackson was "a magnet so powerful as to attract not only all the Strangers but even the old residents of the City who never thought of coming to see us before."[7] According to a young Charles Francis Adams, the general was "the hero of the evening. Everybody wanted to see him, every body to speak to him."[8] That was true at least until the food was served around 9:30 p.m., at which point the crowd swept past Jackson and toward the buffet. Jackson managed to get out a quick toast thanking Mrs. Adams before retiring for the evening. But the evening's festivities had just begun. Flowing with wine and music, the ball picked up steam, with dancing continuing until almost one in the morning. Even though tired from the festivities, John Quincy Adams, methodical as ever, managed to sit down at his desk and write out a journal entry before drifting into a drunken slumber. After describing the party, he happily concluded that "the crowd was great, and the house could scarcely contain the company. But it all went off in good order, and without accident."[9]

Adams might have thought that hosting a ball in his home with all of the major political figures would signal that he was naturally stepping into the president's role. Or perhaps he thought that fêting General Jackson would lend momentum to an Adams-Jackson ticket in the fall. Already circulating was a popular slogan to draft "John Quincy Adams who can write, and Andrew Jackson who can fight."[10] But rather than confirming Adams as the choice to succeed Monroe as president, many guests took the party as confirmation of Jackson's ascendancy.

Adams seemed to sense this. Writing in his diary later that spring, Adams noted that popular opinion overwhelmingly favored the general in the race to the White House. He thought that "if the election went before the people, no man could stand in competition with General Jackson. The 8th of January and the battle of New Orleans was a thing that every man would understand."[11] Adams told New Hampshire congressman William Plumer that he had "no hesitation in saying that he preferred him [Jackson] to any of the other candidates" and found the general not only "strong, but also . . . meritorious." As Plumer wryly noted, Adams "no doubt made a tacit reservation in his own favor."[12] Indulging in some wishful thinking that Jackson might not actually want to be president, Adams told a supporter that "the Vice-Presidency was a station in which the General could hang no one, and in which he would need to quarrel with no one . . . and it would afford an easy and dignified retirement to old age."[13]

Unfortunately for Adams, Jackson was ready for neither retirement nor the vice presidency. The general would increasingly upstage the onetime professor—first in the presidential election of 1824 and then by having his surrogates stymie the Adams administration. This came as a surprise to Adams, who half expected and half hoped that he would be awarded the presidency because of his long record of public service. But American politics was undergoing a seismic shift in the 1820s, redefining who was qualified to vote and to hold office, how elections were conducted, and how the electorate organized itself. Adams was only dimly aware of these changes. He understood that the 1824 presidential election was unusual, but did not see this as a sign of resurgent partisanship.

Seemingly at the pinnacle of power once he captured the presidency, Adams reasoned that this would be the time to use his influence. To justify the moral and political compromises he had made in his career and in the recent election, he would have the opportunity to redeem himself by exercising his political powers for the good of the American people. His critics would soon charge that Adams had moved far beyond the cautionary messages of his July 4 address and the Monroe Doctrine. They would argue that the policies he was now pursuing would expand the Monroe Doctrine, changing it from a defensive unilateral pronouncement into an alliance that placed international responsibilities on America and that came one step closer to drawing the United States into foreign wars. His critics, while overstating the case, had a point. Adams *had* changed his position.

But his critics did not understand that his thinking about America's mission was only partially explained by his foreign policy. To Adams, foreign and domestic policies were intimately connected. In the fight between liberty and oppression, Adams thought the choice was clear. The best way that America could spread its values would be by working to perfect the American experiment and by limiting its involvement with, and interference in, other countries. Intervening in foreign revolutions, even on the side of liberty, would not further the cause of freedom. Rather, Adams argued that it would diminish the nation's capacity to provide for its own citizens. If the purpose of Adams's foreign policy was to keep America's intentions in line with its capabilities, its goal was to allow the United States to become the most progressive nation on earth by devoting its resources to its own development.

In Adams's mind, for representative government to flourish several things needed to happen. First, the country needed security from external threats. The nation would achieve this through economic growth and geographic expansion. As secretary of state, Adams had pushed both commercial treaties and territorial aggrandizement. As president, he did the same. The country's growth also required internal stability. During Adams's presidency, the two main threats to domestic harmony remained slavery and partisanship. Hoping to strengthen the Union, he attempted to avoid these issues. Additionally, Adams envisioned a United States that would show what a state could accomplish. This meant improving the material, intellectual, and spiritual lives of its citizens through active government. Domestically, such a vision would unite the country by building up its infrastructure and promoting economic development in a continually expanding national market. Abroad, it would search out and secure new markets for U.S. goods.

The key to this was a powerful federal government, along Hamiltonian lines, projected over a vast territory, using Madisonian methods. Since the first days of the republic, the idea of an integrated and diverse economy had held a powerful appeal over policy makers.[14] As early as 1787, Hamilton had urged that the United States bind itself "together in a strict and indissoluble Union, [and] concur in erecting one great American system superior to the control of all transatlantic force or influence."[15] Hamilton was even more explicit in his 1791 *Report on Manufactures,* where he urged the federal government to support American independence through subsidizing certain industries, regulating commerce, and imposing a light tariff. Under Hamilton's guidance, these ideas found their way into Washington's Farewell Address of 1796.[16] In 1808, Treasury Secretary Albert Gallatin submitted to Congress his *Report on Roads, Canals, Harbors, and Rivers,* which was designed to improve the country's transportation infrastructure and help agricultural products make their way to market more easily. And in the wake of the War of 1812, Congress passed legislation supporting internal improvements, establishing a national bank, imposing tariffs to protect emerging industries, enlarging the peacetime army, promoting military professionalization, and raising appropriations for the navy. These ideas were popularized by a series of widespread essays and newspaper articles by the publisher and economist Mathew Carey.[17] Chief among his readers was Congressman Henry Clay.[18]

While Adams could claim some credit for promoting a Hamiltonian program as early as 1806, when as a senator he introduced a resolution calling for the Treasury Department to issue a plan for internal improvements, it was Henry Clay who provided political coherence to Carey's program and bestowed on it the term "American System" in a congressional floor speech in 1824. The system was meant to harness the political economy of the country for strategic ends. It consisted of three interwoven measures: a tariff to protect and promote the nation's infant industries; a national bank to help foster trade and investment; and federal subsidies for roads, canals, and other "internal improvements" that would provide the infrastructure necessary to develop new markets for agriculture. As highways reached the West and these regions became more accessible, property values would rise. Governmental proceeds from the sale of public lands would pay off the national debt and provide the funds for maintaining a strong military. Additionally, frontier settlement would provide an ever-increasing domestic market for American manufactured goods.

Clay believed that beyond just providing a market for goods, such a system had the added political benefit of knitting the growing nation together.[19] In this, he was in perfect alignment with Adams. For Adams believed that robust domestic and foreign policies were two sides of the same coin. A country with a strong and diversified economy of agriculture, commerce, and manufacture would be wealthier *and* more unified at home and stronger in its relations with other countries abroad. Adams saw this as the central purpose of his presidency, declaring in 1828 that "independence and union are the ends" and "internal improvement, and domestic industry, the means."[20]

Just as Hamilton and Clay promoted programs that envisioned an industrial community, so too did Adams. But if theirs implicitly linked active government and economic expansion to America's ethical improvements, Adams's did so explicitly. Before becoming president, Adams had mused that "the more of pure moral principle is carried into the policy and conduct of a Government, the wiser and more profound will that policy be."[21] Once elected, he had the opportunity to press such a sweeping vision. "The spirit of improvement is abroad upon the earth," Adams declared in his first Annual Message to Congress. "While dwelling with pleasing satisfaction upon the superior excellence of our political institutions, let us not be unmindful that liberty is power; that the nation blessed with the largest portion of liberty must in proportion to its numbers be the most powerful nation upon earth, and that the tenure of power by man is, in the moral purposes of his Creator, upon condition that it shall be exercised to ends of beneficence, to improve the condition of himself and his fellow men." In his view, it was the responsibility of the federal government not only to foster economic improvement but also to encourage the intellectual and moral improvement of its citizens.[22] The end to which government must work was "the progressive improvement of the condition of the governed."[23]

But before any of that could happen, Adams needed to become president. The presidency was the prize he had been aiming for throughout his life. But the actions he took in pursuit of that prize undercut his principle of disinterested service to the republic and undermined his goal of inspiring national unity. To act in accordance with his principles would have meant abandoning the field to his opponents, whose surrogates were doing everything in their power to secure the election for their preferred candidates. Adams sought to subvert the popular vote, but he was playing by the rules as they were constitutionally defined at the time. Whether or not he was breaking his own ethical rules is another question altogether.

As Monroe's second term progressed and speculation over his successor increased, Adams attempted to maintain his distance from political machinations. In early 1822, he wrote to a South Carolina newspaper editor to assert that he had never solicited public office "by any act of mine direct or indirect." But while he did not seek such honors, he stood "ready to repair to any station which . . . [the public] thought their constitutional authorities might think proper to assign me." Adams presented himself as the Union's selfless patriot—willing, albeit reluctantly, to serve the people in any manner for any office. But he would not work to advance his own chances. "If the old prudential maxim that God helps those that

help themselves is morally applicable to the pursuit of public honors and trust, I shall certainly be the most helpless candidate that
ever was presented to the view of the American people."[24] Being
helpless in this case meant preserving republican propriety. It also
meant ignoring political realities.

Precedent and his own sense of republican propriety demanded
that Adams not actively campaign for the presidency. Alexander
Everett, a Harvard student of Adams's who had accompanied him
to St. Petersburg ten years earlier, asked in 1818 if the secretary of
state was going to do anything to promote his chances of succeeding Monroe. Adams coldly replied, "I should do absolutely nothing." Everett answered that others would not be so scrupulous, and
Adams ought not unnecessarily handicap himself. Adams told his
young friend that this "was not my fault—my business was to serve
the public to the best of my abilities in the station assigned to me,
and not to intrigue for further advancement. I never, by the most
distant hint to any one, expressed a wish for any public office, and
I should not now begin to ask for that which of all others ought to
be most freely and spontaneously bestowed."[25] This was the classical pose of a disinterested statesman who pictured himself innocent of political intrigue, but not naïve about the policies others
pursued.

It was natural for John Quincy Adams to think of himself as
such a statesman. He was raised with a reverence for both ancient
and Enlightenment texts that celebrated the idea of the leader reluctantly summoned to duty. Adams's political role models were
his father and Washington, both of whom he took as exemplars of
Lord Bolingbroke's virtuous patriot king.[26] According to Bolingbroke, the public good required a leader to act as a model of virtue
by transcending faction and self-interest. It was this to which

Adams aspired when he wrote that "if my country wants my services, she must ask for them."[27] He viewed this attitude as neither arrogance nor aloofness, but the suppression of personal ambition to the interests of the state. Adams wrote to a supporter in Pennsylvania that no office "will be in any manner solicited or sought by me, so I shall be prepared to receive the definitive voice of my country concerning it with entire acquiescence and submission."[28] The disinterested statesman did not seek office, but would perform whatever duties his country asked of him.

Adams's advocates worried that his approach diminished his chances. Joseph Hopkinson, an influential supporter from Pennsylvania, wrote to Louisa that "our friend Mr. A. is too fastidious and reserved on a certain subject." His complaint was not that Adams was taking an aloof position, but that he seemed to be actively discouraging others from acting on his behalf. Hopkinson was blunt: "Now, my dear madam, all this won't do. The Macbeth policy—'if chance will make me king, why chance may crown me'—will not answer where little is left to chance or merit, but kings are made by politicians and newspapers; and the man who sits down waiting to be crowned either by chance or just right will go bare-headed all his life."[29]

Adams certainly wanted to be president, but he could not admit that what might be necessary contradicted his image of himself as a disinterested statesmen. After Louisa passed Hopkinson's letter to her husband, he set out his thoughts on ambition and virtue in his diary. The bizarre passage starts with an imagined dialogue between Adams and an unnamed interlocutor—presumably Hopkinson—who studies Shakespeare's *Macbeth*. Pondering the meaning of the tragedy, the two wonder whether it is "unhallowed ambition" that is the cause whereby the protagonist "finally wins the crown and loses his soul?" Adams's unnamed friend tells him that presidential candidates have to put themselves forward if they hope to capture the presidency. Adams answers that he hoped the office would "be assigned to the most able and the most worthy," but admits to no illusions that his competitors "are not equally scrupulous." His code of conduct demanded election by acclamation. "If I am to be a candidate," he told his friend, "it must be by the wishes, ardent and active, of others and not by public interest in my favor."[30] How this was to happen Adams left unanswered, perhaps hoping for "chance" to crown him with the presidency.

For the most part, though, Adams sounded more like Hamlet than Macbeth, fearing failure more than he hoped for success. Adams would later write of Hamlet's "feeling spurring him on, and the reflection holding him back." A description that sounds remarkably like his own hesitant attitude toward electioneering, it is no surprise that Adams regarded *Hamlet* as "a masterpiece of the human mind" and Shakespeare as "a profound delineator of human nature and a sublime poetry."[31] Despite rebuking his wife for suggesting that he was "panting to be President," he asked her to imagine the prospect "that I dread infinitely more than I wish to be President."[32] Expressing vaguely suicidal thoughts, he claimed that he envied Castlereagh "the relief he has found from a situation too much like mine."[33] Just as Shakespeare's Hamlet had found himself paralyzed by the fear of failure, so too Adams, who wrote in his diary, "We know so little of that future which is best for ourselves, that whether I ought to *wish* for success is among the greatest uncertainties of the election."[34] Adams sought the presidency as recognition of his devotion to the country. Standing on the cusp of fulfilling his own and his family's aspirations, he wondered whether he was up to the task.

In his private moments, he admitted that he was as terrified of victory as he was of defeat. He worried that "the alternatives are both distressing in prospect, and the most formidable is that of success. All the danger is on the pinnacle. The humiliation of failure will be so much more than compensated by the safety in which it will leave me that I ought to regard it as a consummation devoutly to be wished, and hope to find consolation in it."[35] These final lines come from Hamlet's famous soliloquy and suggest the trepidation with which Adams viewed the presidency. Consistently, Adams had been told that because of his unique advantages, he had special burdens and responsibilities. While political rejection might earn him some familial sympathy, inability to grasp the nation's highest office would betray his life's purpose. But his path was equally vexed if he did attain the presidency, as he would be exposed to an entire nation's judgment. These, however, were private reflections, as Adams, a New Englander to his core, kept up a stoic front.

This public pose of indifference masked a deliberate strategy. The Adamses turned their home into a political space, receiving callers and often hosting large parties to position themselves at the center of Washington society.[36] Even though Louisa did not relish the role of hostess, she played it superbly, knowing that her husband's quest depended in no small part on her social and political skills. It was her energy and warmth—one guest called her "the most accomplished American lady I have seen," and a senator noted that she was "a very pleasant and agreeable woman"—and not John Quincy's cold reserve that made their home so popular.[37]

As the election drew nearer and it became clear that Adams was not about to be elected by acclamation, he began to play a more active role in his campaign. "I have hitherto discouraged and, as far as I have been able, restrained the exhibition of any such move-ment," Adams told John Heath, editor of Charleston's influential *City Gazette*. But after protests of innocence, Adams noted that he would now allow such electioneering "to take its course."[38] This did not mean that he would openly campaign, but it did mean that Adams was finally willing to move his name, and his campaign, forward.

The first part of his strategy involved answering his critics. As he had written in his *Macbeth* paper, "to parry the daggers of assassins is not to canvass votes for the Presidency."[39] The first of these came from Jonathan Russell, a colleague at the Ghent negotiations and a recently elected congressman from Massachusetts, who accused the secretary of state of trading exclusive navigation rights on the Mississippi River to secure fishing rights off New England during the Ghent negotiations in 1814. The charge was designed to under-cut Adams's support in the West. Adams correctly saw Clay's hand at work. Attempting to make the case clearer than the truth, Rus-sell had falsified two letters he had sent from Ghent. Adams pounced with a passion not seen before. His responses were published in sympathetic newspapers, leaving Russell not only discredited, but disgraced.[40] But this was not enough for Adams. He spent most of the summer of 1822 turning the indictment into a full-length pam-phlet. Writing to a friend, Adams admitted that "persecution makes an egotist in spite of himself and egotism always ends by making itself tedious."[41]

Tedious or not, Adams explained, "I felt a public duty pressing me to lay before the nation information more correct and more true to the general interests."[42] This was not merely a settling of scores or an example of his political intriguing. In letter after letter, Adams expressed a desire to set the record straight so that when the election came, voters would have an undistorted picture of the candidates. Whether sincere or not, this was Adams's way of honoring the ideal of a disinterested statesman while at the same time advancing his candidacy.

More damning were charges that attempted to disqualify him as a successor to the Jeffersonian legacy. While no Virginian himself, Adams knew that his claim to the presidency was based on continuity and precedent. So when Virginia congressman Alexander Smyth published a long letter attacking Adams for votes he had cast as a senator almost twenty years earlier, Adams properly understood this as an attack on his Republican bona fides.[43] Smyth declared that he would never cast a vote for Adams because the latter was not a true Jefferson Republican. Evidence of this was abundant, Smyth charged. Was not Adams's father the man who signed into law the hated Alien and Sedition Acts? Had Adams himself not viciously attacked Thomas Paine? Had not Adams voted against the Louisiana Purchase? In order to counter Smyth's claims, Adams penned a long letter to Smyth's constituents that appeared in the *Richmond Enquirer*. Smyth, Adams claimed, was attempting to administer a political litmus test. Explaining the context of these votes, Adams claimed that he passed with flying colors.

Parroting the old Republican maxim, Adams maintained, "I have held the government of your Union to be a government of limited powers."[44] Given his actions as an outspoken proponent of federal authority while secretary of state, this was a stretch. Attempting to counter this perception and swear his ideological legitimacy as a Jeffersonian, Adams insisted, "I never gave a vote either in hostility to the administration of Mr. Jefferson, or in disregard to republican principles." Adams had certainly proved himself an expansionist in the Jeffersonian mold. But his adherence to limited

government and strict construction of the Constitution was suspect, despite his protests. While this letter might not have convinced Smyth or his constituents, it did show Adams entering the
arena to defend and advance his own chances.

Beyond this, he made other attempts to strengthen his own position and weaken the chances of his rivals. Adams collected political intelligence from supporters throughout the country, knew
which papers were promoting him, gave advice freely, and would
occasionally furnish direct material for publication. He let Joseph Hall, editor of the *Port Folio* in Philadelphia, publish an
anonymous sketch of his life through 1808. He prepared this
himself, and it later was reprinted as an 1824 campaign biography.[45] He also penned a summary of his diplomatic achievements
and sent it to Robert Walsh in Philadelphia, who turned it into
an anonymous article in the *National Gazette* on October 28, 1824.[46]
In addition, he suggested removing Clay, Calhoun, and Jackson
from the political scene with ministerial appointments abroad.
None of them took him up on these magnanimous offers. Such
actions suggest an inclination on Adams's part to advantage
himself within the bounds of what he thought morally and politically permissible.

But even with Adams's increasingly assertive campaign, significant political hurdles remained between him and the presidency.
Lingering Republican doubts about Adams's New England origins
and Federalist sympathies still rankled hard-line Jeffersonian Republicans, including Jefferson himself, who thought that Adams's
Republicanism "is of name only, not of principle."[47] Additionally,
after the Missouri crisis southerners were less willing to have a
nonslaveholder serve as president. By the early 1820s politics were
changing, and the election of 1824 proved the most contentious

since 1800. The first hint of the new political order came in February of the election year.

For the previous two decades, Jeffersonian Republicans had selected their presidential candidate through a congressional party caucus. In 1824, the Republicans had no political opposition to speak of, and nomination amounted to election. Secretary of the Treasury William Crawford was thought to have the most pull with members of Congress and was expected to win. Out of self-interest and in deference to the growing feeling that the party caucus was both outmoded and undemocratic, the other candidates broke with tradition and decided to boycott it. And when in September 1823 Crawford suffered a stroke, the system that had prevailed since the turn of the century was thrown into confusion. When the caucus was held, only 66 of the 240 congressmen and senators attended. While Crawford won their overwhelming support, his victory did more harm than good to the convalescing secretary.

With no single compelling issue to galvanize the public, the election turned on the outsized personalities and ambitions of the men running for president. Adams and Jackson were joined by the Henry Clay, William Crawford, John C. Calhoun, Vice President Daniel Tompkins, and former New York governor DeWitt Clinton. While the latter three did not have enough national appeal, the quartet of Adams, Clay, Crawford, and Jackson certainly did. Each holding, or sharing in the case of Jackson and Crawford, a regional core constituency, these four men split the popular vote. As a result, each fell short of the 131 electoral votes needed to secure the presidency. Jackson led the polling with 151,271 popular and 99 electoral votes; next came Adams with 113,122 votes and 84 electoral ballots; behind him stood Crawford, with 40,856 popular and 41 electoral votes; and finally Clay, who received 47,531 popular and 37 electoral votes.[48] Because Clay had placed fourth in electoral votes, he was constitutionally eliminated from the special House election. But as Speaker of the House for eight of the previous twelve years, he wielded enormous influence in the lower house, and his 37 electoral votes were enough to tip the balance and decide the election in either Jackson's or Adams's favor.

With no clear winner, the Constitution dictated that the House of Representatives would decide among the top three candidates. The Twelfth Amendment stated that in House voting procedure each state would be awarded one vote. In early 1825, there were twenty-four states, so a winner would need thirteen states' votes. In November and December 1824, as the results poured in from all over the country, Adams made the rounds in Washington. In visits to delegates from Illinois, Virginia, Kentucky, and Maryland, all considered crucial to his chances, he was the model of grace, consideration, and good manners. Adams told a Clay ally that he forgave Jonathan Russell's attack on him, declaring that "having repelled that attack . . . I feel no animosity against any person concerned with it."[49] As secretary of state, Adams was in charge of printing federal laws, and he told an Indiana congressman he might change the printer of federal laws in the state to an ally of the congressman's.[50] He soft-pedaled his support for tariffs and internal improvements to a Virginia senator.[51] Hoping to secure more votes from the Empire State, Adams hinted that he might find an important post in his administration for DeWitt Clinton, who commanded a powerful faction in New York.[52] And when Robert Letcher, a congressional ally of Clay's from Kentucky, asked for assurances that Clay "would have a prominent share in the Administration," Adams agreed.[53] Writing in his diary that he was walking over fire, Adams admitted that he was venturing into morally ambiguous territory.[54] But if such maneuverings placed his personal integrity at risk, failure to do so, Adams believed, would threaten the health of the republic given what he believed were the misguided and dangerous policies of his opponents. While this was certainly a convenient argument, that means were subordinate to ends, it also was one that helps explain why, as president, Adams advanced his policies so aggressively. It also goes a long way toward explaining the despondent state Adams fell into as his opponents obstructed the great majority of his projects.

Henry Clay clearly relished playing the role of kingmaker. At a January 1825 dinner party in honor of the visiting Lafayette, Adams, Jackson, and Clay found themselves seated around the same table. Drunk with wine, Clay decided to amuse "himself a little at the expense of the *rivals*." There was an empty chair at the dinner table between Adams and Jackson. Walking around the table and depositing himself between the two candidates, Clay, "in his inimitably impudent significant manner," turned to the pair and declared, "Well, gentlemen, since you are both so near the chair, but neither of you can occupy it, I will step in between you, and take it myself."[55] The dinner party exploded with laughter, though no observers reported either Adams or Jackson found this amusing.

But if Clay enjoyed a joke at Jackson's and Adams's expense, there was little doubt which of the candidates he preferred. As early as mid-December 1824, Clay was telling friends that the choice was obvious—he would support Adams.[56] In a letter written the day *before* his infamous conversation with Adams, Clay catalogued the reasons why he would support Adams. Crawford was ruled out based on his stroke. More importantly, in the contest between Jackson and Adams, Clay's decision was clear. Admitting, and perhaps reveling in, the absurdity of a presidential election being placed in one man's hands, Clay wrote, "I shall, therefore, with great regret on account of the dilemma in which the people have placed us, support Mr. Adams."[57] In another letter, Clay wrote, "I have interrogated my conscience as to what I ought to do, and that faithful guide tells me that I ought to vote for Mr. Adams."[58]

Even though there was no love lost between the two, Clay's support for Adams was a foregone conclusion once he was eliminated from the contest. Clay disapproved of both Jackson and Crawford as potential presidents. While his dislike of Crawford was political and ideological, as the two held opposing views on the role the government should play in stewarding the economy, his hatred of Jackson was intensely personal and centered around his fear that Jackson was rash, vindictive, and violent—and a threat to the republican institutions of the United States. In his writings and speeches, Clay often compared Andrew Jackson to Julius Caesar. The allusion to a self-aggrandizing military hero who had destroyed the Roman Republic was meant to convey the danger he thought Jackson, and blind devotion to the military, posed to the functioning of a peaceful republic.[59] Amazed by and fearful of Jackson's ambitions, Clay wrote, "I can not believe that killing 2500 Englishmen at N. Orleans qualifies for the various, difficult, and complicated duties of the Chief Magistracy."[60]

It was not simply his conscience or his personal animosity toward Jackson that influenced Clay. He also correctly assessed that the odds of being appointed secretary of state, and implicitly designated as the preferred presidential successor, by either Crawford or Jackson were nonexistent. The prospect of succeeding Adams was much better. While there had been many disagreements between Adams and Clay in the previous eight years, there was now little space between the two of them on foreign policy. Supporting Adams's bid offered Clay all of the advantages and none of the disadvantages of either a Jackson or a Crawford administration.

On the night of January 9, 1825, the Great Compromiser paid a call on Adams. Adams had spent the day attending two different church services and speculating about his prospects in anticipation of his meeting with Clay. When the two men sat down, they talked at great length about the peculiar situation in which they found themselves. Unusually, a page and a half of blank space followed the diary page in which Adams recorded meeting Clay. Omissions and blank spaces are rare in Adams's diaries. The absence of record combined with the importance of the occasion does seem suggestive of what else occurred that night that Adams did not record. And yet, despite contemporary and historical charges of a corrupt bargain between Adams and Clay, whereby Clay would pledge his support in exchange for an appointment as secretary of state, there is no evidence to support the assertion that an explicit deal was made.[61] Certainly this was a mutually opportunistic arrangement. But opportunistic can mean more than just politically advantageous. To judge from Adams's record of the conversation, it seemed that Clay was conducting an interview to confirm his own judgment of what lay in the country's, and his, best interests.

"The time had now come," Adams recorded later that night, "at which he [Clay] might be explicit in his communication with me, and he had for that purpose asked this confidential interview. He wished me, as far as I might think proper, to satisfy him with regard to some principles of great public importance, but without any personal considerations for himself." Whatever particulars they discussed, the broad tenets of their politics converged. Their positions on tariffs and internal improvements were indistinguishable. They both favored a strong central government capable of guiding the nation's domestic development and projecting force beyond its borders.[62] It could hardly have surprised Adams when Clay informed him that "in the question to come before the House between General Jackson, Mr. Crawford, and myself, he had no hesitation in saying that his preference would be for me."[63] Clay acted accordingly, voting for Adams and moving the Kentucky delegates to do so as well. On February 9, 1825, in the midst of a heavy snowstorm, Congress elected John Quincy Adams president on the first ballot.[64] Thirteen states voted for him, nine for Jackson, and four for Crawford.

News of Adams's election brought a mixed response. As soon as the tallies in Congress were announced, applause broke out. But it was silenced by loud hisses from the gallery. It was rumored that in one ward of the city "an effigy of Mr. Adams had been prepared and had it not been a stormy day, his opponents among the lower citizens would have burnt it." Interestingly, in light of his future career, the most jubilant at the news of Adams's election were the capital's black residents. Upon hearing the news of his election they "were the only persons who expressed their joy by Hurras."[65]

That night, President Monroe held a reception at the President's House, which was filled to capacity as all of Washington rushed to get a glimpse of the victorious president-elect and the defeated general. Yet just as at the ball Adams had thrown for Jackson a year earlier, the guests at this reception seemed more excited by the general than by the diplomat. When the two finally found themselves face to face, Jackson extended his hand to Adams and congratulated him on his election. As happy as Adams must have been at this moment, the whispering must have bothered him. "More than one, pointing to A. said, there is our 'Clay President,' and he will be

moulded at that man's will and pleasure as easily as clay in a pot-
ter's hands."[66] But if Adams heard the whispers, he chose not to acknowledge them. He returned to his house on F Street, dashed off a
quick note to his father congratulating him, noted to his diary that
this day was "the most important day of my life," and around midnight drifted off to sleep as a band serenaded the president-elect.[67]

While Adams managed to remain outside of the politicking
through late 1824, he eventually had to confront political reality.
And after the popular election's results came in and it was clear
that the winner would emerge from a congressional vote, Adams
campaigned vigorously among the presidential electors, soothed
ruffled feathers, made generous if ambiguous statements, and
promised all things to all people. He played the part of a politician
willing to cut the necessary deals. He had done what was necessary
to obtain the object of his, and his family's, highest ambition. This
was a far cry from his vision of a patriot king. Thinking about the
upcoming election, Louisa had asserted that "in a righteous cause,
I dare both good and ill."[68] Despite his political dexterity, John
Quincy admitted no such contradiction in his actions. But he recognized that the manner in which he obtained the presidency
threatened to undercut his claim to the office and, more seriously,
his ability to govern. Now that he was president of the United States,
he hoped that the promise of what his administration could accomplish would overcome his detractors.

Adams began his presidency with symbolic assurances of continuity and caution. As was tradition, on Inauguration Day 1825, several companies of militia met Adams at his house and escorted
him to the Capitol. Following the cavalry, Adams rode in his own
carriage accompanied by the secretary of the navy and the attorney
general. Both had served with him as members of Monroe's cabi-

net, and both would serve in Adams's cabinet. In the following carriage rode the outgoing President Monroe. Disembarking at the Capitol, they were led into the Senate chamber, where a recently sworn in Vice President Calhoun adjourned the proceedings. From there, Adams marched into the House of Representatives to deliver his inaugural address. The crowd had grown so large at this point that as soon as the president-elect entered the hall, guards closed the doors to the House so quickly that several senators and congressmen were locked out of the proceedings.[69] Dressed in a plain suit of black, which several newspapers approvingly noted was of domestic manufacture, Adams ascended the steps to the Speaker's platform. As soon as silence descended, the president read his address "with a clear and deliberate articulation."[70] Perhaps it was because of the two sleepless nights he had spent prior to the inauguration, or perhaps it was the circumstances surrounding his election a month prior, or perhaps it was just raw nerves that led the former professor of rhetoric to be, according to one observer, "visibly and considerably agitated."[71]

Adams implicitly acknowledged the anger over the results of the recent election and attempted to quiet concerns that he would take his election as a sweeping mandate. He spent most of his address arguing that he was a legacy president who would not impose his own agenda. Rather, Adams asserted that his authority rested on the continuity of his predecessor's policies. He went out of his way to appease his southern critics by casting himself as a strict constructionist, declaring, "My first resort will be to that Constitution which I shall swear to the best of my ability to preserve, protect, and defend."[72] This was the first of thirteen references to the nation's founding document.[73] Adams attempted to mollify his critics by asserting that the "political creed" of the United States was based on frequent elections and limited government. Significantly, he held that the federal government had limited power to impose its will on the states, stating that each of them were "sovereignties of limited powers." As this was a particularly contentious point, he underscored that the federal and state governments were separate entities, "uncontrolled within their respective spheres, uncontrollable by encroachments upon each other."

Additionally, Adams detailed Monroe's accomplishments in order to legitimize his own program. For it was in "the promise and performance of my immediate predecessor [that] the line of duty for his successor is clearly delineated." According to Adams, the whole purpose of his administration would be "to pursue to their consummation those purposes of improvement in our common condition instituted or recommended by him [Monroe]." This he assured the nation would "embrace the whole sphere of my obligations."[74] By stressing the Constitution and James Monroe as the guiding lights of his presidency, Adams hoped both to dispel lingering resentment and legitimize his actions in law and precedent.

Early in his speech, Adams had proclaimed his vision of an efficient government free from political infighting: "The harmony of the nation is promoted and the whole Union is knit together by the sentiments of mutual respect, the habits of social intercourse, and the ties of personal friendship." But according to Adams, such harmony was currently taking place only in the cosmopolitan capital, where representatives from different parts of the nation could meet, exchange ideas, and benefit from mutual understanding. Adams intended to spread this model to the entire country.[75] While this was intended as a conservative speech that stressed the limited powers of federal and state government, it also intimated that Adams's preferences actually lay with a more centralized and expansive government. Placing internal improvements at the center of his agenda, Adams gave notice of his priorities. "To the topic of internal improvement, emphatically urged by him [Monroe] at his inauguration, I recur with peculiar satisfaction."[76] Adams again referred to this as a legacy project of Monroe's. But it seems equally true that he saw internal improvements as his own signature policy. Adams believed that knitting together the country's disparate regions would allow for cross-pollination and efficient transfer of men, materials, and ideas, which in turn would make a more harmonious and prosperous union.

He concluded his speech by noting the peculiar circumstances surrounding his election, which he attempted to turn to his advantage. "Less possessed of your confidence in advance than any of my predecessors, I am deeply conscious of the prospect that I shall stand more and oftener in need of your indulgence."[77] Sketching such a vision of the country's future progress and appealing to Congress for support, Adams hoped to persuade the assembled legislators to join him in building a more politically harmonized and consolidated nation.

The first place Adams sought to build consensus was in his own cabinet, and he meant to do so by appointing individuals who both represented different geographic and ideological constituencies and burnished his Republican credentials. Just as Adams had looked to Monroe for his policy goals, he also drew on Monroe's cabinet for his personnel needs.[78] In retrospect, it seems curious that Adams relied on Monroe for advice rather than on his own father. Monroe of course offered the example of apolitical amalgamation—an example that Adams sought to emulate. Some consultations with the elder Adams, however, who had retained Washington's cabinet to the detriment of his own presidency, might have reminded him of the pitfalls of not selecting his own loyal and like-minded cabinet. Regardless, Adams renominated his predecessor's appointees. Monroe's attorney general, William Wirt, his navy secretary, Samuel Southard, and his postmaster general, John McLean, agreed to stay on. When Crawford declined to remain at Treasury, Adams appointed Richard Rush, the acting American minister in London. With Calhoun now occupying the vice presidency, Adams thought he might be able to lure Jackson into the cabinet, and sent several feelers to the general, who was briefly serving as Tennessee's senator. When Jackson refused, Adams recruited another southerner into his cabinet. He appointed James Barbour of Virginia, a friend of Monroe's and one of the architects of the Missouri Compromise, as secretary of war.

Most significantly, Adams offered Clay the State Department on February 12—just three days after his election in the House of Representatives. In doing so, he undercut any later attempts at national conciliation. The first hint of this was the Senate's 27–10 confirmation vote for Clay, a much wider measure of opposition than either Adams or Clay had anticipated. Clay's confirmation as secretary of state helped turn Crawford's and Jackson's supporters into opposition. Subsequently, Adams appointed Rufus King as minister to London. Having previously served in London as American minister under the first Adams administration in the late 1790s, King was clearly qualified, but his nomination provoked further opposition. Southerners remembered his fiery antislavery speeches over the Missouri Compromise five years earlier, and Republicans took this appointment as confirmation of Adams's covert Federalist leanings. These political miscalculations might have seemed trivial to Adams. But his early missteps stood as harbingers of the political paralysis that was to come.

As president, Adams advanced a series of interrelated programs that were linked by their shared vision of a significantly expanded federal government. While his inaugural address had hinted at the scope of his plans, it was carefully balanced with conservative statements of continuity. But the Annual Message of December 1825 abandoned much of that caution. Adams had given hints of his thinking on domestic matters in the years leading up to his election. Negotiating with the British at Ghent in 1814, he had held that it was a "moral and religious duty of a nation to settle, cultivate, and improve their territory."[79] He returned to this idea regularly over the ensuing decade, fleshing out what such a policy might mean in practice. In an 1822 letter to Massachusetts Federalist senator James Lloyd, Adams wrote of "the future capabilities of our country to constitute a power such as associated man has never yet exhibited upon earth." This was not simply patriotic hyperbole. Adams attributed the growing strength of the United States to "our improvements of physical nature upon this continent." The rest of the letter laid out a program designed to foster that growth by harnessing the nation's latent power. The statesmen's duty, Adams told Lloyd, was "to apply their ingenuity and exercise their influence . . . [and] to aim as far as their abilities extend towards the moral purification of their country from its besetting sins."[80]

As he prepared the Annual Message to Congress of 1825 and read successive drafts to his cabinet, his advisers voiced their strong objections that they found it overly bold and politically unpalatable. Most forcibly, Barbour, the lone southerner in Adams's administration, told the president that he specifically objected to the section on internal improvements. William Wirt also advised Adams against this section, calling it "excessively bold." According to Wirt, the message would play right into the hands of the president's critics, who were already portraying Adams as "grasping for power." Wirt predicted that if this speech were delivered in its current form, the opposition would effectively depict Adams as "wanting a great, magnificent Government."[81] This phrase, long associated with Patrick Henry's warning that Americans had much to fear from centralized and powerful states, still resonated among old Jefferson Republicans.

Moreover, as Wirt had pointed out, the president was proposing measures that would give the administration's critics even more ammunition to depict Adams as deviating from the Jeffersonian tradition. And if this were not enough, Clay repeatedly advised the president that he could not get the votes necessary for his ambitious agenda. Ever the political realist, Clay told Adams that while he "approved of the general principles, [he] scrupled great part of the details."[82] In this case, the details meant making sure not to get too far out in front of the American people. More than anyone else in the cabinet, Clay shared the president's vision of a powerful federal government that could coordinate and direct the country's development. But he was also finely attuned to which way the political winds were blowing. Clay asked why Adams would propose items and policies that the president knew stood little chance of passing.

The president ignored these appeals toward moderation. He informed his cabinet that he was thinking about "a longer range than a simple session of Congress. The plant may come late, though the seed be sown early."[83] Given the opportunity, he wanted to direct history, not merely respond to it. On the eve of announcing his ambitious program, Adams concluded that "thus situated, the perilous experiment must be made. Let me make it with full deliberation, and [be] prepared for the consequences."[84] Not wanting to postpone controversial measures, Adams pushed ahead with his programs. He felt that he owed this duty to the future as well as to the present. This was a strategic viewpoint that stressed long-term results. Unfortunately for Adams, it was not a politically realistic one. Adams possessed the ability to point in the direction he thought the nation ought to head. However, political leadership was as much about pointing the way as it was about persuading others to follow. Repeatedly ignoring the candid advice his politically diverse cabinet offered him and deciding to plunge ahead led Adams to an enormous political miscalculation.

Adams's Annual Message to Congress of December 6, 1825, attempted to persuade Congress of the need for the federal government to support a program of economic, educational, scientific, and social improvement. Both at home and abroad, the president attempted to promote activist republican government "in a more enlarged extent."[85] In foreign policy, Adams declared that the time had come for the United States to play a leading role in inter-American affairs. He discussed the advantages of close commercial relations with the South American republics, announced that he would send representatives to the Pan-American Congress of Republics in Panama, and called for an enlarged and more powerful navy. The navy was particularly important. Citing growing American interests in the Pacific and as far away as mainland China, Adams suggested that "a permanent naval peace establishment, therefore, adapted to our present condition, and adaptable to that gigantic growth with which the nation is advancing in its career . . . will deserve your serious deliberations." Adams appended a report from the secretary of the navy recommending the construction of a new navy port and ten new sloops of war.[86] Adams hoped to create a bulwark of commercial republics that would enrich and protect each other through trade, defense, and ideological sympathy.

Adams's ambitions in foreign policy paled in comparison to his domestic agenda. He proposed a uniform bankruptcy law, a naval academy, a national university and observatory, domestic and international scientific expeditions, and a Department of the Interior. But most important to Adams's American System was his call for a national system of roads and canals, which would tie the country together and provide the basis for the revenues to fund these and other initiatives.

If references to the Constitution formed the backbone of the inaugural address, "improvement" was the theme of the 1825 Annual Message. Invoking "improvements" twenty-seven times in this speech, Adams sought to link the country's increasing prosperity to its continued growth. The nation had spread its commercial reach, improved its finances, expanded its territorial acquisitions, enlarged its military, and increased its population. But past performance was not necessarily indicative of future results. The only way his countrymen could secure the nation's continuing rise was to improve upon their present state of peace and prosperity. That improvement would come through advances in education, governmental funding of scientific endeavor, and innovations in manufacture and agriculture.

The key to such improvements was promoting a culture of innovation through responsible governmental stewardship of the country. And even though states had made important advances—here Adams pointed to Virginia's establishment of its university and New York's enterprise in opening the Erie Canal—their resources were limited and their economic interests were often parochial. Only the federal government could undertake coordinated projects important to the whole country, and Adams appealed to Congress to hold "up the torch of human improvement to eyes that seek the light."[87]

The president anticipated his opponents' charges that he was consolidating power in the federal government and attempted to counter such claims by advancing two separate arguments. Appealing to Congress not to be "palsied by the will of our constituents," Adams explained that only Congress possessed the ability to understand and act on projects "important to the whole and to which neither the authority nor the resources of any one state can be adequate."[88] Such an argument presumed that all federal lawmakers would place allegiance to the Union above their ties to party and to local constituents—a presumption that struck many as particularly imprudent considering Adams secured his victory by subverting the popular vote. Additionally, it rested on the assumption that consolidated power should not be viewed as a harbinger of tyranny and corruption. For too long, Adams argued, liberty and power had been considered antagonistic forces. This was a simplistic belief. This speech argued that liberty, properly harnessed and driven by the federal government, would release the creative powers of the nation.

Adams knew that such positive domestic developments rested on a peaceful, or at least stable, geopolitical environment. So, just as when he was secretary of state, Adams attempted to reduce threats to the nation by securing the Western Hemisphere as America's exclusive sphere of interest. Specifically, this meant ensuring that Europe did not intervene in, colonize, or transfer any territories in the Western Hemisphere. Containing the growth of authoritarian regimes within this sphere, he argued, meant strengthening the republics of the New World.

In the early months of 1825, Adams and Clay launched a number of diplomatic initiatives designed to reduce further the prospect of European influence in the New World. They encouraged a peaceful resolution to the still unresolved conflicts between Spain and its former colonies. They attempted to keep Cuba from falling into foreign hands. They pressed Mexico and Colombia, both attempting to increase their holdings in the Caribbean, to refrain from giving the European powers a pretext for intervention. And remembering the lesson of Florida that unresolved borders made for insecure borders, they tried to acquire Texas from Mexico.

Adams conceived of a program designed to foster the type of norms and behaviors the United States wanted to see in its neighborhood. In his first months in office, Adams instructed Clay to begin negotiating commercial treaties with Mexico, Central America, Buenos Aires, and Brazil. But then a greater opportunity presented itself with the invitation to attend Símon Bolívar's Panama Congress. Bolívar had conceived it with the hope of drawing the Latin American republics closer to each other, developing unified commercial policies for the hemisphere, and establishing a mutual defense treaty. When Clay first broached this issue with the president, Adams noted that attending such a meeting might allow the United States "to establish American principles of maritime, belligerent, and neutral law." He added that promulgating such views would be "a grain of mustard-seed," underscoring his belief that this conference of republics had the potential to grow into something much larger.[89]

Just as Adams's domestic policy focused on offering a positive vision of what the state could accomplish, his foreign policy offered an opportunity to defend and promote the benefits of republicanism. His Annual Message to Congress of March 1826 and Clay's subsequent instructions to the administration's ministers to the Panama Congress advocated avoiding foreign wars, opposing further colonization of the Western Hemisphere, and promoting free trade and noninterference in the internal affairs of other nations. These policies, so they argued, were the most conducive to peace and prosperity.

Not only repeating the themes of the Monroe Doctrine, but going one step further by attempting to set out a guiding set of principles for the republics of the Western Hemisphere, the administration wanted to use the Panama Congress to encourage its neighbors to the south to pursue the same path that the United States had undertaken. This path was fairly straightforward and had distinct stages: postpone a clash with any great power, buy time to grow, develop domestic institutions and industries, and promote liberal trade policies with their fellow republics. Adams and Clay hoped that this sequenced development model would allow the republics to push the monarchies of Europe out of the entire Western Hemisphere.[90]

Adams saw this approach as an extension of his previous thinking and as in line with his recent calls for governmental activism. Critics, however, portrayed it as a dangerous change from his previous stance. The truth was somewhere in between. To Adams, attending the Panama Congress and promoting free trade and republican government were a logical *extension* of his thinking expressed in the Monroe Doctrine. He explained it as in line with the "more enlarged extent" in which the nation was now operating. But he recognized that this could be seen as a departure from refraining from entangling foreign alliances and attempted to explain why circumstances warranted such a departure.

The president acknowledged that "the great rule of conduct for us in regard to foreign nations is, in extending our commercial relations, to have with them as little political connection as possible." But according to Adams this was merely a tactic and not intended to serve as the immutable law governing America's foreign relations. George Washington's advice was "founded upon the circumstances in which our county and the world around us were situated at that time when it was given." At that time, Adams explained, Europe's quarrels were "very remote" and her controversies "were essentially foreign to our concerns." Adams also argued that Washington had anticipated the day when the United States had grown to power and then "might choose peace or war, as our interests, guided by justice, should counsel."[91]

No longer vulnerable, and growing into its financial and industrial power, the United States, Adams believed, had arrived at such a moment. South America's commercial and diplomatic direction was of great interest to the United States, and Adams argued that the United States needed to play a more active role stewarding hemispheric affairs. He took pains to reassure critics that the country would not join a formal alliance and would not pledge itself to act in concert with other countries. But through his advocacy of consultations on inter-American affairs, it is clear that Adams had broadened his understanding of what lay in the nation's interest. He insisted that "far from conflicting with the counsel or the policy of Washington," attending the Panama Congress and playing a larger role in hemispheric matters "is directly deducible from and conformable to it."[92] Adams downplayed the departure from his earlier position, instead arguing that it was a logical, necessary, and moral extension of his previous policies.[93] But he was stretching the meaning of policies he had advanced just three years earlier and attempting to adapt them to new circumstances while justifying them as neither new nor noteworthy. President Adams declared that "the moral influence of the United States may perhaps be exerted with beneficial consequences at such a meeting—the advancement of religious liberty."[94] On the face of it, promoting religious liberty seems like an odd justification for American involvement in an international conference. This is particularly true when taking into consideration Adams's earlier calls as secretary of state for limiting American activities abroad. But it was perfectly in keeping with his recent calls for governmental activism and moral improvement in domestic and foreign affairs.

Adams's agenda rested on three separate but interrelated policies: reducing foreign threats, fostering social cohesion, and promoting domestic development. But while the vision Adams had sketched for his presidency was robust, his legislative strategy for translating it into policy was curiously weak. Shortly after sending his Annual Message of 1825 to Congress, he met with Massachusetts congressman Daniel Webster. When the president finally steered the conversation to his legislative program, he haltingly asked Webster for his help cobbling together a legislative package. Realizing the political difficulties of shepherding through an overly detailed piece of legislation, the president suggested a short bill with expansive language. He did not dictate to Webster how to steer this legislation through the House, but left that to the representative's own devices. With this approach, Adams hoped to encourage Congress to put together a legislative package that was both politically acceptable and in line with his agenda. Instead, the vagueness of Adams's request, coupled with his lack of systematic follow-through, suggests the clumsy moves of a political neophyte who hoped the administration's supporters would sponsor legislation to support the president's recommendations.

But with no legislative leader such as Henry Clay to marshal such a package through the House and Senate, this did not happen. Congressional supporters brought forth piecemeal proposals that served their constituents but did little to advance an integrated system of infrastructure projects, tariffs, land sales, or a federally funded national university. Opponents claimed that the aloof president had no sense of priority and, worse, no clear plan for dealing with the challenges the country faced. With only the high rhetoric of the inaugural and the first Annual Message to Congress and no legislative proposals on hand, the gathering opposition attempted to define the administration—and shoot down its programs. This started in its outsized resistance to the Panama Congress.

Although wary of his opponents, Adams had attempted to entice them into supporting a national unity government. But as they rejected appointments and policies, he sensed that an "inevitable coalition between the Calhoun, Jackson, and Crawford forces" was shifting the political tide against him.[95] Other than a sense of shared grievance from losing the presidential election, this "inevitable coalition" had lacked any galvanizing issues to focus on or rally around. The Panama Congress changed that, with Martin Van Buren leading the opposition. The "Little Magician," as he came to be known, was a courteous and diminutive senator from New York, a master political organizer, and a Jeffersonian Republican who thought the party had deviated too far from Jefferson's original vision. Looking to restore the party's ideological purity and to find a way into power, Van Buren had supported Crawford's recent attempt at the presidency. Writing to a political ally, Van Buren held that ever since the 1824 election he was "looking out for the weak points in the enemies [sic] line" and stood "ready for the assault when opportunity offers."[96]

The Panama Congress offered just the opening that Van Buren had been waiting for—one where a discrete policy issue could be linked to and attacked as symptomatic of the larger vision animating the Adams administration. Under Van Buren's leadership, congressional opponents of the administration attacked the logic of Adams's foreign and domestic policies. They argued that joining an international alliance would undermine the country's sovereignty and make it more likely to fight in foreign wars. They warned that sending American ministers abroad to discuss slavery and the slave trade, as the Panama Congress delegates were called to do, would shatter national cohesion. And they asserted that Adams's plans to coordinate federal projects would not promote but undermine domestic development.

Van Buren charged that the president's actions showed contempt for Congress and for the Constitution. Anticipating Henry Cabot Lodge's opposition to the League of Nations almost a hundred years into the future, Van Buren declared that joining an international alliance with the Latin American republics would put America's sovereignty at risk. More pointedly, Van Buren claimed that Adams was violating the very principles that he had championed as Monroe's secretary of state. The Monroe Doctrine, Van Buren argued, was designed as a message of caution and deliberation. While it stated what was in America's long-term interests, it was also meant to blunt those domestic critics who had pushed for a more aggressive, more activist foreign policy. "This spirit was combated," Van Buren stated, "by ascribing their conduct to a prudent and circumspect policy, designed to effect the greatest good with the least possible hazard."[97] It was this prudent and circumspect policy that had produced Monroe's Annual Message of December 1823. This policy, Van Buren argued, Adams had now forsaken.

Adams's opponents saw in this episode what they expected: a president, once cautious, had been corrupted into overly zealous actions by his dangerous secretary of state. "The policy of Washington was the policy of Jefferson, Madison, and Monroe—a policy in which Mr. Adams concurred during the whole period of his service in the cabinet of the latter, in the Department of State," claimed James Hamilton Jr., another congressional antagonist. "Suddenly, (since an election produced by the memorable coalition, which has put him on the throne) he has become innoculated [*sic*] with 'this Spanish American fever.'" The culprit, Hamilton concluded, was not Adams but Clay. The president "has started from a caution as cold as marble, into the vernal fervors of love, at first sight, for the South Americans. . . . And with this mutation, what a reversal has there been in the whole foreign policy of the country!"[98]

Attacking the Panama Congress from a domestic angle, the opposition declared it a threat to the institution of slavery. Calling attention to the racial issues involved in a conference where American delegates would meet with black delegates from Haiti on an equal footing and discuss the slave trade, Robert Hayne of South Carolina held that "the question of slavery is one, in all its bearings, of extreme delicacy. . . . It must be considered and treated entirely as a DOMESTIC QUESTION." He warned that even considering such a sensitive issue would endanger the domestic tranquility of the country, and explicitly stated that "the Southern States never will permit, and never can permit, any interference . . . in their domestic concerns."[99] In a similar vein, Thomas Hart Benton of Missouri concluded his remarks by underscoring the violence of slave revolts and urged the president to understand that slavery "is a question which ought not to be agitated by us, neither at home nor abroad."[100] It is unclear whether Hayne and Benton thought that debating slavery abroad would inspire slave rebellions in the United States or if they were warning, more darkly, that such discussions would drive the South from the Union.[101]

Regardless, the implications of these speeches were ominous for the administration.

Finally, the opposition attacked the Panama Congress as part of Adams's larger vision for domestic development. In his speech, Hayne attacked Adams's American System, charging that government stewardship of the country's growth amounted to a government that controlled the economy. According to Hayne, such meddling in the market would retard the nation from gradually developing its resources by imposing "the most unnatural and destructive stimulants." The congressman asserted that the American System, "when applied to our domestic policy, mean[s] *restriction and monopoly*."[102]

On top of these accusations of destructive market manipulation, the opposition hammered the administration with charges of political corruption. They did this by bringing up the 1824 election and the corrupt bargain Clay supposedly had struck with Adams. Most egregious was the aging Virginia senator John Randolph, who delivered a six-hour floor speech. Drinking throughout it, Randolph compared the president to Blifil, a condescending hypocrite, and the secretary of state to Black George, a low-class scoundrel—characters in Henry Fielding's famous novel *Tom Jones*. Randolph deplored the "the blue-bonneted puritan of New England sharing the profits of the shuffle with the political Black Legs of the West!"[103] Offended, Clay challenged Randolph to a mostly uneventful duel.[104]

Although the administration and its supporters won the vote on this policy battle, the opposition achieved its desired outcome. John Sergeant and Richard Anderson, the two American diplomats who had finally won approval to attend the Panama Congress, never made it there. Concerned about the risk of contracting tropical fever, Sergeant delayed his trip until early autumn. He ended up missing the conference altogether. Anderson, serving as U.S. minister to Colombia, would have done well to have followed Sergeant's example. Instead, traveling through the summer from Bogotá to Panama, he fell sick and died.

Even if they had attended the conference, it seems unlikely that the administration would have achieved its goals. Of all the countries Bolívar invited, only Mexico, Guatemala, Colombia, and Peru sent delegates. The few agreements reached were soon after rendered moot, as only Colombia ratified the treaties. Moreover, the United States' long delay in sending its delegates gave Great Britain, which had attended the meetings in observer status, an opportunity to push British interests at the expense of American ones. The mission was politically costly for Adams, and he had nothing to show for his victory. Worse, Adams had proved his attorney general correct; he had given his opponents a stick with which to beat the administration.

Beyond the Panama Congress, Adams achieved some diplomatic successes, which included blocking Colombia and Mexico from seizing Cuba and Puerto Rico from Spain, and signing most favored nation agreements with several countries. But these were largely overshadowed by failures to acquire Texas or to settle a boundary dispute between Maine and New Brunswick. Further, a galvanized congressional opposition defeated the president's calls for a new coastal survey, purchase of the raw materials necessary for shipbuilding, and an increase in the construction of navy ships. More galling to a president who had prioritized securing foreign markets for American materials was his failure to gain most favored nation status in the British West Indies. Instead, the British closed their ports to American ships. Admitting that his top priority was defeating Adams in 1828, Van Buren wrote to a fellow New

Yorker that after this diplomatic failure "you may rest assured that the re-election of Mr. Adams is out of the question."[105]

Throughout his term, foreign policy was a second-order priority for Adams. His real focus lay with fostering social cohesion. But just as his efforts at advancing a vigorous foreign policy prompted a backlash, his attempts to assert federal power to promote domestic development exacerbated existing tensions between the state and national levels. This failure can be seen most clearly in the defeat of Adams's plans for humane treatment of the Native American population at the hands of aggressive proponents of land acquisition and states' rights.

Hoping to claim five million acres of fertile lands located within the state's borders, Georgia governor George Troup signed the suspect Treaty of Indian Springs with his part-Creek first cousin William McIntosh on February 12, 1825. The Senate quickly ratified this treaty, and in the rush of business following his inauguration Adams signed it into law. But when he found out that the treaty was forced, he suspended it. While the administration was able to get the Senate to ratify a slightly more equitable subsequent treaty, Troup attempted to nullify it, forcing the issue by ordering a survey of the Creek lands in advance of their distribution. He declared that "if the president believes that we will postpone the survey of the country to gratify . . . the hostile Indians, he deceives himself." When Adams threatened to send in federal troops, Troup warned the secretary of war that in the eventuality of hostilities "you will be considered and treated as a public enemy . . . because you . . . are yourselves the invaders, and, what is more, the unblushing allies of the savages whose cause you have adopted."[106]

The president conceded and allowed Troup to seize all of the Creeks' remaining lands. While Adams had no doubt of the right to federal intervention, he had serious qualms about its expediency. He decided not to force the issue, as violence between the federal government and a state "would be a dissolution of the Union." The country was not ready for that fight, and the president was not willing to risk it. Beyond that, Adams must have realized the force of Troup's arguments even if he despaired of his tone. American encroachment on Indian lands was a constant, and the ability of the government to restrain this lust for new lands had always been a losing battle. In fact, this was just the argument—that American expansion was inevitable and uncontainable—that Adams had made to the Spanish during the Florida crisis several years earlier. He concluded that there was little political support for enforcing the laws of the United States when it came to Indian treaties. "We have talked of benevolence and humanity," Adams wrote in his diary, "but none of this benevolence is felt where the right of the Indian comes in collision with the interest of the white man."[107] Bowing to political realities and not wishing to start a fight that could undermine the authority of the Union, Adams folded his hand.

Adams averted a crisis of sovereignty and civil insurrection, but did so at a high cost. While federal inaction might have been the lesser evil, it set the dangerous precedent of Washington backing down in arguments of state sovereignty. Moreover, capitulating to Georgia's demands encouraged neighboring states to take a similar approach with Indian tribes. And not least for the beleaguered president, it helped solidify the perception of a spineless administration that lacked both the will and the wisdom to deal with a complex problem—qualities that Jackson's supporters would repeatedly invoke in the upcoming election season.[108] Andrew Jackson himself thought that Troup and Georgia had pushed the states' rights line too far. But he realized that Adams would not, or perhaps could not, call in troops and force a confrontation. Jackson guessed that Adams and Clay, "who so oft have denounced mil[itary] chieftains" would not "raise the sword against a sover[e]ign State." He was right.

Constitutional challenge was the tactic the increasingly organized opposition used to defeat the administration's development policies. First to be attacked were Adams's calls for greater investments in higher education. When he recommended the establishment of a national university and a naval academy in his 1825 Annual Message to Congress, he thought he was on firm footing, as George Washington had first recommended the founding of a university and a national military academy in his 1796 Farewell Address. But vocal opponents pointed to James Madison's 1817 veto of internal improvements, in which he had argued that the clause "to provide for the common defense and general welfare" did not warrant extending the powers of Congress beyond those enumerated. Madison insisted that expansive readings of the Constitution "would have the effect of giving to Congress a general power of legislation instead of the defined and limited one."[109] Adams's critics used this argument, asking where in the Constitution federal funding of a national university was sanctioned. The legislation never even made it to the floor of Congress.

Adams's call for the founding of a naval academy, which he reminded Congress was not his design but Washington's, was voted on, but the House deemed it too costly. Critics there also argued that federal appointments to such an academy would become a "vast source of promotion and patronage" which would invariably lead to "degeneracy and corruption of the public morality."[110] This was both a criticism of West Point, already seen as a bastion of well-educated and out-of-touch elites, and a reminder of what many saw as the illegitimate nature of the Adams administration. The opposition portrayed both institutions as expensive, unnecessary, elitist, and constitutionally suspect.

Adams's expansive views on the role of the federal government played right into this characterization. Hoping to foster innovation and discovery, he had promoted the sciences and called on Congress to appropriate money for a national observatory. He committed the cardinal sin of comparing America unfavorably to France and England, admitting "no feeling of pride as an American" when he counted the 130 astronomical observatories dotting Europe, while noting that the United States had not yet built one of "these lighthouses of the skies."[111] While Adams intended the fostering of scientific development as a spur to national competition and greatness, his opponents instead used Adams's statements to depict him as insufficiently convinced of American greatness. "Lighthouses of the skies" earned him the derisive laughter of critics, who depicted him as living in a dream world.

Adams's views might have been enlightened, but in the mid-1820s they were also out of step with the desires of an increasing number of recently enfranchised Americans, who were more worried about their daily well-being than they were interested in ambitious schemes of national improvement that seemed more likely to benefit the intellectual and social elites. Having left Washington shortly after Adams's election, Andrew Jackson unsurprisingly found the new administration detached from the more egalitarian concerns of the public. "Instead of building lighthouses of the skies, establishing national universities, and making explorations round the globe," Jackson complained that the government needed to "pay the national debt . . . then apportion the surplus revenue amongst the several states for the education of the poor—leaving the superintendence of education to the states."[112] Accusing the administration of overstepping its powers, underserving the common man, and ignoring popular will, Jackson predicted that such policy preferences would elicit a "burst of indignation."[113] As the administration's various programs met with failure, Adams learned that Congress was less inclined to ignore its constituents' will than he was.

As president, Adams advocated a significantly expanded role for the federal government, but he chose the wrong means for executing such a bold political proposition. His belief in a post-partisan government rested on the assumption that opposing forces could forge common ground that benefited all and create a more tightly bound nation. This did not happen. Adams failed to respond to the increasingly partisan environment in which he found himself. The result was failure not only of his legislative program, but also of his entire progressive agenda.

As proposal after proposal died in Congress, political momentum shifted from the administration to the president's political adversaries, who seemed in equal parts opposed to Adams and drawn toward Jackson. The developing narrative portrayed the president as not only inept at governing, but also out of touch with the times. In the increasingly egalitarian politics of the late 1820s, being educated, analytical, and intellectual, all qualities the president possessed in spades, was suspect. Jackson, the military hero of the West, carried himself as the opposite: unschooled, uncomplicated, and possessing common sense wisdom born of real experience.

Damning Adams with faint praise, the Republican General Committee of New York City claimed that the president "may be a philosopher, a lawyer, an elegant scholar, and a poet . . . and yet the nation may be little better off for all these endowments and accomplishments. That he is *learned* we are willing to admit; but his *wisdom* we take leave to question." Training at the courts of Europe and in the councils of Washington could not compete with training on the battlefield. "Jackson made law, Adams quoted it" went a popular saying. Adams was a man of learning—effete and out of touch. Jackson, his supporters claimed, was a straight shooter.[114] He was one of us, they rhapsodized, proving the point that anyone could rise and govern, regardless of whether he had attended Harvard.

Differences between Jackson and Adams were based on more than just education and training. The two represented radically divergent views on the nation's future, the role of the federal government, and the mission of the United States. One model advocated centralized planning where separate efforts would be coordinated to produce a vast interconnected system of infrastructure and commerce. The other model was less a coherent set of ideas than a simmering anger against politicians in Washington who thought they could dictate the terms of the country's expansion. The former view, represented by Adams, saw the country reaching its potential only when apolitical public servants imposed order on a decentralized system. The latter vision, championed by Jackson and his supporters, doubted that Washington politicians could plan people's lives better than they could themselves. It saw such a project as an elite plot to keep power out of the people's hands. As a leading historian of the period wrote, "Adams wanted to guide Americans to progress. Jackson expected them to find their own way."[115] Adams's admirers supported such impulses as both enlightened and progressive, while detractors found them elitist, condescending, and removed from the everyday realities that most Americans faced. While the space between Adams and Jackson was perhaps not quite as large as their most zealous partisans declared, their policy preferences did indicate quite different beliefs about the government's proper role as driver of economic, political, and social change.

Behind Adams's proposals was a desire to develop the country. He proposed expanding the economy with an integrated plan of land sales, tariffs, and internal improvements designed to enlarge and enrich the home market.[116] The sale of public lands would pay off the national debt and raise revenue for infrastructure development. The federal government could then underwrite the construction of roads and canals that would open the country's interior and allow farmers to bring their goods to eastern markets with greater ease. What Adams had not considered were the political costs of supporting such a program.[117] Westerners did not want land sold off to the highest bidder; they preferred it sold as cheaply as possible or simply given to them. Leading Jacksonian Thomas Hart Benton opposed the administration's plan as contrary to western interests. He advocated reducing the price of land and, when it went unsold, giving it away to squatters. While Benton's land sale plans were defeated, the administration's position cost it political support in the West and among the working class.

The same was true for the internal improvements that stood as the centerpiece of the president's strategic vision for the country. While his administration was able to promote certain projects, congressmen were more interested in local proposals that would help their own chances of reelection. Instead of creating a national transportation grid, individual projects were approved and funded in a piecemeal fashion. This was not necessarily bad—many projects were undertaken during Adams's presidency. But they were not implemented with any sense of prioritization or coordination, stymying Adams's plan of an interconnected American System.

Strategic or not, the projects that were approved enjoyed much popular and local support and left Jackson's supporters scrambling to find a way to blunt their appeal.[118] They did this by charging the president with misusing governmental funds. Virginia congressman William Cabel Rives accused Adams of using federal dollars "as a source of influence, and a means of operating on the hopes and interests of the community." Here again was the charge of corruption that dogged the administration from its very first moments. By doling out federal money for surveys and projects, Rives charged, "the number of persons brought within the sphere of Executive favor is indefinitely augmented."[119]

This was ironic, as Adams not only eschewed using patronage to build political support, but seemed to go out of his way to alienate anyone who might have supported his administration. In his inaugural address, he paid rhetorical tribute to the idea of nonpartisanship and deplored the "baneful weed of party strife." Since the partisan turmoil that surrounded the War of 1812 had subsided, "no difference of principle ... has existed or been called forth in force sufficient to sustain a continued combination of parties or to give more than wholesome animation to public sentiment or legislative debate."[120] The idea of political harmony was based more on Adams's vision than it was on reality. Even by 1824, it was clear that there were diverging ideas about the role and scope of government. But these had not yet developed into fully organized political parties. Given the virtual disappearance of a two-party system over the previous decade, Adams hoped that he could mollify his opponents. To that end, he sought to make good on the promise of remaining nonpartisan, as indicated by his initial offers of cabinet appointments to Crawford and Jackson.

Unfortunately, the programs Adams pursued undermined this message. The ambitious 1825 Message to Congress, along with his indifference to his cabinet's appeals for restraint, suggests that his stress on continuity was less about content than it was about appearance. This message dwarfed all previous interpretations of the federal government's reach, and in so doing awakened old fears of a tyrannical government. Adams's robust assertion that "liberty is power" might have sounded bold to him, but it sounded ideological alarm bells to his opponents. Through the heated political wars of the 1790s, Jeffersonian Republicans had worried that a centralized government had the means to take away citizens' rights. Now those fears, quasi-dormant during Madison's and Monroe's expansion of governmental powers, reawakened. Following Adams's pronouncement, Jefferson warned of a return of a remote and powerful government, claiming that in Adams's government he detected "the consolidation in itself of powers, foreign and domestic . . . by constructions which, if legitimate, leave no limits to their power."[121] A political struggle took on ideological overtones as the old Jeffersonians darkly warned that unlimited government resulted in tyranny.

Often to his own detriment, Adams attempted to offset these fears by clinging to his vision of a post-partisan government. He would not remove individuals from government office even if they agitated against him. In a May 1825 cabinet meeting, Clay brought up the case of a naval officer described as "a noisy and clamorous reviler of the Administration." Reminding the president that officers of the United States Navy held their commission "at the pleasure of the President," Clay urged Adams to relieve the officer of his post. Not doing so would give the administration "an appearance of pusillanimity." The president reminded his cabinet that dismissing an officer for political motives would be "inconsistent with the principle upon which I have commenced the Administration, of removing no person from office but for cause." Adams estimated that nearly 80 percent of all the customhouse officers in the country, the most traditional post for bestowing political patronage, opposed his election. His political allies had urged him "to sweep away my opponents and provide with their places for my friends." He had refused then and refused to act on this case, explaining, "If I depart from this in one instance, I shall be called upon by my friends to do the same in many."[122]

Even in egregious cases, Adams refused to act in an overtly political manner. Postmaster General John McLean became increasingly partisan through Adams's presidency. Clay charged that McLean employed his office to assist the Jacksonian coalition by "using perfidiously the influence and patronage of his office, which is very great, against the administration."[123] Despite concurring with Clay's judgment that McLean's "appointments of postmasters and his management of contracts are said to be insidiously partial to the opposition, and his conversation is marked with a spirit of hostility exceedingly offensive to the friends of the Administration," President Adams refused to remove him from his post.[124] This was emblematic of Adams's approach, as he dismissed only twelve officials over four years, a record that stood in stark contrast to his predecessors.'[125] And on those few occasions where he did offer appointments, he did so with an expert sense of ineptness, in one instance offending both factions of his New York supporters.[126] This inaction was enough to drive the politically sensitive

Henry Clay to distraction. He warned the president that "friends of the Administration have to contend not only against their enemies, but against the Administration itself, which leaves its power in the hands of its own enemies."[127]

Adams's previous diplomatic and political careers offered every indication that he knew how to negotiate and compromise. Yet, as president, Adams did not seek compromise. Instead, he sought to impose on the country the policies he was convinced were in the nation's best interests. Significantly, he had no plan to convince those who disagreed with or opposed him. He neither prioritized the different aspects of his program nor worked closely with Congress to get them enacted and funded. Perhaps because of his drive to redeem himself from the inauspicious circumstances under which he assumed the presidency, Adams saw compromise as political failure and moral cowardice.

This inflexibility was further reinforced by his refusal to respond to pleas from would-be friends and political realities. Perhaps the most glaring example of Adams's refusal to take advantage of political opportunities was his dealings with Thurlow Weed. Weed, a New York political organizer, was so distressed by what he took to be the administration's political ineptness that he traveled to Washington to offer his aid to the president. In 1826, William Morgan, a resident of upstate New York, disappeared after declaring his intention to publish the secrets of the influential and elite Freemasons' fraternal order. Weed had harnessed the resulting outrage and shaped it into a potent and growing anti-elite political movement as a means to oppose the growing influence of Martin Van Buren in New York. When it became widely known that Andrew Jackson was a Masonic grand master, Adams was presented with a golden opportunity to attack Jackson's populist credentials. Yet

Adams gave Weed a cordial, if cold, reception and silenced his attempts to talk politics. In his memoirs, Weed wrote that the Adams administration failed "owing to Mr. Adams's political impracticability. He was able, enlightened, patriotic, and honest . . . [but] he disregarded or overlooked what Monroe, Madison, and Jefferson had deemed essential, namely, political organization and personal popularity. Mr. Adams, during his administration, failed to cherish, strengthen, or even recognize the party to which he owed his election. Nor . . . with the great power he possessed, did he make a single influential political friend."[128]

Even if Adams had possessed all the political skill in the world, a structural shift in the 1820s toward participatory democracy was changing the nature of governance. Increasingly, states amended their constitutions to abolish property qualifications in a move toward universal male suffrage. The 1828 presidential election witnessed a threefold increase in the number of voters from the 1824 election. Not only did Jackson's populist style play well in this new system, but it also meant that Adams's proposals for centralized planning looked increasingly outmoded. On top of this, Adams often had trouble hiding his public contempt for the political process. Reflecting on his time as president, Adams wrote that he deplored the growing "fashion of peddling for popularity by travelling round the country gathering crowds together, hawking for public dinners, and spouting empty speeches."[129] When he did speak to large gatherings, he felt the need to highlight his erudition, sprinkling obscure literary references and foreign phrases into many of his speeches. In response to one such speech, the Jacksonian *New York Evening Post* commented, with barely suppressed glee, that listening to the president "we supposed it to have been the production of some wicked Jacksonian wag who had undertaken to burlesque the clumsy wit and unwieldy eloquence of the ex-professor." Underscoring the portrayal of an out-of-touch president who spoke over the heads of the ordinary American, the paper concluded that while the speech might have displayed the "President's talent for fine writing," it "passes our comprehension" and left most listeners "in total darkness."[130] Occasionally, Adams elicited popular support at public events, but such appearances were rare and generally scripted and formal affairs. This stood in stark contrast to the success of Jacksonian Hickory Clubs, rallies, parades, and barbecues.

The 1826 congressional elections substantiated perceptions that Adams was needlessly alienating supporters and that Jackson's legislative supporters were increasingly able to stymie the administration. In Pennsylvania, an Adams supporter reported that "to be active & prominent in support of the administration, *is to throw one's self out of the chance of promotion, & the sphere of regard.*"[131] In Kentucky, Clay's brother warned that "the friends of Jackson are desperat [*sic*] and clamerous [*sic*] and consequently active while the friends of the admin. Are inactive and luke warm and with out any concert."[132] Better organized, more energized, and with a more effective message, anti-administration forces picked up enough seats in the elections to take control of Congress. The administration found itself reeling. Adams noted that there was now "a decided majority in both Houses of Congress in opposition to the Administration—a state of things which has never before occurred under the Government of the United States."[133] With an opposition-controlled Congress, government ground to a halt. House members replaced the pro-Adams Speaker with a vocal Jackson supporter. Hostile committees tied up the administration, as they had during the Panama debates, with investigations and by requesting numerous documents from the executive branch. Adams fumed that these demands were "pursued, too, in a spirit of hostility to the Administration."[134]

Nowhere was this spirit more clear than in the opposition's political maneuverings on the tariff. The tariff was a key part of the development plan championed by Adams. But the tariff that emerged out of committee was designed as an electioneering tool by the opposition. It was meant to punish the administration's supporters, reward its opponents, and push swing states into the Jackson camp. A congressman explained, "Why did we frame the bill as we did? Because we had put the duties upon all kind of woolen cloths as high as *our own friends* in Pennsylvania, Kentucky & Ohio would vote for them."[135] The opposition hoped to make the tariff a poison pill for the Adams administration. Jackson supporters, under Martin Van Buren's leadership, believed that New England would oppose the bill because of its heavy taxes on materials imported by the New England states. However, they did not count on the pragmatism of many of the western, mid-Atlantic, and New England congressmen who believed that a tariff, even an imperfect one, would benefit the nation's growing industrial capacity. Much to the surprise of its disingenuous sponsors, the tariff passed by a vote of 105–94. Adams signed the bill into law, realizing that its severe duties on wool imports, essential to the growing textile industry of the Northeast, would hurt him among his supporters. But not wasting a political opportunity, Van Buren immediately used the tariff as another chance to attack Adams's presidency.

To Adams, the political mood was deeply dispiriting. Jackson's supporters were "bitter as wormwood in their opposition, indulging themselves in the warmth of debate in personal reflections as ungenerous as they were unjust."[136] After the midterm elections his disgust grew into resignation, and Adams finally realized that his own programs were probably doomed. He recorded in his journal, "My own career is closed."[137] He tried not to despair, calling on himself to display some stoic fortitude. But after the midterms he could only manage a couple of hours of sleep a night, most of which were spent tossing and turning. He suffered from indigestion even though his appetite had deserted him. He started skipping his daily exercise routines and seemed to revert to the extreme depths of depression he had experienced as a young man. By the summer of 1827, Adams recorded an "uncontrolled dejection of spirits, insensibility to the almost unparalleled blessings with which I have been favored; a sluggish carelessness of life, an imaginary wish that it were terminated, with a clinging to it as close as it ever was in the days of most animated hopes."[138]

Just as the prospect of victory in 1824 had filled him with Shakespearean-like apprehension and foreboding, so now the increasing likelihood of defeat in 1828 filled him with dread and apathy. Often rising before the sun, exercising prior to breakfast with a swim or a brisk walk, and squeezing as much time out of the day as was possible, Adams had been a model of hard work and energy at the outset of his term. Now he found himself absorbed with trivial matters, killing time, and waiting for the end of his term. Much of his energy was spent sitting and thinking about "the severe trials of my life."[139] Added to this was growing disappointment with and apprehension over his eldest child's conduct. Overwhelmed by the pressure of living up to the impossibly high Adams standard, George Washington Adams shirked his father's stern advice and generally avoided answering his letters, dreading the likely response. But instead of relenting, John Quincy only increased the pressure, believing George's behavior weak, and that he merely needed stern words of encouragement. Family concerns exacerbated the strain on the beleaguered and increasingly withdrawn president. The toll showed. A niece confessed that "he looks very badly" and thought "he has the appearance of a man harassed to death with care."[140]

Many saw the election of 1828 as a rematch of 1824. But unlike the 1824 election, where four candidates split the popular and electoral vote, the election of 1828 was fought between only two candidates— Adams and Jackson. The campaign had actually begun in 1825, just months after Adams's inauguration, when Tennessee nominated Andrew Jackson for president. In what one historian dubbed the first modern election, Jackson and Van Buren built a political machine that catered to an expanding electorate by holding torchlight rallies and parades, forming local political clubs, coordinating a sprawling media campaign, liberally spreading money, and making use of symbols and campaign paraphernalia.[141] After a meeting at the President's House with Martin Van Buren, Adams wrote that the senator "is now the great electioneering manager for General Jackson, as he was before the last election for Mr. Crawford . . . [and he] has improved . . . in the art of electioneering." This new political reality could also be seen in the press, where Adams noted the "money expended by the adversaries to the Administration . . . to vitiate the public opinion, and pay for defamation."[142] But even while recognizing this changed political landscape, Adams would not do anything to stop or organize against it, noting in resignation that "Van Buren has now every prospect of success in his present movements."[143]

As the campaign descended into a mudslinging contest that alternatively surprised and offended him, an increasingly dejected Adams withdrew from the public. Opponents charged Jackson with bigamy and murder. Adams, for his part, was accused of pimping for Czar Alexander when serving in Russia. In one memorable campaign ditty, singers warned that "slavery's coming, knavery's coming, plundering's coming . . . if John Quincy not be coming!"[144] Adams's disgust with the campaign's tone and his bitter disappointment with the defeat of his domestic and foreign policy initiatives contributed to an increasing sense of weariness and lethargy. For the first time in years, from August through December of the election year, he stopped writing in his journal. Watching the campaign descend into the gutter and still refraining from a more active role, Adams felt his usefulness ebb, and saw his rejection by the American public as evidence that his good character had been sacrificed and his vision wasted. This rejection at the height of his powers seemed confirmation of failure. When he fell into a depression as a young man about his prospects and direction, his father had been able gradually to ease him back onto the path. But neither his mother nor his father were alive to commune and commiserate with a defeated and rejected Adams. While he might have found some solace in sharing his father's political fate and becoming only the second one-term president, this was cold comfort.

In all of American history, only Adams and his father skipped their successors' inaugurations. The morning that Andrew Jackson was sworn in as the nation's seventh president, a spring breeze blew through Washington. But Adams was not to be found at the Capitol, having chosen to opt out of the day's festivities and instead set out on a solitary horseback ride. Halfway through his route, a stranger approached and asked the former president if he could be so kind as to point him in the direction of John Quincy Adams. Adams informed the rider he had found the man he was looking for. It would be hard to imagine a scene that could have made Adams feel more insignificant and forgotten.

Late at night, nearing the end of his term, Adams sat alone with his thoughts. "I can scarcely conceive a more harassing, wearying, teasing condition of existence," he wrote in his diary. "It literally renders life burdensome." He mused about what his retirement from public life would look like and whether or not he would enjoy it. It hardly mattered. "It cannot be worse than this perpetual motion and crazing cares. The weight grows heavier from day to day."[145] Upon assuming office, many American presidents have expressed surprise at how much the burdens of responsibility weigh on them. This was not the weight that Adams complained of, though surely he felt that burden too. Rather, the oppressiveness that seemed to hang over Adams's final two years in office stemmed from his inability to accomplish his goals and his increasing isolation from the political fray. Analyzing his own presidency with the benefit of almost a decade of hindsight, Adams concluded, "The great object of my life therefore as applied to the administration of the Government of the United States has failed."[146]

John Quincy Adams entered office with the belief that the presidency was a "public trust" that entailed moral as well as political responsibilities. While he did have some successes, by almost any account, including his own, his presidency was an abject failure. This failure sprang from an interplay of personal shortcomings, political miscalculations, and structural shifts to the American polity. Adams's temperament was perfectly suited for the advocacy that policy demanded, but was less agreeable to the compromises of politics. Beyond that, Adams's inability to communicate and sell his policies was fatal for a grand strategy in a democracy. And finally, there was a structural failure. The 1820s were a transitional period in the practice of American politics, and Adams proved unable to cope with the shifting political landscape.

Intelligent, carefully prepared, and long experienced in government, Adams possessed the perfect resume to be president. But he did not have the temperament. Instead of reacting to setbacks with resilience or pugnacity, Adams responded with apathy. Two days after the House voted to elect him president, Adams was already predicting that the defeated opposition would pursue a relentless campaign against him. "To this end," he correctly foresaw, "the Administration must be rendered unpopular and odious, whatever its acts and measures may be." He considered himself forewarned, but it was his next words that were telling: "It is not in man that walketh to direct his steps."[147] John Quincy Adams was a daily reader of the Bible, and he often sprinkled his diary and letters with biblical quotations. This paraphrase of Jeremiah 10:23 conveyed his sense that God controls men's destinies. This could be read as a stoical comment on the impossibility of knowing the future. But it also conveys a certain resignation on the part of Adams about what was coming next and an unwillingness to insert himself in a new kind of politics which he felt above.

Yet Adams was a political survivor who had faced setbacks and opposition throughout his career. Why did he respond with such seemingly uncharacteristic resignation during his presidency? Adams's earlier independence needs to be viewed in terms of his political aspirations. When he abandoned the Federalists, he sensed that the future of the country lay with expansionist sentiment and Jeffersonian politics. He lost his seat in the Senate, but was rewarded with ministerial appointments by Presidents Madison and Monroe. When he clashed with members of Monroe's cabinet, he did so out of principle, but also in regard to furthering his presidential ambitions. In previous political fights, Adams had acted out of either his long-term interests or because he sensed that he was fighting a fight that he could win. As president, he had no further political aspirations. And while his earlier party change might have suggested a certain political nimbleness, few would accuse John Quincy Adams of being too pliant. Rather, his leadership style suggests an overly rigid personality that viewed political actions in stark terms: as right or wrong, good or bad. This trait made him a particularly effective adviser and policy advocate. But it was less useful to a politician trying to make deals and legislate through compromise.

Additionally, the challenges that Adams faced were at least as much political as they were personal. Even before his inauguration, Adams suffered from a crisis of legitimacy. Although he was the second president to have his election decided in the House of Representatives, he knew that he had lost the popular vote.[148] This furnished his opponents with a simple and ruthlessly effective message: Adams was an illegitimate president. "The administration have gone into power contrary to the voice of the nation," Jackson wrote. The question, he declared, was "shall the government or the people rule?"[149] Taking their cues from Jackson and Van Buren, Adams's opponents turned his foreign policy and domestic initiatives against him, casting them as attempts at grasping power.

Unfortunately for Adams, almost everything he did seemed to reinforce this narrative. His public image suffered from charges of a "corrupt bargain" with Henry Clay. His 1825 Message to Congress seemed designed to explicitly challenge existing Republican ideology.[150] And in debates surrounding the Panama Congress, critics charged that Adams had expanded the Monroe Doctrine, changing it from a defensive unilateral pronouncement into a positive alliance that would commit the United States to action.

The cloud under which Adams captured the presidency created a political dilemma. If Adams acted in a partisan manner, he would further the charges of corruption that had dogged him since the election. However, if he avoided acting to reward his supporters and punish his enemies, he would render himself and his political program ineffective. Adams decided that it was more important to refrain from overt political actions than to actively further his programs. He took a deliberate nonpartisan strategy to allay these public concerns, which explains why he largely abstained from removing high-ranking government officials from office based on their political persuasions. Doing so, he had informed his cabinet, "would be thought to indicate an irritable, hasty, and vindictive temper, and give rise to newspaper discussions, of which all the disadvantages would fall upon the Administration."[151]

But in attempting to avoid the appearance of impropriety, Adams abandoned the playing field to his opponents. He was not willing to change the political system as it existed, even as he noted its changing nature. Partially, this was because Adams believed that reviving the party spirit was a betrayal of the country's ideals. But equally strong was Adams's belief that doing so would decisively turn public opinion against his administration. Adams was caught on the horns of a dilemma. If he did nothing, he would almost certainly guarantee his opponent's victory. But if he engaged in the type of political maneuvering he had undertaken to win the presidency, he would both betray his own outdated ideals and furnish his adversaries with confirmation of his supposed corruption. Faced with such a choice, Adams chose the former, realizing that it almost certainly meant political defeat.

As president, Adams could not successfully bridge the gap between his desire to remake the role of the federal government and his refusal to accept the realities of a changed political culture. He justified his new programs in terms of continuity with the past. But he refused to play by the new political rules, explaining that to do so would break with the founders' vision. In his sweeping history of conservatism, Russell Kirk concluded that Adams "adhered to certain innovating beliefs which confused and weakened his conservative prejudices."[152] Kirk's assertion is only partially correct, for Adams was neither a promoter of the status quo nor nostalgic for the past. As president, Adams refused to choose between a traditional and an innovative path. Failing to commit fully might have been an acceptable choice if Adams had been a skilled politician operating in calm political waters. But during his presidency, American politics were in flux, while Adams remained dogmatic. The combination proved fatal to his presidency.

If this were not enough, structural shifts in American politics during the 1820s further challenged Adams's ability to govern effectively. The administration was under constant attack from an oppositional Congress that became more partisan as Adams's term progressed. This was the first time that a president had assumed office without the majority of the popular vote, and this made Adams more vulnerable to his critics. It also meant that the administration was dealing with overtly hostile majorities in Congress for the first time. In this changed political environment, the president had less ability to control the government if he did not command majorities in the legislative branch. The party system, which had seemingly been in decline for over a decade, suddenly came back with force, and it clearly had negative implications for Adams's ability to control the levers of government.

Another major shift that occurred in the 1820s was the growing importance of slavery as a national political issue. While slavery had taken a backseat to other, more pressing political concerns through 1824, Adams's election as president, the first of a northerner since 1796, fanned southern fears. To southerners, the administration's actions, even actions that seemingly had nothing to do with slavery, were explained by an emancipationist's desire to renew an attack on the expansion of slavery.[153] Thus, administration opponents interpreted the Panama Congress as a desire to end slavery in the Western Hemisphere, and they read Adams's opposition to Indian removal in Georgia as a sign of federal infringement on state sovereignty. They saw the failure to acquire Texas as a ploy to limit the expansion of slaveholding territory, and they took the attempts to halt the international slave trade as part of a plan to atrophy the institution of slavery. And above all else, they viewed Adams's plan for internal improvements as the first step toward empowering the federal government to legislate slavery's abolition.

In public messages and in private correspondence, Adams gave no hint of a desire to abolish or even restrict slavery during his presidency. But southern anxiety saw Adams's desire for moral and national improvement in ominous tones. Jeffersonian Republicans had always been ideologically suspicious of a powerful federal government. During and increasingly after Adams's presidency, that same fear turned its focus onto a government that could employ its power to emancipate its slaves. Years later, reflecting on the failure of his presidency, Adams attributed it to "the Sable Genius of the South" that sensed its "own inevitable downfall" and vindictively destroyed his program of national improvements.[154]

John Quincy Adams's presidency, like his tenure as secretary of state, was marked by an astute understanding of the nation's long-term growth needs and a grand strategy for the nation. Where he failed was in the necessary art of politics. He was unable to utilize political skills and tactics to transform his strategy into policy. Most strategists are not politicians. They dwell, with greater or lesser success, on the possible, but do not have to spend their time translating their visions into concrete actions. Thinking about horticulture, Adams wrote that "the design is fascinating, but the practical execution is beset with difficulties."[155] The same was true of a presidency that was good in theory and challenging in its execution. Overwhelmed by opposition, caught in a political dilemma of his own making, and predisposed against compromise, Adams was clear-sighted in the long-term direction of the country. But his reading of the public mood proved inadequate as he sailed adrift on the tides of history, seemingly forgotten and powerless.

5

A STAIN UPON THE CHARACTER OF THE NATION

The Fight against Slavery

ON THE FRIDAY afternoon Missouri was admitted as a state into the Union, John Quincy Adams took a long walk around Washington with John C. Calhoun. In 1820, Monroe's secretaries of state and war were good friends, shared a robust nationalism, and found themselves in agreement on virtually every major policy matter. But on the critical issue of slavery, they were a world apart. Calhoun took it upon himself to educate Adams about how slavery was viewed in the South. What Adams heard shocked him. It was nothing less than a defense of the institution of slavery as a positive good. Adams told his southern friend that he "could not see things in the same light. It is, in truth, all perverted sentiment—mistaking labor for slavery, and dominion for freedom." Later, reflecting on his conversation with Calhoun, Adams worried that "the impression produced upon my mind by the progress of this discussion is, that the bargain between freedom and slavery contained in the Constitution of the United States is morally and politically vicious, [and] inconsistent with the principles upon which alone our Revolution can be justified."[1] He concluded that the fault lay with the Constitution, "which has sanctioned a dishonorable compromise with slavery."[2]

Despite these strong feelings, Adams remained silent in public. As much as he detested slavery, he worried that it was a fight the country could not afford in 1820. It would be possible only once the nation had grown sufficiently powerful and wealthy to avoid being cannibalized by hostile powers as it took on its internal problems. For the present, he believed it was his duty to stay silent on the issue. He concluded that "no man ought to take an active part in that discussion" who was not prepared to take it to its logical conclusion.[3] Silence and compromise were only temporary solutions. Slavery was *the* issue that the nation would eventually need to confront.

Long before he began his post-presidential congressional career, Adams viewed slavery as a blight on the nation's morals and future development. As a senator in 1804, he had called slavery "an offense against the laws of nature and of God."[4] Later he would deplore the slave trade as "a stain upon the character of the nation which endures it, [and] a disgrace to human nature itself."[5] And during the heated exchanges of the Missouri debates, he concluded that slavery was both morally indefensible and a necessary political evil. In private, he called slavery "the great and foul stain upon the North American Union" and noted that "it is a contemplation worthy of the most exalted soul whether its total abolition is or is not practicable."[6] But in public, Adams was careful about the realistic scope for action.

In fact, Adams spent most of his career avoiding taking a strong stand against slavery. And when he did take a public stand, it was generally in defense of the institution. As the lead American negotiator at Ghent, he argued that slaves were property and demanded that Great Britain pay compensation for those who had run away to join the British cause. During his tenure as secretary of state, when the Missouri debates had thrust slavery onto the national scene, Adams chose to remain silent. And as president, in his inaugural address and after, he took pains to reassure southerners that he would uphold the words of the Constitution—including the three-fifths clause. While this restraint can partially be explained by political expediency, it was also because Adams believed that "much more may be done . . . by conciliating than by exasperating means."[7]

But even in 1820 Adams was preparing for a future fight. "I have hitherto reserved my opinions upon it, as it has been obviously proper for me to do. That time may, and I think will, come when it will be my duty equally clear[ly] to give my opinion, and it is even now proper for me to begin the preparation for that emergency."[8] Adams laid out his thinking about whether or not the total abolition of slavery was practical, how it could be accomplished, and what means could be used to accomplish it at the smallest possible cost.

Adams's thoughts on this subject, which he recorded only in private, not only outline his thinking about the nature of the problem, but also sketch the intellectual and political arguments that he would advance in the future. Adams thought that the abolition of slavery was possible, but believed it would come only through "a reorganization of the Union" that would follow the country's dissolution.[9] And this would not occur before a great amount of blood was spilled. Adams believed emancipation a necessity, but realized that its costs would be catastrophic. In his analysis, the destruction wrought by emancipation was, "like all great religious and political reformations . . . terrible in its means though happy and glorious in its end."

However, before a new nation could be organized around the principle of emancipation, the discrepancy between the Constitution's sanction of slavery and the Declaration's message of equality would have to be resolved. Adams's answer to this contradiction was as simple as it was ingenious. He asserted that slavery was inconsistent with America's principles as they were laid out in the Declaration of Independence. Once that inconsistency was rectified, American history would inexorably march forward toward eventual emancipation. "The seeds of the Declaration of Independence are yet maturing," Adams wrote in 1819. "The harvest will be what West, the painter[,] calls the terrible sublime."[10]

Adams had ignored his qualms about slavery earlier in his career both out of political expedience and because he had placed a greater emphasis on preserving and strengthening the Union. As a diplomat, he worked to insulate America from Europe's quarrels. As secretary of state, he crafted a strategy of continental expansion and hegemony. As president, he attempted to anchor the country's long-term development in infrastructure, education, and commerce. But after his defeat for a second presidential term, he began to question whether the compromises he and the country had made were worth it. Adams had thought that preserving, expanding, and strengthening the Union would vindicate republicanism as the form of government best suited to promote progress and liberty. But as it became increasingly clear that expansion of federal territory and power meant the growth rather than the dilution of the South's political clout, Adams reassessed his and the country's priorities.

He harbored no doubts over the destructive consequences of abolishing slavery and reorganizing the Union. He wrote that "this object is vast in its compass, awful in its prospects, sublime and beautiful in its issue. A life devoted to it would be nobly spent or sacrificed."[11] But up to this point, his priorities had necessarily been preserving, securing, and then developing the nation. Yet the final component of his grand strategy required that the United States be not only powerful, but also moral.[12] To expand the republic, prevent it from territorial encroachment, develop its resources, and advance his own political fortunes, Adams, like the Constitution's framers, had been willing to stay silent about slavery. But ultimately he realized that his and the United States' mission was incomplete if it perpetuated and did not destroy slavery.

After stepping down from the presidency, Adams described the danger of letting ends corrupt means—in verse:

> Ambition, when she seeks a certain end,
> Deceives herself with hypocritic art:
> That end obtain'd, her purposes to bend
> Becomes a means, another end to start.
> Such, of the plumeless biped is the fashion:
> Ambition is a never ending passion.[13]

Previously Adams's personal goals of advancement and his sense of priorities had silenced his moral concerns on slavery. But in the years after 1828 Adams's political aspirations no longer required him to temper his long-held but silent belief about the danger slavery posed to the country. Motivated by feelings of personal and political redemption, moral outrage, and a strong belief that slavery was perverting the national mission, Adams reevaluated his and his country's priorities. In his post-presidential career, he relentlessly searched out strategies that would help resolve the nation's great contradiction.

This shift did not happen immediately. When Adams stepped down from the presidency in 1829, he was determined to retire from politics. After Jackson was sworn in, Adams told Henry Clay, "I should consider my public life as closed," and asserted that "it was my intention to bury myself in complete retirement, as much so as a nun taking the veil."[14] He needed to recover from a bruising presidency, and he was excited to turn his attention to the more leisurely pursuits of reading and writing history. No precedent existed for a president to do anything other than slip into a graceful and taciturn retirement.

Yet having been engaged in public service continuously for nearly forty years, and working at the frenetic pace that high office demanded for the past twelve years, Adams faced an abrupt transition into private life. For years, Adams had lamented his packed schedule, often complaining that "in the continual bustle and unceasing occupation" of elected office, he felt "nothing but the want of time."[15] No longer an active participant in American politics, he had almost overnight transformed into "a silent observer of passing events."[16] Trying to process this, the ex-president noted that all of a sudden "my time is now all leisure, like an instantaneous flat calm in the midst of a hurricane."[17]

If Adams had resigned himself to political oblivion, his one consolation was that his sons would carry on the family tradition of public service. "My hopes, such as are left me," he wrote at the end of his presidency, "are centered upon my children."[18] But in the spring of 1829, tragedy struck the Adamses' household. George Washington Adams, John and Louisa's eldest son, committed suicide on April 30. He had been unraveling over the last several years, harried by his father's admonishments, stung by his failures, and slipping into a deep melancholy. He was in debt to his father, his law practice had failed, and he had impregnated a young chambermaid. Shortly after she gave birth to their illegitimate child, George was summoned to the capital to help his parents prepare for their move back to Quincy. The thought of facing his father was apparently too much for the young man, and he threw himself off a ferry in the middle of Long Island Sound. "In the wandering of his mind he had fallen overboard," Adams wrote.[19]

News of his death debilitated his parents. Louisa ran a dangerously high fever, and John was overwhelmed with grief. According to Louisa, George's death wrung John's heart "almost to madness."[20] Job-like in his anguish, Adams called out, "My God, my God, why hast thou forsaken me?" The combination of being turned out of office and losing a son was almost more than he could bear. Things only got worse for the Adams clan. Both John Quincy's younger brother Thomas Boylston and his middle son, John Adams II, succumbed to the Adams family curse of alcoholism within the next four years. In grief, Adams found solace in his wife. Never an easy person to live with, and often harshly critical of Louisa, John Quincy was now filled with tenderness as he read her soothing passages from the Bible. After many solitary walks and tearful discussions with his wife, he took stock of his life and asked for God's grace and guidance. "Let me bow in submission to thy will," he prayed. "Let me no longer yield to a desponding or distressful spirit. Grant me fortitude, patience, perseverance, and active energy, and let thy will be done!"[21]

Gradually, Adams regained control of his emotions and his life. Ralph Waldo Emerson reported that when John Quincy was asked about how he maintained his health and mental sharpness, he replied that "he owed everything to three rules,—(1) Regularity; (2) Regularity; (3) Regularity."[22] He implemented his old regimen of walking, riding, and swimming, and resumed his reading of the Bible, history books, and poetry. He spent afternoons translating the entirety of Cicero's works. There were more practical projects as well. After moving back into the family house in Quincy, he spent time walking the grounds, planting trees, overseeing housework, and supervising the building of new bookcases. His first summer in retirement he reflected that his public life was ended, and that it "only remains for me to use my endeavors to make the remainder of it useful to my family and my neighbors, if possible."[23]

Adams began to pursue literary projects. He worked on a history of political parties in America, started a long-delayed, and quickly abandoned, biography of his father, and drafted several pieces on international affairs. He wrote articles on contemporary England and on the Russo-Turkish War, which included a withering attack on the Ottoman Empire as a power and Islam as a religion.[24] Perhaps his most interesting literary endeavor was in poetry. In an earlier wistful moment, Adams confessed, "Could I have chosen my own genius and condition, I would have made myself a great poet."[25] With time on his hands now, he took up that endeavor. "History, it hath been said, is Philosophy, teaching by example."[26] So began John Quincy Adams's epic poem *Dermot MacMorrogh*. What started with attempts at rhyme and verse in 1829 quickly grew into a 266-stanza, four-canto poem depicting Henry II's twelfth-century

conquest of Ireland. In the tale, MacMorrogh, driven by his unprincipled ambition to become king of Ireland, violates the sanc-
tity of marriage and betrays his country. But in Adams's telling,
Ireland was merely the setting. America was the subject.

The poem reads like a veiled history of Adams's presidency and a
prophecy about what the loosened morals of Jacksonian democracy portended. Perhaps thinking of himself, Adams described
Roderick O'Conner, the previous king of Ireland, as "ill obeyed,
even within his own territory," and lamented that he "could not
unite the people in any measures, either for the establishment of
order, or for defence against foreigners."[27] Just as Andrew Jackson
was accused of stealing another man's wife, MacMorrogh steals
Prince Ororick's wife, Dovergilda. Regardless of with whom the
reader was meant to draw parallels, the point of the poem was explicitly clear: moral decay presaged and led to national decline.[28]

Disillusioned with the drift of the country and depressed by personal tragedies, the ex-president used the poem to argue that private morality and public virtue were intimately connected and that
moral decline in the home meant disaster for the state.[29] "History
as it should be written and read," Adams declared in the preface to
this poem, "is the school of morals, teaching sometimes by examples, but much more frequently by admonition."[30] Adams had spent
his entire life attempting to restrain his and the nation's baser passions. He thought Jackson, in private affairs and public doings, did
the opposite, whipping up excitement and anger and unleashing
them on the community.

While Adams had repeatedly denied any interest in returning to
public life, he had expressed a desire to find an outlet for his "active
energy" and to be "useful" to his community. Withdrawal into private life was part of the classical ideal of the patriotic statesmen.

But a quiet retirement was not in Adams's nature. While he kept his days full and his mind engaged, Adams found his post-political life in Massachusetts bereft of public engagement and meaningful work. No matter how productive Adams was in his writings and daily activities, a life removed from the center of national power seemed idle and useless. It was at this point that Adams was approached with the idea of running for a seat in Congress. The Boston *Courier* first floated the idea of his possible election to the House on September 6, 1830. Coming as it did from a Jacksonian paper, Adams ignored this idea until the incumbent called on Adams to tell him that he was retiring and feared losing his seat to a Jacksonian Democrat unless the former president contested it. Adams was flattered but did nothing until the National Republican nominating convention and two local newspapers endorsed his candidacy.

In early November he was elected to Congress by an overwhelming margin.[31] Adams was elated, claiming that his "election as president of the United States was not half as gratifying to my inmost soul." His election to Congress was everything that his presidential election had not been, and he noted with more than a little satisfaction that these election results were "a call, unsolicited, unexpected, [and] spontaneous."[32] Accordingly, Adams attributed this victory to his life's service and patriotism. His family was less sure. Aghast that his father would demean himself and the office of the presidency by running for Congress, Charles Francis contemptuously commented that his father lacked "the profound wisdom which gives knowledge its highest luster," noting that "he is not proof against the temporary seductions of popular distinction to resist which is the most solid evidence of greatness."[33] But even if he thought his father unwise and undignified, he recognized that the latter could not sit idle. "Quiet is not his sphere," Charles conceded. "When a legitimate sphere of action does not present itself, it is much to be feared that he will embrace an illegitimate one."[34] And even though Louisa was mortified, she knew her husband well. As she later wrote, he could not "bring his mind to the calm of retirement . . . without risking a total extinction of life."[35]

Vindication for his unceremonious defeat at Jackson's hands, anger at the direction the country was heading, and a desire to move past his private grief through public activity were all contributing factors in his decision to reenter politics. Beyond these motivations, Adams had yet another reason for returning to the political arena. Just before he left Massachusetts for Washington in the winter of 1831, Adams wrote that to be both a good and a great man, one must use one's abilities to pursue ends for the benefit of mankind. Looking back on his career, he conceded that his abilities had been, and still were, "very imperfect."[36] This is a harsh assessment of the actions he had taken to secure, expand, and develop the republican institutions of the country. But he now knew that if the republic were to become a good and great nation, it needed to address the moral question of slavery.

When Adams took his seat in Congress in 1831, he realized that the North and the South were diverging over the national interest—and that divergence was a result of their differing attitudes toward slavery. "The real question now convulsing this Union," he told a fellow congressman, "was, whether a population spread over an immense territory, consisting of one great division all freemen, and another of masters and slaves, could exist permanently together as members of one community or not; that, to go a step further back, the question at issue was slavery."[37] Seated next to a young Alexis de Tocqueville at a dinner party in 1831, Adams was asked to describe the nature of the American national character. He told the French aristocrat that there were only two things he had to know: the Puritans explained the North, and slavery the South. Tocqueville asked Adams if he regarded slavery as an evil. The ex-president replied without hesitation that "it's in slavery that are to be found almost all the embarrassments of the present and the fears of the future." When pressed into assessing whether slavery posed an existential threat to the safety of the Union, Tocqueville noted that "Mr. Adams did not answer, but it was easy to see that on this point he had no more confidence than I in the future."[38]

Adams may not have answered Tocqueville that night, but during his congressional career he advanced the argument that slavery threatened the nation's coherence in four distinct ways.[39] When Calhoun and his supporters advanced nullification as a legal theory, Adams challenged its constitutionality in speeches, publications, and writings. When southern congressmen passed a law intending to silence discussion of slavery, he mounted a sustained effort to repeal this act. As southern expansionists advocated an aggressive foreign policy that would extend their political dominance through the addition of new slaveholding states, he fought against annexations that would increase southern power. And as he watched successive Democratic administrations erode the nation's moral authority, he advanced the standards of abolitionism and emancipation.

Legal threats to the supremacy of the Union had a long history, but none was so damaging as the theory of nullification. The Kentucky and Virginia Resolutions of 1798–1799, composed by Thomas Jefferson and James Madison in response to the Alien and Sedition Acts, had argued that ultimate sovereignty lay in the states and granted the states power to declare void what they deemed unconstitutional federal laws. The Kentucky Resolution asserted that "a nullification, by [the states], of all unauthorized acts done under color of [the Constitution], is the rightful remedy."[40] Such sentiment was not confined to South. Angered by the War of 1812, delegates from the New England states who met at the Hartford Convention discussed seceding from the United States. They issued a report in which they argued that any individual state had both the right and the duty "to interpose its authority" between the federal government and its own inhabitants to protect against what it deemed unconstitutional acts.[41] Exercising this right and duty, Governor Troup of Georgia had refused to recognize the Treaty of Washington in 1826. When the Adams administration threatened federal intervention to impose the terms of the treaty, Troup mobilized the Georgia militia. President Adams, not willing to risk civil war, backed down. The most famous, and the most dangerous, formulation of this theory came from Adams's own vice president. In response to the Tariff of 1828, or the Tariff of Abominations, as southerners referred to it, John C. Calhoun built on earlier nullification sentiments to argue that each state reserved the power of "veto" and the "right of interposition" to arrest federal encroachment.[42]

While southerners had certainly been outraged by the passage of a tariff they believed harmed their economic interests and advantaged those of the middle states and New England, the real source of their concern arose from their belief that a powerful federal government could eventually legislate slavery's abolition. This was certainly true of Calhoun, who wrote that opposition to the tariff was merely the occasion "rather than the real cause of the present unhappy state of things. The truth can no longer be disguised, that the peculiar domestick institution of the Southern States . . . has placed them in regard to taxation and appropriations in opposite relation to the majority of the Union." Because the southern advocates of "the peculiar domestick institution" were in the minority in Congress, they required some "protective power" that could thwart the will of the antislavery majority. Dispossessed of that power, Calhoun worried that they would be forced to either rebel or submit to the emancipation of their slaves.[43]

Adams attacked the theory as historically inaccurate, legally dubious, and politically untenable. In order to explain why it was false, he reviewed the history of the country and asserted that in its war against Great Britain, the people of the thirteen colonies bound themselves in Union before they declared independence. The colonies had bound themselves "to be *One People.*"[44] And it was this one people, by act of their representatives, that dissolved the bonds between London and the United States and declared themselves a new nation. This meant that the people of the collective United States, and not of the individual states, were the source of sovereignty in the new nation. Adams maintained that this was an important legal distinction because it meant that while the states were part of a free and independent nation, it did not mean "that any one of them was a free and independent state, separate from the rest."[45] Unfortunately, the Articles of Confederation got this almost exactly backwards by declaring individual states sovereign. In practice, this made them "uncontrollable" and "unlimited."[46]

Historically speaking, claiming sovereignty for the states, and not the people as a whole, was inaccurate. Adams protested that the individual colonies had never been declared sovereign states and pointed out that "the term sovereign is not even to be found in the Declaration."[47] It was only with the Articles of Confederation that states were granted unlimited sovereignty. Not only inconsistent with the language of the Declaration of Independence, this change proved unsound in practice. Under the Articles, the federal government lacked an independent source of revenue, and vied with the individual states for control of foreign and commercial policy. The Confederation could not defend Americans against Indian depredations, Spanish intrigues, and British provocations. It took the Constitution to bring the country back from the edge of a security and financial disaster. The Constitution accomplished this, Adams argued, by making "the states subordinate to the Constitution."[48]

Adams further posited that there were significant legal implications to such an erroneous reading of American history. He pointed out that sovereignty lay with the people of the entire nation, giving "to the People alone ... the right to institute, to alter, to abolish, and to re-institute government."[49] It followed that the people of the separate states formed only one part of the American people and therefore could neither declare acts of the federal government null and void nor separate themselves from the rest of the country, except by declaring a revolution. To hold otherwise, as Jefferson and Calhoun had in their earlier assertions of state sovereignty, was "an erroneous estimate of the extent of *sovereign power!*"[50] Unilateral secession, according to Adams's interpretation, would be based on a misreading of American law and should therefore be interpreted as insurrection.

But if Adams thought the concept of state sovereignty was legally unsound, he realized that its political implications were both real and acute. It would mean that the federal government's authority would rest on the whims and "temporary passions" of each of its constituent members.[51] When a state agreed with a federal law, it would uphold it and enforce it. But when it disagreed with a law, it could "interpose its authority" between the federal government and the state's inhabitants and declare the law null and void. The principle of majority rule would lose its power to selective enforcement of federal law. In speech after speech, Adams attacked this doctrine as a "pernicious and fatal malignity" that would lead to "a dismemberment of the Union."[52] The doctrine of nullification rendered the Union obsolete. He declared it an "absurdity," albeit a particularly dangerous absurdity, that was "neither more nor less than treason, skulking under the shelter of despotism."[53] Americans would no longer be a united people, but instead would be citizens of separate states with no incentive to collectively deliberate and seek consensus.

Adams detected a political motive behind the legal one. He believed that the South was bent on imposing its minority viewpoint on the rest of the Union and achieving political dominance. Adams thought that the South, fearful that a powerful federal government could tamper with slavery, would continue to threaten nullification and, more drastically, the possibility of secession whenever it felt its interests were at risk. Cowed into submission by an aggravated South, the rest of the country would then be held captive by a violent and vocal minority. Already, Adams noted that South Carolina was "attempting to govern the Union as they govern their slaves, and there are too many indications that, abetted as they are by all the slave-driving interest of the Union, the free portion will cower before them, and truckle to their insolence."[54]

As his congressional career progressed, Adams saw this "slave power" conspiracy as the underlying force in American politics.[55] Writing to a political ally in 1836, Adams held that "State rights and negro Slavery, and agrarian rapacity control the current of our public affairs for the present, and for the indefinite future."[56] The southern stranglehold on American politics had a single purpose: placing "on immoveable foundations the supremacy and perpetuity of the slaveholding power."[57] The southern strategy for increasing their hold on power was threefold. First, they would obtain more slaveholding states in order to increase the sphere, and voting power, of slavery. Next, they would attack the growing power of the free states. Finally, they would fortify the institution of slavery to withstand any attack.[58] Threatened by the demographic and financial growth of the North, the South's ambitions became inextricably bound to "supporting, spreading, and perpetuating the peculiar institution."[59]

Adams believed that the methods used by the South to increase its hold on power endangered the nation's republican spirit and institutions. Adams had long been an outspoken advocate of national expansion, and he had not hesitated to extend the country's borders. What he did object to was enlarging the number of slaveholding states, who would in turn elect advocates of slavery to Congress. Already, Adams thought the advantage accorded to the slaveholding states by the Constitution's three-fifths clause unfair. In 1804, he had written that "such a mode of representation is . . . unjust, inasmuch as it is unequal." It was unjust because it established an inequality of rights between fellow citizens based on whether they lived in slaveholding or free states. According special privileges, which amounted to political advantages, to one part of the country's population at the expense of the other was made more egregious by the fact that southern political clout was rewarded "upon the basis of the greatest outrage on the rights of mankind."[60]

Adams thought that for republican government to function, political power needed to accurately reflect demographic reality. But because of the Constitution's three-fifths clause, this was not the case. Between 1810 and 1840, the population of free states had grown from approximately 4.9 million to over 12.2 million—almost 72 percent of the country's entire population. In contrast, the South's population had barely doubled, growing from 2.3 million to 4.7 million, and falling from 32 to 28 percent of the total share of the nation's white population.[61] However, once the slaves from the South were calculated into the total, the South had nearly equal representation in Congress. The three-fifths clause, coupled with the increase of slaveholding states, ensured that advocates of slavery had a disproportionately large voice in the nation's affairs.

Another way in which the South attempted to direct the national debate in its favor was through its use of an unusual parliamentary procedure. Proslavery forces introduced into Congress a gag rule that automatically tabled all abolitionist petitions, preventing them from being read or discussed.[62] Pointing to the history of slave rebellions and worrying about their "imminent peril," southerners claimed they needed to stifle abolitionists' petitions before they entered into public discourse and incited the slaves to violence. Adams saw this as further evidence that a vocal minority, protecting an immoral practice, could block discussion of issues it found distasteful. When the gag rule passed, he protested it, proclaiming, "I hold the resolution to be a direct violation of the Constitution of the United States, the rules of this House, and the rights of my constituents."[63]

Freedom of speech and the right to petition the government for redress of grievances had been enshrined in the First Amendment to the Constitution. Since the creation of the republic, ordinary citizens had taken advantage of those provisions to address petitions to Congress on various matters. While various manumission societies existed in the late eighteenth century, it was not until the Second Great Awakening stimulated the formation of multiple reform movements that abolitionism became a growing force in American society.[64] In 1835, the American Anti-Slavery Society conducted the nation's first direct-mail campaign and attempted to flood the South with antislavery literature. Fearful of such incendiary material, local and federal postmasters confiscated these mailings. The Anti-Slavery Society responded by redirecting its efforts toward federal petitions. What began as a small trickle of abolitionist petitions grew to a flood by the mid-1830s. By 1836, Congress was receiving upwards of thirty thousand abolitionist petitions a year.[65]

In the slaveholding states' determination to block debate in the House, Adams saw ominous threats. The powers of oppression no longer seemed content to stifle liberty only in their own region. They now were intruding into the domain of those states that had already abolished slavery. If congressmen were not even allowed to discuss issues deemed too sensitive to a vocal minority, how could they ever deliberate about the nation's direction? Additionally, without the ability to debate their differing interests honestly, he worried that the free and slaveholding portions of the country, already in tension, would fall into violence. "Freedom of speech is the only safety valve," Congressman Adams told an audience of his constituents, "which . . . can preserve your political boiler from a fearful and fatal explosion."[66] Adams stated that "the right to petition . . . is essential to the very existence of government."[67] The slave conspiracy's attack on this right endangered the practice and the institutions of a free government.

If he wanted to strike a blow against slavery defenders' use of the gag rule, Adams would need northern public opinion to rally around the cause. However, abolitionist sentiment alone would not be effective in rallying public opinion. While the abolitionist movement had been around for decades, by the 1830s it was still considerably outside the mainstream of northern politics.[68] In 1835, a mob pursued the prominent abolitionist William Lloyd Garrison through the streets of Boston, where he was able to avoid a lynching only by spending the night in a local jail. Abolitionists were still largely seen as a group of agitators bent on destroying the Union. It was hardly surprising, then, that in October 1835 Adams wrote that he "hope[d] to have no concern" with "the Slave and Abolition whirligig."[69] This was not completely ingenuous. Opposed to slavery, Adams decided that framing the struggle as one fought over the preservation of the free states' civil liberties would make for a broader-based appeal than casting it as a fight on behalf of abolitionist principles.

Using his expert command of parliamentary procedure, Adams created opportunities to rail against, ignore, and circumvent the gag rule. In so doing, he also hoped to inflame northern opinion against the influence of slavery on the country and its institutions. Pursuing this fight, Adams showed himself to be a master of public opinion. Throughout his career, Adams often had possessed a political tin ear. He seemed to take almost perverse pride in bucking expectations and standing as his own man. In practice this generally meant he was politically isolated. But after the gag rule was passed, Adams found himself standing in a new position as a champion of a popular cause.[70]

On a tour of the western states in 1843, where he had been asked to dedicate an observatory in Cincinnati, Adams drew huge crowds everywhere he went.[71] He entered Dayton "in triumphal procession" and found "a vast multitude of the people assembled."[72] In

Pittsburgh, he found "mass meetings, at which I find myself held up as a show, where the most fulsome adulation is addressed to me face to face in the presence of thousands,—all this is so adverse to my nature that . . . I am like one coming out of a trance or fainting fit, unconscious of what has been passing around me."[73]

All the while, Adams was careful not to get too far ahead of his supporters on slavery, emancipation, or abolitionism. As abolitionists pressed him to take on slavery, he made sure to keep the fight focused on citizens' basic rights and not abolition itself. Among the hundreds of petitions Adams presented to Congress were many that called for the end of slavery in the nation's capital. In a letter to his constituents, he explained that while he supported the right of ordinary citizens to petition their government, he would not personally support this particular measure. He warned that calls for immediate abolition of slavery in Washington were "utterly impracticable" as "the public opinion throughout the Union is against it." Adams warned that even if it were possible to introduce such a bill, he would vote against it "so long as I know it to be not only unwelcome, but odious, to at least four-fifths of the people throughout the Union." Declaring that "I must be governed by their will and not by my own," Adams warned that moving too fast on abolition would do more harm than good to its cause.[74]

If Adams's efforts to fight the gag rule necessitated waiting for northern sentiment to congeal, he also took steps to push it to catch up with his own thinking. Keeping the gag rule constantly in front of his constituents, Adams argued that it trampled not just his rights but also theirs. Explaining an 1837 vote to censure him in a letter to his congressional district, he asked his supporters "not what freedom of speech is left to your representative in Congress, but what freedom of speech, of the press, and of thought, is left TO

YOU?"[75] In the lengthy House proceedings that followed a call for his censure in February 1837, he told southerners that he would not be frightened, politically or physically, from speaking his mind. Clearly anticipating the publication of his speeches to a wider audience than just Congress, he warned his southern colleagues that "this debate will go forth and be read by the whole people, and that, among other things, they will *mark* this *threat* of the gentleman from South Carolina."[76] And in 1839, he told his constituents, "I have felt indignant at the suppression of my right as a member of the House—of the right of my constituents to use the privilege of freeman, to assemble together and to deliberate on freedom and slavery."[77]

Adams's fight against the gag rule culminated in an extraordinary session of Congress where he put the defenders of slavery on trial. In January 1842 Adams brought forward yet another series of petitions he knew would be particularly incendiary. According to the abolitionist Theodore Weld, "Mr. A had said the day before that he should present some petitions that would set them in a blaze, so I took care to be in the house at the time, and such a scene I never witnessed."[78] The most controversial of these was a Massachusetts petition that called for the peaceful dissolution of the Union because southern institutions drained the resources of the North and offered nothing in return. Adams's southern colleagues accused him of treason and called for his immediate censure. This was just what Adams had hoped for, as it gave him a chance to defend his actions. He took the floor of the House for the better part of two weeks and turned his defense into a wide-ranging attack on slavery and slaveholders.

Adams's "trial" was a political stroke of genius because it allowed him to rally public opinion by making his own cause the cause of liberty. He darkly warned that if the supporters of slavery and their northern allies could censure him, they could take away the fundamental right of habeas corpus and trial by jury for anyone. He claimed that if the friends of slavery in Congress could intimidate him, they could silence the voice of the freedom-loving people of the nation. He said that if he bowed to such pressure, it would permanently make northern interests subservient to the members of the "peculiar institution."

This "trial" cemented the impression that Adams was a champion of the abolitionist movement—even though he never formally joined it. When abolitionist Theodore Weld was invited to dine at the Adamses' home on a Sunday evening, he was amazed to find it "a genuine abolition gathering." Breathlessly, Weld wrote to his wife—the equally famous abolitionist Angelina Grimké, author of the best-selling *An Appeal to the Christian Women of the South*—that Adams "talked with as much energy and zeal as a Methodist at a camp meeting."[79] Adams even attempted to organize a caucus composed of the most radical abolitionists in Congress.[80] He relied on Weld for research and speech drafts and practiced his delivery in front of the delighted abolitionist. Yet while Adams gave every indication of being a fellow traveler to abolitionists, during this period he continued to subordinate attacks against slavery to arguments on behalf of constitutional rights.[81] This was part of his strategy of championing a more broadly popular cause instead of promoting a divisive movement. The more northerners he could convince to break party ranks and join together to flex their political muscles, the more quickly he could attack the outsized political power of the slave states.

Northern response to Adams's censure trial was overwhelming. Petitions and letters in support of him poured into Congress. "The hearts of free men are with you," declared one supporter, while another told Adams, "You have awoke a spirit in the North which I trust will prevent them hereafter from unworthily quailing before the slave dictation." Perhaps most satisfying was one admirer who wrote, "I am no abolitionist yet I cannot consent to be an apologist for slavery."[82] This was exactly the response for which Adams had aimed. When the censure resolution finally came to a vote, it was defeated 106 to 93.

Adams's acquittal marked an enormous symbolic victory over slavery's supporters. Weld wrote that "this is the first victory over the slaveholders *in a body* . . . since the foundation of the *government,* and from this date their downfall *takes its date.*"[83] Antislavery congressman Joshua Giddings claimed, "We have triumphed, the north for once has triumphed. . . . I am confident that the charm of the slavepower *is now broken.*"[84] William Lloyd Garrison agreed, claiming it was "a signal victory for the cause of liberty and its advocates."[85] Even Adams's opponents concurred. Virginia congressman Henry Wise, one of Adams's chief antagonists, concluded that the former president was "the acutest, the astutest, the archest enemy of Southern slavery that ever existed."[86] While it took another session of Congress to repeal the gag rule, it was Adams's constant maneuverings that brought about this political victory.

As damaging as southern political ambitions were to the nation's republican institutions, they posed an even greater threat to its foreign policy.[87] Adams observed that the South, for strategic and political reasons, obsessively pursued an expansionist foreign policy that could lead to the annexation of new territories open to slavery. The annexation of Texas, the provocation of war with Mexico, and the abandonment of Oregon north of the 49th parallel made Adams conclude that the South believed that perpetuating slavery's dominion was more important than expanding the sphere of liberty.[88] Unsure of whether "enlargement of territory and multiplication of States" would "finally terminate in the dissolution of the Union itself," Adams was certain that the country could not absorb more territory without further inflaming sectional tensions, sacrificing republican institutions, and becoming an empire of force.[89]

These issues came to a head in the battles over Texas. In the 1830s and 1840s, Adams fiercely opposed admitting Texas into the Union, worrying that such expansion contained the potential to destroy the nation. Critics claimed that his record on Texas acquisition was inconsistent. They charged that he gave away Texas during negotiations with the Spanish, even though as president he had instructed his secretary of state to purchase Texas from Mexico. But when Jackson subsequently attempted to purchase Texas, Adams attacked his effort, claiming his and Jackson's efforts were not the same because Texas was a different place when he was president. Adams's opponents immediately charged him with political opportunism.

While Adams had changed his stance on Texas, domestic and international circumstances had also changed by the 1830s. Mexico won its independence from Spain in 1821 and inherited the northern territory of present-day Texas, New Mexico, Colorado, Utah, Nevada, Arizona, and California. Mexico had at first welcomed American settlers into Texas, hoping that Texas could serve as a buffer between an acquisitive United States and a young and vulnerable Mexican state. This was not the case. As a result, in 1829 Mexico abolished slavery, partially in order to discourage further American settlement. When several Mexican states revolted against President Santa Anna of Mexico in 1835, Texas joined the rebellion. With money, arms, and men flowing in from the southern American states, independence was won, and the Texans appealed to the United States for recognition—or, better yet, annexation. Jackson realized the sensitivity of the issue and recommended recognition of the Republic of Texas, but not annexation. In August 1837, Jackson's successor, Martin Van Buren, did the same, rejecting Texas's annexation appeal.

The question of whether to annex Texas was again revived following the unexpected death of anti-annexation Whig president William Henry Harrison. John Tyler, formerly a Democrat, succeeded him and promptly abandoned Harrison's agenda. It was in this tense political atmosphere that Virginia congressman Henry Wise, Tyler's champion in the House, gave an incendiary pro-annexation speech, proclaiming that "slavery should pour itself abroad without restraint, and find no limit but the Southern ocean."[90] Such sentiment seemed to confirm all of Adams's fears about the true intentions of those pushing for annexation. But if this was an implicit assumption, it was soon made explicit. In April 1844, Calhoun, recently named Tyler's secretary of state, released a strikingly hostile letter he had sent to the British about American designs on Texas. In the letter, Calhoun attacked London's interference with Texas, denounced British antislavery efforts worldwide, praised the institution of slavery as a positive good, and defended annexation on the grounds that it protected America's vital interest in slavery. Whether this was intended primarily as an attempt to force anti-expansionist southern Whigs to rally around slavery, a play for expansionist-minded northern Democrats' support, or an effort to spark an international event with Great Britain and produce a rally-around-the-flag effect mattered little to Adams.[91] Calhoun's letter was an official state paper, and Adams took it to mean that the policy of the United States under Tyler was now to promote the expansion of slavery.

To Adams, such an expansionist foreign policy brought three distinct problems. First, it meant that the United States would now actively work to extend the reach of slavery. Second, the country would be vulnerable to a number of strategic threats. And third, America's mission would be distorted from one of peace to one of war. Addressing the first of these at a speech in Braintree in 1842, Adams called the United States' actions toward Texas "worthy of Machiavel" and argued that their central purpose was to "fortify, beyond all possibility of reversal, the institution of slavery."[92] Texas had denied its legislature the power of emancipating slaves, forbade slave owners from freeing their slaves without state consent, prevented anyone of African or Indian descent from becoming a citizen of the state, and barred freed blacks from entering the state.[93] Particularly galling was the fact that Texas had reinstituted slavery after it had been abolished. Adams warned that the restoration of slavery where it had previously been banished had ominous implications for the rest of the free states of the Union. The end result would see "the preponderancy of Southern slavery" spread "like a garment of praise over the whole North American Union."[94]

Additionally, Adams believed that an expansionist foreign policy would create new vulnerabilities along the country's periphery while stretching its limited resources. London would perceive American annexation of Texas as "shak[ing] her own whole colonial power on this continent . . . like an earthquake; she will see, too, that it endangers her own abolition of slavery in her own colonies."[95] He suggested that this fear could drive the British to shore up their own empire by moving against Spain in Cuba and Puerto Rico. And the justification London would use for aggression was that it simply was mirroring American actions. Additionally, annexation would necessitate expelling the local Indian tribes from their lands and would likely provoke them into a mass uprising. And creating even more areas with potentially restive slave populations would require a larger internal security apparatus. With an understaffed military, Adams argued, the United States was not prepared to fight an Indian war, a conflict against Great Britain, or a servile rebellion.[96]

When President Tyler eventually annexed Texas in March 1845, Adams bemoaned the added political power it would bestow on proslavery forces in the government, lamenting that this was "the heaviest calamity that ever befell myself and my country."[97] To off-set what he saw as a political calamity, Adams pushed for annexing *all* of Oregon from the British during the Polk administration. This did not happen. Even though Polk had made "Fifty-Four Forty or Fight" a centerpiece of his presidential campaign, once in power he backed away from this promise and sought compromise with a powerful British government. While many members of Congress blamed Polk for precipitating hostilities with Mexico by ordering American forces into disputed territory south of the Rio Grande, the House voted 174–14 in favor of war.[98] In this, Adams saw evidence of Polk's willingness to fight for an enlarged slave realm at the cost of abandoning a free realm.

Adams did not think that southern ambitions for expansion would stop at Texas. He predicted that next would come demands for all of Mexico, the West Indies, the Bahamas, Cuba, Puerto Rico, Jamaica, Haiti, the whole Caribbean archipelago, and California. Slavery was an institution that required expansion for its survival. Adams likened this to the Roman Empire's principle of "perpetual aggrandizement, always adding and never ceding," and concluded that this was "but another form of perpetual war." The creed of American foreign policy was now "preserving, protecting, spreading, and perpetuating the institution of domestic slavery."[99] The violent territorial aggrandizement the United States was now pursuing had transformed the Republic into a "colonizing, slave-tainted monarchy . . . [that] extinguished freedom."[100]

To Adams, this transformation was a moral regression. "Our Country if we have a Country is no longer the same," he lamented to his friend and former treasury secretary Richard Rush six weeks before the Union admitted Texas as its newest state. Comparing the corruption of the present with the seeming virtue of an earlier era, Adams wrote that "the Polar Star of our Foreign Relations at that time was Justice, now it is Conquest. Her vital spirit was then Liberty it is now Slavery."[101]

Adams's predictions were prescient. Several years later, John Calhoun gave a speech in the Senate opposing the free-soil provision in the Oregon Territory bill. In this speech, he claimed that the Declaration of Independence's clause that "all men are created equal" was "the most false and dangerous of all political errors."[102] To Adams, nothing was more deplorable than such pernicious corruption of the nation's founding document. "I know well" those who hold "that the Declaration itself is a farrago of abstractions" that "deserves Lynching."[103] Adams argued that "this philosophy of the South has done more to blacken the character of this country in Europe than all other causes put together. They point to us as a nation of liars and hypocrites, who publish to the world that all men are born free and equal, and then hold a large portion of our own population in bondage."[104] He feared that in the eyes of the world, America now represented only hypocrisy.

Adams worried that the republic was quickly becoming an imperial power no different in behavior than any of the monarchies of the old world. As for the mission of spreading liberty to the rest of the world, Adams believed that Great Britain had supplanted the United States and taken up that banner. This was a role reversal from the American Revolution, when the colonies had waged a war on behalf of universal principles and against empire. Ironically, Adams assessed that Great Britain now carried "emancipation and abolition with her in every fold of her flag; while . . . [our] stars, as they increase in numbers, will be overcast with the murky vapors of oppression, and the only portion of your banners visible to the eye will be the blood-stained stripes of the taskmaster."[105] Adams feared that the annexation of more slave lands would turn the United States into a "conquering and warlike nation" where "aggrandizement will be its passion and its policy. A military government, a large army, a costly navy, distant colonies, and associate islands in every sea will follow in rapid succession."[106] It had been one of the founders' fears that a republic encircled by empires would have no choice but to militarize itself, suppress civil liberties, and aggressively seek colonies that would support its economy and strategic position. Now, to Adams's horror, the United States was completing this transformation on its own.

To Adams, this was an inversion of what America was supposed to do. As successive administrations pursued what he considered a policy "of aggression, of conquest, and of slave making," he expressed more and more anger at his country's course.[107] He saw this change as an "ignominious transformation" and a "degradation from the lofty stand we had taken among the nations of the earth, as the first proclaimers of the inalienable freedom of the human race."[108] Adams identified slavery as the chief cause of that degradation. Even though he had never considered himself an abolitionist, he came to see the only moral response as one that pushed for emancipation.

In the midst of one of his numerous congressional fights over slavery, Adams confided in his diary that "the conflict between the principle of liberty and the fact of slavery is coming gradually to an issue."[109] Unsure of whether the issue would be resolved in peace or in war, he never doubted the outcome of this conflict. But there would be an awesome price paid. Adams believed that redemption must come "though it cost the blood of MILLIONS OF WHITE MEN."[110] Sensing the imminent approach of hostilities, Adams called out to the young men of Boston that their "trial was approaching" and warned them to "burnish your armor, prepare for the conflict."[111] In his response to these threats, he attempted to forge the intellectual and moral armor the free nation would need if it were to prevail.

As early as 1804, Adams asserted that putting slavery on the road to extinction would strengthen the nation. He declared that "the more firmly its foundations are fixed on the foundations of freedom and equal rights the more solid and durable will be the fabric."[112] Yet he knew that slavery was legal and, through at least 1828, he did not think the developing nation was strong enough to withstand such an assault. But Adams knew that this compromise could not and ought not to hold indefinitely. To do this, the nation would have to bring its practice in line with its promise, which would mean taking on slavery.

Adams thought that the only legitimate principles of government were "human rights, responsibility to God, and the consent of the people."[113] Through the 1830s and 1840s, Adams justified his increasingly aggressive stance against slavery on these three principles. He asserted that slavery was inconsistent with America's founding principles as they were laid out in the Declaration of Independence, and held that abolishing slavery was a Christian precept that would bring the country closer to fulfilling its religious mission. Additionally, he argued that slavery was thwarting the necessary progress of the nation and its citizens.

The first justification Adams offered for his actions was historic. He believed that slavery had perverted the country's mission, and he called for a return to the nation's first principles. He asserted that these principles were established in the nation's founding document, which was not the Constitution, but the Declaration of Independence. Adams argued that the Constitution must be interpreted as operating within the Declaration's philosophical and legal framework. This framework then pointed the way toward eventual emancipation and equality before the law. He held that once the principles of the Declaration were understood as the foundations of the American polity, it was clear the direction in which American history would march.

In a famous 1839 speech, Jubilee of the Constitution, delivered to the New York Historical Society on the fiftieth anniversary of George Washington's inauguration, Adams laid out this argument in great detail. The entire thrust of the speech was that the Declaration of Independence framed the Constitution, informed its assumptions, and could ultimately be used as a weapon against those who held otherwise.[114] With such a speech, attended by "many hundreds of people" and later published and distributed throughout the country, he knew his audience was the entire nation.[115] He concluded by reminding this broad audience that "the ark of *your* covenant is the Declaration of Independence."[116] Adams believed that eventually the country must bring its laws and institutions in line with the nation's egalitarian principles.[117]

Adams used this historic justification because it held such a powerful appeal to so many Americans. The Declaration's principles—equality under the law, a government subordinated to the natural rights of man, and the right of the people to challenge governments that do otherwise—would have been familiar to Americans because they came explicitly from the Declaration of Independence. In an open letter to the entire country, released shortly after his Jubilee speech, Adams claimed that to renounce the Declaration's principles as false was to "rob the North American Revolution of all its moral principle, and proclaim it a foul and unnatural rebellion."[118] Adams argued that rejecting America's revolution as a moral movement would be to reject the idea of America itself. Appealing to Americans' near-universal veneration of the founders and reverence for the Declaration of Independence, Adams attempted to transform the Declaration from a historic document that justified the American Revolution into a timeless moral standard against which all governments might be judged.[119]

Such an argument not only pointed the way toward a new polity with changed laws and institutions, but also made the explicit point of appealing to Americans' sense of mission. "The truths of the Declaration of Independence are not limited by time or place," Adams wrote. "They belong to the nature of man in every age and every clime. They may be subdued, but they can never be suppressed. They are truths at Constantinople and Pekin, at London and Paris, at Charleston and at Philadelphia."[120] According to Adams, the United States had done something completely novel in world politics by choosing to lay the foundation of its government "upon the unalterable and eternal principles of human rights."[121] Founding a government on these principles meant that sovereigns and subjects, nations and individuals, were all bound by this same respect for human dignity. In 1823, Adams had written that "the influence of our example has unsettled all the ancient governments of Europe. It will overthrow them all without a single exception."[122] More than fifteen years later, he continued to insist that America's mission was to influence the world by example.

Another aspect of Adams's historical justification was the argument that "the great men of the Revolution were abolitionists," albeit gradual ones. Debating on the floor of Congress, Adams held that this included both Washington, whom Adams called "an abolitionist in the most extensive sense of the term," and Jefferson, who in Adams's rendering was "a high authority . . . for the principles of abolition."[123] He pointed out the inconsistency between slavery and the principles of the American Revolution, and asserted that this discrepancy was lamented "by no one with deeper and more unalterable conviction, than by the author of the Declaration himself."[124] Adams even went so far as to claim that "abolition of slavery and the emancipation of slaves was a darling project of Thomas Jefferson."[125] This was of course not true in a technical sense. While Jefferson declared that he detested slavery's effects on American society, and did outlaw American participation in the international slave trade as president, he was also a slaveholder who did not believe in emancipation. For Adams, the point was not whether Jefferson had been a closeted abolitionist, but rather that the principles and the compelling logic of America's revolution, as embodied and enumerated in the Declaration of Independence Jefferson drafted, led the way toward the end of slavery in the United States. Both ironically and seriously, Adams claimed that Jefferson did "not appear to have been aware that [the Declaration of Independence] also laid open a precipice into which the slave-holding planters of his country sooner or later must fall."[126] He used Jefferson, the most venerated figure of the Democratic Party, to argue that those who supported the institution of slavery were standing on the wrong side of history. For, in Adams's argument, the principles Jefferson so memorably laid out in the Declaration presaged the demise of slavery.

What this meant in practice can best be understood by looking at Adams's role in the 1841 *Amistad* trial. In 1839, American forces had apprehended a group of enslaved Africans aboard the Spanish schooner *Amistad* after it had drifted into American waters. The *Amistad* Africans, who had rebelled against their Spanish captors, sued for their freedom. With the international slave trade already abolished, lower courts found that the Africans had been held illegally and, as a result, were entitled to use force to seek their freedom. The Van Buren administration appealed these decisions. When the case came before the Supreme Court, Adams argued in support of the Africans by applying his Jubilee speech interpretation of American history. As he started his defense, he pointed to the copy of the Declaration of Independence hanging on one of the pillars of the courtroom. Eight and a half hours later, he concluded that "the moment you come, to the Declaration of Independence, that every man has a right to life and liberty, an inalienable right, this case is decided. I ask nothing more in behalf of these unfortunate men, than this Declaration."[127] In Adams's hands, the Declaration was transformed into a weapon that could be used against tyranny and oppression. The court agreed, and the Africans were granted their freedom.

Highlighting the preamble of the Declaration of Independence allowed Adams to claim that the republic's founders believed "slavery, in common with every other mode of oppression, was destined sooner or later to be banished from the earth."[128] With foreign revolutions, Adams had been content to advocate gradual rather than radical or sudden change. However, domestically, he now seemed impatient for change, charging his fellow citizens to "turn to yourselves, and, in the Declaration of Independence of your fathers, read that command to you, by the unremitting exercise of your highest energies, to hasten, yourselves, its consummation!"[129] To Adams, abolishing slavery was not a foreign revolution that indirectly affected the interests of the United States. Rather, it was part of an ongoing domestic transformation that Adams believed would justify or discredit the American Revolution. Additionally, he held that slavery was retarding the moral and physical progress of the country. He thought that the longer this problem remained unaddressed, the more it poisoned the country.

Adams's justification for his efforts did not rest solely on a historical argument. As he explained it, abolishing slavery was also a Christian duty that would bring the country closer to fulfilling its religious mission. In the Declaration's principles, Adams saw a reflection of Christianity's most basic and important beliefs. "*Democracy,* pure democracy," he wrote, "is founded on the natural equality of mankind. It is the corner stone of the Christian religion. It is the first *element* of *all* lawful government upon earth."[130] According to this interpretation, what was unique about America was that it had, for the first time in human history, institutionalized the gospel truth of the equality of man as a government's first principle. Adams believed that America was founded on an appeal to certain human rights that superseded all human law. The United States' morality came not from its actions, but from its realization of Christianity's humane and just principles. What gave the American sense of mission such moral weight was its conversion of these universal rights to political principles.

Slavery, Adams contended, was an "unhallowed outrage upon human rights" and wholly inconsistent with Christianity.[131] He pointed to the example of Elijah P. Lovejoy, the Presbyterian minister, newspaper publisher, and abolitionist who had been murdered by an enraged mob in Illinois in 1837. Eulogizing him, Adams claimed that "Slavery was an institution, politically incompatible with a free Constitution, and religiously incompatible with the laws of God."[132] According to Adams, Christianity itself indicated that slavery must perish. He argued that scripture pointed toward such an end, writing that "whoever faithfully studies the Christian system as a code of religion and morals and exercises in reflection upon it the intellectual faculty bestowed upon him by his Maker, cannot possibly fail of coming to the conclusion that all violence, tyranny, and oppression, all exercise of unjust power by man over man, must ultimately fall before it."[133] He claimed that the abolition of slavery "was the great transcendent earthly object of the mission of the Redeemer" and that "the Declaration of Independence was a leading event in the progress of the gospel dispensation." But if it was a divine mission to exterminate slavery from the face of the earth, it was left to mankind to carry out this mission. He enjoined others to follow his lead, claiming that it was "the duty of every free American to contribute" to the struggle on behalf of America's moral mission.[134]

To these historical and religious arguments, Adams added a final argument based on progress. During his presidency, slave interests had destroyed his program of national improvements. Through his congressional career, he watched those same forces continue to do violence to his vision. Often, Adams despaired of the country's direction. But he attempted to encourage his supporters with the knowledge that history did not always march in a straight line. "The improvements in the condition of mankind upon earth have been achieved from time to time by slow progression," he noted. This progression, though, was "sometimes retarded, by long stationary periods."[135] Though occasionally despondent, and often depressed, Adams continued to push an agenda that he thought would promote the nation's development.

In the past, Adams had had trouble explaining difficult policy choices to the American public. During his congressional career, this was not the case. His arguments resonated clearly and were as straightforward as they were thoughtful. There were many reasons for this. Adams was less concerned with playing the role of national conciliator than he had previously been. He was embittered over his defeat to the undereducated and overly aggressive Jackson. He was bewildered by the meaning of his Job-like personal losses. He was angry at the direction of the country. But unlike during his previous withdrawals into debilitating depressions, Adams now harnessed these sentiments into a righteous rage at those he thought were retarding the nation's progress and betraying its mission. Ralph Waldo Emerson commented on that fury, noting that Adams "chose wisely and according to his constitution, when, on leaving the presidency, he went into Congress. He is no literary old gentleman, but a bruiser, and loves the mêlée. When they talk about his age and venerableness and nearness to the grave, he knows better, he is like one of those old cardinals, who, as quick as he is chosen Pope, throws away his crutches and his crookedness, and is as straight as a boy. He is an old roué who cannot live on slops, but must have sulphuric acid in his tea."[136]

Adams clearly had something to rage against. Slavery was such a vexing problem because it was an institution built into America's fabric, yet it was completely at odds with the nation's aspirations. Adams believed that if America were to become a great power, it needed to revitalize its moral foundation. He understood that attacking slavery could lead to the dissolution of the Union. But increasingly in the 1830s and 1840s, Adams saw this as the unfinished business of the country. "The cause of Union and of improvement will remain," he wrote weeks before his presidential term ended. "And I have duties to it and to my country yet to discharge."[137]

Adams had a clear vision of a nation organized around human progress and liberty. But he understood that until slavery was abolished, that vision would remain just that—a vision. As a congressman, it was beyond his grasp to convert such a vision into reality. Shortly after voting against annexing Texas, Adams expressed his contempt for his gardening skills, grousing that he had no results from all his steadfast toil, care, and anxiety. The seedlings he had planted were not growing and seemed to be withering before his eyes. Adams must have felt the same way about the final stage of his career, with almost all of his legislative pursuits coming up short. But, as a gardener, he should have known that growth is measured in the long term.

While he served as secretary of state and president, Adams's different strategies had been stymied by personal and political shortcomings. His disposition was poorly suited for the compromises that democratic politics demanded, and he had little ability to steer public opinion. But what had been liabilities now became assets. Adams believed that "the conflict between the principle of liberty and the fact of slavery is coming gradually to an issue."[138] Because he thought these two antagonistic forces were ultimately irreconcilable, he refused to compromise with slavery's advocates. Knowing when to compromise and when to fight was the key to Adams's political judgment and political success. Assuming the role of the advocate, of the political bruiser and the old roué, Adams argued that slavery was incompatible with the American system of government. Tempered by a lifetime of political setbacks, he finally knew how to fight. His previous failures taught him that he could not move the nation without first moving public opinion. This time, he was finally successful in his efforts, sometimes waiting for the public to catch up and sometimes pushing it forward.

If Adams felt like he failed, he only failed to see the long-term effects of his efforts. During Adams's congressional career all of his fights, save his prolonged battle against the gag rule, were losing ones. But they were not hopeless ones. Stoically, he realized that "this is a cause upon which I am entering at the last stage of my life and with the certainty that I cannot advance in it far; my career must close, leaving the cause at the threshold."[139] Adams had always relished a good fight, especially one where he had something to resist. The one he joined in the twilight of his career gave him a worthy cause to advance and an evil adversary to battle. "The world, the flesh, and all the devils in hell are arrayed against any man who now in this North American Union shall dare to join the standard of Almighty God to put down the African slave-trade," he wrote. Nearly seventy-four when he wrote these words, Adams was an old man. His stamina and his powers of concentration were slowly beginning to fail him, but he would not rest, and he would not retire. "My conscience presses me on," he concluded. "Let me but die upon the breach."[140]

No longer striving to conciliate antagonistic factions, and freed from the responsibilities and distractions of executive office, Adams waged a series of political skirmishes he knew had little chance of short-term success in an increasingly polarized Congress. Yet as he battled against the entrenched interests of slavery, he recognized that his duty required that he "open the way for others. . . . The cause is good and great."[141] His efforts did just that, providing the arguments that others would advance in the war against slavery.

6

THE INFLUENCE OF
OUR EXAMPLE

The Legacy of John Quincy Adams

FITTINGLY ENOUGH, when the end came it found an eighty-year-old John Quincy Adams sitting diligently at his post. He had suffered a stroke a year and a half earlier, made a partial recovery, and returned to Congress. While weakened, he had by no means retired. That afternoon, the House took a vote on a resolution honoring the general officers who had fought in the Mexican-American War. Adams, having condemned the war, opposed the resolution, and voted with the minority of nays in what one observer deemed an "unusually distinct and emphatic manner."[1] At half past one o'clock, when the Speaker of the House proposed reading the tribute to these soldiers for a third time, Adams rose to oppose the motion. But as he stood, his right hand shot out to grasp his desk, and he began falling across his wooden chair. Ohio congressman David Fischer, who was seated next to Adams, managed to catch the collapsing statesman. Along with several other House members, he lifted Adams onto a sofa. Congressmen and strangers crowded around Adams as the House was adjourned, and the fallen representative was carried into the Speaker's chambers. Someone sent for Adams's family. Recovering temporarily, Adams asked for his old friend and colleague Henry Clay, who upon his arrival took Adams's hand in his own, held it silently, and wept. Peering into the faces of those around him, Adams, though he had much trouble speaking, declared, "This is the end of earth; I am composed." Surrounded by colleagues and Louisa Catherine, he gradually faded into unconsciousness and passed away an hour after sunset on February 23, 1848.

Adams lay in state in the Capitol's Rotunda, and a memorial was held in the House of Representatives. As many as fifteen thousand people thronged the Capitol that Saturday, hoping to get a glimpse of Adams's casket. Inside the House Chamber, however, seating was limited. Mourners, including President Polk, his cabinet, members of Congress, the justices of the Supreme Court, the diplomatic corps, officers of the army and navy, members of the Adams family, and various private citizens, filed into the service. As the assembled took their seats, Adams's silver-laced coffin was carried into the chamber, escorted by the House Committee of Arrangements. Among the escorts walked Illinois congressman Abraham Lincoln, serving his first and only stint in Washington prior to his election to the presidency.[2] The House chaplain rose and read passages from the book of Job and concluded, appropriately enough, with some stern yet loving passages addressed to a young John Quincy Adams by his late mother.[3] As the casket was borne out of Capitol, it passed flags flying at half-mast and buildings covered in black mourning drapery.

As Adams's body moved northward toward its final resting place, and the telegraph rapidly spread news of his death, the funeral procession became a national display of grief and tribute.[4] Thirty congressmen, one representing every state in the Union, accompanied Adams on the train ride north. In Baltimore, military bands played dirges, banners waved, and stores closed as thousands saluted the statesman. When the train stopped in New York, all business was suspended. New Yorkers flocked to the route several hours beforehand, and many more took to the rooftops, hoping to claim a spot from which they could watch the solemn procession pass. As the hearse was drawn through the streets by eight white horses, several thousand people formed a four-mile-long funeral procession that marched to the sound of gun salutes and church bells ringing.[5] Two days later, Adams's remains arrived in Boston on a cold, wet, and windy morning. While the rain had turned the streets to mud, and the procession officially had been called off, hundreds still turned out to pay their respects to Adams. From the train depot, six black horses pulled a funeral car carrying Adams to Faneuil Hall, where a public memorial service was held. On Saturday, March 11, Adams's remains were loaded onto a car hitched to a new locomotive engine appropriately named the *John Quincy Adams,* which traveled the final ten miles to Quincy. As the train reached its final destination, its speed slackened. The casket was borne past the Adams family home and the town hall, and finally stopped at the United First Parish Church. After one more funeral service, Adams's remains were placed next to his parents' in a crypt beneath the sanctuary.[6]

Ironically enough, it was only in the aftermath of his death that John Quincy Adams became, temporarily at least, a figure of unity for the whole country. At the congressional service, pallbearers included some lifelong friends and allies, but also Senator Thomas Hart Benton, who had organized opposition in the Senate during Adams's presidency, Senator John C. Calhoun, who had championed nullification and states' rights, and Chief Justice Roger B. Taney, who would find that blacks, whether slave or free, could not be American citizens in the *Dred Scott* case. In the days following his death, congressmen from every corner of the country rose to praise Adams as the epitome of the selflessness, morality, and wisdom. The Speaker of the House intoned that when Adams spoke, "all ears have been wont to listen with profound reverence," while another congressman declared that Adams "stood out far beyond the rest of us, upon a broader and higher elevation."[7] Brushed aside were Adams's violent attacks on the slave power of the South and the complicity of much of the North, as were the calumnies that many of his colleagues had heaped on his head. Instead, colleagues recounted his long, varied, and distinguished career, and mourned his passing as a national loss. As a South Carolina representative avowed, "When a great man falls, the nation mourns: when a patriarch is removed, the people weep."[8]

The first eulogies at the funeral echoed those given in Congress—full of praise for Adams, and seeking to avoid political controversy. As Adams was nothing if not controversial, that choice resulted in rather bland statements. Edward Everett, the great orator and the speaker who preceded Lincoln at Gettysburg in 1863, served as the funeral orator at Adams's memorial service in Boston's Faneuil Hall. "I come, at your request," he told the dignitaries gathered in the wooden chairs before him, "to strew flowers upon the grave of an illustrious fellow-citizen; not to dig there, with hateful assiduity, for roots of bitterness." For that reason, he informed his listeners, he would strip his narrative of "all the interest which it would derive from espousing present or past controversies."[9] Of course, not everyone found Adams's passing a unifying moment for the nation. Future secretary of state William Seward's widely published eulogy presented a distinctly less whitewashed and more political narrative of Adams's life, which explicitly discussed Adams's antagonism to slavery. Seward was the most prominent of the subsequent speakers who would more accurately capture Adams's positions and explicitly highlight controversies. But for that moment, Adams's death would serve as a symbol of unity.[10]

Respect for a fallen colleague and a wish to avoid arousing political controversy only partially explain the immediate and extraordinary national outpouring of grief and praise. More likely, because Adams's life had been so vast, and touched almost every issue of national significance, with his death an entire era of American history seemed to draw to a close. Congressmen noted this, reflecting that "there was no incident in the birth, the life, the death, of Mr. Adams, not intimately woven with the history of the land" and that there was no other American who had ever filled "so large a space in his country's history, or who has stamped so deeply his impress on her institutions."[11] Newspaper accounts of Adams's life and eulogies spoken as his body returned to his native state solemnly proclaimed that "few men have filled a larger space or acted a more important part in the great civil affairs of their country."[12] As Seward concluded the year after Adams's death, "John Quincy Adams sought not merely to consolidate the Republic, but to perpetuate it."[13]

Seward's assessment is largely correct. Before Adams, the United States had an inchoate grand strategy. Almost all of its leading statesmen believed that the country would one day become a powerful and moral force in the world, but they were not able to define the strategies that would be needed to achieve that vision. Different leaders proposed approaches aimed at accomplishing one or more of the country's goals, but Adams was the first to articulate a grand strategy that integrated the nation's political objectives, set priorities among them, and sequenced them. First, as a diplomat, he strove to isolate America from Europe's wars. Then, as secretary of state, he promoted territorial enlargement and continental dominion. Next, as president, he labored to advance the nation's long-term development in infrastructure, education, and commerce. At the end of his career as an antislavery congressman, he worked to reconcile the nation's founding principles with its actions. These actions were linked to a long-term grand strategy designed to reduce security risks to the United States and vindicate republicanism as the form of government best suited to the promotion of human progress and liberty.

Adams's grand strategy included a clear vision of where the country needed to go and a detailed policy road map for how to get there. But in many instances he lacked the ability to convert that vision into political reality. Philip Hone, a friend and admirer of Adams's, captured this tension, writing that, in many respects, Adams was "the most wonderful man of the age; certainly the greatest in the United States,—perfect in knowledge, but deficient in practical results. As a statesman, he was pure and incorruptible, but too irascible to lead men's judgment."[14] This was most apparent during his presidency. Adams advocated a significantly expanded role for the federal government, but he was unable to obtain the political consensus necessary for such an expansion. Adams believed that there could be a post-partisan model of government, resting on his assumption that opposing forces could forge common ground to benefit all. This did not happen, and instead an increasingly organized opposition consistently attacked his foreign and domestic policies. Adams failed to respond appropriately to the increasingly partisan environment in which he found himself. The result was failure not only of his legislative program, but of his entire progressive agenda.

It was not only his naïve beliefs that were to blame. As a politician, Adams seemed predisposed against compromise and often antagonized those who ought to have been natural allies. He did not suffer fools lightly. He was harsh in his assessment of others. And because he possessed both too much and too little self-confidence, his argumentativeness often became overly aggressive. Responding to criticism from his wife, Adams once agreed, "I am a man of reserved, cold, austere, and forbidding manners...with the knowledge of the actual defect in my character, I have not the pliability to reform it."[15] This was a useful quality for an aloof and disinterested statesman, but less so for a politician whose success depended on his political skills. Stratford Canning described Adams as "more commanding than attractive in personal appearance, much above par in general ability, but having the air of a scholar rather than a statesman, a very uneven temper, a disposition at times well-meaning, a manner somewhat too often domineering, and an ambition causing unsteadiness in his political career."[16]

Although Adams's personal temperament may have been an obstacle in politics, he possessed a strategic outlook, which was grounded in the desire to drive events instead of merely responding to them. Adams sensed two seminal changes taking place in world events in his time. First, he recognized that the days of monarchies and tyrannies were numbered. Adams pointed to the inevitable march of history to explain why. "The influence of our example has unsettled all the ancient governments of Europe," Adams wrote a friend. He continued, "It will overthrow them all without a single exception. I hold this revolution to be as infallible as that the earth will perform a revolution around the sun in a year."[17] Adams sensed that the direction of history was moving away from absolute states, and while he did not know exactly when it would happen, he did not think the United States was powerful enough yet to effect that change.

Second, Adams understood that while a republic was the form of government most conducive to human flourishing, it was not inevitable that it would take hold either at home or abroad. He held that "if . . . self government were possessed in perfection by the whole human race, no other government would be needed or could exist." This was obviously not the case, but the fact that self-government was not perfect did not mean that it was dispensable. "Of all governments on earth," Adams lectured a Providence audience in 1842, "the most important, and perhaps the most difficult, is self government."[18] In the case of the United States, this was especially true. Threatened by foreign powers, the nation also faced an internal challenge. But where Adams remained skeptical of the country's ability to impose change beyond its borders, he believed it had the capability and responsibility to change its domestic institutions and ideology.

It would take a far more skilled politician and a far graver national calamity to realize such a transformation. Building on Adams's foundation, Abraham Lincoln resolved the tension between the country's ideals and its laws by asserting that the country's founding document was the Declaration of Independence and not the Constitution. This argument had been an Adams innovation—and one that he advanced publicly for almost twenty years. Lincoln also advanced Adams's assertion that the only way this could happen was for state sovereignty to be subordinated to the federal government.[19] It bears consideration that the logic of the Emancipation Proclamation was first reasoned by Adams on the floor of Congress in 1836, when he asserted that in wartime Congress could interfere with, and even abolish, the institution of slavery. In a stark threat to slavery's allies, he warned that "by war the slave may emancipate himself."[20]

It was not only in the moral realm that Adams stood as the bridge between the founders' vision and Lincoln's nation. Adams was also the first president to promote the federal government as a vehicle to advance national power through manufacturing and infrastructure. This was originally Hamilton's insight, but prior to the Civil War there was never enough support for sweeping measures of governmental activism. But once war had started and secession had occurred, Republican majorities had a free hand to enact their progressive agenda. Lincoln, like Adams, was committed to improving the social conditions of the country and guiding the nation's development. Where Adams had called for a national system of roads and canals to knit the country together, Lincoln signed the Pacific Railway Act, establishing a transcontinental railroad. Eventually, this would integrate the vast American continent into a national economy, fulfilling Adams's vision.

Lincoln also solidified Adams's conception of a Western Hemisphere marked out as an American sphere of influence, by making the United States a two-ocean power and blocking European encroachment during the Civil War. While the United States of the 1820s lacked a credible deterrent to enforce Adams's strategy for creating a preponderance of power, the significance of the Monroe Doctrine for the course of American history was profound.[21] In-

THE INFLUENCE OF OUR EXAMPLE

voked by presidents from Polk through Kennedy, Adams's Monroe Doctrine shaped the official policy of the country for more than a century. In 1845, President James Polk declared that "it should be distinctly announced to the world as our settled policy, that no future European colony or dominion shall, with our consent, be planted or established on any part of the North American continent." Polk justified his acquisitive actions as simply an effort "to reiterate and reaffirm the principle avowed by Mr. Monroe" in the message that Adams had crafted for him.[22] In 1895, the Cleveland administration announced to the British that "today the United States is practically sovereign on this continent and its fiat is law."[23] And in 1904, Theodore Roosevelt enshrined this idea in doctrine, announcing the country's intention to intervene in the Caribbean where and when it saw fit. His justification for this was "adherence of the United States to the Monroe Doctrine."[24]

George F. Kennan thought that Adams's strategies were applicable well into the twentieth century. Testifying before the Senate Foreign Relations Committee in 1966 on American involvement in Vietnam and quoting Adams's July 4 address, the retired diplomat, strategist, and Pulitzer Prize–winning historian concluded his remarks by telling the senators assembled before him, "I don't know exactly what John Quincy Adams had in mind when he spoke those words. But I think that, without knowing it, he spoke very directly and very pertinently to us here today."[25] Kennan's reverence for Adams was not limited to his noninterventionist principles. As America struggled to define its post–cold war role, Kennan wrote in a 1995 issue of *Foreign Affairs,* "This writer, for one, finds Adams' principle, albeit with certain adjustments to meet our present circumstances and commitments, entirely suitable and indeed greatly needed as a guide for American policy in the coming period."[26]

Adams famously proclaimed that "America goes not abroad, in search of monsters to destroy" in a speech that has been quoted ever since to justify noninterference by the United States in the affairs of other nations. Adams was not warning future presidents away from helping aspiring democrats, but rather cautioning his successors that foreign policy was extraordinarily complex and would require trade-offs. Because his United States was then just a rising power on the world stage, it could ignore or stay neutral on world affairs that did not immediately affect it. Fast-forward almost two centuries, and it is hard to imagine the American president having such a luxury. Adams anticipated the democratic upheavals of the twentieth and twenty-first centuries and provided a guide for how best to balance America's impulse to promote change with its instinct to preserve order.

Adams believed that America's mission was to act as the vanguard of human freedom in the world. He also thought that it could best serve that mission through the inspiration of its example rather than through the assertiveness of its policy. America's influence came from its universal appeal to human dignity. Beyond that, America had set in motion a challenge to the established order, but had little power to impose either the timing or the circumstances. Finally, he believed that America's influence was best preserved by promoting its institutions at home and abstaining from direct interference in other nations' revolutions.

Adams's thinking continues to offer powerful lessons for contemporary situations. Adams argued that embracing American power meant being as conscious of its limits as of its reach. He knew that defining American power as limitless could, paradoxically, limit American power, and he therefore consistently worked to scale back overly broad U.S. commitments. Understanding these concepts is particularly important today, as the country weighs its commitments and force structure around the world. An America that is equally committed to projecting its power everywhere limits its ability to do so effectively and decisively.

Additionally, Adams argued that America should advocate change, but not upheaval. The latter, Adams knew, was every bit as full of peril as it was of promise. He was not shy about promoting American values and offering limited support to those struggling against repressive regimes. He was willing to provide explicit American recognition of efforts to promote more open political systems and assure people everywhere that the United States would support their desire for liberty, prosperity, and a better life. Adams believed that the American model was exceptional, and could offer people everywhere hope for a better future. However, Adams frequently reminded his colleagues and the public that there were dangers in supporting violent or sudden upheaval or change in a country. Instead, he argued for gradual change, so as not to cause unintended consequences. Whether or not gradual change is enough to meet the demands of protesters around the world today is yet to be seen, but this philosophy should resonate as our country considers its strategy for dealing with repressive regimes and uprisings against them.

Adams knew that the true source of American power was domestic peace and productivity. He responded to those who advocated a more activist foreign policy by asserting that America's power was in its example, not in its active ability to rid the world of tyranny. He advocated for improvements in infrastructure, investments in higher education, funding for scientific research, and innovations in manufacturing and agriculture. Adams believed that the best way for America to spread its values would be by working to perfect the American experiment, while simultaneously limiting its involvement with, and interference in, other countries. Adams might have argued today that focusing on rebuilding our infrastructure, improving our public schools, and concentrating on job creation and long-term fiscal solvency would further American power more than foreign intervention ever could.

And what of Adams's efforts to shape a powerful and moral nation? In the early republic, American political theory and domestic politics stressed the division of power through checks and balances. But when it came to foreign policy, there was an inconsistency. At least in the Western Hemisphere, America believed in no checks, no balances, and often no restraint. Instead, America pursued, in a vision laid out by the Constitution's framers and executed by John Quincy Adams, a preponderance of power. The reasons for this were clear enough. If America did not, so the framers argued, North America would end up looking like Europe, which would mean no liberty. Yet this logic raises another question: What explains this contrast between the call for strict limits on domestic politics and the belief that American power should not be checked internationally? Perhaps the thinking was that the United States did not need external checks when it had internal ones, but such an answer is hardly satisfying.

Throughout his career, Adams struggled with this question, worrying over the proper role of morality in statecraft. An extended diary entry in March 1820, written while he was serving as secretary of state, typified these concerns. "A remark that I have occasion frequently to make," he began, "is that <u>moral</u> considerations seldom appear to have much weight in the minds of our statesmen, unless connected with popular feelings." Earlier that day, Monroe's cabinet had been debating whether the United States ought to help arm insurgents in Mexico and Peru fighting against the Spanish Empire. But if the South American revolutions provided the immediate context for Adams's comments, the question of America's struggle with slavery also loomed as the backdrop as the Missouri controversy reached a fever pitch that month. Adams admitted that "the path of virtue is, indeed, not always clear, and in the complication of human affairs artifice and simulation itself must occasionally be practised." Such acts were distasteful but, Adams conceded, useful and sometimes even necessary. This, however, was a slippery slope, enabling ends to justify any, and indeed all, means. Adams attempted to circumscribe the use of such "artifices" and "simulations," limiting them to "essentially belonging to the relations of war" and, even there, ensuring that they were only "very sparingly resorted to."[27] Perhaps this was his attempt to carve out separate spheres of domestic and international norms for the United States. Moral behavior would mean one thing inside the United States, but another thing in the international realm. Or perhaps this explanation justified the public actions he had taken on behalf of the country at the expense of the dictates of his personal conscience. Balancing the multiple and often contradictory national impulses left Adams frustrated. In this he was not alone. Adams's belief that it was the unique duty of the American statesman to guide his nation to power while keeping it on a course toward justice presented him with as much of a challenge as it would his successors.

How, then, to evaluate Adams and his strategic vision? The answer of course depends on whether intent or impact is used as a measurement of success. In conception, in comprehensiveness, and in its recalibration of the nation's shifting interests and its most pressing threats, the intellectual underpinnings of Adams's grand strategy were sound. But this vision was not without flaws, as its very successes created daunting challenges. Moreover, if Adams excelled in articulating what was in the nation's interests, he had more trouble translating his vision into policy. But even brilliant strategic minds cannot always rise above their times. It would take an enormously bloody civil war before a much more nimble politician would be able to institutionalize such a vision in concrete policy terms.

If the measure of a grand strategy is the fulfillment of its long-term vision, then its realization depends on its adaptability and transferability. And that requires understanding not only general truths, but also unique circumstances. During his presidency, Adams developed an avid interest in gardening and wrote an essay on tree cultivation, which could just as easily be read as an essay on grand strategy. He noted that the general principles of growing trees were "applicable to all times and to every country." But he also observed that "judgment must be used in adapting the trees to the soils in which they were to grow."[28] As both a theorist and a practitioner of grand strategy in early America, John Quincy Adams developed a vision that tailored universal ideas to the unique experiment that was the early republic.

John Quincy Adams did not live to see the fulfillment of his strategy. This caused him no end of frustration, and left him despondent about his and his nation's future. Often, it seemed that his vision had been rejected and his country's promise thwarted. But in quiet moments, Adams elevated his gaze beyond the present. Writing in his diary at a moment of disappointment, Adams recalled that the classical philosophers he had read as a boy instructed their readers to plant for the future, even if they would not see the fruits of their labor. As it was with the cultivator of the earth, so too with the statesman. "I have had my share in planting laws and institutions according to the measure of my ability and opportunities," Adams reflected, candidly admitting, "I would willingly have had more." As a congressman nearing the end of his life, Adams knew that it was now beyond his abilities to resolve the paradoxes of power and liberty, and of expansion and slavery. "My leisure is now imposed upon me by the will of higher powers, to which I cheerfully submit," he wrote, "and I plant trees for the benefit of the next age, and of which my own eyes will never behold a berry."[29]

NOTES

ABBREVIATIONS

AA   Abigail Adams

AA2   Abigail "Nabby" Adams

AFC   *Adams Family Correspondence*

ASPFR   *American State Papers, Foreign Relations* (Washington, D.C.:
            Gales and Seaton, 1832–1859)

ASPMA   *American State Papers, Military Affairs*

CA   Charles Adams

CFA   Charles Francis Adams

JA   John Adams

JQA   John Quincy Adams

JQA,   John Quincy Adams, *Writings of John Quincy Adams,* ed.
Writings Worthington C. Ford, 7 vols. (New York: Macmillan, 1913–1917)

LCA   Louisa Catherine Adams

LNET   John Quincy Adams, *Life in a New England Town*

MHS   Massachusetts Historical Society

MHS   C. James Taylor, ed., *Founding Families: Digital Editions of the*
[digital   *Papers of the Winthrops and the Adamses*
edition]

INTRODUCTION

1   John Quincy Adams (JQA), Diary 30, April 1, 1816, 44; Diary 30,
April 28, 1817, 177, in John Quincy Adams, *The Diaries of John Quincy*

Adams: A Digital Collection (Boston: Massachusetts Historical Society, 2005), http://www.masshist.org/jqadiaries. All subsequent citations to John Quincy Adams's *Diaries* will appear in the form JQA, Diary 30, April 1, 1816, 44 [electronic edition].

2 John Quincy Adams (JQA) to John Adams (JA), May 29, 1816, in Worthington C. Ford, ed., *Writings of John Quincy Adams,* 7 vols. (New York: Macmillan, 1913–1917), 6:38. All subsequent citations to John Quincy Adams's *Writings* will appear in the form JQA, *Writings,* 6:38.

3 JQA to JA, August 1, 1816, in JQA, *Writings,* 6:58ff.

4 JQA, Diary 30, July 19, 1816, 37 [electronic edition].

5 For a full description of the eruption and its atmospheric as well as social impact, see William and Nicholas Klingaman, *The Year without Summer: 1816 and the Volcano That Darkened the World and Changed History* (New York: St. Martin's Press, 2013).

6 JQA to Abigail Adams (AA), September 20, 1816, in JQA, *Writings,* 6:89.

7 This was based on the American naval Commodore Stephen Decatur's famous toast: "Our Country! In her intercourse with foreign nations may she always be in the right, but our country, right or wrong."

8 JQA to JA, May 29, 1816, in JQA, *Writings,* 6:38.

9 JQA, Diary 30, August 8, 1816, 48 [electronic edition].

10 JQA, Diary 31, February 10, 1819, 31 [electronic edition].

11 JQA to JA, January 3, 1817, in JQA, *Writings,* 6:131.

12 Today this sentiment is often described as "American exceptionalism." Exceptionalism is a twentieth-century term and a politically loaded one at that. Originally, it was meant to connote American separation from the rest of the world and the nation's development of a historically unique polity. Woven in with this meaning was a belief that the United States had a distinct and special providence to change the world. Such an interpretation obviously privileged the good over the darker side of American history, and critics have pointed to the parallels between American history and that of other great imperial

powers. As the term has multiple meanings, its use has become intertwined with the concepts of patriotism and jingoism. For more, see Louis Hartz, *The Liberal Tradition in America: An Interpretation of American Political Thought since the Revolution* (1955; repr., Orlando: Harcourt, 1991); Seymour Martin Lipset, *American Exceptionalism: A Double-Edged Sword* (New York: W. W. Norton, 1996); and "American Exceptionalism: Is It Real, Is It Good?," *American Political Thought* 1, no. 1 (Spring 2012): 3-128.

13 JQA, Diary 46, October 31, 1846, 83 [electronic edition].

14 Any works on John Quincy Adams must begin with Samuel Flagg Bemis's two-volume Pulitzer Prize-winning *John Quincy Adams and the Foundations of American Foreign Policy* (New York: Knopf, 1949) and *John Quincy Adams and the Union* (New York: Knopf, 1956). There are, of course, earlier biographies of John Quincy Adams, though for the most part they are uncritical hagiographies. See William H. Seward, *Life and Public Services of John Quincy Adams, Sixth President of the United States: With the Eulogy Delivered before the Legislature of New York* (Auburn, N.Y.: Derby, Miller, 1849); Josiah Quincy, *Memoir of the Life of John Quincy Adams* (Boston: Phillips, Sampson, 1858); John T. Morse Jr., *John Quincy Adams* (Boston: Houghton Mifflin, 1882); and Bennett Champ Clark, *John Quincy Adams, Old Man Eloquent* (Boston: Little, Brown, 1932). There have been several more recent, and more critical, biographies of Adams, including Marie B. Hecht, *John Quincy Adams: A Personal History of an Independent Man* (New York: Macmillan, 1972); Paul Nagel, *John Quincy Adams: A Public Life, a Private Life* (Cambridge, Mass.: Harvard University Press, 1997); Lynn H. Parsons, *John Quincy Adams* (Oxford: Rowman and Littlefield, 2001); James E. Lewis Jr., *John Quincy Adams: Policymaker for the Union* (Wilmington, Del.: SR Books, 2001); Robert Remini, *John Quincy Adams* (New York: Henry Holt, 2002); and most recently Harlow Giles Unger, *John Quincy Adams* (Boston: Da Capo Press, 2012). Finally, there are a number of other studies that deal with particular aspects of Adams's career—chief among them William Earl Weeks, *John Quincy Adams and American Global Empire* (Lexington: University Press of

Kentucky, 1992); Mary W. M Hargreaves, *The Presidency of John Quincy Adams* (Lawrence: University Press of Kansas, 1985); Leonard L. Richard, *The Life and Times of Congressman John Quincy Adams* (Oxford: Oxford University Press, 1986); and Joseph Wheelan, *Mr. Adams's Last Crusade* (New York: Public Affairs, 2009). In sum, there are a host of good biographies, but none of them argue for consistency, purpose, or a comprehensive strategy in Adams's various endeavors. For a comprehensive bibliography, see Lynn H. Parsons, *John Quincy Adams: A Bibliography* (Westport, Conn.: Greenwood Press, 1993), and David Waldstreicher, ed., *A Companion to John Adams and John Quincy Adams* (Hoboken: John Wiley and Sons, 2013). Particularly useful on the changing historiography of Adams's biography is Waldstreicher's lead essay in *A Companion,* "John Quincy Adams: Life, Diary, Biographers," 241-262. For broader works on the rise of the United States in the nineteenth century that emphasize Adams's role in American foreign policy, see John Lewis Gaddis, *Surprise, Security and the American Experience* (Cambridge: Harvard University Press, 2004); Richard Immerman, *Empire for Liberty* (Princeton: Princeton University Press, 2010); Walter McDougall, *Promised Land, Crusader State* Boston: Houghton Mifflin Company, 1998); Walter Russell Mead, *Special Providence* (New York: Knopf, 2003); and Robert Kagan, *Dangerous Nation: America's Place in the World from Its Earliest Days to the Dawn of the Twentieth Century* (New York: Knopf, 2006).

15 John Lewis Gaddis, "What Is Grand Strategy?," Karl Von Der Heyden Distinguished Lecture, Duke University, February 26, 2009, http://www.duke.edu/web/agsp/grandstrategypaper.pdf.

16 The classical definition of strategy and its relationship to tactics comes from Carl von Clausewitz, *On War,* trans. and ed. Michael Howard and Peter Paret (Princeton: Princeton University Press, 1976). The other great classical theorists of military strategy—Sun Tzu, Machiavelli, Jomini, and Mao Tse-tung—are treated in Michael I. Handel, *Masters of War: Classical Strategic Thought,* 3rd ed. (London: Routledge, 2001). For the nonmilitary or partially military realms,

a more useful definition of grand strategy can be found in Edward
Mead Earle, ed., *Makers of Modern Strategy* (Princeton: Princeton
University Press, 1943). In his introduction to this wartime collection of
essays, Earle defined grand strategy as "the art of controlling and
utilizing the resources of a nation" to either render war unnecessary or
most likely to produce victory (p. viii). Sir Basil Liddell Hart, in *Strategy*
(New York: Faber and Faber, 1967), further broadened the definition of
grand strategy to encompass the calculated relationship of means to
ends meaning it was about not only the effective, but also the efficient
use of one's means. He also argued that grand strategy applied not just
to the military resources of a nation, but to all of the instruments at a
nation's disposal. A succinct description of the evolving definition of
grand strategy is Paul Kennedy's "Grand Strategy in War and Peace:
Toward a Broader Definition," in Paul Kennedy, ed., *Grand Strategies in
War and Peace* (New Haven: Yale University Press, 1991), 1–7. Kennedy
concludes that "given all the independent variables that come into play,
grand strategy can never be exact or fore-ordained. It relies, rather,
upon the constant and intelligent reassessment of the polity's ends and
means" (p. 6). In the realm of statecraft, see Charles Hill, *Grand
Strategies: Literature, Statecraft, and World Order* (New Haven: Yale
University Press, 2010), and, more recently, Hal Brands, *What Good Is
Grand Strategy? Power and Purpose in American Statecraft from Harry S.
Truman to George W. Bush* (Ithaca, N.Y.: Cornell University Press, 2014).

17 Useful historical works dealing with the grand strategy of
statecraft include Paul Kennedy, *The Rise and Fall of the Great Powers:
Economic Change and Military Conflict from 1500 to 2000* (New York:
Vintage Books, 1987); Ludwig Dehio, *The Precarious Balance: Four
Centuries of the European Power Struggle,* trans. Charles Fullman (New
York: Knopf, 1962); Henry Kissinger, *Diplomacy* (New York: Simon and
Schuster, 1994); Gordon A. Craig and Alexander L. George, *Force and
Statecraft: Diplomatic Problems of Our Time,* 3rd ed. (New York: Oxford
University Press, 1995); Williamson Murray, MacGregor Knox, and
Alvin Bernstein, eds., *The Making of Strategy: Rulers, States, and War*

(New York: Cambridge University Press, 1994); and Williamson Murray, Richard Hart Sinnreich, and James Lacey, eds., *The Shaping of Grand Strategy: Policy, Diplomacy, and War* (New York: Cambridge University Press, 2011).

18 The best guide to the art of grand strategy is Winston Churchill, *Painting as Pastime* (London: Odhams Press, 1948). For an excellent example of an individual's grand strategy in practice, see Geoffrey Parker, *The Grand Strategy of Philip II* (New Haven: Yale University Press, 2000). Parker's work, while paying attention to structural and bureaucratic factors, examines Philip's motivations and execution as a way to evaluate his, and Hapsburg Spain's, strategy. Parker uses Philip as a vessel to explore the issues and literature of strategy, leadership, decision making, and organization theory.

19 The John Quincy Adams papers in the Massachusetts Historical Society (MHS) consist of approximately 140 roles of microfilm. The MHS is gradually publishing Adams's private correspondence, but it is thus far incomplete. It is being published in two different forms. First, there is the *Adams Family Correspondence*. As of 2013, eleven volumes had been published, tracking the Adams family from 1761 to 1797. These volumes include many letters from, to, and about John Quincy. Additionally, there is John Quincy's diary, started at the age of twelve. Currently, Harvard University Press has published the first two volumes, which cover the years 1779–1788. There are also two earlier published compilations. Charles Francis Adams, John Quincy's son, compiled and published the twelve-volume *Memoirs of John Quincy Adams: Comprising Portions of His Diary from 1795 to 1848* between 1874 and 1877. Between 1913 and 1917, Worthington Chauncey Ford edited a seven-volume *Writings of John Quincy Adams,* which contains much of his correspondence and some of his personal memoranda. While both of these are good, they are incomplete, and often incomplete in particularly interesting ways—Charles Francis left most of his father's political opinions uncensored but removed most signs of emotional turmoil. The Ford edition only runs through 1823.

20 During his tenure as secretary of state, Adams drafted all official correspondence emanating from the State Department. Much of this can be found in the *American State Papers, Foreign Relations* (hereafter *ASPFR*) (Washington, D.C.: Gales and Seaton, 1832–1859). The official documentary record of major U.S. foreign policy decisions begins in 1861. Prior to that there was a somewhat haphazard record-keeping process. The most important documents and decisions were compiled in the *American State Papers,* but often these were not collected until years after the events and are fragmentary in nature. Many of the most important documents remain in the personal papers of the individuals involved.

21 JQA, Diary 37, December 8, 1825, 26 [electronic edition].

22 For more on the export of the American model, to good effect and otherwise, see Jeremi Suri, *Liberty's Surest Guardian: American Nation-Building from the Founders to Obama* (New York: Free Press, 2011); Tony Smith, *America's Mission: The United States and the Worldwide Struggle for Democracy in the Twentieth Century* (Princeton: Princeton University Press, 1994); and Odd Arne Westad, *The Global Cold War: Third World Interventions and the Making of Our Times* (Cambridge: Cambridge University Press, 2005).

CHAPTER 1 *The Fires of Honorable Ambition*

1 JQA to JA, May 18, 1785, quoted in Richard Alan Ryerson, ed., *Adams Family Correspondence,* vol. 6, *December 1784–December 1785* (Cambridge, Mass.: Harvard University Press, 1993), 153. All subsequent citations to *Adams Family Correspondence* will appear in the form *AFC,* 6:153.

2 JA to AA, July 26, 1784, in *AFC,* 5:399.

3 JQA to William Cranch, December 14, 1784, quoted in C. James Taylor, ed., *Founding Families: Digital Editions of the Papers of the Winthrops and the Adamses* (Boston: Massachusetts Historical Society, 2007),

http://www.masshist.org/ff. Letter available at http://www.masshist
.org/publications/apde/portia.php?id=AFC06d010. Subsequent
citations to the Massachusetts Historical Society's online archive
appear in the form JQA to William Cranch, December 14, 1784, Doc.
no. AFC05d124, MHS [Digital Edition].

4 JQA to Skelton Jones, April 17, 1809, in JQA, *Writings*, 3:298.

5 Henry Adams, *The Education of Henry Adams* (1918; repr., New York:
Modern Library, 1931), 6.

6 Mary Smith Cranch to AA, August 27, 1785, in *AFC,* 6:268ff.

7 Mary Smith Cranch to AA, September 14, 1785, in *AFC,* 6:273.

8 JQA to JA, June 2, 1777, in *AFC,* 2:254.

9 John Quincy Adams, "Ambition for a Young Man," Phi Beta
Kappa lecture, September 5, 1788. A copy of the speech is recorded in
Adams's diary. JQA, Diary 12, September 5, 1788, 219ff. [electronic
edition].

10 For useful blends of philosophy and practicality, see Jeremi Suri,
Henry Kissinger and the American Century (Cambridge, Mass.: Harvard
University Press, 2007), and Gerald Stourzh, *Benjamin Franklin and
American Foreign Policy* (Chicago: University of Chicago Press, 1954).

11 To avoid confusing Adamses, particularly John and John Quincy
Adams, this first chapter refers to the elder Adams as John and to the
younger Adams, for the most part, as John Quincy. In subsequent
chapters, John Quincy Adams is the principal character and will be
referred to, for the most part, as Adams.

12 JA to JQA, April 23, 1794, in *AFC,* 10:151.

13 AA to JQA, June 10, 1778, in *AFC,* 3:37. As for the impact of such
words, see Robert A. East, *John Quincy Adams: The Critical Years* (New
York: Bookman Associates, 1962); David F. Musto, "The Youth of John
Quincy Adams," *American Philosophical Society Proceedings* 113 (1969):
269–282; and Edith B. Gelles, "The Abigail Industry," *William and Mary
Quarterly,* 3rd ser., 45 (October 1988): 656–683. As for John Quincy's
lifelong struggle with depression, a most useful explanation of both
cause and effects can be found in Joshua Wolf Shenk's excellent

Lincoln's Melancholy: How Depression Challenged a President and Fueled His Greatness (Boston: Houghton Mifflin, 2005).

14 David Hackett Fischer, *Albion's Seed: Four British Folkways in America* (New York: Oxford University Press, 1989), 98ff.

15 The Adams family creed remained strong down through the generations. Writing in the third person, Henry Adams recalled being shocked to find out "that there should be a doubt of his being President" (*The Education of Henry Adams,* 16). For more on the transmission of the Adams family creed, see Nagel, *Descent from Glory,* and Richard Brookhiser, *America's First Dynasty: The Adamses, 1735–1918* (New York: Free Press, 2002).

16 JQA to Charles Adams (CA), June 6, 1778, in *AFC,* 3:34.

17 Among the very many good books that document John and Abigail's marriage, see Margaret A. Hogan and C. James Taylor, eds., *My Dearest Friend: Letters of Abigail and John Adams* (Cambridge, Mass.: Harvard University Press, 2010), and Edith Gelles, *Abigail and John: Portrait of a Marriage* (New York: HarperCollins, 2009). There are numerous excellent biographies of both John and Abigail. For overviews, see R. B. Bernstein's essay "John Adams: The Life and the Biographers," 5–35, and Margaret A. Hogan's "Abigail Adams: The Life and the Biographers," 218–238, in David Waldstreicher, ed., *A Companion to John Adams and John Quincy Adams* (Hoboken: John Wiley and Sons, 2013). On John, it would be hard not to recommend David McCullough, *John Adams* (New York: Simon and Schuster, 2001), and Joseph J. Ellis, *Passionate Sage: The Character and Legacy of John Adams* (New York: W. W. Norton, 1993). For more on Abigail, see Woody Holton's excellent *Abigail Adams: A Life* (New York: Free Press, 2009).

18 JA to Robert Livingston, February 5, 1783, in Charles Francis Adams, ed., *The Works of John Adams, Second President of the United States: With a Life of the Author, Notes and Illustrations, by His Grandson Charles Francis Adams* (Boston: Little, Brown, 1853), 8:38.

19 JQA, Letter IV, in John Quincy Adams, *Letters of John Quincy Adams, to His Son, on the Bible and Its Teachings,* ed. Charles Francis

Adams (Auburn, N.Y.: Derby, Miller, 1848), 441. (Hereafter cited as *Letters . . . on the Bible.*)

20 The first and the third quotations come from JQA's article "Misconceptions of Shakespeare, upon the Stage," *New England Magazine* (December 9, 1835): 435-440; the second is from Adams's letter of February 7, 1839, to the actor James Hackett. The letter was subsequently reprinted in the *National Intelligencer* (Washington), November 30, 1839.

21 Both of these quotations come from Henry Steele Commager's thoughtful essay "Leadership in Eighteenth-Century America and Today," *Daedalus* 90 (Fall 1961): 666. In this essay, Commager compares eighteenth-century American leaders to his contemporaries and discusses the factors that produced such extraordinary leaders.

22 This practicality had its roots in the European Enlightenment of the eighteenth century. A terrific overview of the distinct nature of the French, English (to include the Scottish), and American Enlightenments can be found in Gertrude Himmelfarb, *The Roads to Modernity: The British, French, and American Enlightenments* (New York: Vintage, 2004). See also Henry Steele Commager, *The Empire of Reason: How Europe Imagined and American Realized the Enlightenment* (Garden City, N.Y.: Doubleday, 1977), and Henry May, *The Enlightenment in America* (Oxford: Oxford University Press, 1976). For a more specific take on John Adams and the Enlightenment, see Zoltan Haraszti, *John Adams and the Prophets of Progress* (Cambridge, Mass.: Harvard University Press, 1952), and, more recently, Darren Staloff's essay "John Adams and Enlightenment," in Waldstreicher, *A Companion to John Adams and John Quincy*, 36-59.

23 John Adams, Diary, January 3, 1759, http://masshist.org/publications/apde/portia.php?&id=DJA01d216. Also quoted in H. Trevor Colbourn, *The Lamp of Experience: Whig History and the Intellectual Origins of the American Revolution* (Chapel Hill: University of North Carolina Press, 1965), 84.

24 John Adams, *Defence of the Constitutions of Government of the United States of America*, in Charles Francis Adams, *The Works of John Adams*, 6:218. Unfortunately for Adams, his scientific conclusions were decidedly out of step with his contemporaries. See Gordon Wood's excellent chapter, "The Relevance and Irrelevance of John Adams," in his sweeping *Creation of the American Republic, 1776–1787* (Chapel Hill: University of North Carolina Press, 1969).

25 JA to JQA, August 11, 1777, in *AFC*, 2:307.

26 Thucydides, *The Landmark Thucydides: A Comprehensive Guide to "The Peloponnesian War,"* ed. Robert B. Strassler (New York: Simon and Schuster, 1996), I.22.

27 For more on Thucydides and his view on the didactic nature of his work, see Donald Kagan's insightful *Thucydides: The Reinvention of History* (New York: Viking, 2009).

28 JA to AA, August 20, 1777, in *AFC*, 2:321.

29 Thucydides, I.76.

30 JA to JQA, August 11, 1777, in *AFC*, 2:307. For more on Thucydides's *Peloponnesian War* as a manual for statecraft, see Charles Hill, *Grand Strategies: Literature, Statecraft, and World Order* (New Haven: Yale University Press, 2010), 20–24.

31 JQA, Diary 24, April 3, 1795, 24 [electronic edition]. For more on the uses and dangers of history in policy making, see Colbourn, *The Lamp of Experience*, and Ernest May, *"Lessons" of the Past: The Use and Misuse of History in American Foreign Policy* (London: Oxford University Press, 1973).

32 JA to AA, August 28, 1774, in *AFC*, 1:145.

33 AA to Abigail "Nabby" Adams (AA2), February 21, 1791, in *AFC*, 9:193.

34 JA to JQA, April 28, 1782, in Adams, *Writings*, 4:317.

35 JQA to George Washington Adams, Letter I, in *Letters . . . on the Bible*, 9.

36 JQA, Letter II, in *Letters . . . on the Bible*, 22.

37 JQA, Letter VIII, in *Letters . . . on the Bible*, 108.

38 AA to JQA, March 20, 1780, in *AFC,* 3:312.

39 JQA, Letter VI, in *Letters . . . on the Bible,* 84.

40 JA to JQA, May 17, 1781, in *AFC,* 4:117.

41 JA to AA, October 29, 1775, in *AFC,* 1:316ff.

42 JA to AA, April 15, 1776, in *AFC,* 1:384.

43 AA to JA, May 7, 1776, in *AFC,* 1:402.

44 AA2 to JQA, September 28, 1788, in *AFC,* 8:299.

45 JA to JQA, April 26, 1795, in JQA, *Writings,* 1:408.

46 JA to JQA, April 18, 1776, in *AFC,* 1:388.

47 The definition of republicanism was broad and contested in the late eighteenth and early nineteenth centuries and was probably better encapsulated as a set of beliefs. None captured the term's ambiguity better than John Adams, who in 1807 proclaimed that "there is not a more unintelligible word in the English language than republicanism." The literature on republicanism is enormous, but the best overview is Daniel T. Rodgers's essay "Republicanism: The Career of a Concept," *Journal of American History* 79 (June 1992): 11-38. A short list of the most important books in the field that deal with republicanism as a form of government and ideology includes Bernard Bailyn, *The Ideological Origins of the American Revolution* (Cambridge, Mass.: Harvard University Press, 1967); Wood, *The Creation of the American Republic, 1776–1787;* J. G. A. Pocock, *The Machiavellian Moment: Florentine Political Thought and the Atlantic Republican Tradition* (Princeton: Princeton University Press, 1975); Joyce Appleby, *Liberalism and Republicanism in the Historical Imagination* (Cambridge, Mass.: Harvard University Press, 1992); and Drew R. McCoy, *The Elusive Republic: Political Economy in Jeffersonian America* (Chapel Hill: University of North Carolina Press, 1980). For an overview on the role republican thought played in early American education, see Siobhan Moroney, "The Historiography of Early Republican Educational Thought," *History of Education Quarterly* 39, no. 4 (Winter 1999): 476-491.

48 AA to JA, August 19, 1774, in *AFC,* 1:142ff.

49 While it is known that John Adams owned a copy of *Roman History* which he kept in his library, it is unclear whether he owned Rollin's *Ancient History* during the 1770s. See Appendix II, "History in Eighteenth-Century American Libraries," in Colbourn, *The Lamp of Experience*, 212n3.

50 See William Gribbin's useful "Rollin's Histories and American Republicanism," *William and Mary Quarterly*, 3rd ser., 29, no. 4 (October 1972): 611–622. Gribbin concludes that reading Rollin, as so many of America's founding fathers did, helped form—or perhaps reconfirm—their republican worldview.

51 AA to JA, September 21, 1777, in *AFC*, 2:347ff.

52 JQA to JA, June 8, 1777, in *AFC*, 2:261.

53 John Adams, Diary 47, February 24–26, 1778, 10 [electronic edition].

54 JA to AA, June 29, 1774, *The Adams Papers Digital Edition*, Founding Era Collection, Rotunda Database, http://rotunda.upress.virginia.edu /founders/ADMS-04-01-02-0079.

55 JA to JQA, December 28, 1780, in *AFC*, 4:56.

56 JQA to CA, March 2, 1780, in *AFC*, 3:293.

57 John Thaxter to AA, March 6, 1778, Doc. no. AFC02d323, MHS [Digital Edition].

58 JQA to Rev. Henry Coleman, August 25, 1826, Adams Papers, MHS, microfilm, reel 149, quoted in Samuel Flagg Bemis, *Foundations*, 11 (1949).

59 JA to AA, May 14, 1779, in *AFC*, 3:195.

60 JQA to AA, September 27, 1778, Doc. no. AFC03d080, MHS [Digital Edition].

61 JA to Robert Livingston, February 5, 1783, in Charles Francis Adams, ed., *The Works of John Adams, Second President of the United States: With a Life of the Author, Notes and Illustrations, by His Grandson Charles Francis Adams* (Boston: Little, Brown, 1853), 8:38.

62 AA to JQA, January 21, 1781, in *AFC*, 4:68.

63 JA to JQA, May 30, 1781, in *AFC*, 4:146.

64 JQA to AA, July 23, 1783, Doc. no. AFC05d124, MHS [Digital Edition].

65 JA to JQA, December 14, 1781, in Adams, *AFC* 4:263; JA to JQA, February 5, 1782, Doc. no. AFC04d193, MHS [Digital Edition].

66 JQA to AA, September 10, 1783, in *AFC*, 5:242ff.

67 AA to JQA, December 26, 1783, in *AFC*, 5:283.

68 JQA to JA, February 1, 1783, and February 20, 1783, Doc. nos. AFC05d049, AFC05d057, MHS [Digital Edition].

69 JQA to AA, July 23, 1783, Doc. no. AFC05d124, MHS [Digital Edition].

70 JA to AA, July 26, 1783, in *AFC*, 5:218.

71 JA to JQA, June 6, 1784, in *AFC*, 5:338.

72 JA to JQA, June 11, 1784, in *AFC*, 5:342.

73 JQA to JA, June 6, 1784, in *AFC*, 5:340.

74 JQA to JA, June 6, 1784, in *AFC*, 5:340.

75 JQA, Diary 10, March 11, 1785, 23 [electronic edition].

76 JQA to JA, July 30, 1784, Doc. no. AFC05d220, MHS [Digital Edition].

77 AA2 to Elizabeth Cranch, July 30, 1784, Doc. no. AFC05d219, MHS [Digital Edition].

78 JQA to William Cranch, December 14, 1784, in *AFC*, 6:32.

79 AA to Mary Smith Cranch, December 9, 1784, Doc. no. AFC06d006, MHS [Digital Edition].

80 AA to JQA, September 6, 1785, in *AFC*, 6:345.

81 AA2 to Mary Smith Cranch, June 22, 1785, in *AFC*, 6:182.

82 JQA, Diary 10, April 26, 1785, 56ff. [electronic edition].

83 Elizabeth Smith Shaw to AA2, February 14, 1786, in *AFC*, 7:58.

84 JQA, Diary 10, August 19, 1785, 137 [electronic edition]. After a tour of Yale's library, John Quincy added that it was "neither as large nor as elegant" as his father's. JQA to AA2, August 19, 1785, Doc. no. AFC06d083, MHS [Digital Edition].

85 JQA to AA2, April 29, 1786, in *AFC*, 7:157.

86 Elizabeth Smith Shaw to AA, March 18, 1786, Doc. no. AFC07d029, MHS [Digital Edition].

87 Elizabeth Smith Shaw to AA2, February 14, 1786, Doc. no. AFC07d018 [Digital Edition].

88 Elizabeth Smith Shaw to AA, January 2, 1786, in *AFC*, 7:3; Mary Smith Cranch to AA, April 22, 1787, in *AFC*, 8:15ff.

89 AA to Mary Smith Cranch, April 28, 1787, in *AFC*, 8:32.

90 JQA, Diary 11, September 29, 1786, 71ff. [electronic edition].

91 JQA, Diary 11, September 29, 1786, 71ff. [electronic edition].

92 For a detailed analysis of these lectures and their impact, see Richard A. Katula, *The Eloquence of Edward Everett: America's Greatest Orator* (New York: Peter Lang, 2010), esp. 45–56. Better yet are the original lectures in their entirety: John Quincy Adams, *Lectures on Rhetoric and Oratory: Delivered to the Classes of Senior and Junior Sophisters in Harvard University*, 2 vols. (Cambridge, Mass.: Hilliard and Metcalf, 1810).

93 JQA, *Lectures on Rhetoric and Oratory*. This comes from the Inaugural Lecture, 19.

94 JQA, Inaugural Lecture, in *Lectures on Rhetoric and Oratory*, 30.

95 For a detailed description on his daily life at Harvard, see Henry Adams's essay "Harvard College, 1786–1787," which he published in the January 1872 edition of the *North American Review*. The essay draws exclusively from John Quincy's diary to paint a portrait of life, work, ladies, and academic drudgery at Cambridge.

96 JQA, Diary 11, October 30, 1786, 98 [electronic edition].

97 John Quincy Adams, "The Advantages Which Are Derived from a Liberal Education," delivered before the A.B. Society at Harvard, June 26, 1786, Doc. no. DQA02d104, MHS [Digital Edition].

98 JQA, "An Oration, Delivered at the Public Commencement, in the University of Cambridge, in New England, July 18, 1787, by Mr. John Quincy Adams, Son of his Excellency John Adams, L.L.D. the American Minister at the Court of London," *Columbian Magazine, or Monthly Miscellany* (Philadelphia: T. Seddon, W. Spotswood, C. Cist and J. Trenchard, 1787), 625ff.

99   JQA to AA, December 30, 1786, in *AFC*, 7:418.

100   JQA "An Oration, Delivered at the Public Commencement," 628.

101   JA to Cotton Tufts, June 2, 1786, Doc. no. AFC07d080, MHS [Digital Edition].

102   JA to JQA, September 9, 1785, in *AFC*, 6:356.

103   AA to JQA, September 6, 1785, in *AFC*, 6:345.

104   JA to JQA, September 9, 1785, in *AFC*, 6:356.

105   Jeremy Belknap to JQA, August 3, 1787, quoted in Jane Belknap Marcou, *Life of Jeremy Belknap, D.D., the Historian of New Hampshire, with Selections from His Correspondence and Other Writings: Collected and Arranged by His Grand-Daughter* (New York: Harper and Brothers, 1847), 158.

106   See John Quincy Adams, *Life in a New England Town, 1787, 1788: Diary of John Quincy Adams, while a Student in the Office of Theophilus Parsons at Newburyport* (Boston: Little, Brown, 1903), 46, 97, 142. (Hereafter cited as *LNET.*)

107   JQA to AA, August 14, 1790, in *AFC*, 9:89ff.

108   JQA to AA, August 1, 1787, in *AFC*, 8:139.

109   John Quincy Adams, "Ambition for a Young Man," Phi Beta Kappa lecture, September 1788. A copy of the speech is recorded in Adams's diary. JQA, Diary 12, September 5, 1788, 219ff. [electronic edition].

110   JQA, Diary 11, July 11, 1787, 287 [electronic edition].

111   JQA, December 18, 1787, *LNET,* 71.

112   JQA, April 5, 1788, *LNET,* 118.

113   CA to JQA, October 21, 1790, in *AFC*, 9:80.

114   There is an interesting parallel to Lincoln here. See Joshua Wolf Shenk's intriguing *Lincoln's Melancholy.* Lincoln's answer to his own paralyzing fears was to plunge on, even with pain, through the activity of life. "Work work work is the main thing," Lincoln said. This sounds remarkably like John Quincy Adams, who later concluded that the secret to maintaining health and mental agility was owed to "(1) Regularity; (2) Regularity; (3) Regularity."

115 Recorded by Adams's old Newburyport friend Samuel Breck in *Recollections of Samuel Breck, with Passages from His Notebooks, 1771–1862,* ed. H. E. Scudder (Philadelphia: Porter and Coates, 1877), 21. Adams added that "it was a long time before I was cured; or able to transfer my love to another object, which I did very sincerely when I married my present wife, who has fulfilled by her kindness and affection all my expectations and wishes in reference to connubial happiness."

116 JQA, Diary 10, November 3, 1785, 197 [electronic edition].

117 JA to JQA, February 19, 1790, in *AFC,* 9:16; JA to JQA, December 13, 1790, in *AFC,* 9:106.

118 JA to JQA, October 23, 1790, in *AFC,* 9:139.

119 Eliza Smith Shaw to JQA, June 9, 1794, in *AFC,* 10:203.

120 JQA to Thomas Adams, April 2, 1791, in *AFC,* 9:209.

121 Fischer, *Albion's Seed,* 31.

122 Henry Adams, *The Education of Henry Adams,* 7.

123 AA to JQA, November 13, 1782, in *AFC,* 5:38.

124 AA2 to JQA, May 3, 1782, Doc. no. AFC04d215, MHS [Digital Edition].

125 AA to JQA, August 20, 1790, in *AFC,* 9:92.

126 JQA to AA, August 29, 1790, in *AFC,* 9:96.

127 JA to JQA, June 21, 1784, in *AFC,* 5:351.

128 JA to JQA, January 27, 1793, in *AFC,* 9:383.

129 JA to AA, June 29, 1774, in *AFC,* 1:145.

130 JQA Diary 30, July 11, 1817, 222 [electronic edition].

131 JQA, Diary 31, June 4, 1819, 125 [electronic edition].

132 JQA to AA, October 6, 1785, in *AFC,* 6:409.

133 JQA to AA2, November 20, 1790, in *AFC,* 9:147.

134 JQA, Diary 31, July 15, 1820, 391 [electronic edition].

135 Charles Francis Adams (CFA), Diary, September 6, 1824, Aïda DiPace Donald and David Donald, eds. (Cambridge: Belknap Press of Harvard University Press, 1964) 1:315.

136 JQA to AA, July 23, 1783, Doc. no. AFC05d124, MHS [Digital Edition].

CHAPTER 2 *Clans and Tribes at Eternal War*

1 For an excellent analysis of how the first American public officials experimented through trial and error with how to adjust to a style of politics where the people were newly sovereign, see Joanne B. Freeman, *Affairs of Honor: National Politics in the New Republic* (New Haven: Yale University Press, 2001).

2 Legislation approving funding for the creation of a navy for the United States had been passed only in March 1794. The first three ships, however, were not ready until 1797, and the legislation, facing stiff opposition, was watered down to reflect a desire for a small navy. For more on the political debates surrounding a navy, see Craig L. Symonds, *Navalists and Antinavalists: The Naval Policy Debate in the United States, 1785–1827* (Newark: University of Delaware Press, 1980), and Ian Toll, *Six Frigates: The Epic History of the Founding of the U.S. Navy* (New York: W. W. Norton, 2006).

3 George Washington to Edmund Randolph, June 19, 1794, *The Papers of George Washington,* Founding Era Collection, Rotunda Database, http://rotunda.upress.virginia.edu/founders/default.xqy ?keys=GEWN-search-1-9&expandNote=on#match.

4 JQA to JA, July 27, 1794, in *AFC,* 10:218.

5 JQA to JA, July 27, 1794, in *AFC,* 10:218.

6 JA to JQA, August 24, 1794, in *AFC,* 10:227ff.

7 JQA to AA, November 11, 1794, in *AFC,* 10:253ff.

8 JQA to AA, March 30, 1812, in JQA, *Writings,* 4:302ff.

9 JQA to William Vans Murray, July 22, 1798, in JQA, *Writings,* 2:343ff.

10 JQA to AA, January 1, 1812, in JQA, *Writings,* 4:284ff.

11 JQA to Charles Adams, June 9, 1796, in JQA, *Writings,* 1:493ff.

12 David C. Hendrickson's *Union, Nation, or Empire: The American Debate over International Relations, 1789–1941* (Lawrence: University Press of Kansas, 2009) posits the paramount importance of a "unionist paradigm" at the heart of how Americans thought about the interna-

tional system (p. xii). Hendrickson argues that Americans' long history of grappling with the relations between American states conditioned and prepared them for a post-1945 global role. An earlier work of his, *Peace Pact: The Lost World of the American Founding* (Lawrence: University Press of Kansas, 2003), examines the antecedents for federalism and discusses its centrality to American political discourse. For more on unionist thought, see Paul C. Nagel, *One Nation Indivisible: The Union in American Thought, 1776–1861* (New York: Oxford University Press, 1964).

13 Early editions of Paine's work advertised (and subtitled) it as "Being An Answer to Mr. Burke's Attack on the French Revolution."

14 See Jefferson's letter to John Adams, July 17, 1794, in Paul Leicester Ford, ed., *The Writings of Thomas Jefferson* (New York: G. P. Putnam's Sons, 1895), 5:354.

15 JQA, *Columbian Centinel,* July 9, 1791, in JQA, *Writings,* 1:98.

16 JQA, *Columbian Centinel,* June 18, 1791, in JQA, *Writings,* 1:81.

17 Sounding remarkably like Burke, an older John Quincy Adams would argue that "the freedom of France was not of the genuine breed. A phantom of more than gigantic form had assumed the mask and the garb of freedom, and substituted for the principles of the Declaration of Independence, anarchy within and conquest without." Underscoring his fears of the social dislocations and violence that often followed such upheavals, Adams denigrated the French Revolution by depicting it as an attempt to spread revolution worldwide and "overthrow . . . all established governments." JQA, *Jubilee of the Constitution: A Discourse Delivered at the Request of the New York Historical Society, in the City of New York, on Tuesday, the 30th of April 1830* (New York: Samuel Colman, 1839), 86.

18 JQA, *Jubilee of the Constitution,* 77.

19 Thomas Paine to William Short, November 2, 1791, quoted in Moncure Daniel Conway, *The Life of Thomas Paine, with a History of His Literary, Political and Religious Career in America, France, and England, to Which Is Added a Sketch of Paine by William Cobbett,* vol. 1 (New York: G. P. Putnam's Sons, 1893) 132.

20 Thomas Jefferson to James Madison, June 28, 1791, *The Papers of Thomas Jefferson Digital Edition,* Founding Era Collection, Rotunda Database, http://rotunda.upress.virginia.edu/founders/TSJN-01-20-02-0230.

21 James Madison to Thomas Jefferson, July 13, 1791, *The Papers of James Madison Digital Edition,* Founding Era Collection, Rotunda Database, http://rotunda.upress.virginia.edu/founders/JSMN-01-14-02-0037.

22 James Bridges to JQA, January 23, 1792, quoted in Phyllis Lee Levin, *Abigail Adams: A Biography* (New York: St. Martin's Press, 1987), 281.

23 Adams wrote under the pseudonym Marcellus in this address to the *Columbian Centinel* that appeared on May 4, 1793, in JQA, *Writings,* 1:140.

24 JQA, *Jubilee of the Constitution,* 88.

25 JQA, writing as Marcellus in the *Columbian Centinel,* May 11, 1793, in JQA, *Writings,* 1:146.

26 JQA, *Writings,* 1:145.

27 JQA, *Writings,* 1:145–146.

28 Adams's essays were answered by a series of pieces by Americanus, widely known to be James Sullivan, the sitting attorney general of Massachusetts. Sullivan's pieces ran in Boston's *Independent Chronicle* starting on December 19, 1793, and charged that what Columbus had claimed to be neutrality was really covert British leanings. These essays mirrored the 1793 Pacificus (Hamilton)–Helvidius (Madison) debates over the Neutrality Proclamation and, more broadly, the nature and scope of the president's control over foreign policy. Like Adams's Columbus and Marcellus essays, Hamilton's appealed to neutrality. And just as Adams would be accused of being an Anglophile and a crypto monarchist, so Madison accused Hamilton of exhibiting those same tendencies. A more detailed examination of the seven Pacificus essays, which first appeared in the *Gazette of the United States* on June 29, 1793, can be found in Ron Chernow, *Alexander Hamilton* (New York:

Penguin, 2004), esp. 441ff. Madison's response, which came with five essays in the *Gazette* starting on August 24, 1793, is detailed in Ralph Ketcham, *James Madison* (Charlottesville: University of Virginia Press, 1990), 345ff. The timing is interesting, as the first round of Adams's essays appeared before Hamilton's, though the second round—the Marcellus pieces—came several months after the Hamilton-Madison exchange. For a thoughtful, if convoluted, evaluation on the similarities and differences between Adams and Hamilton, see Greg Russell, "John Quincy Adams and the Ethics of America's National Interest," *Review of International Studies* 19, no. 1 (January 1993): 23-38. For a detailed account of the cabinet debates surrounding Washington's Proclamation of Neutrality, see Charles Marion Thomas, *American Neutrality in 1793: A Study in Cabinet Government* (New York: Columbia University Press, 1931).

29 Editing his father's papers, Charles Francis Adams put it best, concluding that the Marcellus and Columbus essays exhibited "abundance of knowledge, closeness of reasoning, and effective retort, as well as . . . that superabounding force of invective which sometimes presses an advantage perhaps beyond the limits of legitimate pursuit" (Charles Francis Adams, ed., *Memoirs of John Quincy Adams: Compromising Portions of His Diary from 1795 to 1848* (Philadelphia: J. B. Lippincott & Co., 1874) 1, 27).

30 JA to William Cunningham Jr., October 14, 1808, in JQA, *Writings,* 1:148.

31 JQA, Diary 20, June 3 and 8, 1794, 1, 2 [electronic edition].

32 AA to JQA, September 15, 1795, *The Adams Papers Digital Edition,* Founding Era Collection, Rotunda Database, http://rotunda.upress .virginia.edu/founders/default.xqy?keys=FGEA-search-1-2& expandNote=on#match, accessed March 1, 2012.

33 JQA, Diary 20, June 10, 1794, 2 [electronic edition].

34 AA to Martha Washington, June 20, 1794, in *AFC,* 10:206.

35 Martha Washington to AA, July 19, 1794, in *AFC,* 10:214ff.

36 AA to JA, January 4, 1794, in *AFC,* 10:10.

37 JA to JQA, May 26, 1794, in JQA, *Writings,* 1:190n2.

38 JA to AA, April 5, 1794, in *AFC,* 10:135.

39 JQA to AA, November 14, 1796. See JQA, *Writings,* 1:495n1.

40 Five thousand Dutch guilders in 1794 corresponds to more than $60,000 in current U.S. dollars. Adjusted for inflation, $4,500 comes out to slightly less than $70,000 in current dollars. See, http://www .measuringworth.com/exchange/ and http://www.pierre-marteau.com /currency/converter.html. Thanks to Professor Colin F. Jackson for help tracking down useful currency converters.

41 JQA to John Gardner, July 15, 1795, quoted in Robert A. East, *John Quincy Adams: The Critical Years, 1785–1794* (New York: Bookman Associates, 1962), 175.

42 Louisa Catherine Adams, *Diary and Autobiographical Writings of Louisa Catherine Adams,* vol. 1, ed. Judith S. Graham, Beth Luey, Margaret A. Hogan, and C. James Taylor (Cambridge, Mass.: Harvard University Press, 2013), 1.37ff.

43 LCA, *Diary and Autobiographical Writings,* 1:42, 43.

44 LCA, *Diary and Autobiographical Writings,* 1:43, 44, 46.

45 AA to JQA, May 20, 1796, *The Adams Papers Digital Edition,* Founding Era Collection, Rotunda Database, http://rotunda.upress .virginia.edu/founders/default.xqy?keys=FOEA-chron-1790-1796-05 -20-1.

46 JQA to AA, August 16, 1796, *The Adams Papers Digital Edition,* Founding Era Collection, Rotunda Database, http://rotunda.upress .virginia.edu/founders/default.xqy?keys=FGEA-search-1-1& expandNote=on#match.

47 John Quincy Adams had actually first been appointed American minister to Portugal by President Washington. However, after his father's election to the presidency in 1796, he was reassigned to the far more important posting to Berlin.

48 Senator Elijah H. Mills, December 24, 1820, quoted in *Proceedings of the Massachusetts Historical Society,* vol. 19, *1881–2* (Boston: Massachusetts Historical Society, 1882), 28.

49 JA to John Taylor, April 13, 1824, Adams Papers, MHS, microfilm, reel 124; Samuel Flagg Bemis, *Foundations*, 81. For an overview of the literature as well as a useful narrative overview of Louisa's life, see Catherine Allgor and Margery M. Heffron, "A Monarch in a Republic: Louisa Catherine Johnson Adams and Court Culture in Early Washington City," in David Waldstreicher, ed., *A Companion to John Adams and John Quincy Adams* (Hoboken: John Wiley and Sons, 2013), 445–467. Also see Lyman H. Butterfield's insightful "Tending a Dragon-Killer: Notes for the Biographer of Mrs. John Quincy Adams," *Proceedings of the American Philosophical Society* 118 (1974): 165–178. For an especially useful treatment of John Quincy and Louisa Catherine's tumultuous and loving marriage, see Jack Shepherd, *Cannibals of the Heart: A Personal Biography of Louisa Catherine and John Quincy Adams* (New York: McGraw-Hill, 1980). And for the often fractious relationship between Abigail and Louisa Adams, see Paul C. Nagel, *The Adams Women: Abigail and Louisa Adams, Their Sisters and Daughters* (New York: Oxford University Press, 1987).

50 JQA to JA, October 23, 1794, in JQA, *Writings*, 1:201ff.; JQA, Diary 21, October 22, 1794, 42 [electronic edition].

51 JQA to JA, October 23, 1794, in JQA, *Writings*, 1:201ff.

52 Douglass C. North, *The Economic Growth of the United States, 1790–1860* (Englewood Cliffs, N.J.: Prentice-Hall, 1961), 25.

53 Adam Seybert, *Statistical Annals: Embracing Views of the Population, Commerce, Navigation, Fisheries, Public Lands, Post-Office Establishment, Revenues, Mint, Military and Naval Establishments, Expenditures, Public Debt, and Sinking Fund of the United States of America: Founded on Official Documents; Commencing on the Fourth of March Seventeen Hundred and Eighty-Nine and Ending on the Twentieth of April Eighteen Hundred and Eighteen* (Philadelphia: Thomas Dobson and Son, 1818), 59ff.

54 Alexander Hamilton, The Defense No. II, July 25, 1795, *The Papers of Alexander Hamilton Digital Edition,* Founding Era Collection, Rotunda Database, http://rotunda.upress.virginia.edu/founders/ARHN-01-18-02-0310.

55 JQA to Sylvanus Bourne, December 24, 1795, in JQA, *Writings,* 1:466ff.

56 JQA to JA, May 22, 1795, in JQA, *Writings,* 1:353ff.

57 JA to AA, June 9, 1795; JA to AA, January 19, 1795, in *AFC,* 10: 445,353.

58 JA to JQA, October 28, 1796, Adams Papers, MHS, microfilm, reel 128; Bemis *Foundations,* 87; Marie B. Hecht, *John Quincy Adams: A Personal History of an Independent Man* (New York: Macmillan, 1972), 108.

59 JA to JQA, March 31, 1797, in Charles Francis Adams, ed., *The Works of John Adams, Second President of the United States: With a Life of the Author, Notes and Illustrations, by His Grandson Charles Francis Adams* (Boston: Little, Brown, 1853), VIII:537.

60 JQA to JA, September 12, 1795, in JQA, *Writings,* 1:409.

61 JQA to JA, May 22, 1795, in JQA, *Writings,* 1:362. Bemis, *Foundations*: 62–65, discusses the influence of these dispatches and Adams's earlier essays in the *Columbian Centinel* on Washington's evolving view of foreign policy. It was not inconsequential. Bemis quotes Washington telling Vice President Adams that "things appear to me exactly as they do to your son." Bemis even suggests that Quincy Adams, unbeknownst to him, served as the key architect of Washington's Farewell Address.

62 JQA, Diary 24, December 1, 1795, 76 [electronic edition].

63 JQA to JA, July 27, 1795, in JQA, *Writings,* 1:388.

64 JQA to JA, September 12, 1795, in JQA, *Writings,* 1:408ff.

65 JQA to Thomas Boylston Adams, February 14, 1801, in JQA, *Writings,* 1:499ff.

66 JQA to Thomas Boylston Adams, February 14, 1801, in JQA, *Writings,* 1:499ff.

67 JQA to Thomas Boylston Adams, February 14, 1801, in JQA, *Writings,* 1:499ff.

68 George Washington to JA, February 20, 1797, in JQA, *Writings,* 2:125ff.

69 JQA to JA, June 24, 1796, in JQA, *Writings,* 1:497ff.

70 JQA to JA, June 24, 1796, in JQA, *Writings,* 1:506.

71 Federalist 11, in Alexander Hamilton, John Jay, and James Madison, *The Federalist* (New York: Penguin, 1961), 86.

72 Hamilton's 1800 *Letter from Alexander Hamilton, concerning the Public Conduct and Character of John Adams, Esq. President of the United States* attacked the public and private demeanor of the president. It also destroyed Hamilton's public standing.

73 JQA to JA, July 27, 1794, in *AFC,* 10:218.

74 JQA to JA, July 21, 1796, in JQA, *Writings,* 2:13.

75 JQA to Timothy Pickering, June 16, 1796, in JQA, *Writings,* 1:508.

76 John Adams, Special Message to the Senate and the House, May 16, 1797, http://avalon.law.yale.edu/18th_century/ja97-03.asp.

77 JQA to William Vans Murray, March 20, 1798, in JQA, *Writings,* 2:272.

78 JQA, Diary 23, November 7, 1797, 77 [electronic edition].

79 For the Adams family's connections to the *Port Folio,* see Linda K. Kerber and John Walter Morris, "Politics and Literature: The Adams Family and the *Port Folio," William and Mary Quarterly,* 3rd ser., 23, no. 3 (July 1966): 450–476. Kerber and Morris very helpfully provide an appendix listing all the Adamses' contributions to the *Port Folio* and note that between 1801 and 1803 John Quincy Adams anonymously contributed translations, verse, expository essays, and book reviews.

80 LCA, March 24, 1801, in LCA, *Diary and Autobiographical Writings,* 1:154.

81 Adams realized the loftiness, and randomness, of such expectations, writing, "I know not whether . . . it be wise to give a great and venerable name to such a lottery-ticket as a new-born infant." See LCA, *Diary and Autobiographical Writings,* 1:170n158.

82 JQA, Diary 24, September 30, 1801, 339 [electronic edition].

83 JQA, Diary 24, January 28, 1802, 355 [electronic edition].

84 JQA to JA, November 25, 1800, in JQA, *Writings,* 2:479ff.

85 JQA, published as Publius Valerius, *The Repertory,* October 30, 1804, in JQA, *Writings,* 3:57ff.

86 JQA, "Reply to the Appeal of the Massachusetts Federalists," in Henry Adams, ed., *Documents relating to New-England Federalism, 1800–1815* (Boston: Little, Brown, 1877), 148.

87 JQA, Diary 31, May 31, 1820, 358 [electronic edition].

88 Quoted in John T. Morse Jr., *John Quincy Adams* (Boston: Houghton Mifflin, 1882), 51.

89 JQA to JA, December 27, 1807, quoted in LCA, *Diary and Autobiographical Writings,* 1:264 n301.

90 JQA to Stephen Row Bradley, September 21, 1824, in JQA, *Writings,* 3:169.

91 LCA, December 1807, in LCA, *Diary and Autobiographical Writings,* 1:264.

92 *Hampshire Gazette,* April 20, 1808.

93 AA to JQA, February 15, 1808, quoted in Woody Holton, *Abigail Adams: A Life* (New York: Free Press, 2009), 349.

94 JQA, Diary 27, July 11, 1807, 297 [electronic edition].

95 JA to JQA, January 8, 1808, in JQA, *Writings,* 1:189n1.

96 JQA to JA, January 27, 1808, in JQA, *Writings,* 1:188ff.

97 JQA to William Branch Giles, November 15, 1808. JQA, *Writings,* 3:242ff. Historians, like Adams's own contemporaries, tend to read him as acting out of either naked ambition or selfless patriotism. The most outspoken advocate for his disinterestedness on this matter remains John F. Kennedy in his 1957 *Profiles in Courage.* On the other side sits David Hackett Fischer, who concludes that to Adams "nothing ever seemed quite as important as his own political future"; Fischer, *The Revolution of American Conservatism: The Federalist Party in the Era of Jeffersonian Democracy* (New York: Harper and Row, 1965), 43. A more judicious treatment can be found in Robert R. Thompson, "John Quincy Adams, Apostate: From 'Outrageous Federalist' to 'Republican Exile,' 1801–1809," *Journal of the Early Republic* 2, no. 2 (Summer 1991). Attempting to deduce Adams's political motives during his time between diplomatic postings, Thompson finds that a complex mixture of classical republican

beliefs, personal ambitions, time spent abroad, and political expediency drove his actions.

98 LCA, December 1807, in LCA, *Diary and Autobiographical Writings,* 1:264.

99 AA to AA2, August 29, 1808, quoted in Holton, *Abigail Adams,* 350.

100 JQA, Diary 27, February 1, 1808, 335 [electronic edition].

101 JQA to William Plumer, October 6, 1810, in JQA, *Writings,* 3:507ff.

102 JQA to AA, June 30, 1811, in JQA, *Writings,* 4:128.

103 After reading a letter from her son detailing the inadequacies of his salary to cover his living expenses, Abigail Adams became so upset that she promptly wrote President Monroe. Wishing to offer Adams a graceful exit if he so chose, the president offered him a seat on the Supreme Court, which he promptly turned down.

104 For more on Russian-American commercial relations, see Norman E. Saul, *Distant Friends: The United States and Russia, 1763–1867* (Lawrence: University Press of Kansas, 1991); Alfred W. Crosby Jr., *America, Russia, Hemp, and Napoleon: American Trade with Russia and the Baltic, 1783–1812* (Columbus: Ohio State University Press, 1965); and David W. McFadden, "John Quincy Adams, American Commercial Diplomacy, and Russia, 1809-1825," *New England Quarterly* 66, no. 4 (December 1993): 613-629. For a terrifically perceptive take on the role that Louisa Catherine played in facilitating her husband's diplomacy in Czar Alexander's court, see Catherine Allgor, "'A Republican in a Monarchy': Louisa Catherine Adams in Russia," *Diplomatic History* 1, no. 21 (Winter 1997): 15-43.

105 JQA, Diary 31, March 21, 1820, 289 [electronic edition].

106 JQA to Richard Rush, November 6, 1817, in JQA, *Writings,* 6:233ff.

107 JQA to AA, January 1, 1812, in JQA, *Writings,* 4:286.

108 JQA to JA, October 14, 1811, in JQA, *Writings,* 4:240ff.

109 JQA to JA, July 13, 1812, in JQA, *Writings,* 4:372.

110 JQA to AA, August 10, 1812, in JQA, *Writings,* 4:388.

111 Robert George Gleig, *A Narrative of the Campaigns of the British Army at Washington and New Orleans, under Generals Ross, Pakenham, and*

Lambert, in the Years 1814 and 1815; with Some Account of the Countries Visited. By the Author of "The Subaltern," 2nd ed. (London: John Murray, 1826), 129.

112 Mary Stockton Hunter to Susan Stockton Hunger, August 30, 1814, quoted in Anthony S. Pitch, *The Burning of Washington: The British Invasion of 1814* (Annapolis: Naval Institute Press, 1998), 115n66.

113 *Federal Republican* (Georgetown), August 30, 1814.

114 Charles J. Ingersoll, *Historical Sketch of the Second War between the United States of America and Great Britain, Declared by Act of Congress, the 18th of June, 1812, and Concluding by Peace, the 15th of February, 1815* (Philadelphia: Lea and Blanchard, 1849), 2:184. Also see Gleig, *Narrative of the Campaigns,* 128.

115 Particularly valuable to understanding the immediate effects of the sack are Michael S. Fitzgerald, "'Nature Unsubdued': Diplomacy, Expansion, and the American Military Buildup of 1815–1816," *Mid-America* 77 (Winter 1995): 5–32, and Paul Woehrmann, "National Response to the Sack of Washington," *Maryland Historical Magazine* 66 (Fall 1971): 222–260. For more general discussions of the influence of the war on the nation, see Steven Watts, *The Republic Reborn: War and the Making of Liberal America, 1790–1820* (Baltimore: Johns Hopkins University Press, 1987); James E. Lewis, *The American Union and the Problem of Neighborhood: The United States and the Collapse of the Spanish Empire, 1783–1829* (Chapel Hill: University of North Carolina Press, 1998); and George Dangerfield, *The Awakening of American Nationalism, 1815–1828* (New York: Harper and Row, 1965).

116 *National Intelligencer,* September 23, 1814.

117 See James Chace and Caleb Carr, *America Invulnerable: The Quest for Absolute Security from 1812 to Star Wars* (New York : Summit Books, 1988).

118 See Aaron L. Friedberg, *In the Shadow of the Garrison State: America's Anti-Statism and Its Cold War Grand Strategy* (Princeton: Princeton University Press, 2000).

119 Michael D. Pearlman, *Warmaking and American Democracy: The Struggle over Military Strategy, 1700 to the Present* (Lawrence: University Press of Kansas, 1999), 73.

120 For a summary of the growth of the American military, see Russell F. Weigley, *The American Way of War: A History of United States Military Strategy and Policy* (Bloomington: Indiana University Press, 1973). For this period, see esp. chap. 3, "The Federalists and the Jeffersonians," 40–55.

121 Thomas Jefferson to James Madison, March 17, 1809, *The Papers of Thomas Jefferson Digital Edition,* Founding Era Collection, Rotunda Database, http://rotunda.upress.virginia.edu/founders/TSJN-03-01-02-0045.

122 JQA to Louisa Catherine Adams, October 11, 1814, in JQA, *Writings,* 5:157.

123 John Quincy Adams, *The Lives of James Madison and James Monroe: Fourth and Fifth Presidents of the United States, with Historical Notes of Their Administrations* (Buffalo: Geo H. Derby and Co., 1850), 278ff.

124 JQA to James Monroe, November 20, 1814, in JQA, *Writings,* 5:202.

125 JQA to Peter Paul Francis De Grand, April 28, 1815, in JQA, *Writings,* 5:314.

126 JQA to Joseph Hall, September 9, 1815, in JQA, *Writings,* 5:376.

127 JQA to AA, January 17, 1814, in JQA, *Writings,* 5:7ff.

128 JQA to William Plumer, October 5, 1814, in JQA, *Writings,* 5:400.

129 War had been declared on almost an entirely party-line vote in the House (79–49). In the Senate, matters were even closer (19–13). Pearlman, in *Warmaking and American Democracy,* notes that "while not the sole partisan war, the War of 1812 was certainly the most partisan political war in U.S. history" (p. 73). For further discussions of the politics of the war, see J. C. A. Stagg, *Mr. Madison's War: Politics, Diplomacy, and Warfare in the Early American Republic, 1783–1830* (Princeton: Princeton University Press, 1983) and Donald Hickey, *The War of 1812: A Forgotten Conflict* (Urbana: University of Illinois Press, 1989).

130 JQA to Alexander Hill Everett, March 16, 1816, in JQA, *Writings,* 5:538.

131 JQA, Diary 30, December 24, 1816, 116 [electronic edition].

132 JQA, Diary 30, April 16, 1817, 170 [electronic edition].

133 LCA, "The Adventures of a Nobody," manuscript dated July 1, 1840, quoted in Shepherd, *Cannibals of the Heart,* 117. Louisa composed several accounts of her life, including "Record of a Life or My Story" and, later, "The Adventures of a Nobody." The former can be found in the Adams Papers, MHS, microfilm, reel 265, the latter in reel 269. For a summary of her compositions, see Michael O'Brien, *Mrs. Adams in Winter: A Journey in the Last Days of Napoleon* (New York: Farrar, Straus and Giroux, 2010), esp. 47ff.

134 JQA, Diary 27, March 26, 1809, 391 [electronic edition].

135 CFA to JA, January 29 and February 26, 1826, Adams Papers, MHS, microfilm, reel 474; Shepherd, *Cannibals of the Heart,* 283.

136 LCA, *Diary and Autobiographical Writings,* 1:45.

137 George Canning, *George Canning and His Friends: Containing Hitherto Unpublished Letters, Jeux d'Esprit, etc. Edited by Captain Josceline Bagot, with Illustrations in Two Volumes* (New York: E. P. Dutton, 1909), 2:362.

138 William Plumer Jr., *Life of William Plumer, Edited with a Sketch of the Author's Life by A. P. Peabody* (Boston: Phillips, Sampson, 1856), 343ff.

CHAPTER 3 *In Search of Monsters to Destroy*

1 Stanislaus Murray Hamilton, ed., *Writings of James Monroe,* vol. 6, *1817–1823* (New York: G. P. Putnam's Sons, 1902), 31. The editor of this volume cites the *Memoirs of John Quincy Adams* as the source of the president's memo to his cabinet on October 25 and 30, 1817. These questions do not seem to be part of the Adams MHS file.

2 JQA, Diary 30, October 30, 1817, 268 [electronic edition].

3 JQA to AA, May 16, 1817, in JQA, *Writings,* 6:181.

4 JQA, Diary 34, June 20, 1823, 86 [electronic edition]. Underlining in original text.

5 Contemporary newspapers suggested as much. Typical was the *New-Bedford Mercury*'s of November 22, 1816: "It is reported that the Hon. John Quincy Adams . . . is to be appointed Secretary of State, vice Mr. Monroe, who will undoubtedly be chosen President. The road to the Presidency has been through the Department of State and in preparing a person for the higher station." See also the *Franklin Herald* (Greenfield, Mass.), November 26, 1816; the *Pittsfield Sun,* November 27, 1816; and the *Baltimore Patriot,* November 8, 1816.

6 JQA, Diary 30, April 16, 1817, 170 [electronic edition].

7 This follows the method set out by John Gaddis in analyzing the "geopolitical codes" of the cold war era. John Lewis Gaddis, *Strategies of Containment: A Critical Appraisal of American National Security Policy during the Cold War* (New York: Oxford University Press, 2005), ix. Gaddis argues that each administration brings a geopolitical code into the White House. This code is its framework for understanding America's capabilities and relationship to the rest of the world. It includes a conception of vital interests and an assessment of threats to those interests. The code becomes strategy with its implementation and justification. Gaddis's argument seeks to apply Alexander L. George's concept of an "operational code" to a geopolitical context. George discusses the philosophical and practical/political questions that shape decision makers' beliefs and, so he argues, influence their actions. See George's excellent "The 'Operational Code': A Neglected Approach to the Study of Political Leaders and Decision-Making," *International Studies Quarterly* 13, no. 2 (June 1969): 190–222.

8 JQA, Diary 31, June 7, 1820, 366 [electronic edition].

9 JQA, Diary 30, September 26, 1817, 258 [electronic edition].

10 See, John Quincy Adams, *Report Upon Weights and Measures* (Washington, D.C.: Gales and Seaton, 1821).

11 Elmer Plischke, *U.S. Department of State: A Reference History* (Westport, Conn.: Greenwood Press, 1999), 75. As an illustrative

example of the excessive demands Congress placed on the secretary of state, Plischke notes that the Census Act of 1820 "spelled out some thirty categories of data to be surveyed and made the Secretary of State responsible for collating the information and having it printed and for providing Congress with 1,550 copies" (p.104).

12 Interestingly, James Madison, in the last months of his presidency, attempted to create a Home Department that could handle many of State's responsibilities. Congress, however, rejected the idea.

13 Paul Nagel, *John Quincy Adams: A Public Life, a Private Life* (Cambridge, Mass.: Harvard University Press, 1997), 268.

14 E. F. Ellet, *The Court Circles of the Republic; or, The Beauties and Celebrities of the Nation from Washington to Grant* (Hartford: Hartford Publishing, 1870), 129ff.

15 Catherine Allgor, *Parlor Politics: In Which the Ladies of Washington Help Build a City and a Government* (Charlottesville: University Press of Virginia, 2000). Especially valuable is her chapter 4, "Louisa Catherine Adams Campaigns for the Presidency," 147–189.

16 This scene is described in Nagel, *John Quincy Adams,* 253.

17 See Charles Jared Ingersoll's description of Adams's regulated walks and swims in William Meigs, *Life of Charles Jared Ingersoll* (Philadelphia: J. B. Lippincott, 1897), 122.

18 JQA, Diary 31, June 4, 1820, 362 [electronic edition].

19 JQA, Diary 30, May 21, 1818, 354 [electronic edition].

20 JQA, Diary 31, June 7, 1820, 365ff. [electronic edition].

21 While Henry Clay was not technically a Virginian—he was from Kentucky—many thought his appointment would appear to extend the Virginia dynasty, as Clay was originally from Virginia. The same was true of William Crawford, who resided in Georgia, though he too was born in Virginia.

22 Monroe to Thomas Jefferson, February 23, 1817, in Monroe, *Writings,* 6:2ff.

23 Ellet, *The Court Circles of the Republic,* 123.

24 Monroe to Andrew Jackson, March 1, 1817, in Monroe, *Writings,* 6:4.

25 Harry Ammon, in *James Monroe: The Quest for National Unity* (New York: McGraw-Hill, 1971), writes that Adams's appointment was an acknowledgment of the "growing importance of the commercial element in the Republican party" (p. 361). This much seems fair. But Ammon then argues that no one, including Adams, thought that the new secretary of state would become a serious contender as Monroe's successor. Both newspaper reports and Adams's private thoughts contradict that contention. See also Stephen Skowronek's interpretation in his *The Politics Presidents Make: Leadership from John Adams to Bill Clinton* (Cambridge, Mass.: Harvard University Press, 1998), 89ff. For political and economic interpretations, see Noble E. Cunningham Jr., *The Presidency of James Monroe* (Lawrence: University Press of Kansas, 1996), esp. 21ff., and William Appleman Williams, *The Contours of American History* (London: (1961; repr., London: Verso, 2011) 140.

26 Monroe to Jefferson, February 23, 1817, in Monroe, *Writings,* 6:4.

27 John Quincy Adams, *The Lives of James Madison and James Monroe: Fourth and Fifth Presidents of the United States, with Historical Notes of Their Administrations* (Buffalo: Geo H. Derby and Co., 1850), 291. Contrast this to Adams's earlier assessment of Monroe in 1818, when he wrote that "there is a slowness, want of decision, and a spirit of procrastination in the President." For the most part, Adams filled his diary with admiration for President Monroe. JQA, Diary 30, January 9, 1818, 294 [electronic edition].

28 George Watterson, *Letters from Washington, on the Constitution and Laws: With Sketches of Some of the Prominent Public Characters of the United States; Written during the Winter of 1817–18. By a Foreigner* (Washington, D.C.: Jacob Gideon, Junr, 1818), 41. Contemporary accounts of his character and appearance revolve around the word "solid." See, for example, Ellet's description of Monroe as "prudent, plodding, generous and patriotic" in *The Court Circles of the Republic,* 99.

29 William Wirt, *The British Spy; or, Letters, to a Member of the British Parliament Written during a Tour through the United States by a Young*

Englishman of Rank (Newburyport: Printed at the Repertory Office, 1804), 96.

30 Historians too diverge on their assessment of Monroe. The standard account argues that Monroe was at best a second-tier president, far inferior to his predecessors. See, for example, Ralph Ketcham, *Presidents above Party* (Chapel Hill: University of North Carolina Press, 1984), who faults Monroe for a "lack of general effectiveness" (p. 128). For recent reassessments, see Harlow Giles Unger, *The Last Founding Father: James Monroe and a Nation's Call to Greatness* (Cambridge, Mass.: Da Capo Press, 2009). Robert Pierce Forbes makes a particularly compelling case for Monroe in his *The Missouri Compromise and Its Aftermath: Slavery and the Meaning of America* (Chapel Hill: University of North Carolina Press, 2007). Much like Eisenhower revisionism, this argument posits that Monroe was the brains of the operation despite attempts to conceal his political genius.

31 For other examples of histories that do a particularly good job at sketching presidents surrounded by strong and talented groups of advisers, see Walter Isaacson and Evan Thomas, *The Wise Men: Six Friends and the World They Made* (London: Faber and Faber, 1986); David Halberstam, *The Best and the Brightest* (New York: Random House, 1972); James Mann, *Rise of the Vulcans: The History of Bush's War Cabinet* (New York: Viking, 2004); and Doris Kearns Goodwin, *Team of Rivals: The Political Genius of Abraham Lincoln* (New York: Simon and Schuster, 2005).

32 *Courier* (New York), March 11, 1817.

33 Quoted in Paul F. Boller Jr., *Presidential Campaigns* (Oxford: Oxford University Press, 1984), 30. John Randolph, always cutting, was said to have remarked that Monroe's popularity arose from "the unanimity of indifference, and not of approbation." William Plumer Jr., *Life of William Plumer, Edited with a Sketch of the Author's Life by A. P. Peabody* (Boston: Phillips, Sampson, 1856), 495.

34 Incensed at not being offered the top cabinet position, Clay turned down appointments to serve as either secretary of war or minister to Great Britain.

35 *Georgetown Messenger,* March 5, 1817, quoted in *Kline's Weekly Carlisle Gazette,* March 19, 1817; *National Intelligencer,* March 5, 1817, quoted in *Weekly Aurora,* March 10, 1817.

36 *Georgetown Messenger,* March 5, 1817.

37 James Monroe, Inaugural Address, March 4, 1817 http://avalon.law .yale.edu/19th_century/monroe1.asp.

38 Monroe, Inaugural Address.

39 Walter McDougall makes this point forcefully in his excellent *Promised Land, Crusader State: The American Encounter with the World since 1776* (Boston: Houghton Mifflin, 1997).

40 For a compelling discussion of the element of time and long-term change in Hamilton's thinking, see Edward Mead Earl, "Adam Smith, Alexander Hamilton, Friedrich List: The Economic Foundations of Military Power," in *Makers of Modern Strategy: Rulers, States, and War* (Princeton: Princeton University Press, 1986).

41 Federalist 11, in Alexander Hamilton, John Jay, and James Madison, *The Federalist* (New York: Penguin, 1961), 87.

42 Nearly all previous accounts of Adams's tenure as secretary of state agree that his primary policy goal was expansion in and across the North American continent, but there are disagreements on both Adams's motivations and on his strategic prioritization. See William Earl Weeks, *John Quincy Adams and American Global Empire* (Lexington: University Press of Kentucky, 1992), especially 37ff.; John Lewis Gaddis, *Surprise, Security, and the American Experience,* 7–33; and James Lewis, *John Quincy Adams: Policymaker for the Union,* (Wilmington: SR Books, 2001) especially his third chapter, "A Dangerous Neighborhood, 1817–1821," 43–69.

43 JQA, Diary 31, November 16, 1819, 205 [electronic edition].

44 Thomas Paine, *Common Sense: Addressed to the Inhabitants of America* (London: H. D. Symonds, 1792), 16.

45 JQA, Diary 30, May 27, 1817, 202 [electronic edition].

46 The term "White House" did not come into widespread usage until the middle of the nineteenth century. Prior to that, in newspapers,

books, and letters Americans generally referred to the Executive Mansion as the President's House. See Esther Singleton, *The Story of the White House* (New York: McClure, 1907), esp. ixff.

47   See the excellent introductory essay in Daniel Preton, ed., *The Papers of James Monroe: A Documentary History of the Presidential Tours of James Monroe, 1817, 1818, 1819* (Westport, Conn.: Greenwood Press, 2003), xvii–xxvii. As a political opponent of the president noted, the tour's "intent is to work out the stain of the Hartford Convention." Jeremiah Mason to Rufus King, *26 June 1817*, quoted in Preton, *The Documentary History of the Presidential Tours of James Monroe*, 163.

48   JQA, Diary 30, September 20, 1817, 256 [electronic edition].

49   The best account of the diplomacy of the Congress of Vienna is still Henry A. Kissinger, *A World Restored: Metternich, Castlereagh and the Problems of Peace, 1812–22* (Boston: Houghton Mifflin, 1957).

50   JQA to JA, August 1, 1816, in JQA, *Writings*, 6:58ff.

51   JQA to William Plumer, January 17, 1817, in JQA, *Writings*, 6:139ff.

52   JQA to William Plumer, January 17, 1817, in JQA, *Writings*, 6:139ff.

53   JQA to JA, August 1, 1816, in JQA, *Writings*, 6:61.

54   JQA, Diary 30, June 1, 1817, 207 [electronic edition]. This comes from JQA's notes from his conversation on the general state of affairs in Europe with the Hungarian Prince Esterhazy.

55   *Annals of Congress*, 15th Cong., 2nd sess., February 15, 1819, 1191–1193; February 16, 1819,1205.

56   *Annals of Congress*, 15th Cong., 2nd sess., February 16, 1819, 1204.

57   Thomas Jefferson to John Holmes, April 22, 1820, http://www.loc .gov/exhibits/jefferson/159.html.

58   *Annals of Congress*, 18th Cong., 1st sess., January 20, 1824, 1113ff.

59   *Annals of Congress*, 15th Cong., 1st sess., March 28, 1818, 1614.

60   *Annals of Congress*, 15th Cong., 1st sess., March 25, 1818, 1482.

61   *Annals of Congress*, 16th Cong., 1st sess., May 10, 1820, 2223ff.

62   Henry Clay, May 19, 1821, originally published in *Kentucky Reporter* (Lexington), May 21, 1821, reproduced in James F. Hopkins, ed., *The*

Papers of Henry Clay, vol. 3, *Presidential Candidate, 1821–1824* (Lexington: University Press of Kentucky, 1963), 79.

63 *Annals of Congress,* 16th Cong., 1st sess., May 10, 1818, 2226ff.

64 "Dispositions of England and America," *Edinburgh Review* 66 (1820), 546. The article Adams responded to was a book review of Robert Walsh's *An Appeal from the Judgments of Great Britain respecting the United States of America: Part First.* An American copy of the January 1820 *Edinburgh Review* can be found in the *Literary and Scientific Repository, and Critical Review,* no. 1 (New York: Wiley and Halsted, 1820).

65 JQA to Robert Walsh Jr., July 10, 1821, in JQA, *Writings,* 7:114, 117.

66 JQA, Diary 31, November 16, 1819, 204 [electronic edition].

67 JQA to JA, May 29, 1816, in JQA, *Writings,* 6:38.

68 JQA, Diary 30, May 5, 1817, 182 [electronic edition].

69 Although Richard Rush signed the act, it was Adams, serving as U.S. minister in London, and Monroe, sitting in the White House, who had sketched the final settlement's main contours. For a detailed account of the correspondence between London and Washington, see Bradford Perkins, *Castlereagh and Adams: England and the United States, 1812–1823* (Berkeley: University of California Press, 1964), esp. 239ff.

70 Rush Memorandum, November 10, 1818. B. Perkins, *Castlereagh and Adams,* 260. Perkins concluded that Great Britain "wanted to reduce the chance of friction even if they could not fix the boundary all the way to the Pacific Ocean" and that "the American political world welcomed the convention" (pp. 267, 272).

71 Richard Rush, *Memoranda of a Residence at the Court of London* (Philadelphia: Carey, Lea and Blanchard, 1833), 379.

72 For Astor's influence on American foreign policy, see, especially, James P. Ronda, *Astoria and Empire* (Lincoln: University of Nebraska Press, 1990).

73 JQA, Diary 30, September 29, 1817, 259 [electronic edition].

74 This reconstruction of the conversation comes from the British Foreign Office archives (F.O. 5, vol. 13). See Katherine B. Judson,

"British Side of the Restoration of Fort Astoria," in *Oregon Historical Quarterly* 20 (1919): 243–260, 305–330.

75 Castlereagh's orders of January 1818 can be found in Alfred LeRoy Burt, *The United States, Great Britain, and British North America from the Revolution to the Establishment of Peace after the War of 1812* (New Haven: Yale University Press, 1940), 414.

76 JQA, Diary 31, January 27, 1821, 502 [electronic edition].

77 *ASPFR*, 4:96.

78 Throughout the eighteenth century, Florida, originally part of Spain's empire, remained a pawn of the European powers. In 1763 the Treaty of Paris, which concluded the French-Indian War, ceded Florida and portions of Louisiana to Britain from Spain, which had participated in the war as a French ally. London divided the territory into East and West Florida, with their respective capitals in St. Augustine and Pensacola.

79 For an exhaustive study of the West Florida case, see J. C. A. Stagg, *Borderlines in Borderlands: James Madison and the Spanish-American Frontier, 1776–1821* (New Haven: Yale University Press, 2009), chap. 2, "West Florida," 52–87.

80 JQA, Diary 30, April 18, 1817, 171 [electronic edition].

81 JQA, Diary 30, May 3, 1817, 181 [electronic edition].

82 JQA, Diary 30, July 22, 1817, 230 [electronic edition]. While Adams recorded this conversation on July 22, it was a re-creation of events that had transpired on June 7, 1818. Sailing across the Atlantic, he took advantage of his leisure time to write a more extensive account of his final weeks in London.

83 Jackson had a long history with the Creeks and Seminoles extending from his encounters with them, as both allies and foes, in the War of 1812. The best account can be found in Robert Remini, *Andrew Jackson and His Indian Wars* (New York: Viking, 2001). Most pertinent to the Seminole War of 1818 was the Treaty of Fort Jackson. Signed on August 9, 1814, following the defeat of the Red Sticks (Upper Creek) at the Battle of Horseshoe Bend in Alabama, this treaty ended

the Creek War. The treaty ceded twenty-three million acres of Creek land in Alabama and Georgia to the United States and served as a major provocation to the subsequent Indian wars.

84 Andrew Jackson to George Graham, December 16, 1817, in John Spencer Bassett, ed., *Correspondence of Andrew Jackson,* vol. 2, *May 1, 1814–December 31, 1819* (Washington, D.C.: Carnegie Institute of Washington, 1927), 340.

85 The historical record is inconclusive, although most scholars conclude that Monroe's and Calhoun's silence on the matter perhaps indicated tacit approval. See especially Bemis, *Foundations* (1949), 314n39; Remini, *Andrew Jackson and His Indian Wars,* 137–140; and William Weeks, "John Quincy Adams' 'Great Gun' and the Rhetoric of American Empire," *Diplomatic History* 14, no. 1 (Winter 1990): 28.

86 John C. Calhoun to Andrew Jackson, December 16, 1817, in Bassett, *Correspondence of Andrew Jackson,* 2:342.

87 The fort was so called because it had previously been inhabited by runaway slaves and Indians. Set up by the infamous British lieutenant colonel Edward Nicholls following the War of 1812 to provide both a haven and a staging ground for attacks on the United States, the fort was located at the intersection of the Chattahoochee and Flint Rivers. The British had used this base as a resupply depot for their Indian allies during the war. As word of it spread, it also became a haven for runaway slaves. A fort defended and armed by blacks and Indians, located only sixty miles from Georgia and supplied with British ammunition, was a clear and present danger to U.S. forces. Accordingly, in July 1816 the fort was destroyed by a naval contingent sent down the Flint River. See, especially, Remini, *Andrew Jackson and His Indian Wars,* 97, 130ff.

88 *American State Papers, Military Affairs* (hereafter cited as *ASPMA*) (Washington, D.C.: Gales and Seaton, 1832–1859), 1:698.

89 *ASPMA,* 1:702.

90 Andrew Jackson to John C. Calhoun, May (4) 5, 1818, in Bassett, *Correspondence of Andrew Jackson,* 2:367. The transcript of the court-

martial may be found in *ASPMA*, 1:721–734. For a full reconstruction of the trial, see Remini, *Andrew Jackson and His Indian Wars*, 153–157. Also see the reports of the House and Senate committees that disapproved of the special court (Remini, *Andrew Jackson and His Indian Wars*, 157n30, and *ASPMA*, 1:735–743).

91 *ASPMA*, 1:713.

92 *ASPFR*, 4:602.

93 Quoted in Remini, *Andrew Jackson and His Indian Wars*, 161.

94 JQA, Diary 30, April 14, 1818, 336 [electronic edition].

95 Quoted in Bemis, *Foundations*, 301. The No-Transfer Resolution referred specifically to the Floridas. It passed the Senate and House on January 15, 1811, declaring that "under the peculiar circumstances of the existing crisis, [the United States] cannot without serious inquietude see any part of the said territory pass into the hands of any foreign Power; and that a due regard to their own safety compels them to provide under certain contingencies, for the temporary occupation of the said territory; they, at the same time, declare that the said territory shall, in their hands, remain subject to a future negotiation." Congress passed this resolution in response to the South American provinces declaring their independence from Spain. There is much room to speculate as to the extent to which this resolution, passed while Adams served as U.S. minister to Russia, shaped and influenced Adams's subsequent thinking regarding the Floridas.

96 JQA, Diary 30, May 8, 1818, 346 [electronic edition].

97 JQA, Diary 30, May 13, 1818, 349 [electronic edition].

98 JQA to Albert Gallatin, May 19, 1818, in JQA, *Writings,* 6:312ff.

99 JQA, Diary 30, July 8, 1818, 370 [electronic edition].

100 JQA to William Plumer, July 6, 1818, in JQA, *Writings,* 6:380.

101 The treaty referred to was Pinckney's 1795 agreement with Spain that obliged both the United States and Spain "expressly to restrain by force all hostilities on the part of the Indian Nations living within their boundaries: so that Spain will not suffer her Indians to attack the Citizens of the United States, nor the Indians inhabiting their

territory; nor will the United States permit these last mentioned Indians to commence hostilities against the Subjects of his Catholic Majesty, or his Indians in any manner whatever." *ASPFR*, 1:547.

102 JQA to James Monroe, July 8, 1818 in JQA, Writings, VII. 283 ff. There is no work that fully explores Adams's view of Indians. George A. Lipsky, *John Quincy Adams: His Theory and Ideas* (New York: Thomas Y. Crowell, 1950), contains a chapter on Adams's view of race. This is a good a good starting place, particularly pp. 121–122, but its focus is on slavery. Lynn Hudson Parsons, in his "A Perpetual Harrow upon My Feelings": John Quincy Adams and the American Indian," *New England Quarterly* 46, no. 3 (September 1973): 339–379, traces Adams's evolving views on American Indians and argues that his attitude shifted from one of hostility to curiosity to outrage over the latter stages of his career.

103 JQA, Diary 30, July 25, 1818, 378 [electronic edition].

104 JQA, Diary 30, July 15, 1818, 373 [electronic edition].

105 JQA, Diary 30, July 17, 1818, 375 [electronic edition].

106 JQA, Diary 30, July 21, 1818, 377 [electronic edition].

107 See Ernest May, *The Making of the Monroe Doctrine* (Cambridge, Mass: Harvard University Press, 1975). Weeks, *John Quincy Adams and American Global Empire;* Weeks, "John Quincy Adams' 'Great Gun'"; Richard H. Immerman, *Empire for Liberty: A History of American Imperialism from Benjamin Franklin to Paul Wolfowitz* (Princeton: Princeton University Press, 2010); and Jay Sexton's insightful *The Monroe Doctrine: Empire and Nation in Nineteenth-Century America* (New York: Hill and Wang, 2011). On the question of whether Adams was an imperialist, it depends on how one defines empire. The question is as political as it is definitional, and the literature on empire is enormous. The most useful starting places are D. K. Fieldhouse, "Imperialism: An Historiographical Revision," *Economic History Review* 14, 187–209(1961); Ronald Edward Robinson, and John Gallagher *Africa and the Victorians: The Official Mind of Imperialism* (New York: St. Martin's Press, 1967); and D. K. Fieldhouse, *The Colonial Empires: A Comparative Survey from the Eighteenth Century* (New York: Delacorte Press, 1967). When applied to

the question of whether or not America was or is an empire, a useful and comparative work is Charles S. Maier, *Among Empires: American Ascendency and Its Predecessors* (Cambridge, Mass.: Harvard University Press, 2006). Before condemning Adams as an imperialist, it is worth considering his complicated response to the Louisiana Purchase. Adams spent much time thinking through how the federal government could constitutionally incorporate new territories. While he supported the acquisition, he voted against it on the basis that it was unconstitutional and that the Constitution provided no formalized process for incorporating territories.

108 JQA, Diary 30, July 21, 1818, 377 [electronic edition]. Adams's letter of November 28, 1818, to George W. Erving also appears in *ASPFR*, 4:539ff.

109 JQA, Diary 30, November 8, 1818, 438 [electronic edition].

110 JQA, Diary 30, November 8, 1818, 438 [electronic edition]. For an argument that Jackson's evidence was less than compelling, and hardly conclusive, see Weeks, "John Quincy Adams' 'Great Gun,'" 29.

111 JQA, Diary 30, November 8, 1818, 438 [electronic edition].

112 *ASPFA*, 4:544. Emphasis in original text.

113 JQA, Diary 30, November 16, 1818, 442 [electronic edition].

114 Rush, *Court of London*, 451.

115 See Bemis, *Foundations* 328, and Weeks, "John Quincy Adams' 'Great Gun,'" 40.

116 John Adams Smith to JQA, January 24, 1819, Adams Papers, MHS, Microfilm, reel 446; Bemis, *John Quincy Adams and the Foundations*, 328.

117 Jefferson to Monroe, January 18–19, 1819, in Paul Leicester Ford, ed., *The Writings of Thomas Jefferson* (New York: G. P. Putnam's Sons, 1899), 10:122.

118 Weeks, "John Quincy Adams' 'Great Gun,'" 41.

119 Bemis offers the authoritative play-by-play account of the negotiations on the boundary line. See, Bemis, *Foundations,* chap. 16, "The Transcontinental Treaty with Spain, 317ff.

120 Thomas Hart Benton, *Thirty Years' View; or, A History of the Working of the American Government for Thirty Years, from 1820 to 1850* (New York: D. Appleton, 1854), 15.

121 Wm. Henry Smith, *Charles Hammond and His Relations to Henry Clay and John Quincy Adams; or, Constitutional Limitations and the Contest for Freedom of Speech and the Press; An Address Delivered before the Chicago Historical Society, May 20, 1884* (Chicago: Chicago Historical Society, 1885), 33.

122 JQA, Diary 31, March 31, 1820, 301ff. [electronic edition]. See both Kagan, 200ff., and Weeks, *John Quincy Adams and America Global Empire*, 166ff.

123 JQA, Diary 31, April 13, 1820, 313ff. [electronic edition].

124 JQA, Diary 31, April 13, 1820, 313ff. [electronic edition].

125 Monroe to Jefferson, May 1820, in Monroe, *Writings,* 6:120.

126 Monroe to Andrew Jackson, May 23, 1820, in Monroe, *Writings,* 6:126ff. It is worth noting that Jackson, at the time, responded to Monroe that he entirely agreed with his assessment.

127 JQA, Diary 31, March 3, 1820, 275ff. [electronic edition].

128 JQA, Diary 31, March 3, 1820, 275ff. [electronic edition].

129 For more on the Republican Party's position on labor, see Eric Foner, *Free Soil, Free Labor, Free Men: The Ideology of the Republican Party before the Civil War* (Oxford, Oxford University Press, 1995 [1970]).

130 JQA, Diary 31, March 3, 1820, 275ff. [electronic edition].

131 In his essay *Two Concepts of Liberty,* Berlin wrote that "if, as I believe, the ends of men are many, and not all of them are in principle compatible with each other, then the possibility of conflict—and of tragedy—can never wholly be eliminated from human life, either personal or social." Isaiah Berlin, *The Proper Study of Mankind: An Anthology of Essays,* ed. Henry Hardy and Roger Housheer (London: Chatto and Windus, 1997), 239.

132 JQA, Diary 31, April 13, 1820, 313 [electronic edition].

133 For more on the role that slavery played in the Missouri Compromise, see Forbes, *The Missouri Compromise and Its Aftermath;* Richard

H. Brown, "The Missouri Crisis, Slavery, and the Politics of Jacksonianism," *South Atlantic Quarterly* 65 (1966): 55–72, Don E. Febrenbacher, "The Missouri Controversy and the Sources of Southern Separatism," *Southern Review* 14 (1978): 653–667, Ronald C. Woolsey, "The West Becomes a Problem: The Missouri Controversy and Slavery Expansion as the Southern Dilemma," *Missouri Historical Review* 77 (1983): 409–432; and Sean Wilentz, "Jeffersonian Democracy and the Origins of Political Antislavery in the United States: The Missouri Crisis Revisited," *Journal of the Historical Society* 4 (2004): 375–401.

134 JQA, Diary 31, November 29, 1820, 456 [electronic edition].

135 JQA to Robert Walsh Jr., July 10, 1821, in JQA, *Writings,* 7:114, 117.

136 In January 1820, the *Edinburgh Review* published a review of Robert Walsh's new book, *An Appeal from the Judgments of Great Britain respecting the United States of America: Part First, Containing an Historical Outline of Their Merits and Wrongs as Colonies, and Strictures upon the Calumnies of the British Writers* (Philadelphia: Mitchell, Ames, and White, 1819). The reviewer snidely asked: "In the four quarters of the globe, who reads an American book? Or goes to an American play? Or looks at an American picture or statue?"; quoted in Arthur Preston Whitaker, *The United States and the Independence of Latin America, 1800–1830* (New York: Russell and Russell, 1962), 351. Adams wrote Walsh that this question—and its derivative, "what has America done for mankind?"—motivated him to deliver his July 4 address.

137 John Quincy Adams, *An Address Delivered at the Request of a Committee of the Citizens of Washington; On the Occasion of Reading the Declaration of Independence on the Fourth of July, 1821* (Washington, D.C.: Davis and Force, 1821), 12, 21. This copy of the speech is the one that Adams submitted to the Committee of the Citizens of Washington, expressly for publication, on July 5, 1821.

138 JQA, *An Address,* 22.

139 JQA, *An Address,* 21, 22ff.

140 JQA, *An Address,* 28, 29.

141 JQA, *An Address,* 29.

142 JQA, *An Address*, 31. Capitalization in original.

143 Poletica to Nesselrode, July 30, 1821, quoted in Bemis, *Foundations*, 357ff. For a more assertive interpretation of Adams's emphasis in this speech, see Kagan, *Dangerous Nation*, 163.

144 JQA to Edward Everett, January 31, 1822, in JQA, *Writings*, 7:199.

145 JQA to Edward Everett, January 31, 1822, in JQA, *Writings*, 7:199.

146 Poletica to Nesselrode, July 30, 1821, quoted in Bemis, *Foundations*, 357.

147 JQA to Charles Jared Ingersoll, July 23, 1821, in JQA, *Writings*, 7:121.

148 JQA to Edward Everett, January 31, 1822, in JQA, *Writings*, 7:199.

149 JQA to Edward Everett, January 31, 1822, in JQA, *Writings*, 7:199.

150 JQA to Robert Walsh Jr., July 27, 1821, in JQA, *Writings*, 7:131.

151 JQA to Edward Everett, January 31, 1822, in JQA, *Writings*, 7:201.

152 JQA to Charles Jared Ingersoll, June 19, 1823, in JQA, *Writings*, 7:488.

153 JQA to Robert Walsh Jr., July 27, 1821, in JQA, *Writings*, 7:131.

154 JQA to Charles Jared Ingersoll, June 19, 1823, in JQA, *Writings*, 7:488.

155 JQA, Diary 31, March 9, 1821, 551 [electronic edition].

156 Ammon, *James Monroe*, 409-410.

157 Walter LaFeber, *The American Age: United States Foreign Policy at Home and Abroad since 1750* (New York: W. W. Norton, 1989), 81. Dexter Perkins, in his *The Monroe Doctrine, 1823-1826* (Cambridge, Mass.: Harvard University Press, 1927), adds the point that when reading Adams's journals it seems clear that the United States was motivated not by trade interests but by political and ideological considerations. These are not mutually exclusive interpretations. Even if principally motivated by ideology, the thought of increased commerce with South America certainly played a role in the administration's desire for closer relations. As most shipping was based out of New England, this is doubly true for Adams.

158 *ASPFR*, 4:846.

159 Monroe to JQA, July 24, 1821, in JQA, *Writings*, 7:138n2.

160 See especially Dexter Perkins's chapter "What Europe Intended" in his *The Monroe Doctrine, 1823-1826*, 104-143.

161 George Canning to Charles Stuart, in March 31, 1823, *Niles Weekly Register.*

162 Stratford Canning to George Canning, May 8, 1823, quoted in D. Perkins, *The Monroe Doctrine,* 1927, 60.

163 JQA, Diary 34, June 20, 1823, 85ff. [electronic edition].

164 Rush, *Court of London,* 459.

165 Rush realized that policy is determined not abroad, but in Washington. When Canning began his "great flirtation," Rush demurred, telling him, "I was willing to take upon myself all fair responsibility attaching to the station which I held; but here was a conjuncture wholly new. It presented a case not seeming to fall within the range of any of the contingent or discretionary duties that could have been in contemplation when I was clothed with my commission as Minister to this Court. For meeting a case thus extraordinary, if I could do so at all, I ought to have some justification beyond any that had yet been laid before me. Such was my opinion; such the conclusion to which I had been forced to come on full deliberation." Rush, *Court of London,* 433–434.

166 George Canning to Liverpool, August 26, 1823, quoted in B. Perkins, *Castlereagh and Adams,* 318.

167 Rush, *Court of London,* 412ff.

168 Rush, *Court of London,* 432.

169 The modern usage comes from then Deputy Secretary of State Robert Zoellick's 2005 speech "Whither China: From Membership to Responsibility?" Zoellick delivered the speech on September 21, 2005, and called for the United States to "encourage China to become a responsible stakeholder. As a responsible stakeholder, China would be more than just a member—it would work with us to sustain the international system that has enabled its success"; http://2001-2009 .state.gov/s/d/former/zoellick/rem/53682.htm.

170 Rush, *Court of London,* 434–435.

171 Jefferson to Monroe, October 24, 1823, in Ford, *The Writings of Thomas Jefferson,* 10:277.

172 James Madison to James Monroe, October 30, 1823, in Monroe, *Writings,* 6:394.

173 Monroe to Madison, October 17, 1823, Rives Collections, Madison Papers, Founding Era Collection, Rotunda Database, http://rotunda .upress.virginia.edu/founders/default.xqy?keys=FGEA-search-1-1&expand Note=on#match.

174 JQA, Diary 34, November 7, 1823, 149 [electronic edition].

175 JQA to Richard Rush, November 30, 1823, quoted in Worthington Chauncey Ford, "John Quincy Adams and the Monroe Doctrine," *American Historical Review* 8, no. 1 (October 1902): 48.

176 JQA, Diary 34, November 17, 1823, 160 [electronic edition].

177 JQA, Diary 34, November 15 and 26, 1823, 157, 172 [electronic edition].

178 JQA, Diary 34, November 26, 1823, 157 [electronic edition].

179 JQA, Diary 34, November 28, 1823, 179 [electronic edition].

180 JQA, Diary 34, November 26, 1823, 172ff. [electronic edition].

181 Monroe to Jefferson, June 23, 1823, quoted in D. Perkins, *The Monroe Doctrine,* 1927: 60.

182 To the author's knowledge, there is no existing copy of Monroe's draft message. Instead, Adams's diary from November 21, 1823, provides the only available evidence of what it contained.

183 JQA, Diary 34, November 21, 1823, 164 [electronic edition].

184 JQA, Diary 34, November 22, 164–165 [electronic edition]. For more on Adams's political motives, see May, *Making of the Monroe Doctrine.* A challenge to May's argument can be found by the James Monroe scholar and biographer Harry Ammon in his "The Monroe Doctrine: Domestic Politics or National Decision?," *Diplomatic History* 5 (Winter 1981): 53–70. The most comprehensive overview of the development of the doctrine and its subsequent impact remains Dexter Perkins's trilogy: *The Monroe Doctrine, 1823–1826* (Cambridge, Mass.: Harvard University Press, 1927); *The Monroe Doctrine, 1826–1867* (Baltimore: Johns Hopkins Press, 1933); and *The Monroe Doctrine, 1867–1907* (Baltimore: Johns Hopkins University

Press, 1937). These volumes were subsequently synthesized into a single work in Perkins's *A History of the Monroe Doctrine* (Boston: Little, Brown, 1963). More recently, Jay Sexton's *The Monroe Doctrine* (2011) tracks the changing interpretation of the Monroe Doctrine and the uses to which it was put in the nineteenth and twentieth centuries.

185 JQA, Diary 34, November 25, 1823, 168ff. [electronic edition].

186 JQA, "Observations on the Communications Recently Received from the Minister from Russia," Department of State, November 27, 1823, quoted in Ford, "John Quincy Adams and the Monroe Doctrine," 43.

187 JQA, "Observations on the Communications Recently Received," 43ff.

188 JQA, Diary 34, November 26, 1823, 174 [electronic edition].

189 JQA, Diary 34, November 27, 177 [electronic edition]. Same sentiment, different government: "A political system which may be antithetical but need not be inimical." Barbara W. Tuchman, *Notes from China* (New York: Collier Books, 1972), 74.

190 James Monroe, Annual Message to Congress, December 2, 1823, in *ASPFR,* 5:250. See also http://avalon.law.yale.edu/19th_century/monroe.asp.

191 JQA to LCA, October 7, 1822, in JQA, *Writings,* 7:316ff.

192 This is, however, perfectly in keeping with Carl von Clausewitz's dictum that "war is nothing but the continuation of policy with other means." Carl von Clausewitz, *On War,* ed. and trans. Michael Howard and Peter Paret (New York: Knopf, 1993), 77.

193 JQA, Diary 34, August 9, 1823, 116 [electronic edition].

CHAPTER 4 *The Spirit of Improvement*

1 Mary S. Lockwood, *Historic Homes in Washington: Its Noted Men and Women* (New York: Belford, 1889), 72; "Mrs. John Quincy Adams's Ball, 1824," *Harper's Bazaar,* March 18, 1871: 4:166–169.

2   Charles Francis Adams, *Diary*, ed. Aïda DiPace Donald and David Donald (Cambridge, Mass.: Harvard University Press, 1964), 32ff.

3   "Mrs. John Quincy Adams's Ball, 1824," 167.

4   CFA, *Diary*, 33.

5   "Mrs. John Quincy Adams's Ball, 1824," 167.

6   Only two members of Congress, Alexander Smyth and John Floyd, were not invited. In his diary Adams wrote that this was owing to "their personal deportment to me." JQA, Diary 34, January 6, 1824, 203 [electronic edition].

7   LCA, *Diary*, Adams Papers, MHS, Microfilm, reel 265, quoted in Jack Shepherd, *Cannibals of the Heart: A Personal Biography of Louisa Catherine and John Quincy Adams* (New York: McGraw-Hill, 1980), 242.

8   CFA, *Diary*, January 8, 1824, 34.

9   JQA, Diary 34, January 8, 1824, 204 [electronic edition].

10   John Bach McMaster, *A History of the People of the United States, from the Revolution to the Civil War*, 7 vols. (New York: D. Appleton, 1900), 5:68.

11   JQA, Diary 34, May 19, 1824, 325 [electronic edition].

12   William Plumer Jr., *The Missouri Compromises and Presidential Politics, 1820–1825, from the Letters of William Plumer, Junior, Representative from New Hampshire*, ed. Everett Somerville Brown (St. Louis: Missouri Historical Society, 1926), 84ff.

13   JQA, Diary 34, May 15, 1824, 320 [electronic edition]. Previously, Adams had recommended that Jackson be appointed minister to Mexico—which, conveniently enough, would have taken the general out of the country in the run-up to the 1824 election. Not that surprisingly, Jackson declined the offer.

14   James Lauritz Larson, *Internal Improvement: National Public Works and the Promise of Popular Government in the Early United States* (Chapel Hill: University of North Carolina Press, 2001).

15   Federalist 11, in Alexander Hamilton, Alexander Hamilton, John Jay, and James Madison, *The Federalist* (New York: Penguin, 1961), 91.

16   For a detailed discussion of Hamilton's views on the United States' political economy, see Edward Mead Earl, "Adam Smith,

Alexander Hamilton, Friedrich List: The Economic Foundations of Military Power," in Peter Paret, ed., *Makers of Modern Strategy: Rulers, States, and War* (Princeton: Princeton University Press, 1986), 217–261.

17 In particular, see Mathew Carey, *The Olive Branch; or, Faults on Both Sides, Federal and Democratic: A Serious Appeal on the Necessity of Mutual Forgiveness and Harmony, to Save Our Common Country from Ruin,* 3rd ed. (Boston: Rowe and Hooper, 1815), and, more significantly, his *Essays on Political Economy; or, The Most Certain Means of Promoting the Wealth, Power, Resources, and Happiness of Nations: Applied Particularly to the United States* (Philadelphia: H. C. Carey and I. Lea, 1822).

18 For the influence of Carey on Clay, see Maurice G. Baxter, *Henry Clay and the American System* (Lexington: University Press of Kentucky, 1995), 24. Also see Robert V. Remini, *Henry Clay: Statesman for the Union* (New York: W. W. Norton, 1991), 228.

19 Both Harry Watson, in *Liberty and Power: The Politics of Jacksonian America* (New York: Hill and Wang, 1990), 77, and Sean Wilentz, in *The Rise of American Democracy: Jefferson to Lincoln* (New York: W.W. Norton, 2005), 243, suggest that Clay's support of the American System arose from both his desire to maintain his political constituency in the West and his sincere belief in national harmony. Both authors, however, give insufficient attention to the Clay-Adams convergence that occurred at the beginning of the Adams administration.

20 *Niles' Weekly Register,* July 19, 1828.

21 JQA, Diary 31, March 29, 1820, 299 [electronic edition].

22 Daniel Walker Howe's excellent *The Political Culture of the American Whigs* (Chicago: University of Chicago Press, 1979) uses Adams's beliefs in societal improvement, governmental stewardship of the market, and the importance of communal morality as early examples of what would become the basis for Whig political culture. While Adams is a somewhat atypical Whig in Howe's rendering, as he never formally joined the party, it is worth noting that all of Adams's Whig-like beliefs and programs were fully developed *before* the rise of the second party system.

23 The two preceding quotations come from Adams's Annual Message to Congress, December 6, 1825, http://millercenter.org/scripps /archive/speeches/detail/3514.

24 JQA to John D. Heath, January 7, 1822, in JQA, *Writings*, 7:191ff.

25 JQA, Diary 30, March 18, 1818, 322 [electronic edition].

26 Ketcham's *Presidents above Party: The First American Presidency, 1789–1829* offers the best study of the ideas and the ideals behind the early presidency. For Ketcham's treatment of Bolingbroke, see especially pp. 57–68.

27 JQA to P. P. C. Degrand, November 15, 1818, quoted in Samuel Flagg Bemis, *John Quincy Adams and the Union* 18.

28 JQA to John Lewis, February 20, 1822, in JQA, *Writings*, 7:209.

29 Joseph Hopkinson to LCA, January, 1823, quoted by Charles Francis Adams in JQA, *Memoirs*, 6:130ff.

30 "The Macbeth Policy," January 23, 1823, in JQA, *Writings*, 7:356ff.

31 JQA to James Hackett, February 7, 1839, reprinted in the *National Intelligencer* (Washington), November 30, 1839; JQA, "Misconceptions of Shakespeare, upon the Stage," *New England Magazine* (December 9, 1835): 435–440. Another observer recorded Adams remarking that the character of Hamlet was "the most beautiful creation . . . of the human imagination"; Philip Hone, *The Diary of Philip Hone, 1828–1851*, ed. with an introduction by Bayard Tuckerman (New York: Dodd, Mead, 1910), pt. 2, 342.

32 JQA to LCA, October 7, 1822, in JQA, *Writings*, 7:316.

33 Castlereagh, the British foreign secretary, had committed suicide in August 1822.

34 JQA, Diary 34, May 8, 1824, 311 [electronic edition].

35 JQA, Diary 33, February 2, 1825, 67ff. [electronic edition].

36 See Catherine Allgor, *Parlor Politics: In Which the Ladies of Washington Help Build a City and a Government* (Charlottesville: University Press of Virginia, 2000), especially chap. 4, "Louisa Catherine Adams Campaigns for the Presidency," 147–189.

37 Anne Royall, *Royall's Sketches of History, Life, and Manners in the United States by a Traveller* (New Haven: Printed for the Author, 1826),

169; Senator Elijah H. Mills to his wife, December 24, 1820, *Proceedings of the Massachusetts Historical Society* 19 (1881–1882): 28.

38 JQA to John Heath, January 7, 1822, in JQA, *Writings,* 7:194.

39 "The Macbeth Policy," January 23, 1823, in JQA, *Writings,* 7:360.

40 For years after Adams's counterattack, the term "to Jonathan Russell" entered into popular discourse and meant to destroy some-one's reputation and career.

41 JQA to Robert Walsh, May 30, 1822, in JQA, *Writings,* 7:260.

42 JQA to James Lloyd, October 1, 1822, in JQA, *Writings,* 7:311.

43 For Smyth's letter, see the *National Intelligencer,* January 7, 1823.

44 "To the Freeholders of Washington, Wythe, Grayson, Russell, Tazewell, Lee and Scott Counties, Virginia." The letter first appeared in the *Richmond Enquirer,* January 4, 1823. Reprinted in JQA, *Writings,* 7:335–354.

45 See *Sketch of the life of John Quincy Adams; taken from the Port Folio of April, 1819. To which are added, the letters of Tell: originally addressed to the editor of the Baltimore American. Respectfully submitted to the serious consideration of those freeholders of Virginia, who desire to exercise the high privilege of voting for a president of the United States at the approaching election* (No place of publication given, 1824). Also see "JQA Loquitur," March 1824, Adams Papers, MHS, microfilm, reel 464.

46 *National Gazette* (Philadelphia), October 28, 1824.

47 Thomas Jefferson to William Johnson, October 27, 1822, http://hdl.loc.gov/loc.mss/mtj.mtjbib024477.

48 Precise numbers are difficult to come by for this election, as states differed in how they counted votes and how they selected their presidential electors. The popular vote numbers are drawn from the eighteen states where presidential electors were elected by popular vote. In Delaware, Georgia, Louisiana, New York, South Carolina, and Vermont the electors were chosen by their respective state legislatures.

49 JQA, Diary 49, December 17, 1824, 718 [electronic edition].

50 JQA, Diary 49, December 19, 1824, 723 [electronic edition].

51 JQA, Diary 49, December 22, 1824, 727 [electronic edition].

52   JQA, Diary 49, December 15, 1824, 714 [electronic edition].

53   JQA, Diary 49, December 17, 1824, 718 [electronic edition].

54   After a subsequent meeting with Letcher, Adams wrote, "Incendo super ignes"—I walk above fire. JQA, Diary 49, December 23, 1824, 729 [electronic edition].

55   Louis McClane to his wife, January 13, 1825, quoted in Remini, *Henry Clay*, 257.

56   For discussions of the timing and motivations behind the Clay-Adams alliance, see Wilentz, *The Rise of American Democracy*, 254–257; Merrill D. Peterson, *The Great Triumvirate: Webster, Clay, and Calhoun* (New York: Oxford University Press, 1987), 126–131; and especially Remini, *Henry Clay*, 253–264.

57   Henry Clay to Francis P. Blair, January 8, 1825, in James F. Hopkins, ed., *The Papers of Henry Clay*, vol. 4, *Secretary of State, 1825* (Lexington: University Press of Kentucky, 1972), 10. All subsequent citations to Clay's letters will appear in the form Clay, *Papers*, 4:10.

58   Clay to Francis Brooke, January, 28, 1825, in Clay, *Papers*, 4:45.

59   For a good summary of Clay's thinking on this subject, see Kimberly C. Shankman, *Compromise and the Constitution: The Political Thought of Henry Clay* (Lanham, Md.: Lexington Books, 1999), 37–40.

60   Clay to Francis P. Blair, January 29, 1825, in Clay, *Papers*, 4:47.

61   See George Dangerfield, *The Awakening of American Nationalism* (New York: Harper and Row, 1965), 225; and Bemis, *John Quincy Adams and the Union*, 40.

62   Howe, in his *Political Culture of the American Whigs*, argues that "the kind of progress that Henry Clay believed in was the same kind of progress John Quincy Adams believed in, one of stability and order" (p.125).

63   JQA, Diary 36, January 9, 1825, 7 [electronic edition].

64   Gaillard Hunt, ed., *The First Forty Years of Washington Society Portrayed by the Family Letters of Mrs. Samuel Harrison (Margaret Bayard) Smith* (New York: C. Scribner's Sons, 1906), 186.

65   Hunt, *The First Forty Years of Washington Society*, 186ff.

66 Hunt, *The First Forty Years of Washington Society,* 183.

67 JQA, Diary 33, February 9, 1825, 77 [electronic edition].

68 LCA, November 30, 1823, in Louisa Catherine Adams, *Diary and Autobiographical Writings of Louisa Catherine Adams,* 2:669.

69 *National Gazette* (Philadelphia), March 8, 1825.

70 *Richmond Enquirer,* March 8, 1825, originally published in the *National Intelligencer.*

71 *National Gazette* (Philadelphia), March 8, 1825.

72 John Quincy Adams, Inaugural Address, http://avalon.law.yale .edu/19th_century/qadams.asp.

73 Robert Forbes, *The Missouri Compromise and Its Aftermath: Slavery and the Meaning of America* (Chapel Hill: The University of North Carolina Press, 2007), 186.

74 JQA, Inaugural Address. See also Michael J. Birkner's biography of Samuel Southard, Adams's secretary of the navy. Birkner quotes Southard as telling a friend that Adams "will consider the line of duty marked out by Mr. Monroe as the one in which it is his duty to walk. The policy of the Government will be unchanged." Birkner, *Samuel J. Southard: Jeffersonian Whig* (Rutherford, N.J.: Fairleigh Dickinson University Press, 1984), 71.

75 For similar sentiments, see Henry Clay's speech, while still serving as Speaker of the House, on the Cumberland Road Bill. Clay had asked, "Is it not the solemn duty of this House, to strengthen . . . the principles of cohesion which bind us to-gether . . . ? Can the imagination of man conceive a policy better calculated than that of which the present measure forms a part, to bring the opposite extremities of our country together—to bind its various parts to each other, and to multiply and strengthen the various and innumerable ties of commercial, social, and literary intercourse?" Quoted in Clay, *Papers,* 4:19ff.; see especially January 17, 1825, 4:25.

76 JQA, Inaugural Address.

77 JQA, Inaugural Address.

78 JQA, Diary 33, February 11, 1825, 79 [electronic edition]. Also see Plumer, *The Missouri Compromises and Presidential Politics,* 139ff., for details.

79 JQA, Diary 29, September 25, 1814, 151 [electronic edition].

80 JQA to James Lloyd, October 1, 1822, in JQA, *Writings,* 7:310ff.

81 JQA, Diary 37, November 28, 1825, 17 [electronic edition].

82 JQA, Diary 37, November 26, 1825, 16 [electronic edition]. For Barbour's initial comments, see Adams's entry of November 23, 1825.

83 JQA, Diary 37, November 26, 1825, 16 [electronic edition].

84 JQA, Diary 37, November 26, 1825, 16 [electronic edition].

85 JQA, Annual Message to Congress, December 6, 1825, http://millercenter.org/scripps/archive/speeches/detail/3514.

86 "Annual Report of the Secretary of the Navy, with the President's Message, Showing the Operations of That Department in 1825," December 2, 1825, *American State Papers, Naval Affairs,* 2:98ff.

87 JQA, Annual Message to Congress, December 6, 1825.

88 JQA, Annual Message to Congress, December 6, 1825.

89 JQA, Diary 33, April 23, 1825, 131 [electronic edition].

90 See Odd Arne Westad, *The Global Cold War: Third World Interventions and the Making of Our Times* (Cambridge: Cambridge University Press, 2005) where he argues that American foreign policy, at its core, amounted to exporting its developmental model. See especially his excellent first chapter, "The Empire of Liberty: American Ideology and Foreign Interventions," 8-38.

91 John Quincy Adams, Special Message to the U.S. Senate, December 26, 1825, quoted in John T. Woolley and Gerhard Peters, The American Presidency Project [online], http://www.presidency.ucsb.edu/ws/?pid=66660.

92 JQA, Special Message to the U.S. Senate, December 26, 1825.

93 Compare Arthur Whitaker, *The United States and the Independence of Latin America, 1800–1830* (New York: Russell & Russell, Inc., 1962), 575, and James E. Lewis Jr., *The American Union and the Problem of Neighborhood : The United States and the Collapse of the Spanish Empire, 1783–1829* (Chapel Hill: University of North Carolina Press, 1998), 215ff.

94   JQA, Special Message to the U.S. Senate, December 26, 1825.

95   JQA, Diary 37, February 8, 1826, 75 [electronic edition].

96   Martin Van Buren to Benjamin Butler, December 25, 1825, quoted in Robert V. Remini, *Martin Van Buren and the Making of the Democratic Party* (New York: Columbia University Press, 1959), 100.

97   *Register of Debates,* Senate, 19th Cong., 1st sess., March 14, 1826, 242.

98   *Register of Debates,* House of Representatives, 19th Cong., 1st sess., April 10, 1826, 2163.

99   *Register of Debates,* Senate, 19th Cong., 1st sess., March 14, 1826, 152ff. Quotation comes from pp. 165–166.

100   *Register of Debates,* Senate, 19th Cong., 1st sess., March 14, 1826, 325.

101   For another contemporary take on the volatility of racial issues in domestic politics, see Benton's *Thirty Years' View; Or, A History of the Working of the American Government for Thirty Years, from 1820 to 1850* (New York: D. Appleton & Company, 1854). 1:65–69.

102   *Register of Debates,* Senate, 19th Cong., 1st sess., March 14, 1826, 152ff. Quotation comes from pp. 166–167.

103   See Peterson, *The Great Triumvirate,* 140. The official record gives a damning but less incendiary version of Randolph's comments; *Register of Debates,* Senate, 19th Cong., 1st sess., 401. For more on the widespread resistance to the American System, and more broadly, the broad disruptions caused by the rapid development of a market economy, see Charles Sellers, *The Market Revolution: Jacksonian America, 1815–1846* (New York: Oxford University Press, 1991).

104   Clay and Randolph met for their duel on April 8, 1826. After an exchange of shots that went wide of their respective targets, either by design or because of shoddy marksmanship, Clay demanded a second round, and Randolph agreed. The secretary of state shot first and fired a bullet through Randolph's large white coat. Randolph, unharmed and unfazed, discharged his pistol in the air, and shaking Clay's hand, blandly remarked, "You owe me a coat, Mr. Clay." Having restored his

sense of honor, Clay replied that he was "glad the debt [was] no greater." Quotes from Peterson, *The Great Triumvirate*,141. Also see Benton, *Thirty Years' View,* 1:76ff.

105 Martin Van Buren to Harmanus Bleecker, February 25, 1827, quoted in Remini, *Henry Clay,* 310.

106 Edward J. Harden, *The Life of George M. Troup* (Savannah: E. J. Purse, 1859), 317, 485.

107 JQA, Diary 37, January 23, 1828, 409 [electronic edition]. For a fuller description of Adams and Native Americans, see Lynn Hudson Parsons, "A Perpetual Harrow upon My Feelings": John Quincy Adams and the American Indian," *New England Quarterly* 46, no. 3 (September 1973): 339-379.

108 Wilentz, *The Rise of American Democracy,* 264.

109 James Madison, Veto Message on the Internal Improvements Bill, March 3, 1817, http://millercenter.org/scripps/archive/speeches/detail /3630. This veto message surprised many, as Madison had spent the years after 1812 calling for energetic and enlarged government. For perspective on Madison's changing interpretations of the federal government's powers, see Larson, *Internal Improvement,* 67-69.

110 *Register of Debates,* 19th Cong., 2nd sess., March 1, 1827, 1499.

111 John Quincy Adams, Annual Message to Congress, December 6, 1825, http://millercenter.org/scripps/archive/speeches/detail/3514.

112 Andrew Jackson to John Branch, March 3, 1826, in Harold D. Moser and J. Clint Clifft, eds., *The Papers of Andrew Jackson,* vol. 6, *1825–1828* (Knoxville: University of Tennessee Press, 2002), 143.

113 Jackson, *Papers,* 6:142.

114 On Jackson's use of symbolism, see John William Ward, *Andrew Jackson: Symbol for an Age* (New York: Oxford University Press, 1955), 63, 65. See also Richard Hofstadter, *Anti-Intellectualism in American Life* (New York: Vintage Books, 1963), 157.

115 Feller, *The Jacksonian Promise: America, 1815–1840* (Baltimore: Johns Hopkins University Press, 1995), 83. See also Watson's assessment in

Liberty and Power that Adams was "determined to use federal power . . . to plan and fund a rapid but orderly transition to a commercial and industrial society" (p. 76). For earlier American versions of this debate, see Drew D. McCoy, *The Elusive Republic: Political Economy in Jeffersonian America* (Chapel Hill: University of North Carolina Press, 1980). And for the contemporary version of this debate, see David Brooks, "The Technocracy Boom," *New York Times,* July 19, 2010, http://www.nytimes .com/2010/07/20/opinion/20brooks.html.

116 *Niles' Weekly Register,* July 19, 1828.

117 Also, Adams probably failed to realize that the issue of land sales was increasingly tied to the issue of slavery. On February 18, 1825, Rufus King, embittered over southern hypocrisy and northern apathy, offered up a resolution calling for the proceeds of public land sales, after the retirement of the federal debt, to be "inviolably applied" to the emancipation and removal from the country of slaves and free blacks. See Forbes's excellent treatment of this, 193–196.

118 See James Lauritz Larson's "Liberty by Design: Freedom, Planning, and John Quincy Adams's American System," in Mary O. Furner and Barry Supple, eds., *The State and Economic Knowledge: The American and British Experiences,* (Cambridge: Cambridge University Press, 1990), especially 89–96, for a persuasive account of the popularity of Adams's programs and the success his opponents had in depicting him as an arrogant enemy of popular democracy.

119 *Register of Debates,* House of Representatives, 19th Cong., 2nd sess., February 20, 1827, 1271ff.

120 JQA, Inaugural Address. March 4, 1825.

121 Jefferson to William B. Giles, December 26, 1825, in Paul Leicester Ford, ed., *The Writings of Thomas Jefferson,* vol. 10 (New York: G. P. Putnam's Sons, 1899), 354.

122 JQA, Diary 33, May 13, 1825, 148 [electronic edition].

123 JQA, Diary 37, November 7, 1827, 331 [electronic edition].

124 JQA, Diary 37, November 30, 1827, 352 [electronic edition].

125 Jefferson, as a point of comparison, dismissed 109 during an eight-year presidency. Madison and Monroe each dismissed 27. Dangerfield, *The Awakening of American Nationalism,* 239.

126 See Dangerfield, *The Awakening of American Nationalism,* 240.

127 JQA, Diary 35, October 28, 1826, 442 [electronic edition].

128 Thurlow Weed, *Autobiography and Memoir,* ed. Harriet A. Weed (New York: Houghton Mifflin, 1884), 1:181.

129 JQA, Diary 39, October 22, 1833, 167 [electronic edition].

130 *New York Evening Post,* October 20, 1827.

131 Webster to Clay, March 25, 1827, in Mary W. M. Hargreaves and James F. Hopkins, eds., *The Papers of Henry Clay,* vol. 6, *Secretary of State, 1827* (Lexington: University Press of Kentucky, 1981), 355.

132 Porter Clay to Henry Clay, February 22, 1827, in Clay, *Papers,* 6:223.

133 JQA, Diary 37, December 3, 1827, 355 [electronic edition].

134 JQA, Diary 37, January 11, 1828, 395 [electronic edition].

135 Silas Wright Jr. to Azariah C. Flagg, December 18, 1827, quoted in Remini, *John Quincy Adams* (New York: Henry Holt and Company, 2002), 114.

136 JQA, Diary 37, December 1, 1827, 353 [electronic edition].

137 JQA, Diary 37, May 13, 1827, 193 [electronic edition].

138 JQA, Diary 37, July 31, 1827, 257 [electronic edition].

139 JQA, Diary 36, December 31, 1828, 95 [electronic edition].

140 Quoted in Charles L. Todd and Robert Sonkin, *Alexander Bryan Johnson: Philosophical Banker* (Syracuse, N.Y.: Syracuse University Press, 1977), 162.

141 For the authoritative account of the elections, see Robert Remini, *The Election of Andrew Jackson* (Philadelphia: J. B. Lippincott, 1963), and, more recently, Lynn Hudson Parsons, *The Birth of Modern Politics: Andrew Jackson, John Quincy Adams, and the Election of 1828* (Oxford: Oxford University Press, 2009), and Donald B. Cole, *Vindicating Andrew Jackson: The 1828 Election and the Rise of the Two-Party System* (Lawrence: University Press of Kansas, 2009).

142 JQA, Diary 37, April 26, 1827, 181 [electronic edition].

143 JQA, Diary 37, May 12, 1827, 193 [electronic edition].

144 1824 campaign song of John Quincy Adams. Audio clip may be heard at http://www.archive.org/details/JohnQuincyAdams-Little KnowYeWhosComin.

145 JQA, Diary 50, March 5, 1827, 62 [electronic edition].

146 JQA to Charles W. Upham, February 2, 1837, quoted in John Quincy Adams, Edward H. Tatum Jr., ed., "Ten Unpublished Letters of John Quincy Adams, 1796–1837," *Huntington Library Quarterly* 4, no. 3 (April 1941): 383.

147 JQA, Diary 33, February 11, 1825, 79 [electronic edition].

148 In fact, John Quincy Adams remains one of only three presidents to have captured the White House while losing the popular vote. In 1876 Rutherford B. Hayes lost the popular vote to Samuel J. Tilden but won the electoral vote and the presidency. In 2000 history repeated itself with George W. Bush defeating Al Gore despite losing the popular vote. In both of these cases, the result hinged on Florida.

149 *Niles' Weekly Register,* October 14, 1826.

150 Political scientist Stephan Skowronek claims Adams lacked the authority to repudiate the past precisely because he was breaking with it. Stephen Skowronek (*The Politics Presidents Make: Leadership from John Adams to Bill Clinton* (Cambridge: Harvard University Press, 1998), 110ff. This charge does sync with the claims of many old Jefferson Republicans, including Jefferson himself, that Adams was a Republican in name only. Skowronek's argument is subtle and catches many of Adams's political missteps, but in its stress on structural changes, or "disjunctions," as he puts it, it perhaps undervalues the contributing role that Adams himself played in his presidency.

151 JQA, Diary 33, May 13, 1825, 148 [electronic edition].

152 Russell Kirk, *The Conservative Mind: From Burke to Santayana* (Chicago: Henry Regnery, 1953), 202.

153 For more on the South's apprehension of John Quincy Adams as an emancipating wolf in sheep's clothing, see Forbes, esp. 193–209.

154 JQA to Charles W. Upham, February 2, 1837, in Tatum, ed. "Ten Unpublished Letters of John Quincy Adams," 383.

155 JQA, Diary 37, June 8, 1827, 217 [electronic edition].

CHAPTER 5 *A Stain upon the Character of the Nation*

1 JQA, Diary 31, March 3, 1820, 278 [electronic edition].

2 JQA, Diary 31, March 3, 1820, 275 [electronic edition].

3 JQA, Diary 31, February 4, 1820, 258 [electronic edition].

4 JQA, "Proposed Amendment to the Constitution on Representation," in JQA, *Writings,* 3:90.

5 JQA to Stratford Canning, June 24, 1823, in JQA, *Writings,* 7:508.

6 JQA, Diary 31, February 24, 1820, 272 [electronic edition]. For more on Adams's evolving attitudes toward blacks, interracial marriage, and slavery, see William Jerry MacLean, "Othello Scorned: The Racial Thought of John Quincy Adams," *Journal of the Early Republic* 4 (Summer 1984): 143–160.

7 JQA to TBA, April 4, 1801, quoted in Linda K. Kerber and John Walter Morris's "Politics and Literature: The Adams Family and the Port Folio," *The William and Mary Quarterly,* Third Series, Vol. 23, No. 3 (Jul., 1966), pp. 450–476.

8 JQA, Diary 31, January 10, 1820, 245 [electronic edition].

9 JQA, Diary 31, March 3, 1820, 275 [electronic edition].

10 JQA, Diary 31, December 27, 1819, 237 [electronic edition].

11 JQA, Diary 31, December 27, 1819, 272 [electronic edition].

12 For a similar point about a different moralizing American statesman, see Arthur S. Link, "The Higher Realism of Woodrow Wilson," *Journal of Presbyterian History* 41 (March 1963): 1–13. Link writes that Wilson "was a realist of a different sort" whose views of domestic and international politics were driven by a desire "to win the long-run moral approval of societies professing allegiance to the common western, humane, Christian traditions" (p. 4).

13 John Quincy Adams, *Dermot MacMorrogh; or, The Conquest of Ireland. An Historical Tale of the Twelfth Century in Four Cantos* (Boston: Carter, Hendee, 1832), 78.

14 JQA, Diary 36, December 31, 1828, 95 [electronic edition]; Diary 36, March 6, 1829, 166 (insert) [electronic edition].

15 JQA, Diary 31, June 4, 1820, 362 [electronic edition].

16 JQA to Henry Clay, May 11, 1829, in Calvin Colton, ed., *The Private Correspondence of Henry Clay* (New York: A.S. Barnes, 1855), 230.

17 JQA, Diary 31, March 5, 1829, 165 (insert) [electronic edition].

18 JQA, Diary 37, May 13, 1827, 193 [electronic edition].

19 JQA, Diary 36, May 4, 1829, 176 [electronic edition].

20 LCA to CFA, May 7, 1829, quoted in Jack Shepard, *Cannibals of the Heart: A Personal Biography of Louisa Catherine and John Quincy Adams* (New York: McGraw-Hill, 1980), 318.

21 JQA, Diary 36, December 31, 1829, 333 [electronic edition].

22 Ralph Waldo Emerson, *Journals*, ed. Edward W. Emerson and Waldo E. Forbes, (Boston: Houghton Mifflin Company, 1909–1914). 8:353.

23 JQA, Diary 36, July 11, 1829, 213 [electronic edition].

24 See *American Annual Register*, vol. 3, for 1827 and 1828, 267ff.; *American Annual Register* for 1829–30, 414ff. The articles on the Russo-Turkish Wars include a fiery comparison of Islam and Christianity. Painting with as broad a brush as possible, Adams selectively quotes from the Koran to assert that, in his view, the two Abrahamic faiths are condemned to a state of perpetual war.

25 JQA, October, 1816, quoted in Paul C. Nagel, *John Quincy Adams: A Public Life, A Private Life* (New York, Knopf: 1997), 231.

26 JQA, *Dermot MacMorrogh*, v.

27 JQA, *Dermot MacMorrogh*, vi.

28 Adams was reading Gibbon's *Decline and Fall of the Roman Empire* as he composed his poem. One of the major themes of Gibbon's work—that erosion in private morality led to a fall in public behavior—seems particularly relevant here.

29 For a different take on this relationship between private morality and public virtue, see Jan Lewis, "The Republican Wife: Virtue and Seduction in the Early Republic," *William and Mary Quarterly,* 3rd ser., 44, no. 4 (October 1987): 689–721. Lewis argues that, prior to the 1830s, marriage was understood as metaphor for the ideal republican relationship of equality and self-sacrifice. In this light, Adams and others would understand marital infidelity as anticipating the end of republican virtue.

30 JQA, *Dermot MacMorrogh,* v.

31 Adams received 1,817 votes, the Democratic candidate 373, and the Federalist just 279.

32 JQA to CFA, November 22, 1831. See Charles Francis Adams, *Diary,* ed. Aïda DiPace Donald and David Donald (Cambridge, Mass.: Harvard University Press, 1964), 4:187n1.

33 CFA, *Diary,* September 28, 1830, 3:328.

34 CFA, *Diary,* May 18, 1831, 4:51.

35 LCA, March 23, 1836, *Diary and Autobiographical Writings of Louisa Catherine Adams,* vol. 2 (Cambridge, Mass: Harvard University Press, 2013), 702.

36 JQA, Diary 38, September 8, 1831, 265 [electronic edition].

37 JQA, Diary 39, December 24, 1832, 12 [electronic edition].

38 George Wilson Pierson, *Tocqueville in America* (Gloucester, Mass.: Peter Smith, 1969), 282ff.

39 This account highlights the concepts that informed Adams's thinking about the threat of slavery and his response to it. For a more straightforward chronological account of Adams's time in Congress, see Leonard L. Richards, *The Life and Times of Congressman John Quincy Adams* (Oxford: Oxford University Press, 1986); William Lee Miller, *Arguing about Slavery: The Great Battle in the United States Congress* (New York: Knopf, 1996); and Joseph Wheelan, *Mr. Adams's Last Crusade: John Quincy Adams's Extraordinary Post-Presidential Life in Congress* (New York: Public Affairs, 2008).

40 Kentucky Resolution—Alien and Sedition Acts, December 3, 1799, http://avalon.law.yale.edu/18th_century/kenres.asp.

41 Theodore Dwight, *History of the Hartford Convention: With a Review of the Policy of the United States Government, Which Led to the War of 1812* (New York: N. and J. White, 1833), 361.

42 John C. Calhoun, "A Discourse on the Constitution and Government of the United States," in Richard K. Crallé, ed., *"A Disquisition on Government and A Discourse on the Constitution and Government of the United States* (Charleston, S.C.: Walker and James, 1851), 283.

43 John C. Calhoun to Virgil Maxcy, September 11, 1830, quoted in William Montgomery Meigs, *The Life of John Caldwell Calhoun* (New York: G. E. Stechert, 1917), 1:419.

44 John Quincy Adams, *An Oration Delivered before the Inhabitants of the Town of Newburyport at Their Request, on the Sixty-First Anniversary of the Declaration of Independence, July 4, 1837* (Newburyport, Mass.: Charles Whipple, 1837), 14.

45 John Quincy Adams, *An Oration Addressed to the Citizens of the Town of Quincy on the Fourth of July, 1831, the Fifty-Fifth Anniversary of the Independence of the United States of America* (Boston: Richardson, Lord and Holbrook, 1831), 17.

46 JQA, *An Oration Addressed to the Citizens of . . . Quincy,* 22.

47 JQA, *An Oration Addressed to the Citizens of . . . Quincy,* 18.

48 JQA, *Jubilee of the Constitution, A Discourse Delivered at the Request of The New York Historical Society, in the city of New York, on Tuesday, the 30th of April 1839* (New York: Samuel Colman, 1839), 43.

49 JQA, *An Oration Delivered before the Inhabitants of . . . Newburyport,* 14.

50 JQA, *An Oration Addressed to the Citizens of . . . Quincy,* 12.

51 JQA, *Jubilee of the Constitution,* 68.

52 JQA, *An Oration Delivered before the Inhabitants of . . . Newburyport,* 15, 17.

53 JQA, *An Oration Delivered before the Inhabitants of . . . Newburyport,* 34, 36.

54 JQA, Diary 36, June 1, 1830, 466 [electronic edition].

55 Adams used the terms "slave power" and "slave conspiracy" interchangeably and loosely. In general, these terms lumped the

southern Democrats and their northern supporters together. They also included southern Whigs who supported slavery and the gag rule. But as the historian Leonard Richards points out in his excellent *Life and Times of Congressman John Quincy Adams,* the driving forces cheering slavery's expansion were the Jacksonians and Tyler Whigs. Richards notes that "it was they he [Adams] invariably had in mind when he lashed out against the 'aggressive slaveocracy'" (p.154). William W. Freehling, *The Road to Disunion: Secessionists at Bay, 1776–1854* (New York: Oxford University Press, 1990), offers a nuanced discussion of southern differences in geography, climate, racial demographics, crop culture, and ethnic differences. Freehling argues that because of these differences, regional solidarity on any issue, including slavery, was problematic. Leonard L. Richards, *The Slave Power: The Free North and Southern Domination, 1780–1860* (Baton Rouge: Louisiana State University Press, 2000), expands on this concept by looking at the evolution of northern supporters of the South.

56 JQA to Robert Walsh, April 16, 1836, Adams Papers, MHS, microfilm, reel 152. Later published in the *New York Times,* October 22, 1852, http://query.nytimes.com/gst/abstract.html?res=FB0F10FE3F5C167493 C0AB178BD95F468584F9.

57 John Quincy Adams, *Address of John Quincy Adams, to His Constituents of the Twelfth Congressional District, at Braintree, September 17th, 1842* (Boston: J.H. Eastburn, 1842), 27.

58 JQA, *Address . . . at Braintree,* 16.

59 JQA, *Address . . . at Braintree,* 29.

60 JQA, "Proposed Amendment," December 1804, in JQA, *Writings,* 3:90.

61 These numbers come from table L-IX of Douglass C. North, *The Economic Growth of the United States 1790–1860* (Englewood Cliffs, N.J.: Prentice-Hall, Inc., 1961), 257. As they are used above, they are only approximations, as North counts Kentucky, Tennessee, Maryland, and Delaware, all slave states, as part of the West and Northeast.

62 The original gag rule was a resolution and needed to be renewed at the start of each congressional session. This allowed Adams and his

allies to rail against the resolution and against slavery until debate was "gagged." Hoping to completely silence Adams on this issue, proslavery forces and their fellow travelers in the House passed the Twenty-First Rule in January 1840, which prohibited even the reception of antislavery petitions.

63 JQA, Diary 48, December 21, 1837, 708 [electronic edition].

64 See James Brewer Stewart, *Holy Warriors: The Abolitionists and American Slavery,* rev. ed. (New York: Hill and Wang, 1996).

65 Stewart, *Holy Warriors,* 81ff.

66 JQA, *An Oration Delivered before the Inhabitants of . . . Newburyport,* 53.

67 *Congressional Globe,* House of Representatives, 26th Cong., 1st sess., appendix, January 22, 1840, 747.

68 See Stewart, *Holy Warriors,* esp. chap. 2, "Immediate Emancipation"; chap. 3, "Moral Suasion"; and chap. 4, "Perfectionism in Politics."

69 JQA to Benjamin Waterhouse, October 15, 1835, Adams Papers, MHS, microfilm, reel 152; Sean Wilentz *The Rise of American Democracy: Jefferson to Lincoln* (New York: W.W. Norton & Company, 2005), 471.

70 Following his 1842 Braintree address, Adams's constituents wrote and performed a song in his honor that included the following verse: "Where Slavery's minions cower Before the servile poewre, He bore their ban; And, like an aged oak, That braved the lightning's stroke, When thunders round it broke, Stood up, A MAN." JQA, *Address . . . at Braintree,* 63.

71 See, John Quincy Adams, *An Oration, Delivered before the Cincinnati Astronomical Society on the Occasion of Laying the Corner Stone of an Astronomical Observatory* (Cincinnati: Shepard and Col, 1843).

72 JQA, Diary 44, November 6, 1843, 124 [electronic edition].

73 JQA, Diary 44, November 20, 1843, 138 [electronic edition].

74 JQA, "Letter to the Citizens of the United States, Whose Petitions, Memorials and Remonstrances, Have Been Entrusted to Me, to Be Presented to the House of Representatives of the United States, at the Third Session of the 25th Congress, May 21, 1839," *Courier* (Boston), June 6, 1839.

75 JQA, "To the Inhabitants of the Twelfth Congressional District of Massachusetts, March 8, 1837," in John Quincy Adams, *Letters from John Quincy Adams to His Constituents of the Twelfth District in Massachusetts, to Which Is Added His Speech in Congress, Delivered February 9, 1837* (Boston: Isaac Knapp, 1837), 13.

76 JQA, *Letters from John Quincy Adams to His Constituents,* 60. This quotation comes from the compilation of Adams's fiery House speech and letters to his constituents explaining his actions. The official record can be read in its entirety in *Congressional Globe,* House of Representatives, 24th Cong., 2nd sess., February 2, 1837, 264ff.

77 JQA, "Letter to the Citizens of the United States."

78 Theodore Weld to Angelina G. Weld and Sarah Grimké, January 23, 1842, in Gilbert Hobbs Barnes and Dwight Lowell Dumond, eds., *Letters of Theodore Dwight Weld, Angelina Grimké Weld and Sarah Grimké, 1822–1844* (New York: D. Appleton-Century, 1934), 2:899ff.

79 Barnes and Dumond, *Letters of Theodore Dwight Weld,* 2:889.

80 JQA, Diary 43, January 15, 1842, 15ff. [electronic edition]. Adams writes that the idea of organizing this caucus was to advance "some concert of action among the friends of the right to petition." The members of this caucus were drawn exclusively from the ranks of the leading abolitionists in Congress.

81 By the 1840s Adams shared with the abolitionists a deeply religious outlook and a belief in civilizational progress. For a more detailed description of white abolitionists' common assumptions, see Ronald G. Walters, *The Antislavery Appeal: American Abolitionism after 1830* (Baltimore: Johns Hopkins University Press, 1976).

82 A. Brown to JQA, January 27, 1842, Adams Papers, MHS, microfilm, reel 520; J. Whittelsey to JQA, July 24, 1842. Adams Papers, MHS, microfilm, reel 523; Edmund Quincy to JQA, January 31, 1842, Adams Papers, MHS, microfilm, reel 520; Samuel Flagg Bemis, *John Quincy Adams and the Union* (New York: Knopf, 1956), 438ff.

83 Theodore Weld to Angelina Weld, February 6, 1842, in Barnes and Dumond, *Letters of Theodore Dwight Weld,* 2:913.

84 Joshua Giddings to his daughter, February 8, 1842, quoted in Richards, *Life and Times of Congressman John Quincy Adams,* 144.

85 William Lloyd Garrison to Richard D. Webb, February 27, 1842, in William Lloyd Garrison, *The Letters of William Lloyd Garrison,* vol. 3, *No Union with Slaveholders: 1841–1849,* ed. Walter M. Merrill (Cambridge, Mass.: Harvard University Press, 1974), 53.

86 Quoted in Barton Haxall Wise, *The Life of Henry A. Wise of Virginia, 1806–1876: By His Grandson, the Late Barton H. Wise* (New York: Macmillan, 1899), 61.

87 To Adams, who always thought of foreign and domestic policy as intimately connected, the fight against the gag rule and the fight against Texas's annexation were the same. As William Freehling astutely points out, "Artificially segregating Whigs' response to the gag and Texas crises . . . hinders awareness that the two issues came to climax at the same time. The same Congress of 1844–5 which abolished the gag rule admitted Texas" (*Road to Disunion,* 410).

88 See Thomas R. Hietala's *Manifest Destiny: Anxious Aggrandizement in Late Jacksonian America* (Ithaca, N.Y.: Cornell University Press, 1985). Using a domestic-political/social-imperialist interpretation of America's expansion, Hietala contends that expansion was used to distract the nation from its inherent internal problems.

89 John Quincy Adams, *The Lives of James Madison and James Monroe, Fourth and Fifth Presidents of the United States, with Historical Notes of Their Administrations* (Buffalo: Geo H. Derby and Co., 1850), 79.

90 *Congressional Globe,* House of Representatives, 28th Cong., 2nd sess., appendix, January 15, 1845, 369. For original, see *National Intelligencer,* April 15, 1842.

91 Richards, *Life and Times of Congressman John Quincy Adams,* 170ff., summarizes these three interpretations of the motivations behind Calhoun's letter. To these, he adds the possibility that it "was just plain stupid."

92 Adams, *Address . . . at Braintree,* 10, 16.

93 Adams, *Address . . . at Braintree*, 11.

94 Adams, *Address . . . at Braintree*, 21, 27.

95 *Register of Debates*, House of Representatives, 24th Cong., 1st sess., May 25, 1836, 4046. In 1833 Great Britain abolished slavery throughout most of its empire. For the effects of emancipation on British politics and foreign policy, see Keith Hamilton and Patrick Salmon, eds., *Slavery, Diplomacy and Empire: Britain and the Suppression of the Slave Trade, 1807–1975* (Brighton, England: Sussex Academic Press, 2009); Howard Temperley, *British Antislavery, 1833–1870* (London: Longman, 1972); and David Turley, *The Culture of English Antislavery, 1780–1860* (London: Routledge, 1991).

96 See Adams's floor speech, May 25, 1836, *Register of Debates*, House of Representatives, 24th Cong., 1st sess., 4040.

97 JQA, Diary 45, February 28, 1845, 59 [electronic edition].

98 For more on Polk's foreign policy, see Robert W. Merry, *A Country of Vast Designs: James K. Polk, the Mexican War, and the Conquest of the American Continent* (New York: Simon and Schuster, 2009).

99 John Quincy Adams, "Address to the Boston Whig Young Men's Club," October 7, 1844. The speech was printed in the *Boston Daily Atlas*, October 9, 1844.

100 JQA, Diary 44, June 10, 1844, 352 [electronic edition].

101 JQA to Richard Rush, October 16, 1845, Adams Papers, MHS, microfilm, reel 154. A copy of the letter sold at private auction can be viewed at http://www.christies.com/LotFinder/lot_details. aspx?intObjectID=3980307.

102 John C. Calhoun, "Speech on the Oregon Bill," June 27, 1848, in Crallé, *The Works of John C. Calhoun*, 507.

103 John Quincy Adams, *Speech of John Quincy Adams, of Massachusetts, upon the Right of the People, Men and Women, to Petition; On the Freedom of Speech and of Debate in the House of Representatives of the United States; On the Resolutions of Seven State Legislatures and the Petitions of More Than One Hundred Thousand Petitioners, relating to the Annexation of Texas to This Union. Delivered in the House of Representatives, in Fragments of the Morning*

Hour, from 16th of June to the 7th of July, 1833, Inclusive (Washington, D.C.: Gales and Seaton, 1838), 83. This portion of the speech was given on Saturday, June 30, 1838.

104 JQA, *Speech of John Quincy Adams,* 83.

105 *Register of Debates,* House of Representatives, 24th Cong., 1st sess., May 25, 1836, 4046.

106 JQA, Diary 44, June 16, 1844, 359 [electronic edition].

107 *Register of Debates,* House of Representatives, 24th Cong., 1st sess., May 25, 1836, 4041.

108 JQA, "Letter to the Citizens of the United States."

109 JQA, Diary 33, December 13, 1838, 687 [electronic edition].

110 Joshua R. Giddings, *History of the Rebellion: Its Authors and Causes* (New York: Follett, Foster, 1864), 218.

111 JQA, "Address to the Boston Whig Young Men's Club."

112 JQA, *Writings,* 3:74. This article first appeared in the *New England Repertory* on November 6, 1804.

113 JQA, *Jubilee of the Constitution,* 51.

114 JQA, *Jubilee of the Constitution,* 11.

115 Boston *Liberator,* May 31, 1839; JQA, Jubilee of the Constitution, 123.

116 JQA, *Jubilee of the Constitution,* 119.

117 Contemporaries understood it as such, with the *Emancipator* declaring, "we do not respond to the revolutionary battle-cry of John Quincy Adams, that the friends of human freedom should stand to their arms" (June 6, 1839).

118 JQA, "Letter to the Citizens of the United States."

119 For a particularly good discussion on the reconceptualization of the Declaration of Independence, see Pauline Maier, *American Scripture: Making the Declaration of Independence* (New York: Knopf, 1997).

120 JQA, "Letter to the Citizens of the United States."

121 JQA, *An Oration Delivered before the Inhabitants of . . . Newburyport,* 19.

122 JQA to Charles Jared Ingersoll, June 19, 1823, in JQA, *Writings,* 7:488.

123 *Congressional Globe,* 25th Congress, House of Representatives, 3rd sess., December 20, 1838, 3rd sess. See also William Seward, *Life and Public*

Services of John Quincy Adams, Sixth President of the United States, with the Eulogy Delivered before the Legislature of New York (Auburn, N.Y.: Derby, Miller, 1849), 292. For Washington's evolving views on slavery, see Harry Wiencek, *An Imperfect God: George Washington, His Slaves, and the Creation of America* (New York: Farrar, Straus and Giroux, 2003).

124 JQA, *An Oration Delivered before the Inhabitants of . . . Newburyport*, 50.

125 JQA, *Address . . . at Braintree*, 25.

126 JQA, *Diary 27*, December 27, 1819, 237 [electronic edition]. This was not necessarily true. For a persuasive account of Jefferson's efforts on behalf of slavery, see Gary Wills's excellent *Negro President: Jefferson and the Slave Power* (Boston: Houghton Mifflin, 2003). Wills argues that "like other southerners, Jefferson had to take every political step he could to prevent challenges to the slave system" (p. xiii).

127 John Quincy Adams, *Argument before the Supreme Court in the Case of the United States, Appellants, v. Cinque, and Others, Africans, Captured in the Schooner Amistad, by Lieut. Gedney, Delivered on the 24th of February and 1st of March, 1841; With a review of the Case of the Antelope, Reported in the 10th, 11th, and 12th Volumes of Wheaton's Reports* (New York: S. W. Benedict, 1841), 89.

128 JQA, *An Oration Delivered before the Inhabitants of . . . Newburyport*, 50.

129 JQA, *An Oration Delivered before the Inhabitants of . . . Newburyport*, 64.

130 JQA, *Address . . . at Braintree*, 21.

131 JQA, *Address . . . at Braintree*, 25.

132 Elijah Lovejoy, Joseph C. and Owen, eds., *Memoirs of the Rev. Elijah P. Lovejoy; Who Was Murdered in Defence of the Liberty of the Press, at Alton, Illinois, Nov. 7, 1837, with an Introduction by John Quincy Adams* (New York: John S. Taylor, 1838), 11.

133 JQA, "Letter to the Citizens of the United States."

134 JQA to J. Edwards, July 13, 1837, quoted in Ralph Ketcham, *Presidents above Party: The First American Presidency, 1789–1829* (Chapel Hill: The University of North Carolina Press), 156.

135 JQA, *An Oration Delivered before the Inhabitants of . . . Newburyport*, 57.

136 Emerson, *Journals*, 6:349–350.

137 JQA, Diary 36, February 28, 1829, 157 (insert) [electronic edition].

138 JQA, Diary 33, December 13, 1838, 687 [electronic edition].

139 JQA, Diary 48, June 19, 1836, 610 [electronic edition].

140 JQA, Diary 41, March 29, 1841, 292 [electronic edition]

141 JQA, Diary 48, June 19, 1836, 610 [electronic edition].

CHAPTER 6 *The Influence of Our Example*

1 This quotation, as do most of the other details in this paragraph, comes from the account in the *National Intelligencer,* February 22, 1848. See also *The Adams Memorial: Containing a Sketch of John Adams, the Elder, together with the Life, Character, Public Services, Last Sickness, Death, and Funeral Obsequies of the Late Venerable John Quincy Adams* (Boston: J.B. Hall, 1848), 12ff.

2 *Journal of the House of Representatives,* 1848, 43:446. See also Abraham Lincoln to Rev. Henry Clicer, June 1, 1848, http://quod.lib.umich .edu/l/lincoln/lincoln1/1:491?rgn=div1;view=fulltext.

3 *National Intelligencer,* February 28, 1848. See also *Congressional Globe,* 30th Cong., 1st sess., 389, and E. F. Ellet, *The Court Circles of the Republic, or the Beauties and Celebrities of the Nation from Washington to Grant* (Hartford: Hartford Publishing Co., 1870), 409ff.

4 The telegraph, developed in America by Samuel Morse, was first demonstrated to the American public in May 1844. For more on what he deems the "communications revolution" of the mid-nineteenth century, see Daniel Walker Howe's comprehensive *What Hath God Wrought: The Transformation of America, 1815–1848* (Oxford: Oxford University Press, 2007).

5 *New-York Daily Tribune,* March 8, 1848.

6 *The Adams Memorial,* 29ff.

7 *Congressional Globe,* House of Representatives, 30th Cong., 1st sess., February 24, 1848, 384 (Speaker Winthrop–Mass.); 386 (Congressman Vinton–Ohio).

8 *Congressional Globe,* February 24, 1848, 385 (Congressman Holmes–S.C.).

9 Edward Everett, *Eulogy on the Life and Character of John Quincy Adams, Delivered at the Request of the Legislature of Massachusetts, in Faneuil Hall* (Boston: Button and Wentworth, 1848), 10.

10 William H. Seward, *Life and Public Services of John Quincy Adams, Sixth President of the United States, with the Eulogy Delivered before the Legislature of New York* (Auburn, N.Y.: Derby, Miller, 1849). For a nuanced portrayal of the sectional and sectarian antagonisms found below the surface of national unity in 1848, see Lynn Hudson Parsons, "The 'Splendid Pageant': Observations on the Death of John Quincy Adams," *New England Quarterly* 53, no. 4 (December 1980): 464–482.

11 *Congressional Globe,* February 24, 1848, 385 (Congressman Hudson–Mass.); 386 (Congressman Vinton–Ohio). The Congressional speeches were subsequently compiled and printed. See, *Token of a Nation's Sorrow. Addresses in the Congress of the United States, and Funeral Solemnities on the Death of John Quincy Adams, who Died in the Capitol at Washington, on Wednesday Evening, February 23, 1848.* Second Edition (Washington: J and G.S. Gideon, 1848).

12 *National Intelligencer,* February 24, 1848.

13 Seward, *Life and Public Services of John Quincy Adams,* 386.

14 Philip Hone, *The Diary of Philip Hone, 1828–1851,* ed. with an introduction by Bayard Tuckerman (New York: Dodd, Mead, 1910), February 24, 1848, pt. 2, 341ff.

15 JQA, Diary 31, June 4, 1819, 125 [electronic edition].

16 Stanley Lane-Poole, *The Life of the Right Honorable Stratford Canning, Viscount Stratford de Redcliffe: From His Memoirs and Private and Official Papers* (London: Longmans, Green, 1888), 1:308.

17 JQA to Charles Jared Ingersoll, June 19, 1823, in JQA, *Writings,* 6:488.

18 John Quincy Adams, *The Social Compact: Exemplified in the Constitution of the Commonwealth of Massachusetts; with Remarks on the Theories of Divine Right of Hobbes and of Filmer, and the Counter Theories of Sidney, Locke, Montesquieu, and Rousseau, concerning the Origin and Nature of*

NOTES TO PAGES 298–305

Government: A Lecture Delivered before the Franklin Lyceum, at Providence, R.I., November 25, 1842 (Providence: Knowles and Vose, 1842), 11.

19 John Quincy Adams, *An Oration Addressed to the Citizens of the Town of Quincy on the Fourth of July, 1831, the Fifty-Fifth Anniversary of the Independence of the United States of America* (Boston: Richardson, Lord and Holbrook, 1831), 34.

20 *Register of Debates,* House of Representatives, 24th Cong., 1st sess., May 25, 1836, 4040.

21 Jay Sexton, *The Monroe Doctrine: Empire and Nation in Nineteenth-Century America* (New York: Hill and Wang, 2011).

22 This comes from President James Polk's Message to Congress of December 2, 1845, as reported in the *Journal of the Senate of the United States of America, 1789–1873,* Tuesday, December 2, 1845, 19–20. The Senate *Journal* has been partially digitized and may be viewed online at http://memory.loc.gov/ammem/amlaw/lwsj.html.

23 Richard Olney to Thomas F. Bayard, July 20, 1895, in *Papers relating to the Foreign Relations of the United States, with the Annual Message of the President, Transmitted to Congress, December 2, 1895,* pt. 1 (Washington, D.C.: Government Printing Office, 1896), 558.

24 This is the famous Roosevelt Corollary to the Monroe Doctrine, http://www.presidency.ucsb.edu/ws/index.php?pid=29545#axzz2fT M991hm.

25 George F. Kennan testimony is in U.S. Congress, Senate, Committee on Foreign Relations, *Supplemental Foreign Assistance Fiscal Year 1966—Vietnam* (Washington, D.C.: U.S. Government Printing Office, 1966), 336.

26 George Kennan, "On American Principles," *Foreign Affairs,* 74, no. 2 (March/April 1995):116–126.

27 JQA, Diary 31, March 29, 1820, 299 [electronic edition].

28 JQA, Diary 37, June 8, 1827, 217 [electronic edition]; JQA, Diary 37, June 4, 1827, 213 [electronic edition].

29 JQA, Diary 36, August 14, 1830, 521 [electronic edition]. Gardening seems to be the preferred hobby of American grand strategists. In a review of Robert Beisner's *Dean Acheson,* John Gaddis wrote that

Acheson enjoyed gardening precisely because it cultivated habits useful to a grand strategist. Gardening, Gaddis wrote, is "a skill that requires patience, sensitivity, and constant care, but that if practiced successfully holds out the reward of growth in desired directions." (John Lewis Gaddis, "The Gardener," *The New Republic Online,* October 16, 2006. The article may be viewed at www.tnr.com.)

ACKNOWLEDGMENTS

THE MOST GRATIFYING PART of publishing this book is getting to acknowledge in print the many people who made it possible. As a young research assistant at the Council on Foreign Relations, during a conversation about contemporary American foreign policy, my boss handed me a small book that framed contemporary policy in terms of its historical evolution. My boss was Walter Russell Mead and the book he handed me was John Lewis Gaddis's *Surprise, Security, and the American Experience.* It is to Walter Mead and John Gaddis that I owe the greatest intellectual debts. Working for Walter was an education and a half. His lessons on hard work, civility, listening to and learning from others, and finding solutions rather than problems have influenced me greatly. John Gaddis is quite simply the best, and certainly the most exacting, teacher I have ever known. In his classrooms, in his lectures, in his books, and in his relationships with his current and past students, John consistently models the highest standards of teaching, scholarship, and mentorship. I am also grateful for his not batting an eye when I decided to take a year off in the middle of graduate school and head to China.

This project began at Yale University, and I count myself especially lucky to have been part of such a vibrant, fun, and stimulating community. I still recall when during my comprehensive exams, Paul Kennedy granted me a "fishing license." He told me that the committee was interested enough in the project that they were willing to let me see what I could catch. Whether discussing the accuracy of *Twelve O'Clock High*, touring the most reputable, and the most secret, burger establishments of New Haven, or opening his home to students, Paul Kennedy showed an innate kindness that was always greatly appreciated. The seriousness with which Charles Hill approaches his many tasks has made his counsel invaluable. Joanne Freeman made sure that my thinking remained grounded in the nineteenth century and pushed me to clarify terms that are more often used than defined. Special thanks to Jonathan Holloway and Aisling Colon for opening their home to me. And whether they know it or not, Donald Kagan, Jonathan Spence, John Mack Faragher, David Blight, Beverly Gage, Michael Oren, and Robert Forbes all helped shape this project. Marcy Kaufman made administrative hurdles anything but, Gregory Eow helpfully responded to all bizarre research questions, and Ann Carter-Drier and Susan Hennigan ensured that Yale's International Security Studies program was a well-run organization. Additionally, generous grants from Yale University, the Smith Richardson Foundation, and the Gilder Lehrman Center enabled much of the research and writing of this book.

The Strategy & Policy Department at the United States Naval War College has been my professional home while I completed this book, and it is hard to think of a place more conducive to writing, thinking about, and teaching strategy. John Maurer brought me on board, and I have been extremely lucky to benefit from his wisdom, thoughtfulness, and constant encouragement. I would also like to thank the many military officers and civilian academics with whom I have been lucky enough to work, teach, and learn. Of these, two military officers, Captain Chris Dennis, USN, and Colonel Michael Hough, USAF, get special thanks for their friendship and for their willingness to educate me on many "queepy" details of military culture. For going above and beyond the call of duty, a thank you to Christine Mello and George Zecher in the S&P front office, and Robin Lima, Dennis Zambrotta, and the rest of the library team.

At Harvard University Press, Joyce Seltzer proved the most thoughtful of editors, pushing me to refine the ideas, flesh out the details, and sharpen the prose in this manuscript. Brian Distelberg answered any and all questions with exceptional professionalism, and Jennifer Bossert helped steer me through the copyediting process. I would also like to thank the two anonymous reviewers of the manuscript, who provided many thoughtful and challenging comments. This is a much better book because of their time and efforts.

Friends, colleagues, and mentors have probably learned more than they ever wanted to know about JQA. Thomas LeBien, Patrick Gaughen, Nikhil Patel, and Michael Morgan deserve more praise than I can offer here for reading multiple drafts and offering sage advice. Will Inboden, Colin Jackson, Josh Rovner, Chris Seiple, and Julia Sweig all encouraged my interest in this project, and I have greatly benefited from their friendship and thoughtful recommendations. Scholarly pursuit requires both solitude and companionship. It has been my good fortune to be surrounded by friends who love to argue, disagree, and critique while simultaneously supporting and encouraging. For making New Haven such a terrific place to live and work, I am grateful to Josh Bradley, Hal Brands, Katie Scharf Dykes, John Frick, John Kent, Kam Lasater, Katheryn Gin Lum, Robin Morris, Aaron O'Connell, Nick Rutter, Ryan Shaw,

ACKNOWLEDGMENTS

Krishanti Vignarajah, Jana Wagner, Litsy Witkowski, Molly Worthen, Puong Fei Yeh, and Justin Zaremby.

Most important are those closest to home. The model for parenting has changed significantly since the Adamses' day, and my parents, Martin and Pamela Edel, take the cake. Their enthusiasm for John Quincy Adams, and really for any project their children undertake, remains infectious. I know I can never pay them back for their constant support, encouragement, and needling. Eliza, Spencer, and Sidney McClelland, are not only the best sister, brother-in-law, and niece, but also remain the most astute of literary critics. And David and Deborah Moriah, as well as Shane Moriah, have been wonderful sources of wisdom and humor.

This book is dedicated to my favorite diplomat, my most scrupulous editor, and my best friend, Kira Jan Moriah. She's had to live with John Quincy Adams for a long time now, and if that weren't hard enough, she's had to put up with me writing this book. And last but not least, our son Caleb and his little brother. Cal was born on the day of my graduate school commencement, and his little brother showed up just as the book was heading into production. Not quite as exciting as a book on fire trucks, but we'll see if they let us read this book as a bedtime story someday.

The views expressed here are solely those of the author. They do not necessarily represent the views of the Naval War College, the U.S. Navy, or the Department of Defense.

INDEX

Abolition, 7, 158, 247, 250–251, 260–261, 266–272, 278–279, 282, 285
Adams, Abigail "Nabby" (sister), 25, 36, 37, 52
Adams, Abigail Smith (mother), 6, 72, 291; on child-rearing, 15–17; 22; on JQA's education, 22–30, 43; relationship with JQA, 33, 36–39, 47, 50–52, 75, 93–95
Adams, Charles (brother), 17, 46, 62
Adams, Charles II (son), 255
Adams, George Washington (son), 89, 239, 255
Adams, Henry, 14, 49
Adams, John (father), 6, 48–53, 193, 206, 256; on child-rearing, 15–17; diplomatic correspondence with JQA, 76–79, 98; *Discourses on Davila*, 65–67; on JQA's career, 83, 94–95; on JQA's education, 19–31, 43; as president, 86–87, 89–90; relationship with JQA, 33–34, 48–49, 58–59, 71–73, 89–90
Adams, John Quincy, on American System, 189–190, 214, 232, 288; appointed minister to Great Britain, 101; appointed minster to the Netherlands, 55, 71; appointed minister to Prussia, 76, 83; appointed minister to Russia, 96; appointed secretary of state, 109–110, 116–118; on

Christianity, 16–17, 23, 280, 284–285; Columbus essays, 70–71; death of, 280–291; *Dermot MacMorrogh*, 256–257; Diary, 7, 30–31, 34, 78, 105, 113, 243; elected to Congress, 258; elected Massachusetts state senator, 90; elected president, 205; elected U.S. Senator, 90; on election of 1824, 192–206; on election of 1828, 236, 239–241; on expansion, 91, 94, 105, 110, 121–123, 128, 133, 156–158, 182–184, 273–276; and Federalist party, 71, 90, 92–96, 117, 199, 210, 243; Harvard College, 36–44; on internal improvements, 189–192, 201, 208–209, 227–228, 231–232; on Islam, 256; *Jubilee of the Constitution* (1839), 279–280; July 4 Address (1821), 159–164, 299; Marcellus essays, 68–70, 78; on neutrality, 8, 62–64, 68–69, 78, 82–86, 90–92, 98, 105, 144, 150, 179; Publicola essays, 66–69; on republicanism, 8, 20, 25–26, 40–43, 54, 58–60, 62, 66, 69–70, 80, 87, 91, 104, 132, 160–164, 167–169, 175, 178, 180–183, 193, 213, 252, 265, 272, 295; and Republican party, 92–94, 117, 198–200, 209, 244, 247; on revolutions, 41, 43, 56–57, 65–70, 88, 125, 129, 132, 160–168, 176, 179, 183, 188, 278, 281, 297, 300; on slavery, 32, 156–159, 184, 247, 249–254,

INDEX

INDEX

INDEX

Troup, Governor George, 225–226, 261
Tuyll, Baron Von, 174–175, 181, 183
Tyler, John, 274–276

University of Leyden, 28
University of Virginia, 214

Van Buren, Martin, 220–221, 224, 235, 238, 240, 244, 274, 283

Walsh, Robert, 199
War of 1812, 2–3, 98–102, 120, 136, 151–152, 161
Washington, D.C., 90, 124, 160, 185, 196, 241, 294; burning of, 99–100
Washington, George, 13, 193, 227; Farewell Address, 128, 165, 177, 190, 218 opinions of JQA, 71–73, 76, 79, 83; as president, 55–57, 63–64, 176, 282
Washington, Martha, 72
Waterloo, 125, 133
Wayne, "Mad" Anthony, 56
Webster, Daniel, 219
Weed, Thurlow, 235–236
Weld, Theodore, 270–272
West Indies (British), 86, 224, 276
West Point, 257
Whig party, 95, 274
Whiskey Rebellion, 56
Wirt, William, 117, 210–212
Wise, Henry, 272, 274

XYZ Affair, 86

Yale College, 38